Contents

Part IV Theory Development: Evolutionary Perspectives

Part V Theory Development: Sociocultural Perspectives

List of Figures and Tables

Figures

Tables

Notes on Contributors

Farid Uddin Ahamed is Professor and Chair at the Department of Anthropology, University of Chittagong, Bangladesh, where he lectures in anthropology, medical anthropology and South Asian ethnography. His research interests include environmental adaptation, bio-medical anthropology, public health, anthropology and development, and the anthropology of marginality, public action and non-governmentality. He currently oversees fieldwork among the hill tribes of Chittagong, and has recently collaborated with Kesson Magid on an investigation of the effects of marriage and fatherhood on salivary testosterone levels in Bangladeshi men, and with Gillian Bentley on an investigation of migration, socioecology and male preferences for female body shape.

Melissa Bateson is a Royal Society University Research Fellow at the Centre for Behaviour and Evolution at Newcastle University. Her research lies in the general area of cognitive ecology with a specific focus on the interaction between evolutionary and mechanistic explanations for choice behaviour in humans and other animals. She has a D.Phil. in animal behaviour and an M.A. in zoology with biological anthropology from the University of Oxford.

Gillian R. Bentley is Professor of Anthropology at Durham University and formerly Royal Society Research Fellow at Cambridge University and University College London. A reproductive ecologist whose research focuses on how environmental factors impact human reproductive function, she is currently collaborating on a number of projects among migrant and non-migrant Bangladeshis, including how developmental conditions affect male hormones, and a comparative study of menopause in older women. She is on the editorial boards of *Journal of Biosocial Science* and *American Journal of Human Biology*, and the Executive Committee of the Human Biology Association. She publishes in both social science and medical journals.

Michael Boroughs, M.A., is a faculty researcher at the Louis de la Parte Florida Mental Health Institute. He completed a Bachelor's degree in Psychology, and a Master's degree in Sociology, with a specialty in Social Psychology, at the University of South Florida. With research experience in programme evaluation in school settings and body image, he is currently a doctoral candidate in Clinical Psychology at the University of South Florida, where his research focuses on body image issues in men.

Rachel M. Calogero received her M.A. in Psychology from the College of William and Mary in Williamsburg, USA, and is currently completing her Ph.D. in Social Psychology at the University of Kent in Canterbury. Between degree programmes, she worked with women in residential treatment for eating disorders. Her diverse research areas include motivated social cognition, antecedents and consequences of self-objectification processes, resistance to change, and eating disorders prevention. She has presented her research regularly at international conferences for the past several years and has published articles in a variety of scholarly journals.

Piers L. Cornelissen is a Reader in Psychology at the University of York. As an undergraduate, he studied medicine at Worcester College Oxford, continuing his clinical training at St. Thomas's Hospital in London. He studied for a D.Phil. with Prof. John Stein at the (then) University Laboratory of Physiology, Oxford, funded by the Wellcome Trust. After 3 years as a McDonnell-Pew postdoctoral Fellow, he lectured at the Psychology Department, Newcastle University until 2006. His inter-disciplinary research interests are divided between investigating body image perception and the neural basis of reading, using combinations of psychophysical and neuroimaging techniques (MEG and FMRI).

Dorothy Einon is Senior Lecturer in Psychology at University College London. Her interests in evolutionary psychology include critical examination of the advantages of male promiscuity and the cross-generational advantages of polygamy, as well as studies of human mate choice, particularly the leg-to-body ratio. She is currently writing a book about the peculiar nature of human love and sexual desire, and the role this may have played in the development of human societies.

Jintu Fan is Professor of Textiles and Clothing at the Hong Kong Polytechnic University. He is known for his invention of the world's first sweating fabric manikin – known as 'Walter' – and for developing the world's first apparel knowledge portal (www.apparelkey.com).

He has published extensively, and has over a hundred and ninety academic papers or patents to his name. In particular, his work on bodily attractiveness is seen as an important contribution to the science and was widely reported in international media. He was the recipient of the Gold Medal Award from the International Invention Exhibition in Geneva in 2004, and the Distinguished Achievement Award of US Fiber Society in 2003.

Adrian Furnham is Professor of Psychology at University College London where he has taught for 25 years. He has written and edited over 50 books, as well as over six hundred scientific publications. He has wide interests in evolutionary, health, and personality psychology. He cycles to work, does not have a mobile phone and loves living in London.

Jeff Galak is a marketing doctoral candidate at New York University's Stern School of Business. His research interests are primarily in the domain of judgement and decision-making, with a focus on adaptation to repeated experiences and choices over time. Much of his work is done in collaboration with his advisor, Leif D. Nelson. Jeff also received his bachelor of science in Marketing and Economics from New York University. Aside from his academic interests, Jeff is an avid cyclist, photographer, and technology geek.

Tom Hildebrandt, Assistant Professor of Psychiatry of the Eating and Weight Disorders Program at the Mount Sinai School of Medicine, has research interests in how evolutionary and sociocultural theories explain extreme forms of weight and shape control, substance use and eating disorder pathology, and male body image. He has particular clinical and research expertise in male body image and the use of appearance and performance enhancing drugs (e.g., anabolic-androgenic steroids). He has authored and presented over twenty-five articles, book chapters and presentations in these areas and is on the editorial board of *Body Image: An International Journal of Research*.

Kerri L. Johnson is a social psychologist in the Department of Communication Studies at the University of California, Los Angeles. Her research examines how perceptual and social processes combine to affect basic person construal (including social categorisation and evaluation). In much of this research, she and her collaborators have focused on the perception and evaluation of sexually dimorphic body cues such as shape and motion.

Janet D. Latner, Assistant Professor of Psychology at the University of Hawaii, has research interests focused on the diagnosis, maintenance, and treatment of obesity and eating disturbances. She has authored and presented over fifty articles, book chapters, and presentations on eating disorders and obesity, has served as an investigator on several nationally funded research projects, and is on the editorial board of *Behaviour Research and Therapy*. Her forthcoming book, *Self-help Approaches for Obesity and Eating Disorders: Research and Practice*, edited by Dr. Latner and G. Terence Wilson, is to be published in 2007 by Guilford Press.

Kesson Magid is a Ph.D. candidate at the Department of Anthropology, University College London. His project compares hormonal profiles in male Bangladeshi migrants to Britain with non-migrants and the children of migrants. The changes in environmental conditions and socioeconomic position accompanying migration is being assessed in relation to reproductive and metabolic hormones. His research interests include human reproductive ecology and androgen effects on cognitive development.

Donald H. McBurney is Professor Emeritus of Psychology at the University of Pittsburgh. His research interests include the psychophysics of taste, evolutionary psychology, a skeptical approach to the paranormal, and critical thinking. He and his colleagues are currently developing a mathematical model of the time course of adaptation to painful stimuli.

Sarah K. Murnen, Ph.D. is a Professor of Psychology, and Women and Gender Studies at Kenyon College. Her teaching and research interests concern feminist perspectives in psychology, as well as research design and statistical analysis. Her published research examines feminist perspectives on the gendered issues of body image/eating disorders, and sexual violence. She and her colleagues have conducted various meta-analyses related to these issues. For example, they have conducted meta-analyses on the effects of athletic participation, traditional femininity, child sexual abuse, and consumption of the media on indices related to eating problems.

Leif D. Nelson is an Assistant Professor of Marketing at the Stern School of Business, New York University. He trained in psychology both as an undergraduate at Stanford University and as a doctoral candidate at Princeton University. His work focuses on well-being: what makes an experience most enjoyable, what eliminates discomfort, and what leads to sustained happiness? Additionally he has studied how hunger makes men prefer heavier women, how bookmakers exploit a gambler bias for picking favourites, how metaphors make north feel uphill, and why Doug earns lower grades than Alvin. He lives in Manhattan with his beautiful wife and his astonishing daughter.

Terry F. Pettijohn II is an Associate Professor of Psychology at Mercyhurst College in Erie, Pennsylvania. He earned his Ph.D. in Social Psychology from the University of Georgia and he conducts research in the areas of interpersonal attraction, relationships, and how environmental conditions influence social preferences. He is a member of the Association for Psychological Science, the American Psychological Association, and the Society of Personality and Social Psychology. His research findings have been published in the journals *Personality and Social Psychology Bulletin,* the *Journal of Social Psychology*, and *Media Psychology.*

Stephen R. Proulx is a theoretical evolutionary biologist at Iowa State University. He uses mathematical models and computer simulations to explore the evolutionary dynamics of a diverse set of phenotypes, including sex ratio, mating preferences, life-history traits, and genome structure.

Isabel Scott is a Ph.D. candidate in Evolutionary Psychology at Bristol University, supervised by Ian Penton-Voak. Her current project involves testing for evidence of 'strategic pluralism' in human mate choice. This entails using socioecological factors, such as disease, resource stress and marriage system, to predict cross-cultural variations in mate preferences, specifically preferences for facial sexual dimorphism. She is also assisting Gillian Bentley with an investigation of the effects of migration upon somatic preferences. This project seeks to predict changes in preferences using age at migration and length of stay in a new socioecology as independent variables, in order to explore the mechanisms via which attraction preferences are acquired.

Glenn H. Shepard is a medical anthropologist at the University of East Anglia. He has worked with diverse indigenous groups in Peru, Brazil, and Mexico studying ethnobiology, ethnoecology, medical anthropology and sensory ecology.

Linda Smolak is Samuel B. Cummings Jr. Professor of Psychology and Professor of Women's and Gender Studies. Her research and teaching interests focus on the developmental psychopathology of body image and eating problems, including the role of gender in the development of these problems. She has published numerous papers on body image development in elementary and middle school aged boys and girls. She has also published several books on body image in children and adolescents, including the forthcoming second edition of *Body image, eating disorders, and obesity in youth* (with J. Kevin Thompson; American Psychological Association).

Sybil A. Streeter received her B.Phil. from the University Honours College at the University of Pittsburgh, with a double major in Psychology and Human Origins and Evolution. She is currently a graduate student in the Department of Psychology at the University of Pittsburgh. Her research interests include evolutionary psychology, perceptions of female physical attractiveness, development of taste preferences, and the role of scent and adult attachment in mating. In addition to research, she is actively involved in undergraduate teaching.

Viren Swami is a Research Associate at the University of Liverpool. His research interests include an eclectic mix of topics, including interpersonal attraction, gender and health, and lay beliefs. His specific interest in physical attraction centres on cross-cultural differences in preferences, particularly the potential of cross-cultural research to inform evolutionary psychological theorising. Despite having authored or co-authored two books on interpersonal attraction (*The Missing Arms of Vénus de Milo* and *The Psychology of Physical Attraction*, with Adrian Furnham), and over thirty-five research papers, he has yet to uncover the secrets of human beauty.

Louis G. Tassinary, Ph.D. J.D., is a Professor of Architecture and an Adjunct Professor of Psychology, as well as the Associate Dean for Research and the Director of Graduate Studies in the College of Architecture, at Texas A&M University. He is the co-editor of, and contributing author to, two editions of *The Handbook of Psychophysiology*. His current research interests are in the areas of perception and evolutionary psychology, with an emphasis on the morphological cues to biological sex, gender and attractiveness. He thinks everyone should read John Spivak's autobiography, *A Man in his Time* (1967).

J. Kevin Thompson, Ph.D., is a Professor of Psychology at the Department of Psychology, University of South Florida. He has worked in the area of body image and eating disorders for 25 years, with current interests in the areas of measurement, adolescent risk factors, media influences, and body image issues in diverse samples. He has been on the editorial board of the *International Journal of Eating Disorders* since 1990. He has authored, co-authored, edited, or co-edited six books in the field, including several published by the American Psychological Association (*Body image, eating disorders and obesity*, 1996; *Exacting beauty: Theory, assessment and treatment of body image disturbance*, 1999; *Body image, eating disorders and obesity in youth*, 2001; *The muscular ideal*, 2007).

Martin J. Tovée did his Ph.D. at the Experimental Psychology Department, Cambridge University, before moving to the Experimental Psychology Department, Oxford University, to work on face recognition. He is currently Reader in Visual Cognition at the Psychology Department, Newcastle University. His research interests lie in the general areas of physical attractiveness and human mate selection, body image and body image distortion in eating disorders, and face recognition and discrimination.

Douglas W. Yu is a behavioural and spatial ecologist at the University of East Anglia, with interests in tropical ecology, the evolution of mutualisms, and tropical conservation. Since 1996, he has worked in collaboration with Glenn Shepard and the Matsigenka people on various topics, including tropical forest beta diversity, conceptions of human attractiveness, and wild meat hunting.

Preface

In the Meno, Plato begins the dialogue by asking Socrates if 'virtue can be taught, or is it rather to be acquired by practice? Or is it neither to be practised nor learned, but something that comes to men by nature or in some other way?' Plato is asking about the causes of human disposition and behaviour, and casting it within the archetypal form of the nature-nurture question. While the latter has typically fallen within the purview of philosophers of science, it also invites commentary from scientists involved in diverse fields of research, including those interested in human interpersonal attraction. The essays in this volume address precisely the divide between biology and culture, in pursuit of answers to the elusive question of human beauty. It represents seminal work from anthropology, psychology and related fields, and provides a fresh perspective for understanding the perception of human physical attractiveness. Many people have helped with bringing this volume together. We are particularly grateful to Daniel Bunyard at Palgrave Macmillan, whose support for the volume provided constant encouragement.

~VS & AF

Part I
Introduction

1
Mutual and Partaken Bliss: Introducing the Science of Bodily Beauty

Adrian Furnham and Viren Swami

> Beauty is Nature's coin, must not be hoarded,
> But must be current, and the good thereof
> Consists in mutual and partaken bliss.
>
> ~ John Milton, *Comus*

It was no easy decision that Paris had to make. According to Ovid's *Heroides*, Paris had been resting against a tree in the valleys of Mount Ida, when he was startled by the sudden appearance of Hermes and, in his wake, the three goddesses: Hera, Athena, and Aphrodite. There had been an 'incident' at the banquet celebrating the marriage of Peleus and Thetis, to which Eris, Goddess of Discord, had been left uninvited. Angered by the snub, Eris turned up anyway and threw a golden Apple of Discord into the proceeding. On the apple was a most simple inscription: *Kallisti*, 'for the fairest one.' Only, the three goddesses, Hera, Athena, and Aphrodite, each claimed the apple as their own.

Zeus, mighty Zeus – king of the Gods, ruler of Mount Olympus, god of the sky and thunder – was reluctant to favour any claim himself, and instead gave the task to Paris, a mere mortal. And so, as Hermes tells him, Paris is to be 'the final judge of beauty.' He must decide which of the three goddesses 'has such beauty/that will conquer the other two.' No, it was no easy decision that Paris had to make. 'My frightened heart took comfort, I became bold/enough to study each one of them./All were worthy; I sighed because only one/could win.'

To sway him in his decision, each of the three goddesses used their powers to bribe Paris. Hera offered to make him king of Europe and Asia; Athena offered wisdom and skill in war. But the decision was no easier: 'How could I choose between power and/a courageous heart?' Finally, Aphrodite – 'she who causes love' – offered Paris the love of the world's most beautiful woman, Helen of Sparta. Aphrodite is effortlessly beautiful, sexual, and charming, and her gift is well-received: Paris awards her the Apple of Discord, at once earning the love of the beautiful Helen and the enmity of the Greeks (Paris' subsequent abduction of Helen from Sparta is the mythological basis for the Trojan War).

In a sense, the Judgement of Paris might be seen as the prototypical beauty contest: the contest which Eris initiates sets the three goddesses against each other, vying for the approval of Paris. But it is a contest in which Aphrodite, Goddess of Love, holds the upper hand: not only is she physically beautiful herself, but she also offers Paris the hand of the most beautiful mortal, Helen of Sparta. But the mythologised Judgement of Paris also serves a different purpose: it highlights the importance of physical beauty, or at least, the fact that human beings have always taken an interest in the beauty of others (although, of course, in the Judgement of Paris, it is a specific beauty that is being judged – the beauty of women).

But the interest does not end there: a consistent theme throughout the history of beauty has been a quest for its secrets. Attempting to define and explain what makes an object or individual beautiful has consumed some of the world's greatest minds. Pythagoras and the ancient Greeks, for example, attempted a mathematico-aesthetical explanation of beauty, when they argued that it just was a matter of having the right proportions. And because these proportions – or 'golden ratios' – were universal, the secret to beauty was the same whether we consider the human face or the dimensions of a building or even music and literature (Armstrong, 2004; Eco, 2004; Swami, 2007).

So convincing was the Pythagorean explanation of beauty that it remained virtually unchallenged until the late 18th century. Leonardo da Vinci, for instance, is said to have designed the proportions of *Mona Lisa* according to Pythagorean notions of beauty; certainly, there can be no denying that his *Vitruvian Man* conformed to quite precise measurements of the human body which he considered ideal. But da Vinci was not alone in doing so: architects and writers, artists and designers, all subscribed to the Platonic thesis that there is an ideal, objective beauty that can be understood and perceived by all individuals. So long as an object has the right proportions, everyone will agree that in it is contained the essence of beauty.

Beginning in the late 18th century, however, a different idea of beauty began to be raised by philosophers like David Hume and Edmund

Burke, for whom beauty was subjective to the individual. Hume's (1757: 208–209) thesis on beauty is often held up as a paradigmatic example of this notion:

> Beauty is no quality in things themselves; it exists merely in the mind which contemplates them; and each mind perceives a different beauty. One person may even perceive deformity, where another is sensible to beauty... To seek in the real beauty, or deformity, is as fruitless an enquiry, as to pretend to ascertain the real sweet or real bitter. According to the disposition of the organs, the same object may be both sweet and bitter; and the proverb has justly determined it to be fruitless to dispute concerning tastes.

For philosophers like Hume, the subjective nature of beauty meant that it could only be understood once individual feelings and emotions had been taken into account. Beauty had firmly been placed in the proverbial eye of the beholder.

The psychology of beauty

The psychological sciences are relative late-comers to these debates. The widespread belief that beauty is idiosyncratic, combined with the maxim that 'beauty is only skin-deep,' ensured that the topic of human beauty remained in psychology's blind spot until recently. After all, if beauty was a matter of personal taste, if each of us has her or his own unique idea of what constitutes beauty, then it makes any scientific analysis of such preferences extremely difficult. Moreover, if beauty is only skin-deep – and, by extension, if we should not judge a book by its cover – then beauty becomes a triviality to be explained away (Langlois et al., 2000).

This is especially true between cultures, where it was thought there was little consensus in judgements of attractiveness and hence no consistent effect of physical beauty on social judgements, interactions and behaviours. In 1871, for instance, Charles Darwin published his *Descent of Man*, in which he amassed an impressive array of evidence highlighting cross-cultural and historic differences in beauty practices. Whether it was 'breasts hanging down to the belt' or 'obliquity of the eye' or 'teeth... stained black, red and blue' (quoted in Swami, 2007), Darwin believed that there existed great variability in idealised beauty from one culture to the next.

Then, in 1966, Walster, Aronson, Abrahams, and Rottmann advertised a 'computer dance,' in which participants would ostensibly be paired on a blind date by a super-computer based on their similarity. In reality, the experimenters paired the participants in a random manner, except that no man was paired with a taller woman. During the dance, participants were asked to rate their date, with Walster et al. (1966) expecting personalities, intelligence or other such variables to be the best predictors of liking. Instead, what they found was that the more attractive participants were favoured as dates over less attractive participants, and overall, physical attractiveness was the best predictor of mutual liking. Indeed, six months after the dance, partners who were similar in terms of physical attractiveness were more likely to still have been dating.

Walster et al.'s (1966) serendipitous finding was the catalyst for interest in physical attractiveness within the psychological sciences. A great many studies began to document the important, though often surreptitious, role that physical attractiveness plays in our daily lives (see Patzer, 2002; Swami & Furnham, 2007). Our first impressions of strangers, for example, are based almost entirely on non-verbal cues (Baron, Byrne, & Branscombe, 2006), particularly physical appearance (Park, 1986). When we meet someone for the first time, we tend to focus on information that we believe will provide cues about that person's personality, principles, and values – which typically means categorising individuals based on their looks.

Over the years, numerous studies and reviews of the literature have shown that physical attractiveness and appearance has a predictable effect on the judgements that people make about others (Dion, 1974; Dion, Berscheid, & Walster, 1972; Eagly, Ashmore, Makhijani, & Longo, 1991; Snyder, Tanke, & Berscheid, 1977). In general, we imbue attractive individuals with perceived positive qualities – including social competence, intelligence, dominance and psychological adjustment – and we shower them with more positive social interactions in a wide variety of everyday domains (Eagly et al. (1991).

These inferences are not only directed at adults: attractive babies tend to receive greater attention (kissing, cooing, smiling, eye contact, even cuddling) from their mothers and nurses than less attractive babies (Corter et al., 1978; Langlois, Ritter, Roggman, & Vaughn, 1991; Stephan & Langlois, 1984). In school, attractive children are more popular than unattractive children (Kleck, Richardson, & Ronald, 1974; Langlois & Styczynski, 1979) and even teachers assume that attractive students are more likely to be academically successful than less attractive students (Adams, 1978; Clifford & Hatfield, 1973). In college, too, attractive students are more likely to receive better grades, regardless of the quality of their work (cf. Landy & Sigall, 1974).

But, of course, it is in adulthood that the pervasive effects of physical attractiveness truly become evident. Attractive individuals are more likely to date and marry (Kalick, Zebrowitz, Langlois, & Johnson, 1998; Udry & Eckland, 1984), and they are also more likely to be helped by strangers in the event of an accident (Benson, Karabenick, & Lerner, 1976; Sroufe, Chaikin, Cook, & Freeman, 1977; Swami, Chan, Wong, Furnham, & Tovée, in press). In the courtroom, attractive defendants benefit from more lenient sentencing than less attractive defendants and are less often perceived as guilty (Castellow, Wuensch, & Moore, 1990; Darby & Jeffers, 1988; Kulka & Kessler, 1978; Solomon & Schopler, 1978; Stewart, 1980, 1984). And compared with less attractive individuals, attractive people are more likely to be hired for jobs (Dipboye, Arvey, & Terpstra, 1977; Swami et al., in press) and receive higher starting salaries (Dipboye, Fromkin, & Wiback, 1975).

The social and evolutionary psychologies of beauty

In short, then, a wealth of evidence suggests that, despite the exhortations of received wisdom and age-old maxims, physical beauty has both an immediate and predictable effect on social interactions (Langlois et al., 2000). Within psychology, two relatively distinct bodies of work have developed in an attempt to answer the question of 'why' attractive individuals are perceived and treated more positively. The first of these stems from social psychological and anthropological work, which highlights the social and cultural contexts in which attractiveness judgements are formed and acted upon. Specifically, this view suggests that a great deal of social learning must take place when it comes to defining standards of attractiveness, and that both individual proclivities and subcultural ideals play important roles in defining what we find attractive.

On the other hand, some psychologists have taken an evolutionary approach to physical attractiveness, arguing that some aspects of perceptions of beauty may be influenced by our common biological heritage. This approach can be traced back to the publication of Don Symons' *Evolution of Human Sexuality* in 1979, in which he applied an explicit evolutionary framework to the science of physical attractiveness. Symons' work inspired a great many other researchers to approach the topic of human beauty from a fresh perspective and, in the past two decades especially, research guided by an evolutionary framework has intensified dramatically (see Swami & Furnham, 2007).

Yet, with very few exceptions, evolutionary and social perspectives on human physical attractiveness have rarely been combined within a more general theoretical framework. In a recent account, Swami and Furnham (2007) lamented this fact, and argued that neither an evolutionary nor a social psychological approach in isolation is sufficient to understand the science of human beauty. Of course, the different paths taken by social and evolutionary psychologists in attempting to understand human beauty stems from their different perspectives. The point remains, however, that in isolation neither perspective can account for the myriad of different factors that affect our attraction to others.

Body beautiful

This, then, is the primary aim of the present volume: we have brought together seminal work from evolutionary and sociocultural perspectives, which explore the questions of *what* our attractiveness preferences are and *why* we find certain others physically attractive. The research and theoretical contributions presented in this volume offer a fresh perspective to understanding the perception of attractiveness, within evolutionary, cognitive, social, motivational, and cultural contexts. The only caveat we introduce is that these contributions focus specifically (though not exclusively) on the human body. The simple reason for this is that much psychological research has been devoted to human facial attractiveness, to the detriment of bodily beauty (see Rhodes & Zebrowitz, 2002).

As might be expected, the human body is an important site of beauty practices (Swami, 2006), and the focus on bodily beauty is not alien to either evolutionary or sociocultural researchers. In terms of the former, for instance, a great deal of research time and expertise has been spent on defining the characteristics of ideal feminine and masculine beauty (see Swami & Furnham, 2007). This body of work has focussed quite specifically on the female waist-to-hip ratio as an index of women's bodily beauty (McBurney & Streeter, Chapter 2), arguing that because a low waist-to-hip ratio was correlated with women's health and fertility in evolutionary history, men should find such ratios attractive today.

Others agree that it is useful to study the human body, but disagree as to the utility of the waist-to-hip ratio as an index of women's physical attractiveness. Fan (Chapter 3) presents the volume-height index as a more accurate predictor of both women's and men's attractiveness, whereas Bateson and colleagues (Chapter 4) take issue with the way in which women's attractiveness has been studied. Instead, they find that overall body weight may be a more important – and accessible – factor in defining what it means to be beautiful, at least for women. The most important conclusion to emerge from these chapters, however, is that there is unlikely to be a single defining characteristic of attractiveness (Fan, Chapter 3; Bateson, Cornelissen, & Tovée, Chapter 4); rather, body shape, body weight and possibly other characteristics (e.g., the leg-to-body ratio, skin tone and so on; Swami, Einon, & Furnham, 2006; Smith, Cornelissen, & Tovée, 2007) all contribute to men's and women's physical attractiveness.

Another important conclusion to emerge from these chapters is that there is great cross-cultural variability in what is perceived as an attractive body. Scott et al. (Chapter 5) examine ideals of body weight in Bangladesh and Britain, and describe how such ideals may be intricately linked with differences in socioeconomic status. Similarly, Tovée, Furnham, and Swami (Chapter 7) document shifting patterns of body weight ideals in South Africa and Britain, and show how this is associated with similarly changing patterns of what is perceived as healthy body weights. Finally, Yu and colleagues (Chapter 6) show how, in a population of Matsigenka Amerindians, mate choice varies within the same individual depending on the sociocultural role of the potential mate. In short, these chapters highlight the way in which socioeconomic and cultural contexts interact with evolved biology to alter perceptions of an attractive body.

The contributions to this volume also make important theoretical advancements in our understanding of human beauty. Einon (Chapter 8) questions whether attractiveness ideals really do reflect an evolved mechanism for choosing fertile mates; rather, she suggests that there may be alternative adaptive explanations for such ideals, which evolutionary perspectives will need to incorporate. Other chapters highlight the importance of incorporating more inclusive perspectives on human physical attractiveness: Johnson and Tassinary (Chapter 9) explore how body shapes affect evaluative social judgements, whereas Nelson, Pettijohn, and Galak (Chapter 10) examine the cognitive and motivational states that give rise to predictable variation in attractiveness ideals.

An important final contribution of this volume comes from the explicitly sociocultural perspective taken by some researchers (Hildebrandt & Latner, Chapter 11; Smolak & Murnen, Chapter 12; Calogero, Boroughs, & Thompson, Chapter 13). These chapters, which focus on research conducted in the West, highlight the many different ways in which social learning and political contexts influence ideals of attractiveness. Importantly, these chapters also explicate the ways in which an unhealthy pursuit of such ideals can sometimes result in 'normative discontent,' including body image and eating disorders. These are topics of study that are rarely considered within the evolutionary psychological scheme, and their discussion here serves to highlight key aspects of the literature in which a combined perspective will be fruitful.

Attempts to provide definitive answers to the persistent quest for human beauty have typically relied on either *objective* or *subjective* perspectives. The dominant paradigm for some years now, derived from evolutionary psychology, argues that there are objective criteria of attractiveness which most, if not all, individuals perceive and agree upon, because these were shaped by their common evolutionary history. However, we believe that the pendulum is now swinging back: most contemporary accounts of attractiveness have highlighted the way in which both sociocultural and evolutionary pathways influence the construction and reconstruction of beauty ideals.

Rather than there being consistent ideals of beauty across individuals or cultures, any true understanding of beauty must analyse the way in which individuals incorporate, either consciously or otherwise, biological and subcultural ideals of attractiveness (Swami & Furnham, 2007). The chapters in this book highlight these themes and illustrate the productive nature of work that combines different perspectives within a single over-arching perspective. As the contributors to this volume argue, bodily attractiveness is a complex phenomenon, which in turn requires comprehensive methods of research and analysis. Certainly, this is a premise known to artists and novelists, such as Giovanni Ruffini:

> The perception of the beautiful is gradual, and not a lightning revelation; it requires not only time, but some study.

References

Adams, G. R. (1978). Racial membership and physical attractiveness effects on preschool teachers' expectations. *Child Study Journal*, 8, 29–41.

Armstrong, J. (2004). *The secret power of beauty*. London: Penguin.

Baron, R., Byrne, D., & Branscombe, N. (2006). *Social psychology*. Boston, MA: Pearson.

Benson, P. L., Karabenick, S. A., & Lerner, R. M. (1976). Pretty pleases: The effects of physical attractiveness, race, and sex on receiving help. *Journal of Experimental Social Psychology*, 12, 409–415.

Castellow, K. S., Wuensch, K. L., & Moore, C. H. (1990). Effects of physical attractiveness of plaintiff and defendant in sexual harassment judgements. *Journal of Social Behaviour and Personality*, 16, 39–50.

Clifford, M. M., & Hatfield, E. (1973). Research note: The effects of physical attractiveness on teacher expectations. *Social Education*, 46, 248–258.

Corter, C., Trehub, S., Boukydis, C., Ford, L., Celhoffer, L., & Minde, K. (1978). Nurses' judgements of the attractiveness of premature infants. *Infant Behavior and Development, 1,* 373–380.

Darby, B. W., & Jeffers, D. (1988). The effects of defendant and juror attractiveness on simulated courtroom trials and decisions. *Social Behavior and Personality, 5,* 547–562.

Darwin, C. (1871). *The descent of man, and selection in relation to sex.* London: Murray.

Dion, K. K. (1974). Children's physical attractiveness and sex as determinants of adult punitiveness. *Developmental Psychology, 10,* 772–778.

Dion, K. K., Berscheid, E., & Walster, E. (1972). What is beautiful is good. *Journal of Personality and Social Psychology, 24,* 285–290.

Dipboye, R. L., Arvey, R. D., & Terpstra, D. E. (1977). Sex and physical attractiveness of raters and applicants as determinants of resumé evaluations. *Journal of Applied Psychology, 62,* 288–294.

Dipboye, R. L., Fromkin, H. L., & Wiback, K. (1975). Relative importance of applicant sex, attractiveness and scholastic standing in evaluation of job applicant resumes. *Journal of Applied Psychology, 60,* 39–43.

Eagly, E. H., Ashmore, R. D., Makhijani, M. G., & Longo, L. C. (1991). What is beautiful is good, but… A meta-analytic review of research on the physical attractiveness stereotype. *Psychological Bulletin, 110,* 109–128.

Eco, U. (2004). *On beauty: A history of a Western idea* (Trans. A. McEwen). London: Secker and Warburg.

Hume, D. (1757). *Four dissertations. IV: Of the standard of taste.* London: Millar.

Kalick, S. M., Zebrowitz, L. A., Langlois, J. H., & Johnson, R. M. (1998). Does human facial attractiveness honestly advertise health? Longitudinal data on an evolutionary question. *Psychological Science, 9,* 8–13.

Kleck, R. E., Richardson, S. A., & Ronald, L. (1974). Physical appearance cues and interpersonal attraction in children. *Child Development, 45,* 305–310.

Kulka, R. A., & Kessler, J. D. (1978). Is justice really blind? The influence of litigant physical attractiveness on juridical judgements. *Journal of Applied Social Psychology, 8,* 366–381.

Landy, D., & Sigall, H. (1974). Beauty is talent: Task evaluation as a function of the performer's physical attractiveness. *Journal of Personality and Social Psychology, 29,* 299–304.

Langlois, J. H., & Styczynski, L. (1979). The effects of physical attractiveness on the behavioral attributions and peer preferences in acquianted children. *International Journal of Behavioral Development, 2,* 325–341.

Langlois, J. H., Ritter, J. M., Roggman, L. A., & Vaughn, L. S. (1991). Facial diversity and infant preferences for attractive faces. *Developmental Psychology, 27,* 79–84.

Langlois, J. H., Kalakanis, L. E., Rubenstein, A. J., Larson, A. D., Hallam, M. J., & Smoot, M. T. (2000). Maxims and myths of beauty: A meta-analytic and theoretical review. *Psychological Bulletin, 126,* 390–423.

Milton, J. (1637/2000). *Comus, or Re-formations of a maske.* Online publication at: http://www.mith.umd.edu/comus/final/. Retrieved January 29, 2007.

Ovid (5 BC/1990). *Heroides* (Trans. H. Isbell). Harmondsworth: Penguin.

Park, B. (1986). A method for studying the development of impressions of real people. *Journal of Personality and Social Psychology, 51,* 907–917.

Patzer, G. L. (2002). *The power and paradox of physical attractiveness.* Boca Raton, FL: BrownWalker Press.

Rhodes, G., & Zebrowitz, L. A. (Eds.) (2002). *Facial attractiveness: Evolutionary, cognitive and social perspectives.* Westport, CO: Ablex.

Smith, K. L., Cornelissen, P. L., & Tovée, M. J. (2007). Color 3D bodies and judgements of human female attractiveness. *Evolution and Human Behavior, 28,* 48–54.

Snyder, M., Tanke, E. D., & Berscheid, E. (1977). Social perception and interpersonal behavior: On the self-fulfilling nature of social stereotypes. *Journal of Personality and Social Psychology, 35,* 656–666.

Solomon, M. R., & Schopler, J. (1978). The relationship of physical attractiveness and punitiveness: Is the linearity assumption out of line? *Personality and Social Psychology Bulletin, 4,* 483–486.

Sroufe, R. A., Chaikin, A., Cook, R., & Freeman, V. (1977). The effects of physical attractiveness on honesty: A socially desirable response. *Personality and Social Psychology Bulletin, 3,* 59–62.

Stephan, C. W., & Langlois, J. H. (1984). Baby beautiful: Adult attributions of infant competence as a function of infant attractiveness. *Child Development, 55,* 576–585.

Stewart, J. E. (1980). Defendant's attractiveness as a factor in the outcome of criminal trials: An observational study. *Journal of Applied Social Psychology, 10,* 348–361.

Stewart, J. E. (1984). Appearance and punishment: The attraction-leniency effect in the courtroom. *Journal of Social Psychology, 125,* 373–378.

Swami, V. (2006). The influence of body weight and shape in determining female and male physical attractiveness. In M. V. Kindes (Ed.), *Body image: New research* (pp. 35–61). New York: Nova Biomedical Books.

Swami, V. (2007). *The missing arms of Vénus de Milo: Reflections on the science of physical attractiveness.* Brighton: The Book Guild.

Swami, V., & Furnham, A. (2007). *The psychology of physical attraction.* London: Routledge.

Swami, V., Einon, D., & Furnham, A. (2006). An investigation of the leg-to-body ratio as a human aesthetic criterion. *Body Image, 3,* 317–323.

Swami, V., Chan, F., Wong, V., Furnham, A., & Tovée, M. J. (in press). Weight-based discrimination in occupational hiring and helping behaviour. *Journal of Applied Social Psychology.*

Symons, D. (1979). *The evolution of human sexuality.* New York: Oxford University Press.

Udry, J. R., & Eckland, B. K. (1984). Benefits of being attractive: Differential payoffs for men and women. *Psychological Reports, 54,* 47–56.

Walster, E., Aronson, V., Abrahams, D., & Rottmann, L. (1966). Importance of physical attractiveness in dating behavior. *Journal of Personality and Social Psychology, 4,* 508–516.

Part II
Methodological Critiques

2
Waist-to-Hip Ratios and Female Attractiveness: Comparing Apples, Oranges, and Pears

Donald H. McBurney and Sybil A. Streeter

An evolutionary approach to female attractiveness predicts that men should prefer honest signals of health, youth, and fertility in potential mates (Buss, 1989). Singh (1993a, 1993b) proposed that the waist-to-hip ratio (WHR) was a signal of female fertility, and thus served as a measure of attractiveness. How revolutionary this approach was can be seen by reviewing what leading books on social psychology said concerning attractiveness before Singh's work. In Baron and Byrne's (1994) leading textbook of the time, the chapter on attractiveness has a section entitled, 'What, exactly, determines attractiveness?' In it they say, '[It] seems to be difficult to specify precisely what cues people utilize to evaluate attractiveness' (Baron & Byrne, 1994: 290). Baron and Byrne (1994) discussed the importance of childlike and mature facial features. They also reviewed work using computer-generated composite faces which showed that average faces were most attractive. Concerning the body, they cited research showing the attractiveness of medium-sized breasts and a slim figure (Baron & Byrne, 1994: 291). Another leading book (Aronson, Wilson, & Akert, 1994: 381) asked the question, 'What is beautiful, anyway?' and answered by stating that, 'From early childhood on, the media tell us what is beautiful ... '.

What made Singh's work so revolutionary was not only that it gave us the WHR as a measure of attractiveness, but it also gave an adaptive explanation of what had previously either been taken for granted or explained essentially atheoretically. We now know that 'female attract-iveness at a glance provides a multitude of information essential for a male's reproductive success' (Singh, 2006: 43). Further, the WHR is closely related to a number of variables associated with a woman's fertility.

Before puberty, boys and girls have similar WHRs of about 1.0. As women approach menopause, their WHRs rise until once again it approaches that of males (Kirschner & Samojlik, 1991). In addition, Singh (1993a, 1993b) reviewed a considerable body of evidence that fertility is associated with the WHR. The rise in estrogen at puberty is not only necessary for fertility, but contributes to a lower WHR. 'Women with higher WHRs and low body mass index (BMI) have more difficulty getting pregnant and have their first live birth at a later age than married women with lower WHR' (Singh, 1993a: 294). Higher WHRs impair the pregnancy rate of *in-vitro* fertilization-embryo transfer (Wass, Waldenstrom, Rossner, & Hellberg, 1997). In a prospective study of women being treated at a fertility clinic for reasons of male infertility, the WHR was the single best predictor of pregnancy rates, including BMI and age. An increase in the WHR of 0.1 yielded a decrease of 30 per cent in achieving pregnancy (Zaadstra et al., 1993). The WHR is also related to conditions not directly related to pregnancy, including diabetes, hypertension, heart attack, stroke, and gallbladder disease (Singh, 1993a).

We believe it is useful to consider the WHR as an example of a fast and frugal heuristic (Gigerenzer, Todd, & the ABC Research Group, 1999) that people can use to solve an adaptive problem efficiently. Gigerenzer and his group (1999) have demonstrated a large number of domains in which people use a rule of thumb to make a decision more rapidly than would be possible by a more complete algorithm. In fact, people are often more accurate when they have less information. We believe this explains why the WHR is so universal and so powerful a signal of a female's desirability.

Critical commentary

Singh's elegant proposal, however, did not go unchallenged. Some have found that the WHR preference may be influenced by the range of WHRs found in local environments, or by scarcity of food resources (Furnham & Alibhai, 1983; Marlowe & Wetsman, 2001; Marlowe, Apicella, & Reed, 2005; Swami & Tovée, 2005, 2006; Wetsman & Marlowe, 1999; Yu & Shepard, 1998). Our purpose in this chapter is not to consider what the 'optimum' WHR is, but rather the role of the WHR as a measure.

Tassinary and Hansen (1998) criticised Singh's line drawings as confounding the WHR with weight. Curiously, however, their own set of line drawings suffered the same problems, as Henss (2000) pointed

out. Tassinary and Hansen (1998) claimed to have found that attractiveness actually increased with WHR, in direct opposition to all other
investigators, before or after. The point we wish to make with regard
to Tassinary and Hansen (1998) simply concerns the way they plotted
their data. It is well known that ratios can be tricky to work with for a
number of reasons. Here, we are concerned with the problems that arise
because of the several ways they can be plotted. In the present case, we
consider the ratio of waist size to hip size.

Now, when plotting attractiveness as a function of WHR with a set
of stimuli that vary both by waist and hip size, one has two choices.
One can use the hip as the parameter, and connect all the data points
that have the same size hip. Or one can use waist size as the parameter, connecting data points having the same waist size. Tassinary and
Hansen (1998) chose to use waist size as the parameter. This choice
determined their conclusion, because if Tassinary and Hansen's (1998)
data are plotted in the conventional manner, we see that they show that
attractiveness increases with lower WHR (Streeter & McBurney, 2003), as
others have found. Figure 2.1 shows Tassinary and Hansen's (1998) data
plotted both ways. The dotted lines show the data the way Tassinary and
Hansen (1998) plotted them, using waist size as the parameter. It appears
that attractiveness increases with WHR. The solid lines show the data

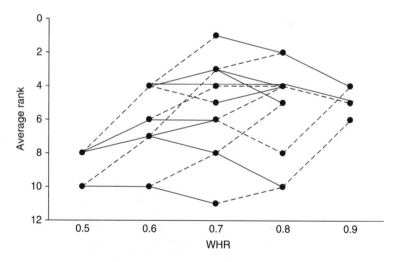

Figure 2.1 Attractiveness as a function of waist-to-hip ratio (data of Tassinary &
Hansen, 1998). Solid lines connect figures with the same hip size. Dotted lines
connect figures with the same waist size (Streeter & McBurney, 2003).

plotted in the conventional way, with hip size as the parameter, and the conventional relationship is demonstrated, namely that attractiveness is greatest at around a WHR of 0.70.

This effect is not an artefact of these data. Consider the area of a rectangle which, of course, equals height times width. If we plotted the area of a set of rectangles as a function of the ratio of their height to width, we could show either that area increased or decreased with the height-to-width ratio, depending on whether we connected data points by height or width. Thus, Tassinary and Hansen's (1998) conclusions depend completely on their choice of method of plotting their data. Which method of plotting the data is appropriate? Fortunately we need not make the choice, because the data of Streeter and McBurney (2003) showed the usual relationship no matter which way they are plotted, when attractiveness is adjusted for the effect of weight (see Figures 2.2 and 2.3). In addition, a replication using Tassinary and Hansen's (1998) line drawings showed the usual preference for a WHR of 0.70, without adjusting for the effect of weight (Forestell, Humphrey, & Stewart, 2004).

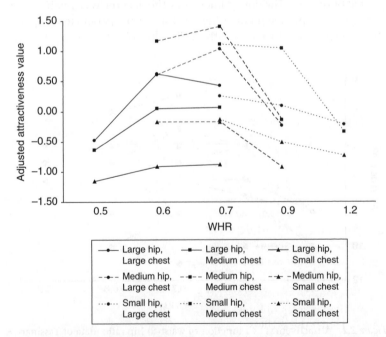

Figure 2.2 Attractiveness values adjusted for the effect of estimated weight as a function of waist-to-hip ratio (Streeter & McBurney, 2003).

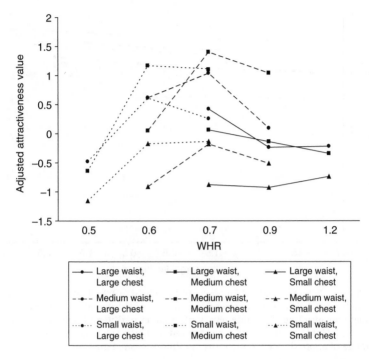

Figure 2.3 Same data as Figure 2.2 plotted by connecting figures with the same waist size, following Tassinary and Hansen (1998) (Streeter & McBurney, 2003).

The relative importance of characteristics

Others have criticised the WHR work on the basis that the line drawings are artificial (Henss, 2000; Swami & Furnham, 2006). We have two responses to that objection. First, several studies (Henss, 2000; Singh, 1994; Streeter & McBurney, 2003) have used photographs and found results consistent with those using line drawings. But, second and more important: artificial stimuli, like artificial laboratory situations in general, often permit an investigator to isolate a variable so that its effects are seen more clearly, rather than less so (Mook, 1983).

Another challenge to Singh's work comes from Tovée and his group (see Bateson, Cornelissen, & Tovée, Chapter 4). They have shown that the WHR may account for less variance than body mass index (BMI), and conclude that the WHR is thus unimportant. This analysis overlooks the fact that whether one variable accounts for more variance than a second in no way invalidates the importance of the second variable. This may

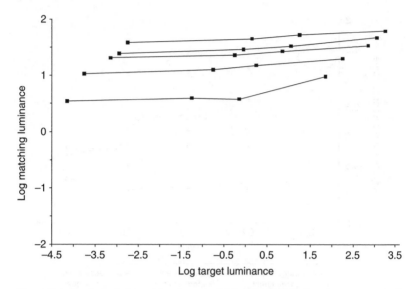

Figure 2.4   Replotted data of Jacobsen and Gilchrist (1988). Luminance required to match the lightness of a target as a function of the overall luminance of the target and surround. Each line represents a target of different reflectance (white to black). Note that the luminance required to match the target varies little over a range of approximately 6 log units (a million-to-one range).

be seen in perception of lightness (i.e., the dimension of white to black). Consider a patch of light surrounded by another (see Figure 2.4). Two variables, level of overall illumination, and the ratio of reflectances of the center and surround, are considered. It is interesting that varying the level of overall illumination over an enormous range has very little effect on the perception of lightness (e.g., Jacobsen & Gilchrist, 1988), as shown by the fact that the lines are practically flat over a range of approximately 6 log units (a million-to-one range).

An everyday example of this point is the robust principle of whiteness constancy; namely, that surfaces appear to have the same level of whiteness whether indoors or in full sunlight. Ratio of reflectances of the target and surround, however, has a very large effect. This set of facts in no way implies that level of illumination can be ignored in favor of ratio of reflectances, for it is absolutely necessary that there be some level of illumination in order to see anything at all.

Many examples come to mind where multiple variables influence a particular dependent measure. Perhaps an everyday example will suffice. The quality of a loaf of bread depends on the amount of flour, sugar, salt, yeast, and water; the extent to which it is kneaded; and the temperature and time of baking. Certain of these variables by themselves will have an all-or-none role in determining the quality of the resulting loaf. It is pointless to ask how much variance each accounts for.

Returning to physical attractiveness, it is quite pointless to consider the *differences in the variance* in attractiveness accounted for by *different variables*. We could vary the apparent age of the figure by varying such signs as wrinkles in the skin and the greying of hair, or we could add large variations in symmetry, visible signs of disease, and so forth. Any of these would no doubt have a considerable effect on attractiveness. For example, Furnham, Lavancy, and McClelland (2001) found that facial attractiveness had a larger effect than WHR on overall attractiveness. This result illustrates that the effect of one particular variable depends strongly on what variables are manipulated and how they are manipulated.

In this connection, it is particularly significant that almost all of the studies of this subject have used young adult women, ignoring variables other than the WHR that signal age. We are aware of one study (Furnham & Reeves, 2006) that varied signals of age along with the WHR. Larger eyes and mouth, and smaller nose increased neoteny, and the reverse decreased it. They found that neoteny was a significant determinant of attractiveness, but the WHR was not. This result makes our point because a previous study (Henss, 2000) using the same pictures, but varying only the WHR, had found significant effects of WHR. Although one can imagine experiments pitting many other variables against the WHR, and one could no doubt show the WHR accounting for any arbitrarily small percent of the variance, nothing would be gained in our understanding of the importance of the WHR.

Statistical analyses

Next, we turn to the question of the equations and transformations used to describe the data in this area. We must distinguish between two very different purposes for using transformations and mathematical equations. The first purpose, and perhaps most familiar to most people today, is to satisfy the assumptions of statistical tests. One common example is taking the logarithm of all data points to normalise a skewed distribution. For example, it is common for a distribution to have a mean close to the lower end of the distribution, with a long tail toward the high end. Transforming all scores to the logarithm of the numbers will tend to make the distribution symmetrical because the numbers 10, 100, and 1,000 have common logarithms of 1, 2, and 3. So if the mean of the distribution were 100, with 10 and 1,000 as one standard deviation below and above the mean, respectively, then the logarithms of the scores would be symmetrical about the mean. Closely related is the use of various equations such as the polynomial, logarithmic, power, and so on, in order to compare sets of data that display non-linear relationships. These are an essential part of the statistical armamentarium. They must not be confused, however, with the second purpose of using transformations and mathematical equations, which is for empirical curve fitting.

The purpose of empirical curve fitting is to determine the mathematical relationship between variables in order to discover fundamental processes revealed by the data. Consider the data from Tovée, Swami, Furnham, and Mangalparsad (2006; see also Tovée, Furnham, & Swami, Chapter 7) (see Figure 2.5). There, a polynomial equation is used to analyse the difference between various populations in the effect of BMI on attractiveness ratings. There is no problem in this application because it served the purpose of statistics. However, it would be a serious mistake to conclude that the polynomial describes any underlying processes relating to attractiveness, in particular the separate roles of BMI and WHR. Note that the curves systematically underestimate attractiveness at a BMI of about 17 to 25 kg/m^2, depending on the particular sample, but especially the case for the British Caucasians (squares) and the Britons of African origin (stars). The polynomial systematically misses the true relationship. But the divergence between the curve and the data becomes most obvious above a BMI of 35, where the fitted line begins to increase, and if shown, would continue to increase dramatically above 45. It is clear that the curve does not reveal any fundamental processes underlying attractiveness.

Empirical curve fitting, on the other hand, has as its goal revealing underlying processes. A particularly well-known example for sensory psychologists would be the question of the validity of S. S. Stevens' power law of sensation, compared to alternatives such as Fechner's logarithmic law, and Helson's adaptation level theory. Stevens said that the magnitude of sensation is proportional to the stimulus magnitude raised to a power [Sensation $= k$(Stimulus Intensity)^n]. Fechner said that sensation is proportional to the logarithm of stimulus intensity [Sensation $= k$(log Stimulus Intensity)]. Helson's equation is too complicated to be instructive here, and the significance of that fact will become relevant soon.

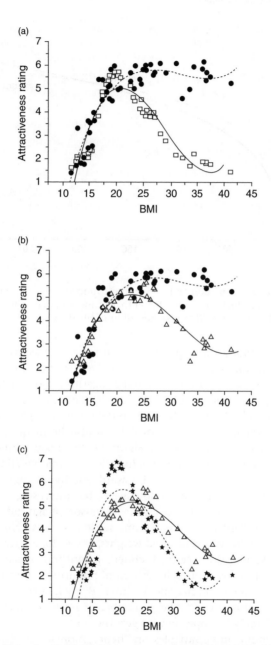

Figure 2.5 Data showing attractiveness ratings as a function of BMI (Tovée, Swami, Furnham, & Mangalparsad, 2006). Although the curves adequately serve the purpose of statistical tests, they do not describe any psychologically meaningful relationship in the data.

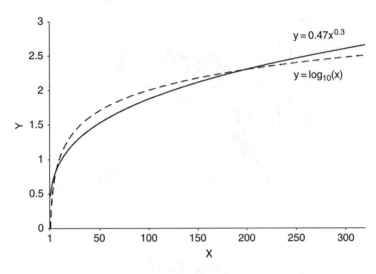

Figure 2.6 A power function and a logarithmic function that are similar to each other. Choosing which function is better to describe a set of data involves theoretical considerations as well as goodness of fit of the data.

Choosing among these approaches, and their respective equations, is more than simply considering the relative fits of data to theoretical curves, because a power function and a logarithmic function can look very similar in particular cases. In such situations, it is necessary to consider the equations in a broader context. For example, data that fit a power function with a slope of 0.3 can also be fit quite well by a logarithmic equation, as shown in Figure 2.6. But a power function with a slope greater than 1 looks nothing like a logarithmic equation, because it is positively accelerating (curved upward, and increasing) rather than negatively accelerating (curved downward, but increasing). In the case of Stevens versus Fechner and scaling of sensory magnitude, it is thus critically important to note that some senses, such as pain of electric shock, and the heaviness of lifted weights, show slopes greater than 1, greatly weakening the case for Fechner's logarithmic equation. If one only wished to consider the dimension of brightness, it would be hard to choose between Stevens and Fechner. But when one realises that brightness is only one of a large number of sensory dimensions that vary considerably in slope, Stevens gets the nod.

Further, adding more variables, and hence, more mathematical terms, will always increase one's ability to fit a particular set of data. As Stevens (1966: 395–396) says with respect to Helson's more complex model,

'[Helson's] formulation contains several constants that are supposed to be evaluated *ad hoc*. Consequently a decisive test of the quantitative model becomes rather elusive. But notwithstanding our dismay at the hyperflexibility of the quantitative model, we must admit that a wide spectrum of applications has been recounted...Into a loose tent and a loose theory much can be crowded.'

So how would we approach empirical curve fitting in the case of BMI, WHR, and attractiveness? First, we avoid functions such as the polynomial, where one can account for more of the variance simply by adding more parameters. In fact, a polynomial equation can account for any arbitrary amount of the variance by adding more variables (Weisberg, 2005).

Closely related is the tack taken by Fan and colleagues (Fan, Chapter 3; Fan, Liu, Wu, & Dai, 2004), who have considered the contribution to attractiveness of many variables other than WHR. They found that attractiveness can be well described as a power function of BMI (for stimuli with a BMI of 16 or greater, which simplifies the relationship by considering only normal-weight and heavier figures). This is a large improvement over the polynomial equation used by the Tovée group because it avoids the problem raised above. Fan et al. (2004) then defined another variable, the volume-height index (VHI) that was slightly better than the very similar BMI in predicting attractiveness.

Fan et al. (2004) additionally found the ratio of waist-height to chin-height (WHC) to be slightly more important than WHR. (This ratio is larger when legs are longer, and is an indicator of youth.) This approach of considering many different variables may be suitable for accounting for overall attractiveness, especially in the context of clothing design, but does not invalidate the importance of any particular measure, as we discussed above. Consideration of more variables will always reduce the relative contribution of any particular variable.

Second, we look for dimensions that are relatively simple: BMI (or VHI) and WHR qualify. Tovée and his group have taken a different approach. They treated the outline of the torso as a waveform, and used the mathematical technique of waveform analysis to investigate contributions of shape to attractiveness (e.g., Tovée, Hancock, Mahmoodi, Singleton, & Cornelissen, 2002). They measured 68 slices of the torso and legs and plotted the size measures against position as a waveform. Fourier analysis of this waveform deconstructed the waveform into its constituent parts. Such a process, however, permits an arbitrary number of components of shape to be considered, without any *a priori* consideration. For this reason, it shares with the polynomial function the arbitrariness of its results, which is fine if one's purpose is simply statistical. But Tovée et al. (2002) then look for some theoretical basis for the various principal components of the waveform analysis, which brings us to the next consideration.

The third consideration in doing empirical curve fitting is crucially important, and that is to find theoretical reasons for the relationship. Once again BMI and WHR are both systematically related to important health outcomes, and the list is similar, but not the same. Higher BMI is related to a long list of diseases (Weeden & Sabini, 2005, and references therein), including hypertension, adult-onset diabetes, coronary artery disease, and stroke. Reproductive problems in women associated with BMI include complications of pregnancy, menstrual irregularities, amenorrhea, polycystic ovarian syndrome, increased morbidity for mother and child, and increased risk of congenital abnormalities.

Higher WHR is negatively predictive of female reproductive health (Weeden & Sabini, 2005, and references therein), including higher plasma testosterone, polycystic ovary syndrome, and lower rate of pregnancy. WHR was the best predictor of pregnancy rates among the tested variables, including BMI (Weeden & Sabini, 2005). Although the list of health outcomes for WHR and BMI partially overlap, the considerable differences suggest that these are two different but important measures, each of which gives different information about women's health.

A striking example of the different information provided by BMI and WHR has recently been given by Lassek and Gaulin (2006). These authors point out that the hips and thighs of women store particular fats that are essential for the development of a baby's brain during gestation and lactation. Because these fats are scarce in the diet, they must be stored before pregnancy, and they are depleted over the woman's fertile lifetime. WHR, but not BMI, provides a visible signal of the stores of these essential fats. Although BMI affects the size of hips and thighs, it is not possible to evaluate a woman's store of these crucial fats by looking at hips and thighs alone. For that purpose it is necessary to evaluate WHR. Thus, Lassek and Gaulin's (2006) finding suggests another reason for the importance of WHR as a signal of fertility.

Conclusion

In summary, Singh's proposition that WHR is a measure of female attractiveness because of its usefulness as a signal of fertility remains a powerful example of the evolved human mind. Those who have proposed that other measures are capable of predicting more of the variance confuse curve fitting for the purpose of statistics with curve fitting to reveal underlying psychological functions.

Much in the popular press is made about the relative health benefits of 'pear-shaped' bodies over 'apple-shaped' ones. We contend that using BMI gives information mainly about the plumpness of the fruit, whereas WHR gives information about the kind of fruit. Plumpness can be an important determinant of quality when in the produce aisle. Pitting BMI against WHR, however, is more like contrasting apples with oranges. We believe that in the case of judging attractiveness it is more important to compare apples to pears.

References

Aronson, E., Wilson, T. D., & Akert, R. A. (1994). *Social psychology: The heart and the mind*. New York: Harper Collins.

Baron, R. A., & Byrne, D. (1994). *Social psychology: Understanding human interaction* (7th ed.). Boston, MA: Allyn & Bacon.

Buss, D. M. (1989). Sex differences in human mate preferences: Evolutionary hypotheses tested in 37 cultures. *Behavioral and Brain Sciences, 12*, 1–49.

Fan, J., Liu, F., Wu, J., & Dai, W. (2004). Visual perception of female physical attractiveness. *Proceedings of the Royal Society London B, 271*, 347–352.

Forestell, C. A., Humphrey, T. M., & Stewart, S. H. (2004). Involvement of body weight and shape factors in ratings of attractiveness by women: A replication and extension of Tassinary and Hansen. *Personality and Individual Differences, 36*, 295–305.

Furnham, A., & Alibhai, N. (1983). Cross-cultural differences in the perception of female body shapes. *Psychological Medicine, 13*, 829–837.

Furnham, A., & Reeves, E. (2006). The relative influence of facial neotony and waist-to-hip ratio on judgements of female attractiveness and fecundity. *Psychology, Health and Medicine, 11*, 129–141.

Furnham, A., Lavancy, M., & McClelland, A. (2001). Waist-to-hip ratio and facial attractiveness: A pilot study. *Personality and Individual Differences, 30*, 491–502.

Gigerenzer, G., Todd, P. M., & the ABC Research Group. (1999). *Simple heuristics that make us smart*. New York: Oxford University Press.

Henss, R. (2000). WHR and female attractiveness: Evidence from photographic stimuli and methodological considerations. *Personality and Individual Differences, 28*, 501–513.

Jacobsen, A., & Gilchrist, A. (1988). The ratio principle holds over a million-to-one range of illumination. *Perception and Psychophysics, 43*, 1–6.

Kirschner, M. A., & Samojlik, E. (1991). Sex hormone metabolism in upper and lower body obesity. *International Journal of Obesity, 15*, 101–108.

Lassek, W. D., & Gaulin S. J. C. (2006). Changes in body fat distribution in relation to parity in American women: A covert form of maternal depletion. *American Journal of Physical Anthropology, 131*, 295–302.

Marlowe, F. W., & Wetsman, A. (2001). Preferred waist-to-hip ratio and ecology. *Personality and Individual Differences, 30*, 481–489.

Marlowe, F. W., Apicella, C. L., & Reed, D. (2005). Men's preferences for women's profile waist-hip-ratio in two societies. *Evolution and Human Behavior, 26,* 458–468.

Mook, D. G. (1983). In defense of external invalidity. *American Psychologist, 38,* 379–389.

Singh, D. (1993a). Adaptive significance of female physical attractiveness: The role of waist-to-hip ratio. *Journal of Personality and Social Psychology, 65,* 293–307.

Singh, D. (1993b). Body shape and women's attractiveness: The critical role of waist-to-hip ratio. *Human Nature, 4,* 297–321.

Singh, D. (1994). Is thin really beautiful and good? Relationship between waist-to-hip ratio (WHR) and female attractiveness. *Personality and Individual Differences, 16,* 123–132.

Singh, D. (2006). Universal allure of the hourglass figure: An evolutionary theory of female physical attractiveness. *Clinics in Plastic Surgery, 33,* 359–370.

Stevens, S. S. (1966). On the operation known as judgment. *American Scientist, 54,* 385–401.

Streeter, S. A., & McBurney, D. H. (2003). Waist-hip ratio and attractiveness: New evidence and a critique of 'a critical test.' *Evolution and Human Behavior, 24,* 88–98.

Swami, V., & Furnham, A. (2006). The science of attraction. *The Psychologist, 19,* 362–365.

Swami, V., & Tovée, M. J. (2005). Female physical attractiveness in Britain and Malaysia: A cross-cultural study. *Body Image, 2,* 115–128.

Swami, V., & Tovée, M. J. (2006). Does hunger influence judgments of female physical attractiveness? *British Journal of Psychology, 97,* 353–363.

Tassinary, L. G., & Hansen, K. A. (1998). A critical test of the WHR hypothesis of female physical attractiveness. *Psychological Science, 9,* 150–155.

Tovée, M. J., Swami, V., Furnham, A., & Mangalparsad, R. (2006). Changing perceptions of attractiveness as observers are exposed to a different culture. *Evolution and Human Behavior, 27,* 443–456.

Tovée, M. J., Hancock, P. J. B., Mahmoodi, S., Singleton, B. R. R., & Cornelissen, P. L. (2002). Human female attractiveness: Waveform analysis of human body shape. *Proceedings of the Royal Society London B, 269,* 2205–2213.

Wass, P., Waldenstrom, U., Rossner, S., & Hellberg, D. (1997). An android body fat distribution in females impairs the pregnancy rate of in-vitro fertilization-embryo transfer. *Human Reproduction, 12,* 2057–2060.

Weeden, J., & Sabini, J. (2005). Physical attractiveness and health in Western societies: A review. *Psychological Bulletin, 131,* 635–653.

Weisberg, S. (2005). *Applied linear regression.* Hoboken, NJ: Wiley-Interscience.

Wetsman, A., & Marlowe, F. (1999). How universal are preferences for female waist-to-hip ratios? Evidence from the Hadza of Tanzania. *Evolution and Human Behavior, 20,* 219–228.

Yu, D. W., & Shepard, G. H. (1998). Is beauty in the eye of the beholder? *Nature, 396,* 321–322.

Zaadstra, B. M., Seidell, J. C., Van Noord, P. A., te Velde, E. R., Habbema, J. D., Vrieswijk, B., et al. (1993). Fat and female fecundity: Prospective study of body fat distribution on conception rates. *British Medical Journal, 306,* 484–487.

3
The Volume-Height Index as a Body Attractiveness Index

Jintu Fan

The study of bodily attractiveness is important to evolutionary psychology and contributes more generally to an understanding of beauty. The fundamental questions within this literature are: how do we judge bodily beauty, and what are the physical cues for bodily attractiveness? And finally, are these cues related to health and reproduction? This chapter reviews past works on bodily attractiveness, introduces a new body index – the volume-height index (VHI) – and discusses the influence of VHI and other body parameters on bodily attractiveness.

Review of past works on bodily attractiveness

The ancient Greeks believed that the world is beautiful because there is a certain proportion, order and harmony in its elements (Gaut & Lopes, 2001). For centuries, classical Greek body proportions were considered ideal (Horn & Gurel, 1981). For both the Greek male and female ideals, the height of the figure was approximately seven-and-a-half head lengths, with the fullest part at the hipline and wrist level dividing the total length exactly in half. The fullest part of the bust or chest was located two head lengths from the crown. The waistline, which coincides with the bend of the elbow, was two-and-two-third head lengths from the crown, whereas the knees and ankles were five-and-a-half and seven head lengths from the crown, respectively. Male and female proportions differed only in circumference ratios. For the ideal female, the width of the hip in frontal view was almost the same as the shoulder width; the shoulder width of the ideal male, by contrast, was greater than the width of his hips.

Despite the wide appeal of these Greek body proportions, the concept or perception of the ideal body has never been static. It varies from time to time and from culture to culture. From the 15th through the 17th centuries, a plump body shape was considered sexually appealing and fashionable, at least in the West. The ideal woman was portrayed as plump, big-breasted and, as a consequence, maternal. This observation has recently been confirmed by Swami, Gray, and Furnham's (2007) empirical study on 17th century paintings by Pieter Pauwel Rubens. By measuring the waist-to-hip ratio (WHR) of the nude female beauties in the paintings by Rubens, they showed that the mean WHR of Rubens' women was 0.776, suggesting that the ideal female figure during that period was plumper than it is today (Swami et al., 2007).

Indeed, by the 19th century, the ideal had shifted to a more voluptuous, corsetted figure, idealising a more hourglass shape. In contemporary Western culture, thinness – coupled with somewhat inconsistently large breasts and a more toned, muscular physique – has become the ideal of feminine beauty (Thompson, Heinberg, Altabe, & Tantleff-Dunn, 1999). Detailed discussions of the ideal female body image of today are provided in Calogero, Boroughs, and Thompson (Chapter 13).

In addition to historical factors, cultural differences play an important role in the concept of bodily beauty. For example, traditional Chinese culture associated plumpness with affluence and longevity, whereas Arab cultures associate heavier body weights with female fertility (Nasser, 1988). In one study, Yu and Shepard (1998) investigated men's preferences for women's bodies in a culturally isolated Matsigenka village in southeast Peru, and discovered that the body preferences of the Matsigenka males were strikingly different from those prevalent in a more modern, Western culture. Matsigenka males ranked the 'over-weight' female figure as most attractive, healthy and preferable for marriage.

Within this literature, and in spite of historical and cultural factors, the WHR and body mass index (BMI) have been widely regarded as the most important cues to female bodily attractiveness. Earlier researchers suggested that a low WHR (i.e., a curvaceous body) corresponds to the optimal fat distribution for female health (Folsom et al., 1993; Singh, 1993a, 1993b) and high fertility (DeRidder et al., 1990; Zaadstra et al., 1993), and hence female attractiveness. In Singh's (1993a, 1993b, 1994a, 1994b, 1995a) studies, ratings of attractiveness were elicited using a set of line-drawn figures of women's bodies with varying WHR and three body weight categories. Singh found that men and women aged between 18 and 85 years regarded normal-weight female figures with a low WHR (typically centred around 0.70) as more attractive than those with a higher WHR with the same or lower body weight. In addition, the normal-weight figures were judged as being more attractive than the underweight figures, which were more attractive than the overweight. Additionally, an overweight woman with a low WHR was judged to be more attractive than a slim woman with a high WHR.

Singh's findings were supported by Furnham, Tan, and McManus (1997), who found the WHR to be the most parsimonious measure of bodily attractiveness. In this and other studies, an optimal WHR for attractiveness of 0.70 was suggested, corroborating Singh's conclusions (Furnham et al., 1997; Singh, 1993a, 1993b, 1994a, 1994b, 1995a). Furnham, Dias, and McClelland (1998) further investigated the effect of breast size on judgments of female attractiveness and found that the effect of breast size was dependent on overall body weight and WHR. For females with a low WHR, large breasts enhanced attractiveness ratings, whereas for females with a high WHR, the reverse was true.

Recent studies by Tovée and colleaguess (Tovée & Cornelissen, 1999, 2001; Tovée, Maisey, Emery, & Cornelissen, 1999; Tovée, Hancock, Mahmoodi, Singleton, & Cornelissen, 2002), however, have shown that BMI, rather than WHR, is much more important to female bodily attractiveness. Their analyses showed that BMI accounted for over 70 per cent of the variance in attractive ratings, whereas WHR only accounted for less than 5 per cent. They further argued that the perimeter-area ratio (i.e., the path length around the perimeter of a figure divided by the area within the perimeter) provides a good visual proxy of BMI, and the importance of WHR in Singh's findings was due to the fact that the WHRs of Singh's line-drawn figures co-varied with BMI (see Bateson, Cornelissen, & Tovée, Chapter 4).

Tovée and Cornelissen (2001) believe that the reason for WHR being so poor a predictor of attractiveness could be due to the difficulty in accurately judging WHRs. Tovée et al. (2002) further argue that features such as the WHR may be used to discriminate broad categories, such as male from female or pregnant from non-pregnant women (i.e., a between-category discrimination), and discrimination within the category of potential partners may use cues such as BMI and other cues, such as the proportions of the body or body shape. These arguments remain open to debate. Since the WHR is one of these body proportions and since BMI is an indicator of overall fitness and easy to estimate by viewers, one might argue that BMI is first used to discriminate broad categories in terms of underweight or emaciated, medium weight, and overweight. Discrimination within each category then requires other traits, including skin

tanning (Smith, Cornelissen, & Tovée, 2007) and other body proportional parameters such as the WHR, leg-to-body ratio (LBR), bust size,
and the position of the hips (Fan, Dai, Qian, Chau, & Liu, 2006).

3D body images as stimuli for body attractiveness research

Until recently, work on bodily attractiveness have used line-drawn
figures (Singh, 1993a, 1993b, 1994a, 1994b, 1995a) or front- and
side-view photographic images (Tovée & Cornelissen, 2001; Tovée et
al., 1999, 2002). These findings have not been tested using three-
dimensional (3D) stimuli. Could previous findings be the result of the
limitation in stimulus sets and are there possibly other body parameters
important in bodily attractiveness? In order to answer these questions, it
is essential to use 3D body images as stimuli for attractiveness judgment.
We (Fan, Liu, Wu, & Dai, 2004), therefore, used 3D body-scanning technology to obtain 3D body images and various body measurements of
different types of female bodies (Figures 3.1a and 3.1b show examples of
the scanned bodies). Recently, colour 3D female body images obtained
by digital camcorder were also used for the investigation of body attractiveness (Smith et al., 2007).

3D body scanning technology

3D body scanning technology is a major technological development in
body metrics that has developed in the late 1980s and 1990s. A comprehensive review of the development of this technology was recently
provided by Fan, Yu, and Hunter (2004). 3D body scanning technologies
use different kinds of techniques for making non-contact measurements
of the human body. The most common techniques are phase measurement profilometry and laser triangulation techniques. Phase measurement profilometry (PMP) is applied in the commercial [TC]2 body
scanner, in which structured lights are projected onto the body surface
to create a curved, two-dimensional patterned grating. The patterned
images on the body surface are then captured by CCD cameras to be used
to derive the 3D profile of the body surface. Laser triangulation techniques are applied in a number of other commercial body scanners such
as Cyberware, Techmath. With this technique, a laser beam is projected
by a sensor towards the body surface, and the direction of the reflected
laser beam is used to derive the distance between the sensor lens and the
incident point on the body surface. From this distance and the known
position of the sensor lens, the 3D coordinates of the incident point is

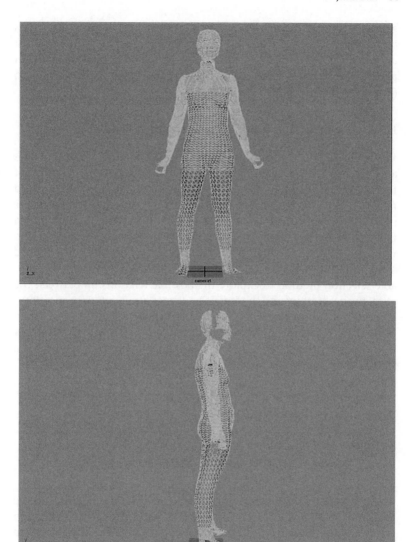

Figure 3.1 An example of a movie still in front view (a) and side view (b).

determined. By determining numerous points on the body surface to form a point-cloud, 3D body measurements are then achieved.

3D body scanning technology has an important application in the clothing industry, in terms of improving garment sizing, improving garment fitting, and computerised pattern generation for mass customisation fitting (Fan, Yu, et al., 2004). The huge potential of applying 3D body scanning technology for psychological research, in particular for studies of human physical attractiveness, is also recognised (Treleaven, Furnham, & Swami, 2006).

Discovery of VHI as a body attractiveness index

We applied 3D body scanning technology to obtain 3D body images and investigated the relationship between the attractiveness ratings of these 3D stimuli and the various body measurements and their derived ratios. In our first experiment (Fan et al., 2004), scanned bodies images of 31 Caucasian women were made into short movie clips and shown to 54 Hong Kong Chinese participants (29 men and 25 women), who were asked to rate the images for attractiveness. Thereafter, we applied a multiple linear regression method and an associated stepwise variable selection method to explore the possible relationship between the attractiveness ratings and the female body measurements or proportions. The multiple linear regression method is a statistical method for establishing the relationship between a dependent variable and a number of independent variables. The stepwise variable selection method is a statistical technique to choose statistically significant independent variables. In our study, the logarithm of the attractiveness ratings were considered as a dependent variable and the numerous body measurements or proportions were considered as independent variables.

When bodily attractiveness ratings were regressed onto BMI and WHR, we found:

$$\log(AR) = 3.314 - 0.888\log(BMI) - 2.212\log(WHR) \tag{1}$$
$$(R^2 = 0.821, p < 0.15)$$

where, $\log(AR)$ is the logarithm of attractiveness ratings, $\log(BMI)$ is the logarithm of BMI and $\log(WHR)$ is the logarithm of WHR. Equation (1) means the logarithm of attractiveness ratings is linearly related to the logarithm of BMI and the logarithm of WHR. The total variance of attractiveness ratings explained by Equation (1) is 82.1 per cent, with $\log(BMI)$ accounting for 80.4 per cent and $\log(WHR)$ accounting for the additional 1.7 per cent.

When the body attractiveness ratings were regressed onto body volume and height, we found for female observers:

$$\log(AR) = -4.431 - 1.367\log\left(\frac{V}{H^{2.16}}\right) \quad (R^2 = 0.9010, p < 0.05) \tag{2}$$

where, V is the body volume and H is the body height. For male observers:

$$\log(\text{AR}) = -4.046 - 1.382 \log \left(\frac{V}{H^{1.99}} \right) \quad (R^2 = 0.8899, p < 0.05) \quad (3)$$

It was clear from this study that about 90 per cent of the variance of the attractiveness ratings made by either female or male participants was explained by the body volume divided by the square of the height. We, therefore, defined a new index, which we named the Volume-Height Index (VHI):

$$\text{VHI} = \frac{V}{H^2} \quad (4)$$

Comparing the percentage of fits of Equations (1), (2) and (3), VHI is clearly a better predictor of women's bodily attractiveness than BMI and WHR. Since no other body measurement or ratio was found to have a stronger relationship with bodily attractiveness ratings than VHI in our analysis of the data, we concluded that VHI was the most important determinant of women's attractiveness, at least in terms of the body.

The discovery of VHI from the analyses of our experimental data also explains why BMI (i.e., body mass divided by the height squared), but not body mass divided by the height to the power of other magnitudes, has been identified in the earlier research by Tovée and colleagues as being an important determinant of women's bodily attractiveness. Mathematically speaking, there is a possibility of body mass divided by the height to the power of other magnitude being a better predictor of bodily attractiveness than that to the power of two. However, our analysis showed that BMI (body mass divided by the height to the power of two) is not simply a choice of convenience, but most probably because of the strong relationship between BMI and VHI. Our study (Fan, Dai, et al., 2006) showed that:

$$\text{VHI} = 0.586\text{BMI} + 6.713 (R^2 = 0.526, p < 0.01) \quad (5)$$

The physical meaning of VHI is in fact the ratio of average cross-sectional area over height or, in other words, the ratio of the horizontal dimension over the vertical dimension. Therefore, it is possible that when people judge the attractiveness of others, they make an estimate of the ratio of the subjects' horizontal dimension over the vertical dimension. Although BMI and VHI are correlated, the finding that VHI, rather than BMI, is the better visual cue to bodily attractiveness is important, because it means that women's bodily attractiveness could be enhanced by modifying the perception of body volume without changing the body mass.

Validation of the effects of VHI on women's bodily attractiveness

In the first experiment described above, the number of female body images was necessarily limited. Further work (Fan, Dai, et al., 2006) was, therefore, carried out to scan an additional 71 Chinese women with BMIs ranging from 14.1 to 44.0 kg/m^2 (the corresponding VHIs ranged from 13.3 to 50.5 l/m^2). Based on an analysis of a total of 102 female body images (i.e., the 31 Caucasian women scanned earlier and the additional 71 Chinese women), we confirmed that there is only a weak negative correlation between WHR and attractiveness ratings ($r = -0.43$, $p < 0.01$). Moreover, as can be seen from Figures 3.2 and 3.3, VHI is clearly a better predictor of attractiveness ratings than BMI.

For the range of BMI concerned, the relationship between BMI and attractiveness ratings could be best fitted by a power law curve, or in

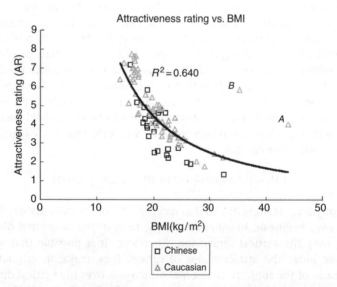

Figure 3.2 Plot of female attractiveness ratings versus BMI for 102 real female stimuli.

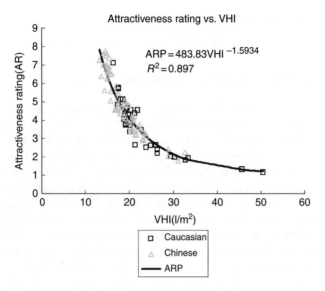

Figure 3.3 Plot of female attractiveness ratings versus VHI for 102 real female stimuli.

other words, the attractiveness rating is related to BMI to the power of a certain magnitude. We had:

$$AR = 295.2BMI^{-1.4018} \quad (R^2 = 0.640, p < 0.01) \tag{6}$$

with the percentage of fit being 64.0 per cent. The relationship between VHI and attractiveness ratings could be fitted by the following equation:

$$AR = 483.8VHI^{-1.5934} \quad (R^2 = 0.897, p < 0.01) \tag{7}$$

with the percentage of fit being 89.7 per cent.

VHI was a particularly useful cue for more 'masculine' female bodies, such as those indicated by points A and B in Figure 3.2, who have relatively high body mass indices but relatively low body volume (for point A, BMI = 43.97, VHI = 20.46 and AR = 4.01; for point B, BMI = 35.30, VHI = 17.09 and AR = 5.85). However, even without these two subjects and using a power law curve to fit the relationship between BMI or VHI and attractiveness ratings, VHI is still a better predictor of attractiveness. If fitted with a power law curve without points A and B, for VHI, we have:

$$AR = 483.83 \cdot VHI^{-1.5934} \quad (R^2 = 0.897, p < 0.01) \tag{8}$$

whereas for BMI, we have:

$$AR = 1247.2BMI^{-1.8883} \quad (R^2 = 0.753, p < 0.01) \tag{9}$$

Optimal VHI for women's bodily attractiveness

For the 102 female stimulus subjects, the highest attractiveness rating was accorded to the woman with a VHI of $14.7 \, l/m^2$. There was a trend of decreasing attractiveness ratings with a further reduction in VHI. Since there were only six female subjects in the sample having VHIs less than $14.7 \, l/m^2$, and since it is practically impossible to recruit many female subjects with VHIs of less than $13.0 \, l/m^2$ (i.e., underweight and emaciated women), 20 digitally manipulated virtual female figures were generated using commercially available software to test whether there is an 'optimal' VHI value. These virtual images were generated by compressing the horizontal dimensions of average female body images The virtual female figures had VHIs ranging from 4.7 to $17.0 \, l/m^2$. For the virtual female figures, the highest attractiveness rating was accorded to the figure with a VHI value of $14.1 \, l/m^2$. We, therefore, concluded that there is an optimal VHI value of about $14.0 \, l/m^2$ for women's bodily attractiveness.

Figure 3.4 shows the plot of attractiveness ratings against VHI for both the 102 real subjects and the 20 virtual images. Assuming that there is continuity at the peak, the relationship between VHI and attractiveness ratings could be best fitted with two half bell-shaped exponential curves (i.e., as VHI deviates from its optimum value, attractiveness rating initially reduces slowly, then very quickly and then further deviations of VHI do not reduce attractiveness ratings any further):

$$\begin{cases} AR = e^{1.99e^{-0.05(VHI-14.2)^{1.07}}} & (VHI \geq 14.2) \quad (R^2 = 0.906, p < 0.01) \\ AR = e^{1.99e^{-0.2(14.2-VHI)^{0.86}}} & (VHI < 14.2) \quad (R^2 = 0.850, p < 0.01) \end{cases} \tag{10}$$

Judging from the similarity between the trend shown in Figure 3.4 and that of attractiveness ratings with changing BMI found in the work of Tovée and colleagues, and from the fact that there is a linear relationship between BMI and VHI, a similar trend of attractiveness with changing VHI might be expected if the stimuli used by Tovée and colleagues (1999) was analysed in the same manner. Moreover, since Tovée and colleague's stimuli were rated by Caucasian observers, whereas ours were rated by Chinese viewers, it is reasonable to believe that VHI is used in a similar manner by both Chinese and Caucasian observers in judging bodily attractiveness. In other words, VHI is used as a cue to bodily attractiveness by people in both Eastern and Western culture.

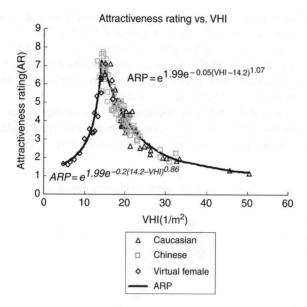

Figure 3.4 Plot of female attractiveness ratings versus VHI for 102 real female subjects and 20 virtual female images.

While the general trend of the effect of VHI may be culturally invariant, the optimal value of VHI may be different for viewers cross-culturally. From Tovée et al.'s (1999) data, and based on the general relationship between BMI and VHI, the optimum VHI as rated by Caucasian viewers would be about 16.0 to 17.5 l/m² (corresponding to a BMI of about 18 to 19 kg/m²), which is higher than the optimum VHI of 14.2 l/m² found in our work with Chinese viewers. This difference in the optimum VHI for different ethnic groups may be the result of differences in the optimal VHI for health and longevity in different ethnic groups (Kopelman, 2000; Tovée & Cornelissen, 2001; Winkelgren, 1998). Future cross-cultural research is needed to examine this possibility.

Effects of VHI on male bodily attractiveness

Applying the same methodology, we have also investigated the relationship between male bodily attractiveness and various body measurements and their derived ratios (Fan, Dai, Liu, & Wu, 2005). Twenty-five Caucasian men and 69 Chinese men with BMIs ranging from 17.4 to 30.7 kg/m² (the corresponding VHI ranged from 15.2 to 44.2 l/m²) were scanned to obtain 3D body measurements, which were then used to create 3D wire-frame male body images and short movie clips. When the 94 images were rated for physical attractiveness, we again found that VHI was the best predictor of men's bodily attractiveness, followed by the waist-to-chest ratio (WCR), and finally the abdominal region (or WHR, with an optimal WHR of 0.8) and BMI.

Figures 3.5(a) and 3.5(b) plot the attractiveness ratings versus VHI. As can be seen, the relationship between VHI and attractiveness ratings was best fitted with a bell-shaped exponential curve:

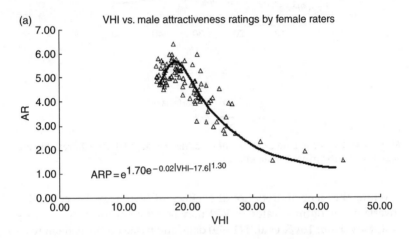

(a) VHI vs. male attractiveness ratings by female raters

$$ARP = e^{1.70e^{-0.02|VHI-17.6|^{1.30}}}$$

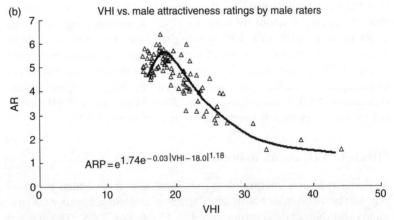

(b) VHI vs. male attractiveness ratings by male raters

$$ARP = e^{1.74e^{-0.03|VHI-18.0|^{1.18}}}$$

Figure 3.5 Plot of VHI versus male attractiveness ratings by female (a) and male observers (b).

$$\begin{cases} \text{ARF} = e^{1.70e^{-0.02|\text{VHI}-17.6|^{1.30}}} & (R^2 = 0.731, p < 0.01) \\ \text{ARM} = e^{1.74e^{-0.03|\text{VHI}-18.0|^{1.18}}} & (R^2 = 0.748, p < 0.01) \end{cases} \qquad (11)$$

where, ARF are attractiveness ratings by female observers and ARM are attractiveness ratings by male observers. We found an 'optimum' VHI for ARF of $17.6 \, l/m^2$ and for ARM of $18.0 \, l/m^2$, respectively. As VHI deviates from these optimum values, ratings of attractiveness reduces in a similar trend as that for female bodily attractiveness.

Effects of other body parameters on attractiveness

The finding that VHI has the strongest relationship with bodily attractiveness does not mean other body proportions are not important for physical attractiveness. In fact, for the ideal body, VHI alone is not sufficient. In further analysing our data, we have shown that proportionally longer legs, less deviation from a WHR of 0.7, a narrower bust-width and greater bust-depth (or a larger bust) and a higher position of the hips in relation to waist all enhance femininity and, by implication, women's bodily attractiveness (Fan, Dai, et al., 2006; Fan et al., 2004). Our finding that proportionally longer legs are more attractive for female bodies corroborates recent work by Swami, Einon, and Furnham (2006), which also showed that females having longer legs were considered to be more attractive. The reason that females having longer legs, optimum WHR, larger bust and more lifted hips are more attractive most probably derives from the fact these are cues to health, fitness and reproductive potential.

With regard to male bodily attractiveness, we have shown that physical attractiveness is related to WCR (waist to chest ratio) and WHR (Fan, Dai, et al., 2005). A lower WCR is preferred as it corresponds to an 'inverted triangular' shape (i.e., a narrow waist and a broad chest and shoulders), which is consistent with physical strength and muscular fitness. In addition, the optimum WHR for the range of male bodies that we investigated was approximately 0.80. This is smaller than the optimum value of WHR for males found by Singh (1995b), who investigated the role of WHR in male body attractiveness by analyzing the attractiveness ranking of 12 line drawing stimuli of male figures and found that the stimuli having WHR of 0.90 was the most attractive. Further investigation is needed to examine whether such differences are caused by differences in the viewer's background or due to the fact that line drawings lack ecological validity. It is interesting to note that, unlike the longer female legs, our analysis did not reveal that longer male legs had any significant effects of men's bodily attractiveness. This again corroborates recent findings by Swami, Einon, et al. (2006).

Conclusion

Ever since ancient times, there has been a long debate on whether there exists an objective beauty (i.e., whether there are properties in an object which are sufficient or necessary for an object to be judged beautiful) or whether beauty is simply 'in the eye of the beholder.' Our finding that bodily attractiveness is overwhelmingly dependent on a single parameter which we have called the VHI adds to the belief that bodily beauty is not simply a matter of personal preference, but is a perception of optimum body proportions which indicate health and fertility.

Although VHI may appear to be just a slight modification to the more commonly used parameter of BMI, the discovery that VHI, rather than BMI, is the most direct and important visual cue to bodily attractiveness, is significant for at least two reasons. First, it may mean that VHI is a better indicator of people's fitness levels than BMI. This can in fact be easily understood; for example, a heavy person with a solid muscular body is fit, although she or he may have a relatively high BMI. Further research is, therefore, encouraged to examine whether VHI is indeed a better health or fitness indicator than BMI.

Secondly, it means that bodily attractiveness can be enhanced by changing the volume of the body without changing the body weight. This again is easily understandable, as we all know that many women use pressure garments, such as body shapers, to tighten their body to improve attractiveness. We also know that one's body image can be enhanced by wearing garments which change the perception of body size and height.

One might argue that VHI is too inconvenient to measure, so it cannot become a popular indicator of fitness and attractiveness, as in the case of BMI. However, with the increasingly wide application and availability of 3D body scanning technology, this will not be a major impediment in the near future. Indeed, in some countries, 3D body scanning technology has been used to conduct population sizing surveys (see Treleaven et al., 2006). It can be envisaged that, in the near future, everyone may have her or his own card containing body scanning data, which will not only be useful for garment fitting, but also provide measures of personal health or fitness level.

The finding that VHI is the most important visual cue to bodily attractiveness, however, does not mean that other body proportions are not important. For ideally attractive bodies, not only VHI, but also other body proportions should be optimum. For women, we have shown that proportionally longer legs, optimum WHR, larger busts, and more lifted hips contribute to bodily attractiveness. For men, we have shown that a lower WCR and optimum WHR enhance bodily attractiveness in addition to VHI.

The discovery of VHI has further implications for our understanding of the perceptual processes governing human beauty. For female bodies, VHI alone explained about 90 per cent of the variance in attractiveness rating; for male bodies, VHI alone explained about 70 per cent of the same variance. Why should bodily attractiveness be so overwhelmingly dependent on such a simple parameter as the VHI? Is it because our minds first estimate the horizontal dimension over the vertical dimension of the body, which VHI represents, for assessing body attractiveness, before using other body proportions to 'fine tune' the judgements? Further research is needed to examine this speculation.

The importance of VHI for bodily attractiveness also has a significant implication for future research in the field. In the past, many studies have been carried out in trying to identify body proportions related to fitness or attractiveness. Body proportions, such as BMI, WHR, WCR, and LBR, were identified as potentially important parameters. Since these body proportions may co-vary with VHI, it is necessary to first extract the effect of VHI before the effect of other body proportions can be identified. Research on the effects of other body proportions on bodily attractiveness should, therefore, be re-visited in the light of our findings.

In summary, then the present investigation demonstrates, for the first time, the usefulness of 3D body scanning technology in psychological and health research. As pointed out by Treleaven et al. (2006), 3D body scanning is poised to become a mainstream psychological tool of major value, and researchers studying physical attractiveness will need to incorporate such technologies into their research if they are to fully understand the perception of human beauty.

References

DeRidder, C. M., Bruning, P. F., Zonderland, M. L., Thijssen, J. H. H., Bonfrer, J. M. G., Blankenstein, M. A., et al. (1990). Body fat mass distribution, and plasma hormones in early puberty in females. *Journal of clinical Endocrinological and Metabolism, 70*, 888–893.

Fan, J. T., Yu, W., & Hunter, L. (2004). *Clothing appearance and fit: Science and technology*. Cambridge: Woodhead Publishing Limited.

Fan, J. T., Dai, W., Liu, F., & Wu, J. (2005). Visual perception of male body attractiveness. *Proceedings of Royal Society of London Series B, 272,* 219–226.

Fan, J. T., Liu, F., Wu, J., & Dai, W. (2004). Visual perception of female physical attractiveness. *Proceedings of the Royal Society London B, 271,* 347–352.

Fan, J., Dai, W., Qian, X., Chau, K. P., & Liu, Q. (2006). *Effects of shape parameters on female body attractiveness.* Unpublished manuscript.

Folsom, A. R., Kaye, S. A., Sellers, T. A., Hong, C., Cerhan, J. R., Potter, J. D., et al. (1993). Body fat distribution and 5-years risk of death in older women. *Journal of the American Medical Association, 269,* 483–487.

Furnham, A., Dias, M., & McClelland, C. (1998). The role of body weight, waist-to-hip ratio, and breast size in judgments of female attractiveness. *Sex Roles, 39,* 311–326.

Furnham, A., Tan, T., & McManus, C. (1997). Waist-to-hip ratio and preferences for body shape: A replication and extension. *Personal and Individual Differences, 22,* 539–549.

Gaut, B., & Lopes, D. M. (2001). *The Routledge companion to aesthetics.* London: Routledge.

Horn, M. J., & Gurel, L. M. (1981). *The second skin* (3rd ed.). Boston, MA: Houghton Mifflin Company.

Kopelman, P. G. (2000). Obesity as a medical problem. *Nature, 404,* 635–643.

Nasser, M. (1988). Culture and weight consciousness. *Journal of Psychosomatic Research, 32,* 573–577.

Singh, D. (1993a). Adaptive significationce of female physical attractiveness: Role of the waist-to-hip ratio. *Journal of Personality and Social Psychology, 65,* 293–307.

Singh, D. (1993b). Body shape and women's attractiveness: The critical role of waist-to-hip ratio. *Human Nature, 4,* 297–321.

Singh, D. (1994a). Is thin really beautiful and good? Relationship between waist-to-hip ratio (WHR) and female attractiveness. *Personality and Individual Differences, 16,* 465–481.

Singh, D. (1994b). Body fat distribution and perception of desirable female body shape by young black men and women. *International Journal of Eating Disorders, 16,* 289–294.

Singh, D. (1995a). Female health, attractiveness and desirability for relationships: Role of breast asymmetry and WHR. *Ethology and Sociobiology, 16,* 465–481.

Singh, D. (1995b). Female judgement of male attractiveness and desirability for relationships: Role of waist-to-hip ratio and financial status. *Journal of Personality and Social Psychology, 69,* 1089–1101.

Smith, K. L., Cornelissen, P. L., & Tovée, M. J. (2007). Color 3D bodies and judgements of human female attractiveness. *Evolution and Human Behavior, 28,* 48–54.

Swami, V., Einon, D., & Furnham, A. (2006). An investigation of the leg-to-body ratio as a human aesthetic criterion. *Body Image, 3,* 317–323.

Swami, V., Gray, M., & Furnham, A. (2007). The female nude in Rubens: Disconfirmatory evidence of the waist-to-hip ratio hypothesis of female physical attractiveness. *Imagination, Cognition and Personality, 26,* 139–147.

Thompson, J. K., Heinberg, L. J., Altabe, M., & Tantleff-Dunn, S. (1999). *Exacting beauty: Theory, assessment, and treatment of body image disturbance.* Washington, DC: American Psychological Association.

Tovée, M. J., & Cornelissen, P. L. (1999). The mystery of human beauty. *Nature, 399,* 215–216.

Tovée, M. J., & Cornelissen, P. L. (2001). Female and male perceptions of female physical attractiveness in front-view and profile. *British Journal of Psychology, 92*, 391–402.

Tovée, M. J., Maisey, D. S., Emery, J. L., & Cornelissen, P. L. (1999). Visual cues to female physical attractiveness. *Proceedings of the Royal Society of London Series B, 266*, 211–218.

Tovée, M. J., Hancock, P., Mahmoodi, S., Singleton, B. R. R., & Cornelissen, P. L. (2002). Human female attractiveness: Waveform analysis of body shape. *Proceedings of the Royal Society of London Series B, 269*, 2205–2213.

Treleaven, P., Furnham, A., & Swami, V. (2006). The science of body metrics. *The Psychologist, 19*, 416–419.

Winkelgren, I. (1998). Obesity: How big a problem? *Science, 280*, 1364–1367.

Yu, D. W., & Shepard, G. H. (1998). Is beauty in the eye of the beholder? *Nature, 396*, 321–322.

Zaadstra, B. M., Seidell, J. C., van Noord, P. A. H., te Velde, E. R., Habbema, J. D. F., Vrieswijk, B., et al. (1993). Fat and female fecundity: Prospective study of effect of body fat distribution on conception rates. *British Medical Journal, 306*, 484–487.

4

Methodological Issues in Studies of Female Attractiveness

Melissa Bateson, Piers L. Cornelissen, and Martin J. Tovée

Evolutionary models of mate choice predict that we should be sensitive to the cues in a potential partner that signal honest information about their mate quality (i.e., their health and reproductive potential). Individuals displaying cues indicative of high quality should be judged as more sexually attractive than those signalling lower quality. In recent years, much research in evolutionary psychology has focussed on applying this approach to understanding variation in the attractiveness of female body shapes. Several features of a body's size and shape have been suggested as potential indices of mate quality based on biological data linking these indices to measures of health and fertility.

In order to prove the relationship between a specific index of body shape and attractiveness, the research strategy typically adopted has been to generate a series of bodies varying in the index of interest and investigate whether this variable explains attractiveness judgements. These studies tend to use artificial stimuli in the form of either line-drawn figures or digitally manipulated photographs for two reasons. First, if stimuli are generated artificially then it is possible to exaggerate the variation in the index of interest, thus ensuring that the variation is sufficient to affect attractiveness judgements. Second, it is assumed that if only the index of interest is varied and other features that might play a role in attractiveness judgements are not explicitly altered, then it follows that any correlated variation in attractiveness judgements must prove that the explicitly varied index must be the cue used in making these judgements.

These two goals produce two interrelated problems. First, extreme variation in an index may result in unrealistic bodies. Second, variation in one index of body shape is difficult or impossible to achieve without simultaneously varying other indices. This co-variation problem can make it difficult to disambiguate which physical feature is responsible for producing a change in the attractiveness percept. In this chapter we discuss these problems inherent in the use of artificial stimulus sets, and demonstrate how they can lead to misleading conclusions about which physical features are the true focus of attractiveness judgements. We explore how these problems can be reduced by the use of stimulus sets based on naturally occurring variation in female body shape.

Distinguishing perceptual cues from physical features

The above introduction highlights some important distinctions that are often overlooked in studies of female attractiveness and that we feel it is crucial to clarify. The simple indices used by scientists to quantify variation in human body shape are not the same as either the biological traits that we presume underlie variance in mate quality, or the visual cues that subjects attend to when they make attractiveness judgements. Furthermore, it is possible that both the precise nature of the indices used to quantify shape variation and the visual cues used by observers to determine attractiveness may be affected by the nature of the stimuli available, and may vary from one study to the next. For example, different indices of shape and different visual cues are available depending on whether two- or three-dimensional information is available for the stimulus bodies.

A common problem in research on attractiveness is the confusing of indices of shape with the visual cues that may be used by observers to identify these. First, the assumption is made that a specific index is being used by observers to judge an underlying biological trait. Then the images are rated for attractiveness and the ratings are correlated not with either the trait itself or the index in question, but with a putative visual cue to the index. This can lead to problems. If an index accurately reflects mate quality, it is this that has to be correlated with attractiveness preferences for the behaviour to have any validity. It would be possible, for example, for a putative visual cue to be moderately correlated with an index. The visual cue might then be moderately correlated with attractiveness ratings. As we see below, it would be wrong to then assume a significant link between attractiveness and the underlying biological trait on this basis, as a direct correlation between attractiveness and the trait may be weak and non-significant.

In women, the two indices which have received the most attention in attractiveness studies are weight scaled for height (kg/m^2) and lower body shape. The former index is called the body mass index or BMI

(Bray, 1978), while for shape, research has focused on the ratio of the waist to the hips (the WHR). There are several alternative measures to BMI. Fan, Liu, Wu, and Dai (2004) have suggested the volume-height index (VHI) based on their three-dimensional laser-scanned images (see also Fan, Chapter 3). Given that a body tissue has a density on average of 1.06 kg/l, an increase in body mass will tend to come with a corresponding increase in volume (i.e., as a body's mass rises and falls, so will the volume the body occupies) (Garrow, 1999). As a result, features such as BMI and VHI are highly correlated. For example, in our own laser-scanned images, the Spearman correlation between weight and volume, and between BMI and VHI is better than 0.90 (Tovée & Cornelissen, unpublished data). So both BMI and the VHI scale can be seen as scaling an approximation of relative body mass. However, if we assume that the observer making an attractiveness judgement is attempting to estimate body fat composition, then a possibly more accurate way of measuring the actual body fat of a subject is through the skin calliper technique which directly measures body fat deposition and is strongly correlated with both BMI and attractiveness judgements (Smith, Cornelissen, & Tovée, 2007).

WHR can also be measured in more than one way. There is the *actual* WHR, which is the distance *around* a woman's waist divided by the distance around the hips. This is the WHR measure that some artificial insemination studies have correlated with female fertility (Waas, Waldenstrom, Rossner, & Hellberg, 1997; Zaadstra et al., 1993). WHR can also be taken from a two-dimensional photograph by measuring the distance *across* the waist and dividing it by the distance *across* the hips. The difference between the two WHR measures is important. *Actual* WHR is the index that has been linked to fertility; the WHR as measured across the front is just one possible visual cue to this (see Figure 4.1). If we are trying to correlate physical attractiveness to indices that are linked to health and fertility, it is more direct to correlate attractiveness with actual WHR, rather than this indirect cue, in the same way that it is more direct to link attractiveness to a measure of body fat (such as BMI) and not one of its possible visual cues.

The two measures of WHR are correlated, but only at around $r = 0.60$ (compare with the correlation of around 0.97 between the BMI and its visual cues) (Tovée & Cornelissen, 2001). So a weak correlation between attractiveness and WHR as seen from the front is likely to be an even weaker correlation between attractiveness and actual WHR (previous studies using photographs of real women have found a very weak or non-significant relationship between attractiveness and 'front' WHR

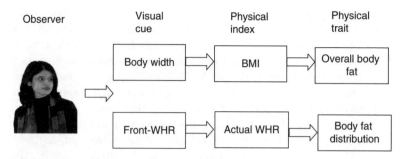

Figure 4.1 A schematic diagram illustrating the difference between visual cues to a feature and the physical features themselves.

and a non-significant relationship with actual WHR (e.g., Thornhill & Grammer, 1999; Tovée, Maisey, Emery, & Cornelissen, 1999). Thus, the confusion between two measures can lead to an over-estimation of the importance of the role of actual WHR in determining attractiveness judgements. In the studies discussed below, WHR is always front WHR, yet the studies fail to make any discrimination between actual WHR and front WHR.

We now turn to exploring the way in which images have been manipulated to produce variation in specific features, and how this manipulation can generate results which may prove misleading or difficult to interpret.

Artificial manipulation of features

The initial evidence for WHR as a predictor of attractiveness judgements came from studies using a set of line-drawn figures of women (Singh, 1993; Henss, 1995; Furnham, Tan, & McManus, 1997). The line-drawn figures are arranged in three series: underweight, normal, and overweight. Within each series, the WHR is varied by altering the torso width around the waist. The problem with this approach is that when the figures are modified by altering the width of the torso around the waist, this not only alters the WHR, but also the apparent BMI. As the value of the WHR rises, so does that of the apparent BMI, and so it is not possible to say whether changes in attractiveness ratings are made on the basis of WHR or BMI, or both (Tovée & Cornelissen, 1999).

One attempt to overcome this co-variation in the line-drawn images has been to 'inflate' the size of the arms and legs as the waist width narrows (Furnham, Petrides, & Constantinides, 2005). The rationale for this shape change is that the change in the apparent weight of the figure from altering the width of the lower torso is countered by altering the size of the arms and legs. This approach has two flaws. First, it is an unrealistic representation of how fat is distributed on the body (e.g., Garn, 1955; Garn & Harper, 1955; Garn, Sullivan, & Hawthorne, 1987). Second, eye-movement studies suggest that when observers make attractiveness judgements they concentrate their gaze on the upper and middle parts of the torso and do not look at the arms (George, Cornelissen, Hancock, & Tovée, 2007; Singleton, Cornelissen, & Tovée, 2004). Thus, this arm-based compensation for the effect of altering the waist width may not be considered when observers are making their attractiveness judgements, and as a result there would be no perception of a constant body mass across the range of shape changes in the drawings.

The co-variation problem is also found in studies using modified photographic images of women, where their WHR has been artificially altered by thickening or narrowing their torsos (e.g., Henss, 2000). Altering the torso width also alters their apparent body mass and so, once again, the WHR and apparent BMI are co-varied. Streeter and McBurney (2003) used the same technique to produce a set of images varying in WHR based on a single digital photograph. They use a very much wider WHR range than previous experiments, ranging from 0.50 to 1.20. This range of shapes includes pregnant women, which is a departure from the shape ranges used before. Previous studies have looked at judgements discriminating between potentially fertile women (i.e., excluding pre-adolescent and pregnant women).

They asked 95 undergraduates to rate their image set for attractiveness on a seven-point scale. Streeter and McBurney (2003) were aware of the co-variation problem and, therefore, also asked their observers to estimate the weight of the women in the images, so that they could try and control for body mass. Unlike previous studies, they report a non-linear relationship between attractiveness and WHR. The attractiveness of the images was higher in the middle WHR range (centred at about 0.70), and declined towards either end of the WHR range.

The images are not a good representation, as the digital manipulation's need to alter the WHR of a body over such a wide WHR range makes the resultant bodies unrealistic (see Figure 4.2). The degree of image distortion increases with the degree of image manipulation; so at either ends of their WHR range, the degree of obvious distortion also increases. So an obvious apprehension is that their result may be influenced by the 'plausibility' of their image manipulation (i.e., can their

Figure 4.2 Examples of the Streeter and McBurney (2003) stimuli. As can be seen there are number of problems with their image manipulation. For example, the fact that the head remains a constant size gives a strong cue to the degree to which the body has been altered. The manipulation also impacts on features such as the hands which are elongated and distorted in some of the images. Finally, and most importantly, the manipulation of the body produces shapes that are just not credible as human bodies.

results simply be explained by the images that appear less realistic being rated more highly?).

To explore this possibility, we asked a group of 13 observers (6 male and 7 female) to perform a 2-alternative forced-choice experiment. They were presented with the 27 images from this set viewed in a random sequence on a 17-inch flat panel monitor. The observers were informed that the images had been digitally manipulated and asked to make a 2-alternative forced-choice on whether each of the images were realistic or unrealistic. We also measured the distance across the waist and hips of the woman in the images, and so calculated a WHR value for each image. A plot of the realism of the images against the WHR is shown in Figure 4.3a. The 'base' image of a female model with a WHR of 0.70 is naturally regarded as the most realistic. The more this shape is modified, the less realistic the images become. On a separate sequence of present-ations, the observers were asked to rate the images for attractiveness on a scale of 1 to 7 (1 = Unattractive, 7 = Attractive). The relationship between realism and attractiveness is very strong (Spearman correlation, $r = 0.70$, $p < 0.001$; see Figure 4.3b).

As stated earlier, Streeter and McBurney (2003) reported an inverted U-function for the ratings of attractiveness plotted against WHR (i.e., the extremes of the WHR range are rated as less attractive). We found the same relationship (see Figure 4.3c). The shape of this relationship is important because the two dips in attractiveness (where there is a large change in the perception of attractiveness) correspond to the extremes of the WHR range where the images 'appear unrealistic.' The evidence suggests that this change in perceived attractiveness is an artifact of the distortion of the images inherent in their manipulation of WHR. Thus, the apparent change in attractiveness with changing WHR is actually a change in attractiveness with changing 'realism' (which in turn co-varies with WHR). This is not to say that WHR may not play a role in attractiveness judgements, but it does not seem justified to make such an assertion based on this image set.

Another image set recently used to test attractiveness is that used by Rozmus-Wrzesinska and Pawłowski (2005). They focused on the fact that because WHR is a ratio rather than an absolute value, a small, and thus potentially attractive, WHR can result either from a small waist or from large hips. Rozmus-Wrzesinska and Pawłowski (2005) argue that because the biological information contained in waist size and hip size is different, we might expect men to pay more attention to either waist or hip size depending on which provides the better predictor of repro-ductive potential in a given environment. Specifically, they argue that in food-limited populations large hips, which are associated with fat reserves, are the best cue to reproductive success, whereas in populations that are not limited by food, waist size is a better cue to a woman's fertility and general health. On this basis, they hypothesised that West-ernised men should be more sensitive to changes in WHR when these are produced as the result of changes in waist size than as the result of changes in hip size.

To test their hypothesis, Rozmus-Wrzesinska and Pawłowski (2005) generated two series of images of female bodies in which: (a) hip width

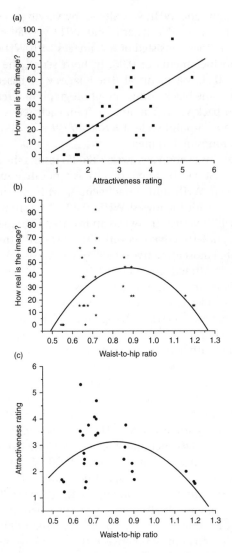

Figure 4.3 Ratings based on the Streeter and McBurney (2003) images. Panel A shows the relationship between judgements of how realistic the images are plotted against the WHR of the images. The WHR of the woman model in the unaltered image is 0.70. As the magnitude of the change in WHR increases, the degree to which the image is seen as unrealistic increases. Panel B shows the relationship between attractiveness judgements and WHR. As in Streeter and McBurney (2003), the images become less attractive at either end of the WHR range. Panel C shows the relationship between the attractiveness ratings and the realism of the images. As can be seen, there is a very strong correlation between these two features.

was held constant, and WHR was altered by varying waist width, and; (b) waist width was held constant, and WHR was altered by varying hip width. Each series consisted of five images with WHR ranging from 0.60 to 0.80 in increments of 0.05. In both series, the central image with a WHR of 0.70 was identical. The images were based on morphed versions of the same black-and-white photograph of a female model in both front and back view. The images from each series were rated for attractiveness on a 5-point scale (1 = *Not attractive*, 5 = *Very attractive*) by two different groups of 170 men.

Rozmus-Wrzesinska and Pawłowski's (2005) results show that in series (a), in which waist width varied, there was a negative monotonic relationship between WHR and attractiveness, with the most attractive image being that with the lowest WHR (0.60). By contrast, in series (b), in which hip width varied, there was an inverted U-shaped relationship between WHR and attractiveness with the image with the central WHR (0.70) being rated most attractive overall (see Figure 4.4a). There was also a greater range in attractiveness ratings in series (a) than in series (b).

On the basis of these findings, Rozmus-Wrzesinska and Pawłowski (2005: 304) conclude: 'Our results indicate that men are very sensitive to WHR differences based on waist change and much less sensitive to WHR differences based on hip changes.' Thus, 'Women with the same WHR but manipulated either by waist or hip size are perceived differently by men.' However, we believe that these conclusions are not justified on the basis of the results presented, because Rozmus-Wrzesinska and Pawłowski (2005) failed to control for variation in apparent body mass in their stimuli. BMI is known to be a strong negative predictor of attractiveness in laboratory studies (Tovée, Hancock, Mahmoodi, Singleton, & Cornelissen, 2002; Tovée, Reinhardt, Emery, & Cornelissen, 1998; Tovée et al., 1999), a finding that is supported by field data showing that Western women with slimmer hips, but not lower WHRs, have a higher frequency of sexual intercourse (Brody, 2004). Here we will present evidence that the difference in attractiveness ratings between series (a) and (b) reported by Rozmus-Wrzesinska and Pawłowski (2005) is explained by differences in apparent BMI between the two image sets.

In series (a), in which hip width was held constant and waist width was varied, apparent BMI must increase as WHR increases. In contrast, in series (b), in which waist width was held constant and hip width was varied, apparent BMI must decrease as WHR increases. Rozmus-Wrzesinska and Pawłowski (2005) did not quantify BMI for their images; however, they did ask their subjects to rate which of the images in the series was the heaviest and which the slimmest. In agreement

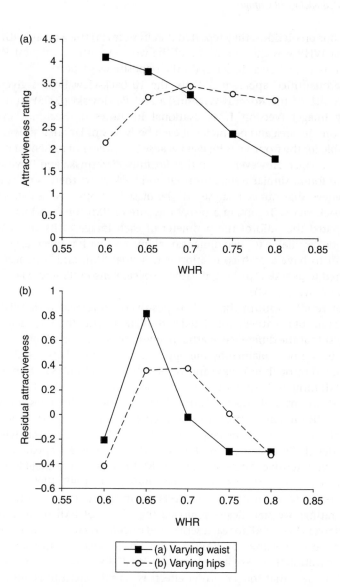

Figure 4.4 Attractiveness as a function of WHR. Panel A shows the original mean attractiveness ratings for the back views of the images reported by Rozmus-Wrzesinska and Pawłowski (2005). Panel B shows the residual attractiveness for the same images once the effects of apparent BMI have been statistically removed.

with our predictions, they reported that in series (a) the woman with the lowest WHR was the slimmest and the woman with the highest WHR the heaviest, whereas in series (b) the opposite was true.

We quantified apparent BMI for the 10 back-view images given in Figure 4.1 of the Rozmus-Wrzesinska and Pawłowski (2005) study by using ImageJ (version 1.34s; National Institutes of Health, USA) to measure the area and perimeter of each body. A similar analysis was not possible for the front-view images because they were not presented in the original paper. However, given that Rozmus-Wrzesinska and Pawłowski (2005) found similar results for front and back views there is no reason to believe that our re-analysis will be biased by only using data from the back views. To obtain a proxy measure of BMI for each image, we computed the ratio of the perimeter of each image to its area (PAR), an index available for two dimensional images that has previously been shown to have a high correlation with actual BMI, and is henceforth referred to as PAR (Tovée et al., 1999, Tovée, Benson, Emery, Mason, & Cohen-Tovée, 2003).

Our results confirm that PAR is positively correlated with WHR in series (a), but negatively correlated with WHR in series (b). We, therefore, suggest that the difference in attractiveness ratings reported for series (a) and (b) can be explained by the opposite associations between BMI (as measured through its proxy) and WHR in the two stimulus sets. In series (a), BMI influences attractiveness in the *same* direction as WHR resulting in a strong overall effect on attractiveness, whereas in series (b), BMI and WHR influence attractiveness in *opposite* directions, producing an overall weaker effect. The fact that the image with lowest attractiveness in series (b) is that with the lowest WHR and highest apparent BMI fits with extensive data showing that BMI explains considerably more variance in attractiveness than WHR (Tovée et al., 1998, 1999, 2002).

In order to control for the effects of apparent BMI on attractiveness ratings we statistically removed the effects of BMI by regressing attractiveness on PAR for each series, and calculating the residual attractiveness not explained by PAR for each image. Figure 4.4b shows this residual attractiveness plotted against WHR for series (a) and series (b). It is clear that the pattern of effects is very different in Figures 4.4a and 4.4b: in Figure 4.4b there is now a similar, non-monotonic relationship between WHR and residual attractiveness for both the series (a) and series (b) data, with peaks at WHRs of 0.65 and 0.70 respectively. Once PAR (the proxy for BMI) is controlled for, the difference between series (a) and (b) reported by Rozmus-Wrzesinska and Pawłowski (2005) disappears.

Although the data presented by Rozmus-Wrzesinska and Pawłowski (2005) do not support the hypothesis that men are differentially sensitive to absolute waist and hip size, we agree with their basic suggestion that there is likely to be more to female attractiveness than BMI and WHR. For example, Tovée et al. (2002) carried out a principal component analysis (PCA) based on 60 front-view digital photographs of real women sampled from a controlled BMI range. The image of each woman's torso was divided into 31 slices of equal thickness, and a waveform was generated by plotting the width of each slice against its position in the body. The PCA was then used to derive independent descriptors of this waveform. The analysis identified four statistically independent descriptors of shape. These results are consistent with a number of factors (such as hormone levels, overall body fat, nutrition, exercise, etc.) contributing independently to the determination of body shape. If this is the case, then simple width and ratio measures alone are inadequate for capturing the biologically meaningful variation in female body shape, and are thus unlikely to be the only cues used to judge attractiveness.

Natural images

An alternative to using images in which features have been artificially manipulated is to use the natural variation of these features within a population. This approach has the advantage that such images, by definition, will fall within the naturally occurring range of size and shape found within the female population, and will not have the problem of individual images looking unrealistic. So one simple solution is to use digital photographs of women taken under standardised conditions and build up an image library, from which sets of body images may be selected varying in their range of size and shape.

A commonly used image set consists of 100 nude photographs produced by the Japanese photographer Akira Gomi (e.g., Thornhill & Grammer, 1999). However, this image set was not produced for scientific study, and the pictures have some manipulations which introduce noise into an experiment. For example, the focal distance at which the photographs were taken was varied. The aim of the photographer was that each woman should appear to be roughly the same 'size' in each photograph. As the pictures were taken against a plain background, there are no cues to the relative distance at which the photographs were taken. As a result, all information about the relative size of the women is lost, making judgements about relative height and weight more difficult.

Another problem is the relative range of physical features in an image set. For example, if the range of BMI values used is significantly greater than that of the WHR range (relative to the range of values found in a normal population), then BMI may appear a stronger predictor than it actually is. In our initial studies we used the widest range of BMI and WHR in our library of photographs and found that BMI was the primary predictor of attractiveness judgements (Tovée et al., 1998, 1999). In subsequent studies, we have varied the relative range of BMI and WHR to determine how the relative ranges altered the results. For example, we varied the relative ranges such that the range of WHR was three times that of BMI, but BMI was still the primary predictor (Tovée et al., 2002).

However, it may be argued that a two-dimensional image cannot adequately capture a three-dimensional shape. For example, in Caucasian women, the pattern of fat on the buttocks is not visible in a photograph taken in front-view. To counter this problem, some studies have used either laser-scanned three-dimensional body shapes (Fan et al., 2004) or video sequences of bodies rotating through 360° (Smith, Tovée, et al., 2007). However, it should be mentioned that the results from the rating of two- and three-dimensional representations are very similar.

For example, ratings of the three-dimensional video sequences from Smith, Tovée, et al. (2007) and two-dimensional digital photographs of the same women have very highly correlated attractiveness ratings. The correlations between the two- and three-dimensional attractiveness ratings ranged from $r = 0.88$ to 0.96 (comparing the three-dimensional ratings with the three ratings obtained from two-dimensional views of the front, side, and back; Smith, 2006). This is consistent with a previous study which showed a very high correlation of 0.90 between attractiveness ratings of two-dimensional photographs taken from front and profile (Tovée & Cornelissen, 2001). It seems that the cues used to make attractiveness judgements are salient from any view-point, and the additional information an observer may acquire from varying his or her view-point may provide information that is largely redundant.

Principled manipulation of images

Of course, there may be occasions when a manipulation of the relative range of features in a controlled manner may be desired. It is important that any such change has to be biologically plausible and also not co-varying other physical features which are potentially important to attractiveness judgements. For example, in order to address properly the question of whether simple changes in waist and hip size exert differential effects on attractiveness independent of their effects through BMI and WHR it would be necessary to generate a stimulus set in which BMI and WHR are held constant, but waist and hip width are allowed to vary. Streeter and McBurney (2003; see also McBurney & Streeter, Chapter 2) claim that this is impossible to achieve in a factorial design. However, while this may be true with simple images based on line drawings or with crude uni-dimensional manipulation of photographs, we believe that it would be possible to produce such a stimulus set either by selecting images from a large sample of real bodies, or by synthesising images using information about naturally occurring variation in body shape (see Figure 4.5).

If one wishes to synthesise a set of biologically plausible, artificial body shapes (as in Figure 4.5), it is necessary to use objective information about female body shape derived from real women. As we described above, Tovée et al. (2002) carried out a PCA of female torso shape, and found that 4 PCs adequately described the shape variation. Each PC described a different shape dimension over which the body shapes varied. For example, PC1 represented changes in overall body width and PC2 captures a significant change in the shape of the hip region, varying from thickset to slender. It is then possible, to use these 4 PCs to construct a new set of stimulus bodies (Smith, Tovée, et al., 2007). This is possible because the PCs are statistically independent shape descriptors that can be linearly re-combined to create new shapes, each of which

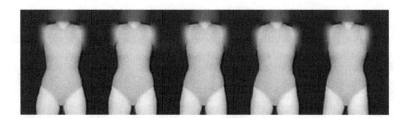

Figure 4.5 A sequence of five synthesised images created by applying four independent descriptors of shape derived from a principal components analysis of the variation in natural body shape to an average female torso (see Smith, Tovée et al., 2007, for details). The images were chosen from the full set of 625 images such that BMI_{PAR} is approximately constant (the variation equates to only 4 per cent of that in the complete image set), but WHR increases from a minimum of 0.65 on the left to a maximum of 0.78 on the right (equal to 69 per cent of the variation in the complete image set). This figure illustrates the complex shape changes that are necessary to effect a dissociation between BMI and WHR.

is uniquely specified by its particular combination of PCs. In this way, it is possible to create a carefully controlled set of body shapes that are based on the natural shape variation in the original sample, and which take into consideration the contours of the entire torso.

Conclusion

The co-variation of features and the lack of realism in most artificial image sets make it impossible to determine the underlying cause of variation in attractiveness ratings. It is not possible to determine easily the effect of changing an individual index of body shape because several indices are typically co-varied when any single index is systematically manipulated. Additionally, the extreme caricaturing of physical shape used in some studies can make figures seem unrealistic, adding an additional stimulus parameter to the experiment that may confuse the pattern of results yet further. To avoid these problems we suggest that image sets for use in attractiveness studies should be based on natural images. A simple approach is to use unmodified digital photographs that can be utilised to capture the natural variation in body shape present in a population. Alternatively, biometric measures from a sample population of women can be used to construct artificial images in a statistically principled way. Using this latter approach, it is theoretically possible to construct image sets in which various indices of body shape such as BMI and WHR are uncorrelated.

References

Bray, G. A. (1978). Definition, measurement, and classification of the syndromes of obesity. *International Journal of Obesity, 2,* 99–112.

Brody, S. (2004). Slimness is associated with greater intercourse and lesser masturbation frequency. *Journal of Sex and Marital Therapy, 30,* 252–261.

Fan, J., Liu, F., Wu, J., & Dai, W. (2004). Visual perception of female physical attractiveness. *Proceedings of the Royal Society London B, 271,* 347–352.

Furnham, A., Petrides, K. V., & Constantinides, A. (2005). The effects of body mass index and waist-to-hip ratio on ratings of female attractiveness, fecundity, and health. *Personality and Individual Differences, 38,* 1823–1834.

Furnham, A., Tan, T., & McManus, C. (1997). Waist-to-hip ratio and preferences for body shape: A replication and extension. *Personality and Individual Differences, 22,* 539–549.

Garn, S. M. (1955). Relative fat patterning: An individual characteristic. *Human Biology, 27,* 75–89.

Garn, S. M., & Harper, R. V. (1955). Fat accumulation and weight gain in the adult male. *Human Biology, 27,* 39–49.

Garn, S. M., Sullivan, T. V., & Hawthorne, V. M. (1987). Differential rates of fat change relative to weight change at different body sites. *International Journal of Obesity, 11,* 519–525.

Garrow, J. (1999). Clinical assessment of obesity. In British Nutritional Foundation Task Force on Obesity. *Obesity: The Report of the British Nutrition Foundation Task Force.* (pp. 17–22). Oxford: British Nutritional Foundation, Blackwell Science.

George, H., Cornelissen, P. L., Hancock, P. J. B., & Tovée, M. J. (2007). Eye-movements in the perception of female attractiveness. Manuscript in preparation.

Henss, R. (1995). Waist-to-hip ratio and attractiveness: A replication and extension. *Personality and Individual Differences, 19,* 479–488.

Henss, R. (2000). Waist-to-hip ratio and female attractiveness: Evidence from photographic stimuli and methodological considerations. *Personality and Individual Differences, 28,* 501–513.

Rozmus-Wrzesinska, M., & Pawłowski, B. (2005). Men's ratings of female attractiveness are influenced more by changes in female waist size compared with changes in hip size. *Biological Psychology, 68,* 299–308.

Singh, D. (1993). Adaptive significance of female physical attractiveness: Role of waist-to-hip ratio. *Journal of Personality and Social Psychology, 65,* 293–307.

Singleton, B. B. R., Cornelissen, P. L., & Tovée, M. J. (2004). On what visual areas are human attractiveness judgements based? Paper presented at the Annual Meeting of the Human Behavior & Evolution Society (HBES-2004).

Smith, K. L. (2006). *The visual cues to female physical attractiveness, health and fertility.* PhD Thesis. Newcastle University.

Smith, K. L., Cornelissen, P. L., & Tovée, M. J. (2007). Colour 3D bodies and judgements of human female attractiveness. *Evolution and Human Behavior, 28,* 48–54.

Smith, K. L., Tovée, M. J., Hancock, P., Bateson, M., Cox, M. A. A., & Cornelissen, P. L. (2007). An analysis of body shape attractiveness based on image statistics: Evidence for a dissociation between expressions of preference and shape discrimination. *Visual Cognition, 15,* 1–27.

Streeter, S. A., & McBurney, D. H. (2003). Waist-hip ratio and attractiveness: New evidence and a critique of 'a critical test.' *Evolution and Human Behavior, 24,* 88–98.

Thornhill, R., & Grammer, K. (1999). The body and face of woman: One ornament that signals quality? *Evolution and Human Behavior, 20,* 105–120.

Tovée, M. J., & Cornelissen, P. L. (1999). The mystery of female beauty. *Nature, 399,* 215–216.

Tovée, M. J., & Cornelissen, P. L. (2001). Cue-invariance in the perception of female physical beauty. *British Journal of Psychology, 92,* 391–402.

Tovée, M. J., Maisey, D. S., Emery, J. L., & Cornelissen, P. L. (1999). Visual cues to female physical attractiveness. *Proceedings of the Royal Society B, 266,* 211–218.

Tovée, M. J., Reinhardt, S., Emery, J. L., & Cornelissen, P. L. (1998). Optimum body-mass index and maximum sexual attractiveness. *The Lancet, 352,* 548.

Tovée, M. J., Benson, P. J., Emery, J. L., Mason, S. M., & Cohen-Tovée, E. M. (2003). Measurement of body size and shape perception in eating-disordered and control observers using body-shape software. *British Journal of Psychology, 94,* 501–516.

Tovée, M. J., Hancock, P. J. B., Mahmoodi, S., Singleton, B. R. R., & Cornelissen, P. L. (2002). Human female attractiveness: Waveform analysis of body shape. *Proceedings of the Royal Society B, 269*, 2205–2213.

Waas, P., Waldenstrom, U., Rossner, S., & Hellberg, D. (1997). An android body fat distribution in females impairs the pregnancy rate of in-vitro fertilization-embryo transfer. *Human Reproduction, 12*, 2057–2060.

Zaadstra, B. M., Seidell, J. C., Noord, P. A. H. V., Velde, E. R. T., Habbema, J. D. F., Vrieskwijk, B., et al. (1993). Fat and female fecundity: Prospective study of effect of body fat distribution on conception rates. *British Medical Journal, 306*, 484–487.

Part III

Attractiveness Research Across Cultures

5

An Evolutionary Perspective on Male Preferences for Female Body Shape

Isabel Scott, Gillian R. Bentley, Martin J. Tovée,
Farid Uddin Ahamed, and Kesson Magid

Cross-culturally, humans make systematic use of physical attractiveness to discriminate among members of the opposite sex, and physical cues to youth, health, and fertility may be particularly important to men (Buss, 1989). Nevertheless, there is controversy over whether attraction preferences are adaptive, particularly in novel environments, and whether they are universal or flexible depending on cultural circumstances (Singh & Luis, 1995). To date, a good deal of research into somatic (i.e., body) attractiveness has focused on two particular characteristics: waist-to-hip ratio (WHR) and the body mass index (BMI). WHR is calculated as the circumference of the waist divided by circumference of the hips, and provides an index of a woman's 'curvaceousness.' BMI is calculated as an individual's weight (kilogrammes) divided by height (metres) squared, and provides an estimate of body fatness.

The evolutionary rationale for the existence of somatic preferences is that it allows men to distinguish women of high mate value. There are a number of traits indexed both to mate value and somatype, including fertility, health, youth, and access to resources. In the West, all of these traits are positively associated with slimness and curvaceousness. BMI rises with age across a range of ethnic groups (Department of Health, 1999), but falls with socioeconomic status among women (Department of Health, 1999; Sobal & Stunkard, 1989), so that slimmer women are on average younger and wealthier. Low WHR (i.e., having a narrow waist relative to hips) is observed predominantly among reproductive-aged women (Lanska, Lanska, Hartz, & Rimm, 1985) and is more common among women in non-manual professions (Department of Health, 1999; Lahti-Koski, Pietinen, Männistö, & Vartiainen, 2000). In contrast, high

WHR is associated with lower levels of reproductive hormones – at least among Polish women (Jasienska, Ziomkiewicz, Ellison, Lipson, & Thune, 2004) – as well as reduced chances of ovulation and conception (Ley, Lees, & Stevenson, 1992; Wass, Waldenstrom, Rossner, & Hellberg, 1997; Zaadstra et al., 1993). Obesity (as studied in the West) reduces fertility (Zaadstra et al., 1993), increases morbidity and mortality (Manson et al., 1995) and, along with high WHR, is linked to elevated risks for a range of chronic diseases including diabetes and heart disease (Björntorp, 1988; Hartz, Rupley, & Rimm, 1984; Lahti-Koski et al., 2000).

When restricted to within-population comparisons, and most importantly *when BMI is controlled for*, the association between low WHR and high fertility – or more specifically, probability of conception – is claimed to be universal (or at least there is little evidence to contradict it; DeRidder et al., 1990; Jasienska et al., 2004; Lanska et al., 1985; Sugiyama, 2004; Zaadstra et al., 1993). To the best of our knowledge, in all societies studied to date, women of reproductive age have lower average WHRs than males, children or non-reproductive aged women in the same population. In addition, Pawłowski and Grabarczyk (2003) report that centre-of-mass is lower in females with low WHR, a characteristic which the authors suggest is designed to compensate for the destabilising effects of pregnancy and child-carrying upon the balance and mobility of bipedal animals. Such facts have been taken to suggest that females with a 'locally' low WHR represent a high fertility phenotype the world over.

While we acknowledge that (locally) low WHR probably signals (locally) high fertility, we argue here that the inference that low WHR (by Western standards) represents the optimal phenotype for mate value, and that WHR preferences should be universally low, is premature. This argument is supported by a number of considerations. First, an increasing body of data suggests that local anthropometric norms of female WHR are highly variable and that, whereas male and female WHR ranges were once seen as mutually exclusive, when viewed in a cross-cultural context there may be a degree of overlap (Marlowe, Apicella, & Reed, 2005). In addition, fertile women (by local standards) do have high WHR (by Western standards) in some societies (Sugiyama, 2004). If low WHRs represent a universally optimal phenotype for reproductive success, then it seems unlikely that such variation would be maintained.

Secondly, there is the issue of BMI. While research from developing countries is relatively scant, the limited data available suggest that the relationships between weight and other indices of mate value may be reversed in environments of caloric stress and uncertainty. In poorer countries (including those in South Asia; Sobal & Stunkard, 1989), there is a positive association between obesity and socioeconomic status (SES) which is, in turn, associated with more secure access to resources. In such societies, high BMI should increase the probability of a woman maintaining energy balance during periods of deprivation, which in turn increases the chances of carrying a pregnancy to term and producing offspring (Kramer et al., 1995; Steer, 2005). A higher preconception maternal BMI is also correlated with a higher birth weight for the resulting child and hence a better chance of survival in a low resource environment (Baker, Michaelsen, Rasmussen, & Sorensen, 2004; Bhargava, 2000; Mohanty et al., 2006).

In addition, the potential long-term health penalties resulting from overweight are likely to be compensated by the 'more immediate positive consequences of being plump' (Anderson, Crawford, Nadeau, & Lindberg, 1992; Hosegood & Campbell, 2003), while the relationship between age and weight gain common in the West is also unlikely to be present in much of the developing world, where maternal depletion syndrome (negative energy balance brought about by frequent reproductive cycling) is much more common (King, 2003; Shell-Duncan & Yung, 2004; Tracer, 2002). Consequently, in developing countries women with high BMI are likely to be healthier, wealthier, and possibly younger and more fertile as well.

However, within those populations that have been studied, the correlation between fatness and WHR is positive (e.g., Lahti-Koski et al., 2000; Department of Health, 1999), possibly a consequence of metabolic adjustments (see below). This means that, while a low WHR/high BMI combination might be optimal for fertility, few women will exhibit such a phenotype. In such situations, the advantages associated with low WHR may be 'trumped' by those of high BMI (Marlowe & Wetsman, 2001; Tovée, Swami, Furnham, & Mangalparsad, 2006), although in order for this to be the case, BMI must be considered to be more critical to mate value than is WHR.

A third consideration is that, in energetically stressful conditions, features associated with an 'android' phenotype (i.e., high WHR) may be advantageous in their own right. Irrespective of current body weight, a high WHR appears to promote efficient storage of fat for utilisation in times of caloric deprivation. Various authors (e.g., Kuh & Schlomo, 2004) have suggested that a tendency toward central adiposity (commonly referred to as a 'thrifty' phenotype) is an adaptation to anticipated energetic stress. Such body types are suggested to result from foetal responses to intrauterine maternal under-nutrition. This is argued to be an evolved phenomenon of adaptive value in our ancestral past when food shortages were more common, or where particular food resources were in short supply or only seasonally available (Gluckman & Hanson, 2005; Prentice, 2005; Simmons, 2005; although other authors challenge the notion of severe food shortages prior to the development of agriculture, e.g., Benyshek & Watson, 2006; Cordain, Miller, & Mann, 1999). In such uncertain environments, the reproductive benefits of the low WHR phenotype may have to be 'traded-off' against the metabolic costs.

A final point to take into consideration is that the relationship between fertility and mate value is likely to be non-linear, and that optimal levels of fertility should vary between populations. Life history theory emphasises that because finite resources are available from the environment, trade-offs must be made between effort devoted to survival and to reproduction, and that maximal fertility is not necessarily optimal. Recent research suggests that women raised in more stressful environments not only adapt their metabolic activity, but also end up with adult levels of reproductive steroids that are significantly lower than women who grow up in resource-rich environments (Ellison et al., 1993a, Ellison, Panterbrick, Lipson, & Orourke, 1993b).

As with metabolism, population variation in base-line sex hormone levels may reflect developmental influences during pre-pubertal years (Núñez-de la Mora et al., in press – a, b). This suggests that developmental adjustments leading to a reduced probability of conception may constitute an adaptation to environments where resources are scarce. While it may seem counterintuitive to suppose that mate value should be increased by a reduction in fertility, a mate that fails to time her pregnancies correctly may have low reproductive success. In contrast, women who appropriately adjust their fertility schedules to fluctuations in resource-availability are likely to reproduce more successfully and, therefore, should be considered as more desirable partners. Women born into stressful environments may have a longer waiting time to conception, but still appear to be able to conceive and maintain relatively high levels of lifetime fertility, and may carry more pregnancies to term or have more surviving offspring as a consequence (Vitzthum et al., 2002; Vitzthum, Spielvogel, & Thornburg, 2004).

In summary, then, both android and gynoid body shapes are associated with phenotypic costs and benefits, and so the optimal body shape for reproductive success is likely to depend on local ecological conditions. The low WHR phenotype is advantageous insofar as a woman with low WHR is more likely to conceive, and may be morphologically better adapted to pregnancy. High WHR on the other hand, is associated with high BMI, metabolic thrift, and potentially adaptive adjustments to fertility and to mobility when non-pregnant, all of which may contribute to mate value where resources are scarce.

We, therefore, suggest that local variations in norms of body shape represent adaptive phenotypic adjustment to local environments, in particular to resource availability and energetic demands. Moreover, we hypothesise that male preferences should track such norms, so as to select mates of high reproductive value. This need not imply that preferences centre precisely on local averages. Rather, preferences for WHRs that are slightly lower than local norms will select females that are of reproductive age, and that have high probabilities of conception by local standards. Preferences should be *indexed* to local norms, however, if they are to track females with metabolic and reproductive schedules appropriate to the current environment.

Whether such preferences should be hardwired or flexible depends largely on the frequency of change in resource availability in our ancestral past. If change occurred relatively frequently over generations or even decades, then it might well have been adaptive to be able to take a flexible approach to mate choice, with preferences responding either to local cultural norms or exposure to local anthropometry. If changes took place over significantly longer periods, then genes for certain preferences might have co-evolved with genes for different types of body shape. We suggest that the former account is more plausible, largely because of the documented existence in humans of developmental adjustments to anticipated diet, as outlined in previous paragraphs. We, therefore, hypothesise that male body shape preferences will be plastic and amenable to adjustment, as well as reflecting local environmental conditions and norms of body shape.

Research findings to date are largely supportive of the hypotheses outline above. Studies suggest that in populations experiencing nutritional stress, males prefer plumper women (Anderson et al., 1992) and deem images of overweight women to be maximally attractive (Furnham & Alibhai, 1983; Marlowe & Wetsman, 2001; Sugiyama, 2004; Wetsman & Marlowe, 1999; Yu & Shepard, 1998). In contrast, most of the findings from developed countries show male preferences for thin or moderate-weight women (Furnham, Tan, & McManus, 1997; Henss, 1995; Singh, 1993; Smith, Cornelissen, & Tovée, 2007; Tovée & Cornelissen, 2001; Wetsman & Marlowe, 1999).

While earlier research indicated a cross-cultural preference for low WHR (centred at around 0.70) among Caucasians, Hispanics, Indonesians and African Americans, Britons, Israelis, and Kenyans (Furnham, McClelland, & Omer, 2003; Gitter, Lomranz, Saxe, & Bar-Tal, 1983;

Singh, 1993, 1994; Singh & Luis, 1995), in recent years, evidence of indifference to or aversion to low WHRs has begun to emerge from a number of non-Western populations, including the Matsigenka of Peru (Yu & Shepard, 1998), the Hadza of Tanzania (Marlowe & Wetsman, 2001; Wetsman & Marlowe, 1999), South African Zulus (Tovée et al., 2006) and rural Malaysians (Swami & Tovée, 2005). Direct evidence of *plasticity* in somatic preferences remains relatively scarce, but is mostly positive. Research by Yu and Shepard (1998) on the responses of the Matsigenka to exposure to American culture and socioecology, and a study by Tovée et al. (2006) on the effects on preferences of migrants from Africa to Britain, both offer preliminary support for the adjustment of preferences to local conditions, while recent research shows that even comparatively small changes in food intake can produce a measurable and significant shift in male preferences for female weight and size (Swami & Tovée, 2006). Further (albeit indirect) evidence for plasticity of preferences is apparent in the literature connecting women's idealisation of thinness with development and modernisation at the population level (Brewis & McGarvey, 2000), and in studies relating economic factors to the kind of female somatype depicted in the media (Pettijohn & Jungeberg, 2004; see also Nelson, Pettijohn, & Galak, Chapter 9). To date, however, no research of which we are aware has attempted to relate changes in WHR preference to changes in local anthropometric norms.

Changing mate preferences: Migrant Bangladeshi pilot study

To measure the possibility of plasticity in male preferences for female body shape, we initiated a pilot study in 2005 among 30 Bangladeshi migrants to London, of whom 6 were second-generation migrants, and compared the responses to 40 residents still living in Sylhet District, Northeast Bangladesh. We chose this particular area of Bangladesh since over 95 per cent of British migrants originate from here, thus ensuring ethnic and geographic homogeneity (Eade & Momen, 1996). The length of time in Britain for first-generation migrants ranged from 1 to 41 years, with a mean of 13 years. Age differences between the groups were not significant (mean age residents = 34.3, migrants = 32.6, $p = 0.54$).

Socioeconomically, Bangladesh rates as one of the poorest countries in the world with one of the lowest gross national product indices; approximately 47 per cent of the population live below the poverty line (gross national income per capita Britain = US\$37,600, Bangladesh = US\$470; World Bank, 2005). The population under study here represents the relatively affluent middle-class, namely middle-class men who originate from relatively wealthy families that are often landowners and able to afford servants within their own country. These families do not suffer from nutritional or energetic stress themselves, but are nevertheless embedded within a society in which caloric deprivation is commonplace, and do experience poorer health and sanitation conditions relative to London.

Bangladeshis are of specific interest in this context given the high proportion of individuals (both men and women) with an android body shape that places them at higher risk for metabolic syndrome later in life. Statistics in many countries show that South Asian immigrants, including Bangladeshis, have significantly higher rates of central adiposity, obesity, type 2 diabetes, and cardiovascular disease (Department of Health, 1999; Misra & Vikram, 2004; Vikram et al., 2003). According to data from the Health Survey for England (Department of Health, 1999), while the average WHR for women aged 16–34 in Britain was 0.76, the average for Bangladeshi women of the same age was 0.81. Moreover the average pre-menopausal Bangladeshi WHR is higher than that of British women aged 35–54, despite the lower incidence of obesity amongst Bangladeshi migrant women compared to all other ethnic groups in Britain. It seems likely, therefore, that males in Bangladesh have generally been exposed to a high proportion of people with a high WHR compared to men in Britain.

During the course of the survey, participant information was collected on a range of SES markers, including birthplace (rural or urban), overcrowding (twice number of adults in household plus number of children, divided by number of rooms in household), ownership of a range of consumer goods (car, microwave, freezer, CD player, video, computer, satellite television), and highest educational level achieved. Of these, all but one was patterned in a way consistent with expectations, with migrant males scoring higher for SES markers than residents (see Table 5.1). The exception was educational achievement, with 85 per cent of residents in Sylhet achieving degree level or higher, compared with only 40 per cent of migrants. It was, therefore, decided to control for educational achievement.

Participants were presented with an anonymous questionnaire requesting demographic information including age, education, employment, housing and migration. They were then shown a booklet containing 35 composite photographic images in colour of real women wearing leotards and tights in front and side view simultaneously (with heads obscured). These women had documented BMIs ranging from 11.6

Table 5.1 Demographic and socioeconomic indicators.

	Average age mean (median)	% married	% describing birthplace as rural	Average over-crowding	Average ownership consumer goods	% with degree or higher
Residents	34.3 (30)	53	72.5	2.3	3.1	85
Migrants	32.6 (26)	43	33.3	1.8	5.9	40

to 36.1 kg/m^2, and documented WHRs from 0.68 to 0.90. To control for order effects two books were used, with images randomised in different orders. Men were asked to rate each image for attractiveness, health, wealth, and fertility, on a scale of 0 to 9 (0 = lowest, 9 = highest), and to estimate the age of the women in the photo. All photographic images used for the study were developed and tested in prior studies (Tovée, Hancock, Mahmoodi, Singleton, & Cornelissen, 2002; Tovée, Maisey, Emery, & Cornelissen, 1999). These images were first piloted among a few Bangladeshis to ensure they would not be offensive or culturally inappropriate for Muslim men of different ages living in different locations.

To check for significant differences between groups, three statistics were generated for each respondent. First, the 'peak BMI value for attractiveness' was calculated for each male respondent. For each respondent, a graph was plotted with the BMI of each woman in the photographs on the x-axis and the respondent's rating of her attractiveness on the y-axis. A cubic polynomial was fitted to the graph, which was then used to calculate the BMI at which attractiveness ratings peaked, demonstrating the respondent's most preferred female body weight. Secondly, an average was taken for each respondent's ratings of the seven obese women in the image set (those with BMI > 30), which provided an index of his appraisal of the attractiveness of obese women. Thirdly, the correlation between WHR and attractiveness ratings was calculated for each respondent, which provided an index of whether, and how strongly, he preferred low values of WHR. A General Linear Model (GLM) was used to assess the impact of group membership on BMI of peak attractiveness, attractiveness of obese women, and preference for low WHR, controlling for both age and educational attainment.

We also tested for group differences in the perceived relationships between BMI, WHR and each of health, fertility, SES and age. In order to do this, further statistics were generated for each participant. As before, cubic polynomials were used to calculate the BMI at which health, fertility and SES ratings were perceived to peak by each respondent. The

BMI value at which age was perceived to be minimised was also calculated (the minimum average age rating for any image was 28 years). In addition, averages were taken of the perceived healthiness, SES, fertility and age of the obese images, and the correlation between WHR and each of health, SES, fertility and age were calculated. These ratings were then treated as dependent variables in a GLM, controlling for respondents' age and education as before. Data were analysed using three statistical software packages: SPSS (version 12 for GLMs), OriginLab (version 7.5 for interpolating graphs and calculating maximal ratings), and MiniTab (version 14 for best subsets regressions).

Results

Attractiveness ratings as a function of BMI and WHR respectively are shown in Figures 5.1a and 5.1b. The relationship between attractiveness and BMI is non-linear for both migrants and Sylhet residents, peaking

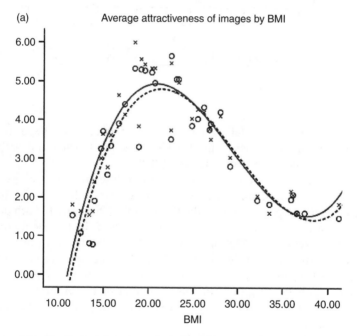

Figure 5.1(a, b) Attractiveness as a function of BMI and WHR respectively. Each point represents the average ratings of one image by either the sedentee or the migrant group.

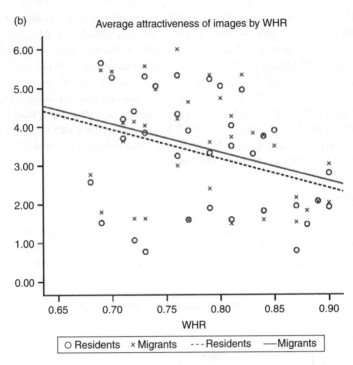

Figure 5.1 (Continued).

at around BMI 20, and falling away sharply on either side. The relationship between attractiveness and WHR is weak, but linear and negative, indicating a slight preference for low WHR.

Despite the absence of discernable group differences in the graphs (Figures 5.1a and 5.1b), when confounds were controlled, the findings were largely supportive of the adaptive flexibility hypothesis, with peak BMI for attractiveness significantly higher in the Sylhet resident group (mean for residents = 22.8, migrants = 19.8, $p < 0.001$) and preference for low WHR significantly higher in the migrant group (mean for residents = −0.20, migrants = −0.31, $p < 0.05$). There were no significant differences between groups in their appraisal of the attractiveness of obese women (mean for residents = 1.95, migrants = 1.58, $p = 0.46$; see Tables 5.2 and 5.3).

The relationship between BMI, WHR and average ratings of the images for health, fertility, SES and age are plotted in Figures 5.2 and 5.3. Results of GLM testing for group differences showed that significant differences

Table 5.2 (a, b, c) GLMs for BMI of peak attractiveness, average attractiveness of obese images and correlation between WHR and attractiveness.

	Unstandardised coefficient (*B*)	SE of *B*	*t* value	*P*
(a) General Linear Model for BMI of peak attractiveness				
Constant	25.7	1.56	16.52	0.00
Age	−0.08	0.04	−2.16	0.03
Education	−1.50	0.40	−3.78	0.00
Groups	3.05	0.82	3.71	0.00
(b) General Linear Model for average attractiveness of obese images				
Constant	3.57	0.94	3.79	0.00
Age	−0.03	0.02	−1.28	0.20
Education	−0.47	0.25	−1.91	0.06
Groups	0.37	0.50	0.74	0.46
(c) General Linear Model for correlation between WHR and attractiveness				
Constant	0.07	0.10	0.72	0.47
Age	−0.01	0.00	−2.23	0.03
Education	−0.09	0.03	−3.70	0.00
Groups	0.11	0.05	2.06	0.04

Table 5.3 (a, b, c) Mean values, by group, of BMI of peak attractiveness, attractiveness of obese women and preference for low WHR.

	Marginal mean* for residents	Marginal mean for migrants
(a) BMI of peak attractiveness	22.82	19.78
(b) Average attractiveness of obese women	1.95	1.58
(c) Correlation between WHR and attractiveness	−0.20	−0.31

* Marginal means are the mean response of the group once confounds are controlled for. Thus when age and education are factored out, Sylhet residents viewed attractiveness to peak at BMI 22.82, gave obese women an average rating of 1.95 out of 9 for attractiveness, and the average perceived relationship between WHR and attractiveness had a correlation coefficient of −0.19

between groups were limited exclusively to SES ratings. Group differences mirrored differences in attraction judgements, with the migrant group regarding SES as peaking at a reduced BMI compared to the Sylhet residents, and obese women and women with high WHR to be less wealthy (see Tables 5.4 and 5.5).

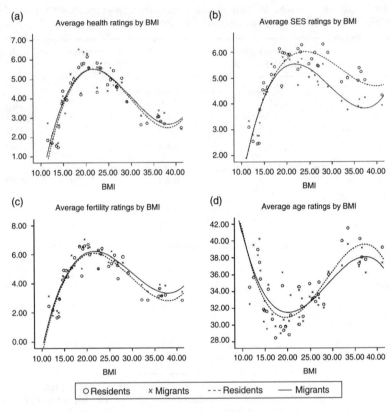

Figure 5.2 (a, b, c, d) Average ratings for health, wealth fertility and age by BMI. Each point represents the average ratings of one image by either the sedentee or the migrant group.

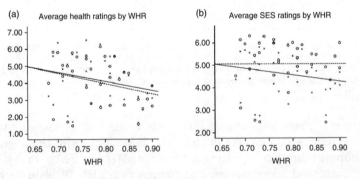

Figure 5.3 (a, b, c, d) Average ratings for health, wealth, fertility and age by WHR.

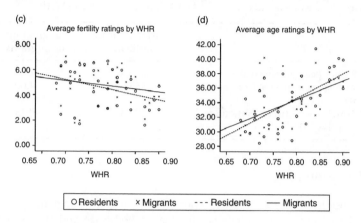

Figure 5.3 (Continued).

Table 5.4 (*a, b, c*) GLMs for BMI of peak perceived SES, average perceived SES of obese images and correlation between WHR and perceived SES.

	Unstandardised coefficient (*B*)	SE of *B*	*t* value	*P*
(a) General Linear Model for BMI of peak perceived SES				
Constant	24.44	2.21	11.09	0.00
Age	−0.02	0.05	−0.30	0.76
Education	−0.55	0.56	−0.98	0.33
Groups	2.60	1.19	2.18	0.03
(b) General Linear Model for average perceived SES of obese images				
Constant	4.51	0.89	5.09	0.00
Age	−0.01	0.02	−0.51	0.61
Education	−0.08	0.23	−0.35	0.73
Groups	1.01	0.47	2.13	0.04
(c) General Linear Model for correlation between WHR and perceived SES				
Constant	0.12	0.11	1.10	0.28
Age	−0.00	0.00	−1.77	0.08
Education	−0.05	0.03	−1.81	0.08
Groups	0.17	0.06	2.89	0.01

Table 5.5 (a, b, c)   Mean values, by group, of BMI of peak perceived SES, perceived SES of obese women and correlation between perceived SES and WHR.

	Marginal mean for residents	Marginal mean for migrants
(a) BMI of peak perceived SES	25.23	22.63
(b) Average perceived SES of obese women	5.00	4.00
(c) Correlation between WHR and perceived SES	0.03	−0.15

Discussion

The results of the experiment showed that migrant Bangladeshi men exhibited changing preferences for female body size and shape, with migrant attitudes mirroring previously documented Western preferences. In addition, preferences were adjusted in a direction consistent with principles of maximising mate choice. Bangladeshi residents rated optimal attractiveness at a significantly higher BMI than migrants, and the correlation between WHR and attractiveness was more negative in the migrant group, indicating a stronger preference for a low WHR or curvaceousness. This accords with the fact that, within the Bangladeshi population, heavier, larger-waisted women are likely be of higher relative mate value than their counterparts in Britain, as outlined in the paragraphs above. Our findings, therefore, support an account of somatic attraction in which preferences are flexible and adapt to new environments in such a way as to maintain an orientation towards women of high mate value.

In addition, the experiment involved an exploration of the proximate causes of group differences in preferences. Both mental modelling and exposure effects constitute possible mechanisms via which differences are mediated. Various authors have suggested that attraction may respond to anthropometric means in the local population (Sugiyama, 2004; Symons, 1979) and numerous studies from the facial attractiveness literature have shown that mere exposure to facial types is sufficient to adjust preferences in that direction (Buckingham et al., 2006; Rhodes et al., 2003). To date, however, little research appears to have investigated similar phenomena for bodies, presumably due to the widely acknowledged fact that preference for overweight women is inversely associated with their prevalence (Anderson et al., 1992). WHR preferences, however, may well respond to local norms of body shape, particularly if they are the optimal value for reproductive success, and our findings are consistent with this hypothesis. As stated earlier, the average WHR for Bangladeshi women is significantly higher than that for Caucasian women in Britain. Further, among the Sylhet residents in our study, preference for low WHR was correlated with access to foreign media, as indexed by ownership of television, video, home computer and satellite television ($r = 0.33$, $p < 0.05$) and hence presumably images of Western women. Our results, therefore, are consistent with the hypothesis that exposure to females of particular body shapes influences preferences.

An alternative to the hypothesis of mere exposure is that of mental modelling. This states that the association between particular somatypes and certain attractive traits is reliable within populations, but differs between them, and hence that within populations (either at the level of the individual, or as part of a process of cultural evolution) certain somatypes come to be psychologically associated with particular traits, and are therefore seen as attractive. Our data indicated that only SES perceptions differed significantly between the groups, with Sylhet residents viewing both SES and attractiveness to be optimised at significantly higher BMIs and WHRs than migrants, while perceptions regarding the relationship between somatype and each of health, fertility, and age were the same between groups. Moreover, as outlined above, our subjects' perceptions regarding environment, SES and somatype (i.e., that the association between BMI and wealth was more positive in Bangladesh than in Britain) were probably reasonably accurate (Islam, Akhtaruzzaman, & Lamberg-Allardt, 2004; Sobal & Stunkard, 1989). The results, therefore, indicated that perceptions about SES were a plausible mechanism through which group differences in attraction were generated, a suggestion consistent with the hypothesis that resource availability – specifically caloric resources – is of primary importance to inter-population differences in male preferences for female body shape.

It should be noted, however, that there are a number of limitations to our study, which further research might be able to rectify. The first of these is that our method of testing for mental representations of the relationships between somatype and other traits relied on participants' ability to articulate such representations, and to consciously recognise cues of particular traits (i.e., health, wealth, etc.). Our findings, therefore, do not exclude the possibility that males are able to track the somatic correlates of traits such as health and fertility across different environments, but are simply unaware of what their preferences signify. Indeed, prior research suggests that when males are asked to make conscious judgements about the relationship between somatype and traits such as health and fertility, like our subjects, they do not provide particularly accurate models (Furnham et al., 1997, 2003; Garfinkel & Garner, 1982; Henss, 1995; McGarvey, 1991; Powers, 1980; Singh, 1993).

This provokes the question of why males should be more cognisant of the somatic correlates of wealth than of health or fertility. One suggestion is that, cross-culturally, there exist invariant correlates of health and fertility (such as, for example, feminine facial features and good hair and skin) but that wealth markers vary greatly from population to population. If this is the case, then males need not be aware that a particular body-type was more fertile in order to track fertile phenotypes across a range of environments. All that would be required would be that certain (e.g., facial) signals should be considered attractive by all males, and that exposure to a population in which a particular somatype was reliably associated with such signals should generate a preference for that somatype. Wealth cues, on the other hand, would have to be re-learnt in each new environment, and one, therefore, expects an element of awareness of the relationship between SES and somatype. It may, therefore, be the case that some or all of the other traits under investigation (i.e., health, fertility and age) are responsible for group differences in preferences, but that SES is the only trait for which participants are able to articulate accurate models. This hypothesis could, in principle, be easily tested by priming participants with stimuli in which various somatic variables are positively or negatively correlated with cues of health, wealth, fertility and age, and subsequently testing both for somatic preferences, and for judgements about the relationships between somatype and other traits.

A further shortcoming in this study is that our results are consistent with a number of hypotheses regarding the ultimate explanation for flexible variation in preferences. As outlined above, in Britain slim but curvy women are on average younger, healthier, wealthier and more fertile than average while, in much of Bangladesh, these trends are likely to be reversed. With a large, multi-population sample, it would be possible to treat population relationships between somatype and each of these factors (wealth, health, etc.) as independent variables, and preferences as a dependent variable, and hence to determine which factors were genuinely salient. As there are only two groups in this experiment however, it is impossible to determine which, if any, of these factors is being tracked by male preferences. Moreover, it remains a possibility that other factors not considered here may exert an effect on the adjustment of preferences, and indeed various authors have proposed other traits that may be important. For example, a higher androgen/oestrogen ratio may be associated with increased assertiveness and competitive ability as well as increased WHR, which may be of benefit in societies in which women compete directly for resources (Cashdan, 2003; Marlowe et al., 2005). As described by Einon (Chapter 8), curvaceousness may facilitate heat loss (see also Barber, 1995), which is of benefit in hot, arid climates but may impose costs in environments where heat conservation in important (although this would not of course explain the current findings). High WHR may indicate an 'ability to digest fibrous foods' (Sugiyama, 2004), which could be important in societies in which these constitute a staple part of the diet. And regional variation in fertility, child-carrying practices and other mobility requirements, such as those associated with foraging, water-carrying and so on, may also impact both on the salience of mobility to survival, and on what is the ideal fat distribution for mobility (Barber, 1995; Marlowe et al., 2005). All of these hypotheses are in principle easily testable, and require further investigation in a cross-cultural context.

In addition to the further research suggested above, we feel that there are a number of questions of interest that could easily be addressed by supplementary studies. Our findings indicated that, within groups, education was a highly significant predictor of preferences for Western ideals. Future research could address in more depth the subject of intra-group variation in preferences, attempt to identify further intra-group factors, and explain how and why they exert an effect on preferences. Secondly, while we did not collect data on length of stay in Britain or age at migration in this study, it would be of great interest to examine the interaction of these two factors in determining preferences. It would be interesting to examine whether there is a 'critical window' of development during which preferences are acquired, and/or whether preferences are capable of modification throughout adult life. Third, given that exposure to Western media has been proposed to impact on preferences, but that such exposure presumably correlates with other socioecological factors, it would be informative to compare the effects of exposure to media images with exposure to 'ordinary' individuals of varying somatype, to determine which of these has the greatest effect of preferences. Should one or the other have a disproportionate influence, this would be relevant to the ongoing debate regarding the responsibility of the media for body image problems among women. Fourth, to determine whether exposure effects and/or mental modelling are pertinent to WHR preferences, we suggest lab-based priming experiments, in which individuals are exposed both to stimuli sets with particularly high/low WHRs, and to stimuli sets in which WHR is positively or negatively correlated with other cues of mate quality, in order to determine the proximate processes responsible for adjustments to preferences.

Finally, a comprehensive investigation of the effects of different stimuli should be undertaken. To date, researchers have employed line drawings, greyscale and colour photographs, front, profile and 3D perspectives, varying ranges for both BMI and WHR, and different ethnic groups in their depiction of women for experiments. To the best of our knowledge, no one has thus far attempted to present such a variety of stimuli to a single, homogenous group. Such a project would confirm (or otherwise) that apparent group differences in preference are genuine and not an artifact of some other factor. (Indeed, in the current study, the use of colour photographs, while contributing to the realism and impact of the stimuli, would have revealed the skin tone, and hence the ethnicity, of the women depicted. While there is no theoretical reason, of which we are aware, to suppose that there should be an interaction between ethnicity of stimuli and subjects' preferred body shape, neither are we aware of any research that has specifically investigated this possibility, and therefore cannot rule out that it was responsible for group differences.)

Conclusion

In conclusion, we agree that males evidently possess an evolved ability to assess women's attractiveness on the basis of physiological indicators that are linked to various criteria of mate value. However, a great deal of evidence is also accumulating to show that this ability is highly plastic depending on the kind of environment in which humans are living. Rather than a universal male preference for a low WHR ratio centred around 0.70, as posited by early research on the issue of male preference for female body shape, male preferences for a specific WHR and BMI appear to differ depending on the amount of resources available in their environment. Where resources are more abundant, as is typical for Western and/or urbanised cultures, men seem to prefer women with a slim but curvy figure, but where resources are scarce or uncertain, male preferences are for a higher WHR and a higher BMI.

In certain circumstances, the high WHR/BMI phenotype could signal higher mate value in a woman and potentially an evolved capability to use scarce resources more efficiently. Although such a phenotype is associated (in modern environments) with lower levels of oestrogen and potentially reduced fecundity, the benefits to females of metabolic thrift may sometimes outweigh the drawbacks of a longer waiting time to conception compared to those measured in contemporary women. We argue for the existence of fluctuation in nutritional security in our ancestral past, as evidenced in the developmental flexibility of the physical body, which is capable of anticipating both plenty and scarcity, and that there is hence a rationale for flexibility in preferences as well. We further suggest that male preferences should respond to local socioecological conditions by tracking females of high mate value across a range of environments, and that mechanisms exist which enable them to do so. A combination of further cross-cultural/correlational and experimental investigations is required in order to confirm our suggestions.

References

Anderson, J. L., Crawford, C. B., Nadeau, J., & Lindberg, T. (1992). Was the Duchess of Windsor right? A cross-cultural review of the socioecology of ideals of female body shape. *Ethology and Sociobiology*, *13*, 197–227.

Baker, J. L., Michaelsen, K. F., Rasmussen, K. M., & Sorensen, T. I. (2004). Maternal prepregnant body mass index, duration of breastfeeding, and timing of complementary food introduction are associated with infant weight gain. *American Journal of Clinical Nutrition*, *80*, 1579–1588.

Barber, N. (1995). The evolutionary psychology of physical attractiveness: Sexual selection and human morphology. *Ethology and Sociobiology*, *16*, 395–424.

Benyshek, D. C., & Watson, J. T. (2006). Exploring the thrifty genotype's food shortage assumptions: A cross-cultural comparison of ethnographic accounts of food security among foraging and agricultural societies. *American Journal of Physical Anthropology*, *131*, 120–126.

Bhargava, A. (2000). Modelling the effects of maternal nutritional status and socioeconomic variables on the anthropometric and psychological indicators of Kenyan infants from age 0–6 months. *American Journal of Physical Anthropology*, *111*, 89–104.

Björntorp, P. (1988). The associations between obesity, adipose tissue distribution and disease. *Acta Medica Scandinavica*, *723* (Suppl.), 121–134.

Brewis, A. A., & McGarvey, S. T. (2000). Body image, body size, and Samoan ecological and individual modernization. *Ecology of Food and Nutrition*, *39*, 105–120.

Buckingham, G., DeBruine, L. M., Little, A. C., Welling, L. L. M., Conway, C. A., Tiddeman, B. P., et al. (2006). Visual adaptation to masculine and feminine faces influences generalized preferences and perceptions of trustworthiness. *Evolution and Human Behavior*, *27*, 381–389.

Buss, D. M. (1989). Sex differences in human mate preferences: Evolutionary hypotheses testing in 37 cultures. *Behavioural and Brain Sciences*, *12*, 1–49.

Cashdan, E. (2003). Hormones and competitive aggression in women. *Aggressive Behavior*, *29*, 107–115.

Cordain, L., Miller, J., & Mann, M. (1999). Scant evidence of periodic starvation among hunter-gatherers. *Diabetologia*, *42*, 383–384.

Department of Health. (1999). *The health survey for England 1999*. Online publication   at: http://www.dh.gov.uk/PublicationsAndStatistics/Published Survey.

DeRidder, C. M., Bruning, P. F., Zonderland, M. L., Thijssen, J. H. H., Bonfrer, J. M. G., Blankenstein, M. A., et al. (1990). Body fat mass, body fat distribution and plasma hormones in early puberty in females. *Journal of Clinical and Endocrinological Metabolism, 70*, 888–893.

Eade, J. A., & Momen, R. (1996). *Bangladeshis in Britain: A national database*. London: Centre for Bangladeshi Studies.

Ellison, P. T., Lipson, S. F., Orourke, M. T., Bentley, G. R., Harrigan, A. M., Panterbrick, C., et al. (1993a). Population Variation in Ovarian-Function. *Lancet, 342*, 433–434.

Ellison, P. T., Panterbrick, C., Lipson, S. F., & Orourke, M. T. (1993b). The ecological context of human ovarian-function. *Human Reproduction, 8*, 2248–2258.

Furnham, A., & Alibhai, N. (1983). Cross-cultural differences in the perception of female body shapes. *Psychological Medicine, 13*, 829–837.

Furnham, A., McClelland, A., & Omer, L. (2003). A cross-cultural comparison of ratings of perceived fecundity and sexual attractiveness as a function of body weight and waist-to-hip ratio. *Psychology, Health & Medicine, 8*, 219–230.

Furnham, A., Tan, T., McManus, C. (1997). Waist-to-hip ratio and preferences for body shape: A replication and extension. *Personality and Individual Differences, 22*, 539–549.

Garfinkel, P. E., & Garner, D. M. (1982). *Anorexia nervosa: A multidimensional perspective*. New York: Bruner and Mazel.

Gitter, A., Lomranz, J., Saxe, L., & Bar-Tal, D. (1983). Perception of female physique characteristics by American and Israeli students. *Journal of Social Psychology, 121*, 7–13.

Gluckman, P., & Hanson, M. (2005). *The fetal matrix: Evolution, development and disease*. Cambridge: Cambridge University Press.

Hartz, A. J., Rupley, D. C., & Rimm, A. A. (1984). The association of girth measurement with disease in 32,856 women. *American Journal of Epidemiology, 119*, 71–80.

Henss, R. (1995). Waist-to-hip ratio and attractiveness: A replication and extension. *Personality and Individual Differences, 19*, 479–488.

Hosegood, V., & Campbell, O. M. (2003). Body mass index, height, weight, arm circumference, and mortality in rural Bangladeshi women: A 19-y longitudinal study. *American Journal of Clinical Nutrition, 77*, 341–347.

Islam, M. Z., Akhtaruzzaman, M., & Lamberg-Allardt, C. (2004). Nutritional status of women in Bangladesh: Comparison of energy intake and nutritional status of a low income rural group with a high income urban group. *Asia Pacific Journal of Clinical Nutrition, 13*, 61–68.

Jasienska, G., Ziomkiewicz, A., Ellison, P. T., Lipson, S. F., & Thune, I. (2004). Large breasts and narrow waists indicate high reproductive potential in women. *Proceedings of the Royal Society of London B, 271*, 1213–1217.

King, J. C. (2003). The risk of maternal nutritional depletion and poor outcomes increases in early or closely spaced pregnancies. *Journal of Nutrition, 135* (Suppl. 2), 1732–1736.

Kramer, M. S., Coates, A. L., Michoud, M. C., Dagenais, S., Hamilton, E. F., & Papageorgiou, A. (1995). Maternal Anthropometry and Idiopathic Preterm Labor. *Obstetrics and Gynecology, 86*, 744–748.

Kuh, D., & Schlomo, Y. B. (Eds.) (2004). *A life course approach to chronic disease epidemiology* (2nd ed.). London: Oxford University Press.

Lahti-Koski, M., Pietinen, P., Männistö, S., & Vartiainen, E. (2000). Trends in waist-to-hip ratio and its determinants in adults in Finland from 1987 to 1997. *American Journal of Clinical Nutrition, 72*, 1436–1444.

Lanska, D. J., Lanska, M. J., Hartz, A. J., & Rimm, A. A. (1985). Factors influencing anatomical location of fat tissue in 52,953 women. *International journal of Obesity, 9*, 29–38.

Ley, C. J., Lees, B., & Stevenson, J. C. (1992). Sex- and menopause-associated change in body fat distribution. *American Journal of Clinical Nutrition, 55*, 950–954.

Manson, J. E., Willet, W. C., Stampfer, M. J., Colditz, G. A., Hunter, D. J., Hankinson, S. E., et al. (1995). Body weight and mortality among women. *New England Journal of Medicine, 333*, 677–685.

Marlowe, F., & Wetsman, A. (2001). Preferred waist-to-hip ratio and ecology. *Personality and Individual Differences, 30*, 481–489.

Marlowe, F., Apicella, C., & Reed, D. (2005). Men's preferences for women's profile waist-to-hip ratio in two societies. *Evolution and Human Behavior, 26*, 458–468.

McGarvey, S. (1991). Obesity in Samoans and a perspective in its aetiology in Polynesians. *American Journal of Clinical Nutrition, 53*, 86–94.

Misra, A., & Vikram, N. K. (2004). Insulin resistance syndrome (metabolic syndrome) and obesity in Asian Indians: Evidence and implications. *Nutrition, 20*, 482–491.

Mohanty, C., Prasad, R., Reddy, A. S., Ghosh, J. K., Singh, T. B., & Das, B. K. (2006). Maternal anthropometry as predictors of low birth weight. *Journal of Tropical Pediatrics, 52*, 24–29.

Núñez-de la Mora, A., Chatterton, R. T., Choudhury, O., Napolitano, D., & Bentley, G. R. (in press – a). Childhood conditions determine adult progesterone levels. *PLOS Medicine.*

Núñez-de la Mora, A., Chatterton, R. T., Choudhury, O., Napolitano, D., & Bentley, G. R. (in press – b). The impact of developmental conditions on adult salivary estradiol levels: Why this differs from progesterone? *American Journal of Human Biology.*

Pawłowski, B., & Grabarczyk, M. (2003). Center of body mass and the evolution of female body shape. *American Journal of Biology, 15*, 144–150.

Pettijohn, T. F., & Jungeberg, B. J. (2004). Playboy Playmate curves: Changes in facial and body feature preferences across social and economic conditions. *Personality and Social Psychology Bulletin, 30*, 1186–1197.

Powers, P. S. (1980). *Obesity: The regulation of weight.* Williams & Wilkins: Baltimore.

Prentice, A. M. (2005). Early influences on human energy regulation: Thrifty genotypes and thrifty phenotypes. *Physiology and Behavior, 86*, 640–645.

Rhodes, G., Jeffery, L., Watson, T. L., Clifford, C. W. G., & Nakayama, K. (2003). Fitting the mind to the world: Face adaptation and attractiveness aftereffects. *Psychological Science, 14*, 558–566.

Shell-Duncan, B., & Yung, S. A. (2004). The maternal depletion transition in northern Kenya: The effects of settlement, development and disparity. *Social Science and Medicine, 58,* 2485–2498.

Simmons, R. (2005). Developmental origins of adult metabolic disease: Concepts and controversies. *Trends in Endocrinological Metabolism, 16,* 390–394.

Singh, D. (1993). Adaptive significance of female physical attractiveness: Role of waist-to-hip ratio. *Journal of Personality and Social Psychology, 65,* 293–307.

Singh, D. (1994). Body fat distribution and perception of desirable female body shape by young black men and women. *International Journal of Eating Disorders, 16,* 289–294.

Singh, D., & Luis, S. (1995). Ethnic and gender consensus for the role of waist-to-hip ratio on judgment of women's attractiveness. *Human Nature, 6,* 51–65.

Smith, K. L., Cornelissen, P. L., & Tovée, M. J. (2007). Color 3D bodies and judgements of human female attractiveness. *Evolution and Human Behavior, 28,* 48–54.

Sobal, J., & Stunkard, A. J. (1989). Socioeconomic status and obesity: A review of the literature. *Psychological Bulletin, 105,* 260–275.

Steer, P. (2005). The epidemiology of preterm labor – a global perspective. *Journal of Perinatal Medicine, 33,* 273–276.

Sugiyama, L. S. (2004). Is beauty in the context-sensitive adaptations of the beholder? Shiwiar use of waist-to-hip ratio in assessments of female mate value. *Evolution and Human Behavior, 25,* 51–62.

Swami, V., & Tovée, M. J. (2005). Female physical attractiveness in Britain and Malaysia: A cross-cultural study. *Body Image, 2,* 115–128.

Swami, V., & Tovée, M. J. (2006). Do judgements of food influence preferences for female body weight? *British Journal of Psychology, 97,* 353–363.

Symons, D. (1979). *The evolution of human sexuality.* Oxford: Oxford University Press.

Tovée, M. J., & Cornelissen, P. L. (2001). Female and male perceptions of female physical attractiveness in front-view and profile. *British Journal of Psychology, 92,* 391–402.

Tovée, M. J., Maisey, D. S., Emery, J. L., & Cornelissen, P. L. (1999). Visual cues to female physical attractiveness. *Proceedings of the Royal Society of London B, 266,* 211–218.

Tovée, M. J., Swami, V., Furnham, A., & Mangalparsad, R. (2006). Changing perceptions of attractiveness as observers are exposed to a different culture. *Evolution and Human Behavior, 27,* 443–456.

Tovée, M. J., Hancock, P., Mahmoodi, S., Singleton, B. R. R., & Cornelissen, P. L. (2002). Human female attractiveness: Waveform analysis of body shape. *Proceedings of the Royal Society of London B, 269,* 2205–2213.

Tracer, D. P. (2002). Somatic versus reproductive energy allocation in Papua New Guinea: Life history theory and public health policy. *American Journal of Human Biology, 14,* 621–626.

Vikram, N. K., Misra, A., Pandey, R. M., Dudeja, V., Sinha, S., Ramadevi, J., et al. (2003). Anthropometry and body composition in northern Asian Indian patients with type 2 diabetes: Receiver operating characteristics (ROC) curve analysis of body mass index with percentage body fat as standard. *Diabetes, Nutrition and Metabolism, 16,* 32–40.

Vitzthum, V. J., Spielvogel, H., & Thornburg, J. (2004). Interpopulational differences in progesterone levels during conception and implantation in humans. *Proceedings of the National Academy of Sciences USA, 101,* 1443–1448.

Vitzthum, V. J., Bentley, G. R., Spielvogel, H., Caceres, E., Thornburg, J., Jones, L., et al. (2002). Salivary progesterone levels and rate of ovulation are significantly lower in poorer than in better-off urban-dwelling Bolivian women. *Human Reproduction, 17,* 1906–1913.

Wass, P., Waldenstrom, U., Rossner, S., & Hellberg, D. (1997). An android body fat distribution in females impairs the pregnancy rate of in-vitro fertilisation-embryo transfer. *Human Reproduction, 12,* 2057–2060.

Wetsman, A., & Marlowe, F. (1999). How universal are preferences for female waist-to-hip ratios? Evidence from the Hadza of Tanzania. *Evolution and Human Behaviour, 20,* 219–228.

World Bank Key Development Data and Statistics. (2005). Online publication at: http://siteresources.worldbank.org/DATASTATISTICS/Resources/GNIPC.pdf.

Yu, D. W., & Shepard, G. H. (1998). Is beauty in the eye of the beholder? *Nature, 396,* 321–322.

Zaadstra, B. M., Seidell, J. C., van Noord, P. A. H., te Velde, E. R., Habbema, J. D. F., Vrieswijk, B., et al. (1993). Fat and female fecundity: Prospective study of effect of body fat distribution on conception rates. *British Medical Journal, 306,* 484–487.

6
Masculinity, Culture, and the Paradox of the Lek

Douglas W. Yu, Stephen R. Proulx, and Glenn H. Shepard

Explaining why males vary in their attractiveness and ability to garner mates is a long-standing problem in evolution (Darwin, 1871, Fisher, 1930). A well-accepted solution posits that 'attractive' traits, such as bright feathers, are costly to produce and, thus, truthfully signal high mate quality (Andersson, 1994). High quality males may confer direct or indirect benefits to their offspring. Direct benefits are essentially phenotypic in nature, such as nuptial gifts, parental care, or territory, and if such benefits vary across males, then female choice is easy to explain (Kokko, Jennions, & Brooks, 2006; Thornhill, 1976). Indirect benefits are genetic; a mate is chosen because it can pass on 'good' (versions of) genes, such as those involved in disease resistance (Evans & Magurran, 2000; Jennions & Petrie, 2000; Milinski, 2006; Møller & Alatalo, 1999).

Evolutionary psychological explanations for male attractiveness in humans have tended to emphasise indirect benefits, as revealed by symmetry and markers of immunocompetence. In a well known study, Penton-Voak et al. (1999, 2000), using computer-generated composite photographs, found that some women consider masculine male faces to be more attractive in the week of highest fertility, but judge feminine male faces to be more attractive (and indicative of a caring partner) during the rest of the menstrual cycle. This was interpreted as evidence for a mixed-mating strategy (also known as the ovulatory-shift hypothesis) in which females pair long-term with caring, more effeminate males, but engage in extra-pair matings (EPM) with masculine males for the latter's 'good genes.'

Much like what initially happened with Singh's (1993) waist-to-hip ratio hypothesis of bodily attractiveness, Penton-Voak et al.'s (1999, 2000) results have spawned a small industry replicating and extending the original results (Danel & Pawłowski, 2006; Gangestad

& Simpson, 2000, Gangestad, Simpson, Cousins, Garver-Apgar, & Christensen, 2004; Gangestad, Thornhill, & Garver-Apgar, 2005a, 2005b; Haselton & Gangestad, 2006; Haselton & Miller, 2006; Havlicek, Roberts, & Flegr, 2005; Provost, Kormos, Kosakoski, & Quinsey, 2006; Roney, Hanson, Durante, & Maestripieri, 2006; Scheib, Gangestad, & Thornhill, 1999; Waynforth, Delwadia, & Camm, 2005). Nonetheless, many studies with *non*-humans, mostly birds and insects, have shown that the 'good-genes' explanation for male attractiveness should be applied with a bit of caution. There exist alternative explanations, and corresponding empirical support, for why females should be selected to mate outside the pair (Jennions & Petrie, 2000; Newcomer, Zeh, & Zeh, 1999). For instance, by accepting sperm from multiple males, females increase the probability that the genotypes in their eggs will be matched with particular paternal genotypes that are more compatible (Kempenaers, Congdon, Boag, & Robertson, 1999; Newcomer et al., 1999; Tregenza & Wedell, 2002), or females might be trying to reduce the risk of male infertility (Krokene, Rigstad, Dale, & Lifjeld, 1998; Sheldon, 1994). Another possibility starts with the acknowledgment that some males are more attractive but only arbitrarily so. Nonetheless, a female who mates with such males will have sons who look like their fathers, thus producing what are known as 'Fisherian sexy sons,' after the population geneticist Ronald Fisher, and such sons will also enjoy heightened attractiveness in a self-fulfilling and self-perpetuating way (Jones, Quinnell, & Balmford, 1998).

A different class of criticism suggests that apparent good-genes effects might result instead from biased female investment. For example, female zebra finches and mallards have been found to provision eggs fathered by attractive males with, respectively, more testosterone (Gil, Graves, Hazon, & Wells, 1999) and more food (Cunningham & Russell, 2000; but see Petrie, Schwable, Brande-Lavridsen, & Burke, 2001; Cunningham & Russell, 2001). The offspring of such extra-pair males should enjoy heightened fitness, but because of the confounding effect of female investment, it is not possible to conclude that the genotype of the male has contributed to that increase.

Experiments with birds have also shown that even basic assumptions of the masculinity/immunocompetence theory do not always hold. Experimentally increasing testosterone does not reduce immunocompetence in red-winged blackbirds or greenfinches (Hasselquist, Marsh, Sherman, & Wingfield, 1999; Lindstrom, Krakower, Lundstrom, & Silverin, 2001; but see Duffy, Bentley, Drazen, & Ball, 2000, for a positive result in starlings), and in one population of house sparrows, Cordero,

Wetton, and Parkin (1999) have found that males with smaller badges are not cuckolded more frequently (but see Møller & Ninni, 1998).

More generally, female preference for more masculine males might simply reflect selection pressure on the female to reduce total matings, since mating is a costly activity. Under this interpretation, the evolution of masculinity is the result of male–male competition for those matings (reviewed in Kokko et al., 2006). Also, mathematical models have found that selection for female choice to select males offering indirect benefits is in fact weak. There can even be selection against the evolution of female choice if the costs of expressing choice are high (see Kokko et al., 2006; Milinski, 2006).

Most fundamentally, because it is usually assumed that females prefer the costliest and showiest marker phenotypes (e.g., the largest horns), females impose what is known as 'directional selection' on a trait to increase (or decrease) in some value. Evolutionary biology tells us that directional selection acts by removing gene variants ('alleles') from the population, so the genes coding for sexually selected traits should become less and less variable over time. As a result, all males will become similarly showy, and selection on females to express choosiness over genetic differences in males will itself be relaxed, leading ultimately to the trait of female choice selecting *itself* out of existence.

This dynamic is called the Paradox of the Lek (Borgia, 1979; Kirkpatrick & Ryan, 1991; Taylor & Williams, 1982), where a lek is a term from ornithology describing an aggregation of males competing for female attention. Resolving the Paradox of the Lek is a not-so-minor industry in evolutionary biology, and whole careers have been spent on the challenge. Currently, the leading explanation for how variation in sexually selected traits is preserved (and consequently, how female choice is preserved) suggests that sexually selected traits, such as the brightness of feathers, are especially sensitive to *overall* physiological condition. If physiological condition happens to depend in part on underlying genetic variation, which is reasonable, then sexually selected traits can be said to reflect or 'capture' part of the overall genetic variation in an organism, and as there are a lot of genes in an organism, genetic variation in sexually selected traits can be maintained by the low, background mutation rate that exists over the whole genome (Rowe & Houle, 1996). Empirical tests have provided support for the 'genic capture' model (David, Bjorksten, Fowler, & Pomiankowski, 2000; Kotiaho, Simmons, & Tomkins, 2001; Wilkinson & Taper, 1999).

Any theory of human mate choice that invokes indirect benefits must confront the many theoretical challenges that attend this model and must especially deal with the Paradox of the Lek. Even though there is much to like about the 'genic capture' model, it must be remembered that masculinity in humans has not yet been shown to be condition-dependent. Thus, the first research priority for evolutionary psychology should be to test the genic capture model. Is variation in phenotypic condition expressed as variation in masculinity, and *more so* than in non-sexually selected traits? And if so, is variance in condition itself dependent on genetic variation?.

So far, there is some evidence for the first requirement. Penton-Voak, Jackson and Trivers (2004) found that Jamaican women preferred more masculine faces than did Japanese or British women, as predicted by the higher parasite load in Jamaica. Also, Thornhill and Gangestad (2006) found that increased facial masculinity in males correlates with a lower incidence of respiratory (but not stomach) illness and a lower usage of antibiotics, even after controlling for body size (see Cotton, Fowler, & Pomiankowski, 2004, for a review of the empirical challenges of determining condition dependence).

A second way to approach the lek paradox is to define a complete set of conditions under which female preferences might maintain genetic variation in masculinity. For this purpose, let us take at face value the findings from Penton-Voak et al. (2000) and others that suggest that female preference is (at least) bi-directional in that the desired degree of masculinity in a mate appears to vary depending on whether the male is chosen for marriage or for extra-pair matings. Because they act in opposition, we will show here that preferences for different kinds of partners by the same female could maintain genetic variance in masculinity.

However, to do this, we must formalise Penton-Voak et al.'s (2000) mixed-mating strategy hypothesis in order to lay out all the assumptions and conditions and to devise tests. When we do this with a simple mathematical model, we will see that the mixed-mating strategy, as described, is implausibly applied to Western societies, even though the choice tests have been conducted with Westernised females. That is, the mixed mating hypothesis appears incomplete, which leads us to the other part of our chapter.

A theory of mate choice in humans must also delimit the choices that a female has available to her. For example, by interpreting within-individual variation in preferences as indicators of long-term versus short-term mate choice, Penton-Voak et al. (2000) and others have implicitly assumed women are free to choose their long-term partners, which largely reflects a recent and Western conception of marriage. In contrast, in almost all traditional societies (and in many industrialised countries), parents have varying degrees of influence over the daughter's choice of spouse (Beckerman, 2000). Thus, any study of variation in female preferences for long-term versus short-term partners must take into account kinship and marriage systems, inheritance rules, social class, gender relations, and other sociocultural factors influencing mate choice (McGraw, 2002).

Following a previous study (Yu & Shepard, 1998, 1999) of how cultural change can affect men's perceptions of female bodily attractiveness among the Matsigenka, an Amerindian population of southeastern, Amazonian Peru, we tested the hypothesis that marriage systems and socioeconomic systems (i.e., 'culture') might affect how women choose mates, for themselves, and, for their daughters. If we find such an effect, then we can conclude that not just biological but cultural rules can plausibly produce trade-offs that preserve genetic variation, and more generally, that cultural variation can guide human evolution, as has been shown convincingly for the evolution of tolerance to cow's milk sugar, lactose (Tishkoff et al., 2007).

For the Matsigenka, the preferred marriage partner is the cross-cousin (or failing that, an individual from outside the village, exogamy), and residence is matrilocal (or uxorilocal), meaning that a man moves to the village or hamlet of his wife's family (Shapiro, 1984). Furthermore, parents, guided by kinship rules (see below), have a strong influence over the daughter's choice of marriage partner. Parents wish to ensure that a son-in-law will become a reliable food provider, through hunting and swidden agriculture, for the extended family as the parents age. Glenn Shepard has observed instances of 'lazy' sons-in-law being kicked out by parents, and many instances of threats to do so. On the other hand, we have also observed that, though hardly encouraged, extramarital liaisons are not uncommon, are not typically met with harsh punishment or ostracism for either men or women, and we have no reason to believe that parents influence the choice of these extra-marital partners.

Thus, we test the *a priori* hypothesis that in traditional Matsigenka culture, parents will prefer masculine men for sons-in-law, in contrast to the results of Penton-Voak et al. (2000), where feminine males are given the marriage advantage. We are suggesting that more masculine men, on average, are better hunters and garden-makers and, therefore, that masculine males confer greater *direct* benefits in the form of increased food provision, which implies that wives are more likely than girlfriends to capture those benefits. Therefore, we are not assuming any 'good genes' effects of masculinity. Finally, we judge the plausibility of our empirical results by formally examining the conditions under which observed Matsigenka female preferences could maintain genetic variance in masculinity.

Study population

The study was carried out in 1999 with 45 Matsigenka women living in the department of Madre de Dios, Peru. Three of the women are long-term residents of native communities along the Madre de Dios River bordering Manu National Park, and the rest of the subjects are residents of the villages of Tayakome ($n = 13$), Yomybato ($n = 28$), and Sotileja ($n = 1$), within Manu Park itself, a 1.8 million hectare tropical rainforest biosphere reserve. The age range was 13 to 50 years (mean $\pm$ SE, 26 $\pm$ 1.3).

Tayakome is located on the Manu River, a day and a half journey by boat from the park entrance, whereas Yomybato is reached only after a further 2–6 days' journey up a small stream, and Sotileja is several days walk from Yomybato. Sotileja was first visited by a non-Matsigenka in 1995, and the Sotileja women in our sample were visiting Yomybato at the time of our census. All the communities practice swidden agriculture, supplemented with fruit, fish, and game (Shepard, 2002).

The Madre de Dios and Tayakome communities are more Westernised than the Yomybato and Sotileja communities in that the former are more fluent in Spanish, less dependent upon bow-and-arrow hunting, more dependent upon hook-and-line fishing, have easier access to manufactured goods via the cash economy, and, because of their proximity to a major river course, have more frequent contact with outsiders. Perhaps the simplest index of isolation is that when given a choice, cultural anthropologists, to a person, have chosen to work in Yomybato rather than in Tayakome. It is possible that such cultural and economic differences among villages could influence judgements of the attractiveness of prospective sons-in-law. Thus, we analysed the responses first by pooling across all communities and then by separating the more Westernised from the more isolated communities.

Interviews

The images used in the study are computer-generated composite photographs of Japanese faces from Perrett et al. (1998), where examples can also be seen. We used three of their Japanese images based on the subjects' volunteered observations about the similarity between East Asian and Matsigenka physical features. The face stimuli created by

Perrett et al. (1998) included one un-manipulated composite male face (M), one masculinised by 50 per cent (MM), and one feminised by 50 per cent (MF), using the morphometric difference between composite male and female photos (M and F) as a gauge of the direction and extent of masculinity.

All interviews were conducted in the Matsigenka language. We presented each subject individually with two pairings of faces (MF versus M, and M versus MM), and for each pair, the subject was asked to choose the most attractive (*tyapaita*) of the two. Following the same procedure, we also asked each subject to choose the preferred son-in-law (*tiñeri*). The order of the questions (attractiveness and son-in-law) and the order of the picture pairings within questions were randomised across subjects. That is, half the respondents were asked about sons-in-law first, and the other half were asked about attractiveness first. In total, therefore, each subject chose from four pairs of faces, two for each question. For each pair, we scored whether the subject chose the more masculine or the more feminine face. This means that M was more masculine when paired against MF but more feminine when paired against MM. We did not attempt to control for the subject's menstrual cycle, except in the sense that both questions were asked at the same time.

Correcting for pseudo-replication

Using all the responses is a form of pseudo-replication, since each individual would be counted twice. We, therefore, corrected for pseudo-replication by counting only those individuals whose responses reveal an internally consistent masculine or feminine preference within a given question. That is, for a given question (attractiveness or son-in-law), we score an individual as having a 'he-man' preference only if she responded *both* MM > M and M > MF, and as having a 'she-man' preference if she responded both MF > M and M > MM, thereby counting each individual respondent, at most, once per question. Individuals with mixed responses *within question* are thus dropped. To confirm that our procedure does not introduce artefacts, we also analysed the data without correction for pseudoreplication (i.e., we used the entire dataset).

Results

Despite the rather severe reduction in sample size caused by omitting all non-internally consistent responses, we find that women's perceptions and judgements change significantly with the cultural context of the

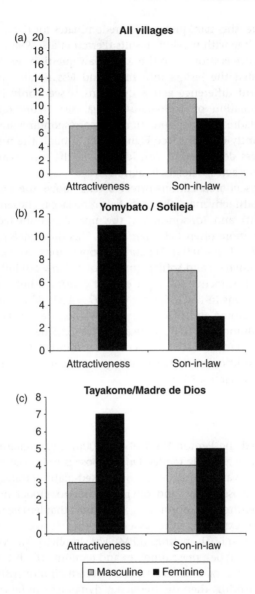

Figure 6.1 Preference for masculinised or feminised male faces as a function of question asked. Only internally consistent answers were included in this analysis (see Results). Thus, the number of responses is not equal across categories. (a) Pooled over both villages (Fisher's Exact Test, 1-tailed, $p < 0.05$); (b) Yomybato/Sotileja villages only ($p < 0.05$); (c) Tayakome/Alto Madre villages only ($p > 1.0$). Figure 6.1b is significantly different from 1c (Mantel-Haenszel chi-square = 3.990, $p < 0.05$).

question. The 'she-man' preference predominates for the attractiveness question, in line with previous results (Perrett et al., 1998), but the 'he-man' preference is stronger in the son-in-law question (see Figure 6.1a).

We separated the results into more and less isolated populations. The significant difference across questions is seen only in the more isolated population of Yomybato/Sotileja (see Figure 6.1b). In the Tayakome/Madre de Dios population, the corresponding preferences are not significantly different (see Figure 6.1c), though the preference for feminine faces does weaken considerably in the son-in-law question. This difference across villages is significant.

The non-pseudoreplication-corrected data shows the same patterns ($n = 90$). For attractiveness, the more feminine face is chosen more often (62.2 per cent), and, for son-in-law, the more masculine face is chosen only slightly more often (53.3 per cent). This difference is significant ($G = 4.41$, $df = 1$, $p < 0.05$). Separating populations, we also find that women of Yomybato and Sotileja (more isolated, $n = 58$) judge feminine males as more attractive (62.1 per cent of contrasts) but prefer masculine males as sons-in-law (56.9 per cent, $G = 4.21$, $df = 1$, $p < 0.05$). In contrast, Tayakome and Madre de Dios women (less isolated, $n = 32$) also find feminine faces to be more attractive (62.5 per cent), but do not prefer masculine faces (46.9 per cent) for son-in-law ($G = 0.58$, $df = 1$, $p > 1.0$). This difference between villages is again significant (Mantel-Haenszel chi-square=4.35, $p < 0.05$).

Model

We formalised the Penton-Voak et al. (2000) 'mixed-mating strategy' hypothesis with a simple model. Our purpose is to lay out more clearly the assumptions and consequences of a mixed-mating strategy involving variation in masculinity, and obviously not to model human mate choice in its entirety. To begin with, we assume that female mating preferences can be expressed either as a long-term association (marriage) or as short-term extra-pair matings (EPM). For simplicity, we consider only two male phenotypes: masculine (m) and feminine (f). If the two types only differ in their mating success, and not in their propensity or ability to care for offspring, then the frequency dynamics can be written as:

$$p_{t+1} = M(p_t)(1 - C_m(p_t)v) + (1 - M(p_t))C_f(p_t)v \qquad (1)$$

where p is the fraction of m males (and $1 - p$ the fraction of f males) in the population. $M(p)$ is the proportion of marriages to m males, C_i is the probability a type i male is cuckolded, and v is the average proportion of offspring fathered through EPMs. Thus, the first term represents the marriage success of m males, multiplied by the expected proportion of offspring fathered by the m male (i.e., the probability of not being successfully cuckolded). The second term is the proportion of marriages to f males multiplied by the expected proportion of offspring fathered by cuckolding m males (i.e., the probability of successfully mating with females married to f males).

In order for the two types of males to co-exist, each must increase in frequency when rare. Mathematically, this requires that:

$$\left. \frac{d_{p_{t+1}}}{d_{p_t}} \right|_{p_t=0} > 1$$
$$\left. \frac{d_{p_{t+1}}}{d_{p_t}} \right|_{p_t=1} < 1$$

In order to evaluate these two conditions, some information about the marriage preference function $[M(p)]$ and the cuckoldry functions $[C_i(p)]$ is required. While the exact forms would be difficult to measure and are unknown, the data from Penton-Voak et al. (2000) and from the current study can be used to make assumptions about the general properties of these functions.

In the Penton-Voak et al. (2000) study, the masculine male was considered to be more attractive for EPMs while the feminine male was more attractive for marriage. Under this scenario, the mating preference function and the cuckoldry function will act in opposition, creating a stable polymorphism where both types of male are maintained. So, when m males suffer a marriage disadvantage, they marry at less than their own frequency, making $M(p) < p$, for all p. Further, for mating systems in which females examine a fixed number of males before mating (i.e., the best of n mating system; Janetos, 1980), the mating success of disfavored rare males will be approximately 0, so that $M'(0) = 0$. If m males also have a cuckoldry benefit then the probability of cuckolding an f male will be greater than the probability of being cuckolded by an f male; hence $C_f(p) > C_m(1-p)$. We expect that $C_f'(0) > 0$ and $C_m'(1) = 0$. Using these assumptions, the conditions for polymorphism become:

$$C_f'(p)v > 1$$
$$(1 - C_f(1)v)M'(1) > 1$$

In other words, in the Penton-Voak et al. (2000) system, rare m males must receive more than one female equivalent of offspring through cuckolding in order to spread, and rare f males must on average marry more than one female and escape being cuckolded. A marriage advantage could be achieved if feminine males have more wives or, in a socially monogamous society, if feminine males had higher 'quality' wives.

In the Matsigenka study, we found that the more masculine male was preferred as the son-in-law, which could translate into higher marriage success, depending on the degree of parental influence over the daughter's choice of a long-term mate. As a result, in the Matsigenka system, feminine males, who are considered more attractive, would have to have an EPM advantage to counteract any masculine marriage advantage.

Even if the assumptions are relaxed to include cuckoldry functions that do not have zero derivatives, a marriage advantage is required for polymorphism if one male type has an EPM advantage. For instance, we can break down the female decision to engage in EPMs into two components: a decision to engage in cuckoldry, followed by the choice of a partner. Both of these components may depend on the frequency of the two types of male in the population. We define $C_i(p) = \mu_i \rho(p)$, where μ_i is the probability that a female married to a type i male chooses to engage in EPMs, and $\rho(p)$ is the probability that she does so with an m male. This necessarily leads to $\rho(0) = 0$ and $\rho(1) = 1$. When there is no marriage advantage $[M(p) = p]$, the condition for polymorphism becomes:

$$\rho'(0)\mu_f v + (1 - \mu_m v) > 1 \tag{2}$$

$$\rho'(1)\mu_m v + (1 - \mu_f v) > 1 \tag{3}$$

If m males have an EPM advantage, then $\rho'(0) > 1$ while $\rho'(1) < 1$ and $\mu_f > \mu_m$. Thus, inequality (2) is met, but inequality (3) is not. So, even under these more general conditions, a marriage advantage for the male type less likely to achieve EPMs is necessary for both types to be present at equilibrium.

The model can be further generalised to allow for differences across the male types in the degree of offspring care proffered and/or the quality of the offspring. For example, in the Penton-Voak et al. (2000) system, f males might care more for offspring, but m males might produce offspring with higher survivorship. If the benefit of offspring survivorship outweighs the benefit of better offspring care ($v_m > v_f$), then for a polymorphism to be maintained, f males must compensate by having a larger marriage advantage.

The maintenance of the two male phenotypes can be understood intuitively by recognising that the male type that has an advantage in gaining marriage partners also provides a sort of resource for the other type. For instance, in the Penton-Voak et al. (2000) model, f males produce marriages that are vulnerable to cuckoldry by m males. This means that marriages with f males as partners are a resource for m males. On the other hand, if there are mostly m males and a few f males, the f males will outcompete the m males for marriages so much that the f males' higher rate of being cuckolded will not reduce their fitness below the m males. By switching the subscripts, the same logic holds for the Matsigenka scenario: m males must have a marriage advantage in order to persist in the face of cuckoldry by f males.

Discussion

To our knowledge, this is the first experimental study of human mate choice to include parental preferences, even though parents in many cultures have had historically, and continue to have, influence over the long-term mate choices of their daughters and sons (Beckerman, 2000). We found statistical evidence consistent with the interpretation that Matsigenka women preferred masculine faces for sons-in-law or did not show a preference for feminised faces in that role. This result contrasts with the standard result, in which the preferred long-term mate is a feminised male. We tentatively attribute this difference to the different sociocultural roles on offer: husband or son-in-law. The most straightforward interpretation for these results is that masculine men are, on average, perceived as better resource providers, as we suggested earlier. In fact, one woman from Yomybato pointed at the MF image and stated that she already had a daughter (i.e., she assumed the feminised face was a female) and needed a son-in-law to marry her.

We should, however, emphasise several limitations of our protocol. Sample sizes were unavoidably small, given the small population size. Also, cultural sensibilities meant that we could not ask women to choose potential partners for themselves but were limited to asking them to indicate the most attractive male. Moreover, we could not take the respondents' menstrual cycles into account. Following Penton-Voak et al. (2000), it is possible that when fertile, Matsigenka women find masculine men more attractive. If so, then feminine males would not have an EPM advantage, which our model predicts would lead to fixation of masculinity in the absence of any other countervailing processes. Finally, we purposely made our interviews as simple as possible by using only one face for each degree of masculinity, by asking only two kinds of questions per respondent.

Thus, we certainly cannot conclude that cultural rules are in fact trading off a marriage advantage in masculine males against an EPM advantage in feminine males, thus maintaining genetic variation in masculinity amongst the Matsigenka. However, the combination of our data and our model does allow us to state that this is a plausible and internally consistent hypothesis that should be considered when trying to explain the striking within-village variation in male masculinity that we have observed among the Matsigenka (Yu & Shepard, personal observation). Our take-home message is that such studies should be conducted in as many independent cultures as possible. Efforts are in fact underway to collect relevant data now, and our group has been collecting hunter success data among the Matsigenka as a partial test of the *masculine equals better resource provider* hypothesis (Ohl et al., 2007).

McGraw (2002) used lonely hearts advertisements to show that heterosexual American women living in cities with high costs of living are more likely to advertise explicitly for wealthier mates. In other words, cultural variability in female mate preference can be found to exist even within Western society, and this variability correlates with an environmental predictor. Additionally, we found that the preference for masculinised faces in the son-in-law role varied with the village's degree of Westernisation, which is perhaps a reflection of cultural change such as that documented in Yu and Shepard (1998).

More generally, by laying out the conditions under which variation in masculinity can be maintained, our model gauges the overall plausibility of the Penton-Voak et al. (2000) hypothesis that human females engage in a mixed-mating strategy. However, in the Westernised societies where Penton-Voak et al. (2000) conducted their interviews and where they suggest that women are choosing masculine men as short-term mates, feminine males would have to enjoy a marriage advantage in order to preserve variance in masculinity and, ultimately, female choice itself. Because the West is socially monogamous, such a marriage advantage would have to take the form of feminine males marrying higher quality females, or of divorcing and remarrying as each wife's fertility drops, thereby achieving higher lifetime fecundity.

The problem is that for such a mechanism to work in, for example, the United States, the football quarterback would not marry the head cheerleader, the movie action hero would not wed the fashion model, and neither would have more lifetime wives than a feminine male. As this does not accord with our impression of how Western societies function, one way that Penton-Voak et al.'s (2000) findings can be reconciled with the maintenance of female choice in a socially mono-gamous society is for feminine males to produce more viable children on average, in a married setting. This prediction can be used as a test, albeit a limited one, of our model. In fact, Roney et al. (2006) have found that women are able to use facial portraits alone to detect male interest in infants (and prefer those men for long-term relationships), and the same women prefer males with higher testosterone levels for short-term relationships. However, testosterone levels were not negatively correl-ated with infant interest in Roney et al.'s (2006) study, suggesting the existence of a second axis of male variation that might replace our femininity/masculinity axis.

In traditional Matsigenka societies, a marriage advantage for mascu-line males was easily achievable until recently because polygamy – typic-ally a man marrying two sisters – was practiced widely. However, in order for a mixed-mating strategy to preserve variance in masculinity in the Matsigenka, masculine males must have a marriage advantage, and feminine males must be more likely to be chosen as extra-pair mates (or produce offspring of higher quality). Again, these predictions can be used as a test of our hypothesis. The latter prediction is consistent with the finding that feminine males are judged to be more attractive, but we have only sparse additional support for this assumption. We know one male in the Yomybato community who has a feminine face (to our eye). He has fathered at least one out-of-wedlock child, and when we asked two women about the secret of his romantic success, they responded that, unlike other men, he smiles at them, listens, and makes nice small talk. This male, instead of hunting for a living, later chose to study to be a community health worker.

If a caring or gentle manner is correlated with femininity (as also suggested by Penton-Voak et al.'s 2000 results), it perhaps is no surprise that feminine males might have an EPM advantage in Matsigenka society. Of course, the mother of his child might have been attracted by his potential to earn cash income, although he had not earned any cash income at the time, nor had he yet made his career decision. Addi-tionally, Vickers (1975) noted that in the one case of adultery among the Amazonian Siona-Secoya for which he had comprehensive hunting data for both males involved, the cuckolded husband brought home 30 per cent more meat than did the cuckolder. On the other hand, Siskind

(1973) has suggested that meat has been used to trade for sex in the Sharanahua, which would reward better hunters with higher fitness. Clearly, the idea that feminine men might have an EPM advantage needs further investigation, but the possibility appears to be more feasible than a marriage advantage for feminine males in a monogamous Western society.

Our results also suggest that Matsigenka mothers and daughters might disagree over the desirability of a particular suitor, a conflict not unheard of. In practice, however, we note that kinship rules and small village size limit the range of potential long-term mates, perhaps mitigating such conflicts. The Matsigenka kinship system is of the Dravidian type, and the preferred marriage partner is the cross-cousin (Johnson & Johnson, 1975). Cross-cousins are the offspring of the mother's brother or the father's sister and are potential marriage partners throughout life. When asked to identify individuals on the basis of kinship terminology, cross-cousins will without hesitation refer to each other as *nohina/nohime* ('spouse') or *nohinatsori/nohimetsori* ('step spouse') (Shepard, personal observation). In contrast, parallel cousins (e.g., father's brother's offspring) are considered to be siblings, with whom marriage would be equivalent to incest. On the other hand, village exogamy is also practiced, and here, there is more scope for parents and daughter to express masculinity (or other) preferences.

We stress that our mixed-mating strategy model should be understood as only one of many potential resolutions for the Paradox of the Lek, albeit one that applies most directly to humans. Other mechanisms, such as 'genic capture' model described above, temporally shifting female preferences, migration between groups with different preferences, balancing selection for masculinity (Swaddle & Reierson, 2002), and insufficient time for fixation should be seen as complementary rather than as mutually exclusive. Formal modelling of these processes in human societies can provide a framework for testing and measuring the relative importances of these alternative mechanisms, for generating new ideas, and for finding ways to use human genetic data. Hence, by no means should we be concluding that the problem of variation in male attractiveness has been explained in humans (*pace* Gangestad & Simpson, 2000).

If it is the case that human female mate choice can vary in response not only to biological factors but also to cultural rules governing marriage, then we have found a plausible mechanism by which cultural change can guide evolutionary dynamics. The lesson for evolutionary psychology is that studies of human mate choice should include the possible effects of parental preferences. Moreover, cultural variation in the degree of parental influence can potentially provide the raw material with which to compete alternative theories of human mate choice, biologically based or not (Beckerman, 2000).

Cultural variation has already been documented in several other aspects of human psychology, such as body-shape preference (Yu & Shepard, 1998, 1999), colour classification (Davidoff, Davies, & Roberson, 1999), mathematical ability (Gordon, 2004), and propensity to engage in cooperation (Henrich et al., 2005, 2006). As we have seen here, cultural rules could potentially contribute to the maintenance of human genetic diversity. Studies carried out among the world's remaining indigenous and tribal peoples, stewards of at least half of humanity's cultural-linguistic diversity (Harmon, 1995), are especially important (and given the fast pace of globalisation, urgent) for assessing the full range of human cultural variability.

To conclude, as outsiders to the field of evolutionary psychology, we are struck by what appears to be the total absence of formal modelling. Evolutionary psychology is psychology, to be sure, but it is also evolution, and evolutionary theories sometimes require mathematical expression to reveal hidden assumptions and non-intuitive results. Verbal models are particularly poor at capturing the complexity of evolution in mate choice, due to the many simultaneously interacting players.

We are also surprised at the low frequency of studies that take advantage of the wealth of genetic data available for humans (with the clear exception, of course, of immune system genes, e.g., Wedekind, Seebeck, Bettens, & Paepke, 1995), and it is our impression that failure to embrace the new techniques that are being adopted in other areas of behavioural ecology (Owens, 2006) has hindered progress in evolutionary psychology. To judge by the literature we have surveyed for this chapter and by the other chapters in this book, technological innovation in evolutionary psychology appears to involve primarily the design of new stimuli and the use of more sophisticated statistics. More can be done.

On the other side of the disciplinary spectrum, the concentration of studies amongst Westernised populations (and mostly university students at that) continues to plague the field. In our case, this work represents the collaboration of a field biologist, a theoretical biologist, and a cultural anthropologist. Evolutionary psychologists working on the subject of human beauty would do well to collaborate across disciplines with biologists, behavioural economists, and anthropologists.

Acknowledgements

The authors thank L. V. White for statistical advice, D. Perrett and I. Penton-Voak for supplying the images, several anonymous reviewers and Sophie Miller for insightful comments, Peru's Instituto Nacional de Recursos Naturales (INRENA) for granting permission to work in Manu Park, the Asociación Peruana para la Conservación de la Naturaleza (APECO) for logistical support, the communities of Tayakome and Yomybato for their hospitality, and E. O. Wilson and the A. L. Green Fund for financial support.

References

Andersson, M. (1994). *Sexual selection*. Princeton: Princeton University Press.

Beckerman, S. (2000). Mating and marriage, husbands and lovers: Commentary on Gangestad & Simpson. *Behavioral and Brain Sciences, 23*, 590–591.

Borgia, G. (1979). Sexual selection and the evolution of mating systems. In M. S. Blum, & N. A. Blum (Eds.), *Sexual selection and reproductive competition in insects* (pp. 19–80). New York: Academic Press.

Cordero, P. J., Wetton, J. H., & Parkin, D. T. (1999). Extra-pair paternity and male badge size in the House Sparrow. *Journal of Avian Biology, 30*, 97–102.

Cotton, S., Fowler, K., & Pomiankowski, A. (2004). Do sexual ornaments demonstrate heightened condition-dependent expression as predicted by the handicap hypothesis? *Proceedings of the Royal Society B, 271*, 771–783.

Cunningham, E. J. A., & Russell, A. F. (2000). Egg investment is influenced by male attractiveness in the mallard. *Nature, 404*, 74–77.

Cunningham, E. J. A., & Russell, A. F. (2001). Sex differences in avian yolk hormone levels: Reply. *Nature, 412*, 498–499.

Danel, D., & Pawłowski, B. (2006). Attractiveness of men's faces in relation to women's phase of menstrual cycle. *Collegium Antropologicum, 30*, 285–289.

Darwin, C. (1871). *The descent of man, and selection in relation to sex*. Princeton: Princeton University Press.

David, P., Bjorksten, T., Fowler, K., & Pomiankowski, A. (2000). Condition-dependent signaling of genetic variation in stalk-eyed flies. *Nature, 406*, 186–188.

Davidoff, J., Davies, I., & Roberson, D. (1999). Colour categories in a stone-age tribe. *Nature, 398*, 203–204.

Duffy, D. L., Bentley, G. E., Drazen, D. L., & Ball, G. F. (2000). Effects of testosterone on cell-mediated and humoral immunity in non-breeding adult European starlings. *Behavioral Ecology, 11*, 654–662.

Evans, J. P., & Magurran, A. E. (2000). Multiple benefits of multiple mating in guppies. *PNAS USA, 97*, 10074–10076.

Fisher, R. A. (1930). *The genetical theory of natural selection*. Oxford: Clarendon Press.

Gangestad, S. W., & Simpson, J. A. (2000). Trade-offs, the allocation of reproductive effort, and the evolutionary psychology of human mating. *Behavioral and Brain Sciences, 23*, 624–644.

Gangestad, S. W., Thornhill, R., & Garver-Apgar, C. E. (2005a). Adaptations to ovulation: Implications for sexual and social behavior. *Current Directions in Psychological Science, 14,* 312–316.

Gangestad, S. W., Thornhill, R., & Garver-Apgar, C. E. (2005b). Women's sexual interests across the ovulatory cycle depend on primary partner developmental instability. *Proceedings of the Royal Society B, 272,* 2023–2027.

Gangestad, S. W., Simpson, J. A., Cousins, A. J., Garver-Apgar, C. E., & Christensen, P. N. (2004). Women's preferences for male behavioral displays change across the menstrual cycle. *Psychological Science, 15,* 203–207.

Gil, D., Graves, J., Hazon, N., & Wells, A. (1999). Male attractiveness and differential testosterone investment in zebra finch eggs. *Science, 286,* 126–128.

Gordon, P. (2004). Numerical cognition without words: Evidence from Amazonia. *Science, 306,* 496.

Harmon, D. (1995). The status of the world's languages as reported in the Ethnologue. *Southwestern Journal of Linguistics, 14,* 1–33.

Haselton, M. G., & Gangestad, S. W. (2006). Conditional expression of women's desires and men's mate guarding across the ovulatory cycle. *Hormones and Behavior, 49,* 509–518.

Haselton, M. G., & Miller, G. R. (2006). Women's fertility across the cycle increases the short-term attractiveness of creative intelligence. *Human Nature, 17,* 50–73.

Hasselquist, D., Marsh, J. A., Sherman, P. W., & Wingfield, J. C. (1999). Is avian humoral immunocompetence suppressed by testosterone? *Behavioral Ecology and Sociobiology, 45,* 167–175.

Havlicek, J., Roberts, S. C., & Flegr, J. (2005). Women's preference for dominant male odour: Effects of menstrual cycle and relationship status. *Biology Letters, 1,* 256–259.

Henrich, J., Boyd, R., Bowles, S., Gintis, H., Fehr, E., Camerer, C., et al. (2005). 'Economic Man' in cross-cultural perspective: Ethnography and experiments from 15 small-scale societies. *Behavioral and Brain Sciences, 28,* 795–855.

Henrich, J., McElreath, R., Barr, A., Ensimger, J., Barrett, C., Bolyanatz, A., et al. (2006). Costly punishment across human societies. *Science, 312,* 1767–1770.

Janetos, A. C. (1980). Strategies of female mate choice: A theoretical analysis. *Behavioral Ecology and Sociobiology, 7,* 107–112.

Jennions, M. D., & Petrie, M. (2000). Why do females mate multiply? A review of the genetic benefits. *Biological Reviews, 75,* 21–64.

Johnson, O. R., & Johnson, A. W. (1975). Male-female relations and the organization of work in a Machiguenga community. *American Ethnologist, 2,* 634–638.

Jones, T. M., Quinnell, R. J., & Balmford, A. (1998). Fisherian flies: Benefits of female choice in a lekking sandfly. *Proceedings of the Royal Society of London B, 265,* 1651–1657.

Kempenaers, B., Congdon, B., Boag, P., & Robertson, R. J. (1999). Extrapair paternity and egg hatchability in tree swallows: Evidence for the genetic compatibility hypothesis? *Behavioral Ecology, 10,* 304–311.

Kirkpatrick, M., & Ryan, M. J. (1991). The evolution of mating preferences and the paradox of the lek. *Nature, 350,* 33–38.

Kokko, H., Jennions, M. D., & Brooks, R. (2006). Unifying and testing models of sexual selection. *Annual Reviews of Ecology, Evolution and Systematics, 37,* 43–66.

Kotiaho, J. S., Simmons, L. W., & Tomkins, J. L. (2001). Towards a resolution of the lek paradox. *Nature, 410,* 684–686.

Krokene, C., Rigstad, K., Dale, M., & Lifjeld, J. T. (1998). The function of extrapair paternity in blue tits and great tits: Good genes or fertility insurance? *Behavioral Ecology, 9,* 649–656.

Lindstrom, K. M., Krakower, D., Lundstrom, J. O., & Silverin, B. (2001). The effects of testosterone on a viral infection in greenfinches (*Carduelis chloris*): An experimental test of the immunocompetence-handicap hypothesis. *Proceedings of the Royal Society of London B, 268,* 207–211.

McGraw, K. J. (2002). Environmental predictors of geographic variation in human mating preferences. *Ethology, 108,* 303–317.

Milinski, M. (2006). The major histocompatibility complex, sexual selection, and mate choice. *Annual Reviews of Ecology, Evolution, and Systematics, 37,* 159–186.

Møller, A. P., & Alatalo, R. V. (1999). Good-genes effects in sexual selection. *Proceedings of the Royal Society of London B, 266,* 85–91.

Møller, A. P., & Ninni, P. (1998). Sperm competition and sexual selection: A meta-analysis of paternity studies of birds. *Behavioral Ecology and Sociobiology, 43,* 345–358.

Newcomer, S. D., Zeh, J. A., & Zeh, D. W. (1999). Genetic benefits enhance the reproductive success of polyandrous females. *PNAS USA, 18,* 10236–10241.

Ohl, J., Shepard, G. H., Jr., Kaplan, H., Peres, C. A., Yu, D. W. (manuscript in review). Reconciling the conflict between biological conservation and indigenous rights in a Neotropical park. *Conservation Biology.*

Owens, I. P. F. (2006). Where is behavioural ecology going? *Trends in Ecology and Evolution, 21,* 356–361.

Penton-Voak, I. S., & Perrett, D. I. (2000). Female preference for male faces changes cyclically: Further evidence. *Evolution and Human Behavior, 21,* 39–48.

Penton-Voak, I. S., Jacobson, A., & Trivers, R. (2004). Populational differences in attractiveness judgments of male and female faces: Comparing British and Jamaican samples. *Evolution and Human Behavior, 25,* 355–370.

Penton-Voak, I. S., Perrett, D. I., Castles, D. L., Kobayashi, T., Burt, D. M., Murray, L. K., et al. (1999). Menstrual cycle alters face preference. *Nature, 399,* 741–742.

Perrett, D. I., Lee, K. J., Penton-Voak, I., Rowland, D., Yoshikawa, S., Burt, D. M., et al. (1998). Effects of sexual dimorphism on facial attractiveness. *Nature, 394,* 884–887.

Petrie, M., Schwable, H., Brande-Lavridsen, N., & Burke, T. (2001). Sex differences in avian yolk hormone levels. *Nature, 412,* 498.

Provost, M. P., Kormos, C., Kosakoski, G., & Quinsey, V. L. (2006). Sociosexuality in women and preference for facial masculinization and somatotype in men. *Archives of Sexual Behavior, 35,* 305–312.

Roney, J. R., Hanson, K. N., Durante, K. M., & Maestripieri, D. (2006). Reading men's faces: Women's mate attractiveness judgments track men's testosterone and interest in infants. *Proceedings of the Royal Society B, 273,* 2169–2175.

Rowe, L., & Houle, D. (1996). The lek paradox and the capture of genetic variance by condition dependent traits. *Proceedings of the Royal Society of London B, 263,* 1415–1421.

Scheib, J. E., Gangestad, S. W., & Thornhill, R. (1999). Facial attractiveness, symmetry and cues of good genes. *Proceedings of the Royal Society of London B, 266,* 1913–1917.

Shapiro, J. R. (1984). Marriage rules, marriage exchange and the definition of marriage in lowland South American societies. In K. Kensinger (Ed.), *Marriage practices in lowland South America* (pp. 1–32). Chicago: University of Illinois Press.

Sheldon, B. C. (1994). Male phenotype, fertility, and the pursuit of extra-pair copulations by female birds. *Proceedings of the Royal Society of London B, 257,* 25–30.

Shepard, G. H. (2002). Primates in Matsigenka subsistence and worldview. In A. Fuentes, & L. Wolfe (Eds.), *Primates face to face* (pp. 101–136). Cambridge: Cambridge University Press.

Singh, D. (1993). Adaptive significance of female physical attractiveness: The role of waist-to-hip ratio. *Journal of Personality and Social Psychology, 65,* 293–307.

Siskind, J. (1973). *To hunt in the morning.* New York: Oxford University Press.

Swaddle, J. P., & Reierson, G. W. (2002). Testosterone increases perceived dominance but not attractiveness in human males. *Proceedings of the Royal Society B, 269,* 2285–2289.

Taylor, P. D., & Williams, G. C. (1982). The lek paradox is not resolved. *Theoretical Population Biology, 22,* 392–409.

Thornhill, R. (1976). Sexual selection and paternal investment in insects. *American Naturalist, 110,* 153–163.

Thornhill, R., & Gangestad, S. W. (2006). Facial sexual dimorphism, developmental stability, and susceptibility to disease in men and women. *Evolution and Human Behavior, 27,* 131–144.

Tishkoff, S. A., Reed, F. A., Ranciaro, A., Voight, B. F., Babbitt, C. C., Silverman, J. S., et al. (2007). Convergent adaptation of human lactase persistence in Africa and Europe. *Nature Genetics, 39,* 31–40.

Tregenza, T., & Wedell, N. (2002). Polyandrous females avoid costs of inbreeding. *Nature, 415,* 71–73.

Vickers, W. T. (1975). Meat is meat: The Siona-Secoya and the hunting prowess-sexual reward hypothesis. *Latinamericanist, 11,* 1–5.

Waynforth, D., Delwadia, S., & Camm, M. (2005). The influence of women's mating strategies on preference for masculine facial architecture. *Evolution and Human Behavior, 26,* 409–416.

Wedekind, C., Seebeck, T., Bettens, F., & Paepke, A. (1995). MHC-dependent mate preferences in humans. *Proceedings of the Royal Society of London B, 260,* 245–249.

Wilkinson, G. S., & Taper, M. (1999). Evolution of genetic variation for condition-dependent traits in stalk-eyed flies. *Proceedings of the Royal Society of London B, 266,* 1685–1690.

Yu, D. W., & Shepard, G. H. (1998). Is beauty in the eye of the beholder? *Nature, 396,* 321–322.

Yu, D. W., & Shepard, G. H. (1999). The mystery of female beauty. *Nature, 399,* 216.

7

Healthy Body Equals Beautiful Body? Changing Perceptions of Health and Attractiveness with Shifting Socioeconomic Status

Martin J. Tovée, Adrian Furnham, and Viren Swami

There has been considerable debate over the utility of the possible visual cues used to judge human physical attractiveness and their evolutionary origins. In theory, of course, the human body can (and should) be considered as more than just the sum of its various components (see Johnson & Tassinary, Chapter 9), but for reasons of brevity and simplicity, academic debate has tended to centre on one particular body measurement, the waist-to-hip ratio (WHR). This almost exclusive focus on the WHR can be traced back to a series of papers published in the early 1990s by Devendra Singh, in which he argued that the WHR was *the* key component to understanding a woman's physical attractiveness.

The popularity of his hypothesis stems from its simplicity: Singh (1993) argued that low female WHRs (typically centred around 0.70) are attractive because they are correlated with better health and fertility outcomes. In evolutionary terms, Singh argued, men who wanted to maximise their reproductive potential (in lay terms, siring the most surviving offspring) should have mated with healthy, fertile women. But because women do not explicitly advertise their reproductive potential, men evolved a simple means of overcoming this problem: they paid close attention to her WHR. So, by mating with women who have low WHRs, men in evolutionary history presumably enhanced their reproductive success; and for lack of the self-same advertising, contemporary men continue to use this tried-and-tested method for assessing a woman's healthiness and fertility.

Singh has continued to defend his hypothesis (e.g., Singh, 2002, 2006), but others have been somewhat more sceptical (including the authors of several chapters in this volume). For one thing, a growing body of work has raised methodological concerns about the line-drawn stimuli that Singh used to derive his conclusions (Tassinary & Hansen, 1998; Wilson, Tripp, & Boland, 2005; see also Bateson, Cornelissen, & Tovée, Chapter 4). Others have questioned whether secular trends in ideal WHRs really show the stability that Singh (1993) claimed it does (Freese & Meland, 2002; Voracek & Fisher, 2002, 2006). For example, Pieter Pauwel Rubens, the Flemish painter famed for his exuberant Baroque style, certainly seemed to prefer as models women with WHRs (and body weights) that were much higher than the esteemed figure of 0.70 (Swami, Gray, & Furnham, 2007).

It is also possible to question many of the key assumptions underlying Singh's evolutionary hypothesis (see Einon, Chapter 8). For instance, Singh (1993) argued that the ideal mate for our male ancestors would have had a low WHR. However, those ancestral humans are likely to have inhabited an environmental context characterised by food short-ages, and especially a lack of carbohydrates. In such a situation, those individuals who were able to quickly increase their body mass (including truncal obesity, or higher WHRs) with increasing supplies of carbo-hydrates are likely to have had an advantage in terms of health and possibility fertility (Woods, 2006). Indeed, this tendency towards higher WHRs with changing dietary patterns is shared by all hunter-gatherer populations throughout the world, from the Canadian Inuit to South Pacific Islanders (e.g., Clastres, 1972; Junshi, Campbell, Junyao, & Peto, 1990; Mann, 1981; Milton, 1984; O'Keefe & Cordain, 2004; Salzano & Callegari-Jacques, 1988). It is also corroborated by the archaeological record of Venus figurines from the Late Stone Age, that is, small figur-ines and representations depicting stylised obese women with extreme WHRs (Swami & Furnham, 2007).

Two other critiques of Singh's (1993) WHR hypothesis have been particularly damaging. First, one research team (Bateson et al., Chapter 4; Smith, Cornelissen, & Tovée, 2007; Tovée & Cornelissen, 2001; Tovée, Hancock, Mahmoodi, Singleton, & Cornelissen, 2002; Tovée, Maisey, Emery, & Cornelissen, 1999; Tovée, Reinhardt, Emery, & Cornelissen, 1998) has levelled a stringent critique of the idea that the WHR acts as a 'first-pass filter' of women's attractiveness. Rather, body mass index (BMI), or weight scaled for height, appears to be a much more important determinant of women's bodily attractiveness than the WHR (in addi-tion to the body of work produced by Tovée and colleagues, see also Fan, Liu, Wu, & Dai, 2004; Puhl & Boland, 2001; Wilson et al., 2005). And this finding remains stable even when different nationalities and cultures are sampled (e.g., Scott, Bentley, Tovée, Ahamed, & Magid,

Chapter 5; Swami & Tovée, 2005, 2007; Swami, Antonakopoulos, Tovée, & Furnham, 2006; Swami, Caprario, Tovée, & Furnham, 2006; Swami, Knight, Tovée, Davies, & Furnham, 2007; Swami, Neto, Tovée, & Furnham, in press; Tovée, Swami, Furnham, & Mangalparsad, 2006). In short, then, whatever the role of the WHR in defining women's attractiveness, it is certainly not the most important cue.

Second, there is a large and continually growing body of evidence documenting cross-cultural, cross-ethnic, and cross-national differences in what is considered an attractive WHR (for reviews, see Swami, 2006, 2007). While low WHRs are typically judged to be attractive, healthy, and fertile in contexts of high socioeconomic status (SES) (e.g., Furnham, Lavancy, & McClelland, 2001; Furnham, Moutafi, & Baguma, 2002; Furnham, Petrides, & Constantinides, 2005; Furnham, Swami, & Shah, 2006; Henss, 2000; Singh, 1993; Streeter & McBurney, 2003), high WHRs are judged more positively in contexts of low SES (Marlowe & Wetsman, 2001; Sugiyama, 2004; Swami & Tovée, 2005; Wetsman & Marlowe, 1999; Yu & Shepard, 1998). To put it simply, a heavier, more tubular female body is considered the height of beauty in contexts of low SES, and this is even the case when participants in otherwise affluent environments are made to feel 'poor' (Nelson & Morrison, 2005; Swami & Tovée, 2006; see also Nelson, Pettijohn, & Galak, Chapter 10).

Is it possible to explain these combined findings? We believe it is, but only once the commitment to exalted measurements, or 'golden ratios,' are dropped. Thus, one evolutionary psychological argument suggests that humans are capable of calibrating their attractiveness preferences to local conditions (Marlowe, Apicella, & Reed, 2005; Sugiyama, 2004). In a very general sense, this seems obvious enough: human beings have an unparalleled ability to adapt to some of the most inhospitable conditions and climates. But more specifically, they may also be able to 'tailor' their attractiveness ideals in response to changing socioeconomic conditions, resource availability and so on (Marlowe et al., 2005; Sugiyama, 2004; Swami & Tovée, 2005, 2006, 2007; Tovée et al., 2006). Cultural norms, such as gender role stereotypes (Furnham & Nordling, 1998; Swami, Antonakopoulos, et al., 2006; Swami, Caprario et al., 2006) and dietary factors (Swami, Neto, et al., in press), may also play a role in influencing what is considered a locally attractive body shape.

An important aspect of this hypothesis is based on the idea that different environments will favour different optimal values for a particular feature dimension (Anderson, Crawford, Nadeau, & Lindberg, 1992; Brown & Konner, 1989; Ember, Ember, Korotayev, & de Munck, 2005). For example, in a recent study, we reported attractiveness ideals for

Caucasian and British-African observers in Britain, Zulu observers in rural South Africa and Zulus who had migrated to Britain (Tovée et al., 2006). Our results showed that the Caucasian observers preferred a comparatively slim body size, whereas the Zulu observers in South Africa preferred a heavier body mass (i.e., clinically overweight women). Zulu migrants, on the other hand, showed preferences that were intermediate between those of the Caucasian and rural Zulu participants. Finally, the British-African observers, who were born and raised in Britain, showed the same preferences as their Caucasian counterparts.

These results suggest, first, a cross-cultural difference in what is considered an attractive body size, and secondly, that those differences are malleable and subject to change. But why should there be this difference? And why should there be this change? We hypothesised that the difference was based largely on variations in what was a healthy body mass for the particular environment in question. That is, a heavier body weight may have been perceived as more attractive in rural South Africa because of the combined effects of a heavier body weight being healthier in that context, as well as the social connotations associated with a thin figure (e.g., HIV/AIDS infection). However, we previously published no data on whether perceived health mirrored the perception of attractiveness for any of these observer groups; that is, we provided no direct evidence in support of our explanation. In this chapter, we expand on the earlier data set to include data on the perceptions of health for the British Caucasian and two Zulu observer groups, and compare their relationship with attractiveness judgements to determine whether a healthy body really is an attractive body.

A summary of the methods and participants

As previously discussed (Tovée et al., 2006), we recruited three groups of participants from Britain and South Africa. The first group comprised 100 British Caucasians, equally divided between the sexes, who were recruited from the relatively affluent environment of Greater London. The second group consisted of 35 South Africans (19 male, 16 female) from Mshwati-Mpolweni, in KwaZulu-Natal (Eastern Seaboard of South Africa). This group were made up of ethnic Zulus with little command of any other language, intermittent education, and were employed either as subsistence farmers or as temporary labourers and domestic workers in nearby towns like Howick. The third group were comprised of 52 Zulu migrants into Britain (25 male, 27 female), all of whom were born in South Africa and moved to Britain in the 18 months before taking part in the study. There were no significant differences in the age ranges of the three groups (British Caucasians, $M = 24.76$, $SD = 6.96$; South African Zulus, $M = 25.60$, $SD = 4.47$; South African migrants, $M = 26.56$, $SD = 6.87$) [$F(2, 186) = 1.31$, $p > 0.05$].

Participants in each of the three groups were asked to rate grey scale images of 50 real women in front view. To generate the images, consenting women were videoed standing in a set pose at a standard distance, wearing tight grey leotards and leggings in front view. Images were then frame-grabbed and stored as 24-bit images (see, e.g., Swami & Furnham, 2007; Tovée et al., 2002). The heads of the women in the images were obscured, so that they could not be identified and so that facial attractiveness would not be a factor in the subject's ratings. Although previous studies have manipulated the relative ranges of BMI and WHR to explore the relative contributions of these features to attractiveness judgements (e.g., Tovée et al., 1999, 2002), in this study the ranges of BMI and WHR used were not constrained, and represented the widest range in the available image library. The ranges seem not inconsistent with population data reported by epidemiological studies, such as the *Health Survey for England 2003* (United Kingdom Department of Health, 2003).

The images of the women were printed on sheets of paper measuring 210×297mm, so that each image covered the entire page. Participants were presented with booklets to record their ratings, where the first page consisted of brief instructions and a worked example of a rating, and where the final page requested participants' demographic details (age, gender, ethnicity, weight, and height). Other pages in the booklet provided a 9-point Likert scale, which appeared below a question of either 'How beautiful is the person in the photograph?' or 'How healthy is the person in the photograph?' and on which participants were asked to record their ratings. The order in which the observers rated the images for health or attractiveness was randomised between participants. All participants were tested individually, with the only difference in procedure between the different settings being the language used (English for all groups except the rural South African sample, for whom the questionnaire was translated into Zulu). Within the image set, individual images were presented in a randomised order.

Sex differences between participants

To explore whether there were differences between the two sexes in our observer groups, we carried out Spearman Rank correlations. For the attractiveness ratings, we found high correlations between the women and men in each group, suggesting they were ranking the images in a highly similar manner (British Caucasians, $r = 0.94$, $p < 0.001$; South African Zulus, $r = 0.78$, $p < 0.001$; Zulu migrants, $r = 0.66$, $p < 0.001$). This result is consistent with the correlations between attractiveness ratings by women and men found in previous studies (e.g., Tovée & Cornelissen, 2001; Tovée et al., 2002). For the health ratings, we also found high correlations between the ratings by women and men (British Caucasians, $r = 0.97$, $p < 0.001$; South African Zulus, $r = 0.93$, $p < 0.001$; Zulu migrants to Britain, $r = 0.94$, $p < 0.001$).

The relationship between perceptions of health and attractiveness

As can be seen from Figure 7.1, there is a strong linear relationship between attractiveness and health ratings for all of three of the observer groups. We quantified this relationship as the correlations between attractiveness and health ratings for each group. The ratings are very highly correlated in each group: for the Caucasian observers, the correlation was $r = 0.98$, $p < 0.001$; for the South African Zulus, it was $r = 0.84$, $p < 0.001$, and; for the Zulu migrants, it was $r = 0.95$, $p < 0.001$. This implies a very strong relationship between perceptions of attractiveness and health. Moreover, as can be seen in Figures 7.2 and 7.3, the relationship between these ratings and either BMI or WHR were also very similar.

Multiple regression results

Multiple polynomial regressions were used to model the contributions of BMI and WHR to the ratings of attractiveness and health. As in previous studies (e.g., Tovée et al., 1998, 1999, 2002), we modelled the data using a multiple regression model, to estimate the variance of attractiveness and health ratings explained by BMI and WHR. The model, run separately for the different groups, was:

$$y = a + b_1 x_1 + b_2 x_2 + b_3 x_3 + b_4 x_4 + e$$

where y is the attractiveness or health rating, a is the intercept, x_1 is the WHR, x_2 is the BMI, x_3 is the BMI^2, x_4 is the BMI^3 and e is random error. Figure 7.2 shows plots of the attractiveness and health ratings as a function of BMI, with all sets being significantly explained by BMI ($p < 0.001$ in all cases). Figure 7.3 shows the corresponding relationship between attractiveness and WHR. None of the observer groups showed a significant relationship between attractiveness ratings and

114

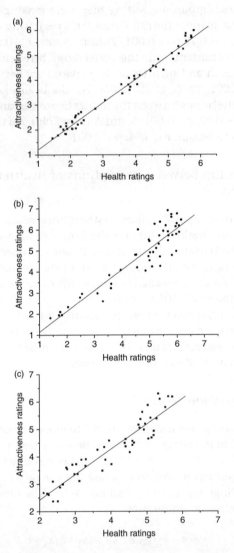

Figure 7.1 Comparison plots of the attractiveness ratings against the health ratings by the three observer groups. Each point represents the average rating for a particular body by all the observers in one of the observer groups. (a) illustrates the correlation between attractiveness and health ratings for the British Caucasian observers; (b) illustrates the correlation between attractiveness and health ratings for the Zulu observers in South Africa, and; (c) illustrates the correlation between attractiveness and health ratings for the Zulu migrants in Britain.

115

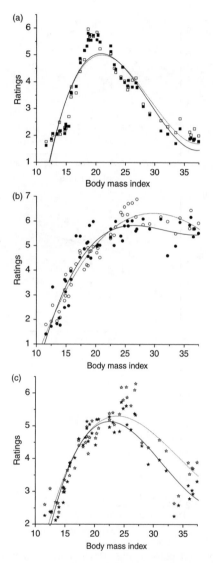

Figure 7.2 Comparison plots of the attractiveness and health ratings by the three observer groups as functions of BMI. Each point represents the average attractiveness rating for a particular body by all the observers in one of the observer groups. (a) illustrates a comparison of the British Caucasian ratings on attractiveness (filled squares and continuous line) and attractiveness (open squares and dotted line); (b) illustrates a comparison of the South African Zulu ratings of attractiveness (filled circles and continuous line) and health (open circles and dotted line), and; (c) illustrates a comparison of the Zulu migrant ratings of attractiveness (filled stars and continuous line) and health (open stars and dotted line).

116

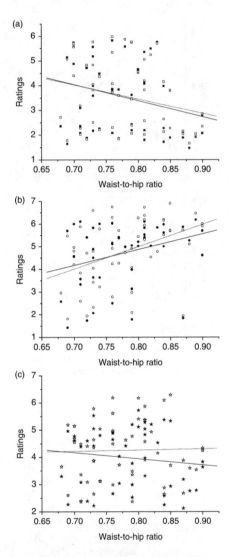

Figure 7.3 Comparison plots of the attractiveness and health ratings by the three observer groups as functions of WHR. Each point represents the average attractiveness rating for a particular body by all the observers in one of the observer groups. (a) illustrates a comparison of the British Caucasian ratings on attractiveness (filled squares and continuous line) and attractiveness (open squares and dotted line); (b) illustrates a comparison of the South African Zulu ratings of attractiveness (filled circles and continuous line) and health (open circles and dotted line), and; (c) illustrates a comparison of the Zulu migrant ratings of attractiveness (filled stars and continuous line) and health (open stars and dotted line).

Table 7.1 Summary of the proportion of variance accounted for by BMI and WHR in the regression analyses of attractiveness and health judgements, plus the peak BMI for each group and the gradient of the relationship between attractiveness and WHR.

Group	Rating task	BMI variance	WHR variance	Peak BMI	WHR gradient
British	Attractiveness	84.1	7.4	20.85	−6.54
Caucasians	Health	81.7	6.4	21.11	−5.78
South African	Attractiveness	82.5	7.5	26.52	+6.18
Zulus	Health	82.5	11.3	30.07	+9.86
Zulu migrants	Attractiveness	86.2	1.7	23.99	−2.38
to Britain	Health	76.9	0.1	25.56	+0.46

WHR ($p > 0.05$), suggesting that, for this image set, WHR has only a weak effect on attractiveness ratings. Similarly, only the South African Zulu data showed a significant relationship between WHR and health ratings ($p < 0.05$), with both the Caucasian and migrant data returning associations that were not significant. The variance explained by BMI and WHR in the best subsets analysis from this model is shown in Table 7.1.

Between-group differences

There is a striking difference in the shape of the relationship between the sets of ratings and BMI between the three groups (see Figure 7.2). The British Caucasian group shows a roughly inverted-U shape: attractiveness and health ratings are lower for the low and high BMI values, and higher for the middle BMI values. In contrast, the attractiveness and health functions for the South African Zulu group has shifted towards higher BMI values, and does not show the fall-off in attractiveness with higher BMI values (see Figure 7.2). Instead, attractiveness and health ratings remain high, and the functions are largely flat over the middle and high BMI values. Finally, the Zulu migrants show a function intermediate between these two patterns; that is, the ratings decline for the higher BMI values, but not to the same extent as that seen in the Caucasian group (see Figure 7.2).

To determine the statistical significance of these differences, we fitted a third-order polynomial to each of the BMI functions for each observer, allowing the BMI at peak attractiveness to be calculated for each participant. There were significant differences between the different groups for attractiveness [$F(2, 186) = 45.50$, $p < 0.001$]. A post hoc Tukey HSD showed that the South African Zulus had the preference for the highest BMI, followed by the Zulu migrants and finally the British Caucasians; all three groups were significantly different from each other (see Table 7.1). The same pattern was found for the health ratings. First, there were highly significant differences between the three groups [$F(2, 186) = 107.58$, $p < 0.001$], and a *post hoc* Tukey HSD showed the same pattern of results as the attractiveness ratings (see Table 7.1).

Discussion: What is healthy is beautiful...

The present results highlight two important contributions to the scientific study of human beauty. First, it would appear that perceptions of what constitutes healthy and unhealthy bodies are largely determined by overall body size. That is, for the set of photographic stimuli that was used in this study, the primary predictor of ratings of health was BMI, with WHR having a very small or negligible effect on those judgements. To the extent that these findings mirror those found when participants are asked to judge the same set of stimuli for attractiveness (e.g., Smith et al., 2007; Swami & Tovée, 2005, 2006, 2007; Tovée & Cornelissen, 2001; Tovée et al., 1998, 1999, 2002, 2006), our results strongly suggest that the WHR is not the 'first-pass filter' of women's attractiveness that Singh argues it to be. Rather, judgements of both health and attractiveness, at least for women, appear to be determined in large part by BMI, with WHR playing a much smaller role.

Second, the ratings of health and attractiveness were very highly correlated for all three observer groups (see Figure 7.1). Moreover, the relationship between both sets of ratings and the feature dimensions examined in this study were very similar *within* each group, although there were considerable differences *between* groups. More specifically, the peaks for both sets of ratings by the rural South African Zulu group was shifted to a higher BMI compared to the British observers, and, most strikingly, the former ratings do not show a dip for bodies with higher BMI values (see Figure 7.2). That is, rural South Africans appear to judge overweight and obese women as being just as attractive and healthy as normal-weight women.

There was also a difference in the pattern of ratings with changing WHR. The Caucasian group showed a preference, in their ratings of attractiveness and health, for a more curvaceous figure (a low WHR), but the opposite appears true of the South African Zulus (see Figure 7.3). This latter change may be, at least partially, a by-product of their preference for heavier bodies, which also tend to be less curvaceous (Tovée et al., 2006). In addition, the health and attractiveness ratings of the

Zulu migrants seem to be intermediate between those of their coun-terparts in Britain and South Africa (see Figures 7.2 and 7.3). In other words, the migrant group appear to find attractive and healthy women who have a higher BMI than those preferred by British Caucasians, but with a lower BMI than those preferred by rural Zulus.

In general, these findings provide preliminary support for the evolu-tionary psychological hypothesis that judgements of attractiveness are, at least in part, based on the perceived health of an individual. We previ-ously suggested that the difference in what is considered an attractive body weight in Britain and rural South Africa may be explained in terms of an 'adaptation' (in the loose sense of the word) to the different environmental pressures (Tovée et al., 2006). Specifically, we proposed that the optimal BMI for health is different in Britain and rural South Africa, and to the extent that judgements of attractiveness are based on perceived health, those health differences may be the basis of the attractiveness shift.

This hypothesis is consistent with the ratings of health for our images, which suggest that 'what is healthy is also attractive.' These findings take on added importance because they suggest a link between what is *perceived* as healthy and judgements of attractiveness, and not simply what clinical and epidemiological records suggest are healthy body sizes. Of course, individuals appear to be highly adept at perceiving the health status of the self and others (e.g., Hunt, McEwen, & McKenna, 1984; Hunt et al., 1980; Martikainen et al., 1999), which suggests that the perceptions of healthy body sizes in the present study may be grounded in the lived experiences of women and men.

Consider, for example, the case of rural South Africa, where there are long-standing problems with infectious diseases, including meningitis, diarrhoea, septicaemia, and tuberculosis. When combined with the reported low levels of immunisation, this makes potentially serious infections a significant possibility (South African Department of Health, 1998). More pertinently, the health consequences linked to these serious diseases include weight loss, and so a lower body mass may signal infec-tion. However, the association between weight loss resulting in thin-ness and serious infections will only likely have an influence on related perceptions (e.g., those of attractiveness) if they are acknowledged and assimilated by particular cultural groups. To date, the best evidence of such cultural assimilation comes from studies on the perceived effects of HIV/AIDS infection in South Africa.

HIV/AID is a common infection in South Africa (Blacker, 2004; Caldwell, 1997) and is now the single largest killer of women and men in the country (Bradshaw et al., 2003; Hosegood et al., 2004). In 2005, for example, it was estimated that 16.5 per cent of the population of KwaZulu-Natal, the area of sampling the present study, were HIV-positive, the highest level of any province in South Africa (Shisana et al., 2005). The potential effect of HIV/AIDS on the perception of health and its role in mate choice is increased when one considers that other important causes of illness and death (such as pulmonary or respiratory diseases) are associated with older adults, whereas the prevalence of HIV infection and the rate of AIDS deaths are highest in young and middle-aged adults (i.e., those who are most likely to be actively seeking partners; Bradshaw et al., 2003; Shisana et al., 2005).

A growing body of work highlights the fact that HIV/AIDS is recognised as a significant risk in partner choice by young people in rural South Africa (Bernardi, 2002; Varga, 1997). One potential cue to HIV-infection is low body weight: HIV/AIDS infection causes a characteristic loss of body mass, called wasting syndrome (Cohan, 1994; Kotler & Grunfeld, 1995). This moderate-to-severe weight loss can occur before the onset of other symptoms (Polsky, Kotler, & Steinhart, 2004), and so a lower body weight may signal HIV-infection (either on its own or in conjunction with other symptoms), and could support a mate strategy that favours heavier bodies (Tovée et al., 2006). Indeed, there is evidence that, in South Africa, some communities – especially rural groups – associated thinness with HIV/AIDS infection (Kruger, Puoane, Senekal, & van der Merwe, 2005; Puoane et al., 2002).

In short, then, a mate choice strategy in South Africa that favours heavier body weights may arise because low BMIs are associated with perceived illness and infection. To the extent that such perceptions are grounded in cultural understandings of infection, obesity, and thinness (Kruger et al., 2005), they may also give rise to better reproductive outcomes. That is, by finding attractive (and hence, mating with – theoretically, speaking at least) women with higher BMIs, men in rural South Africa may increase their chances of mating with healthy women, and thus increase the survival probabilities of their children. In contrast to the conditions in rural South Africa, the prevalence of HIV/AIDS is comparatively low in Britain (European Centre for Epidemiological Monitoring of AIDS, 2003), and the general mortality rate in young women is very low. Rather, in Britain, a low BMI is associated with lower levels of cancer (Calle et al., 2003; Garfinkel, 1985), as well as better long-term health for women (Manson et al., 1995; Willet et al., 1995). Taken together, then, a mate choice strategy that favours a lower female BMI in Britain would appear to enhance an individual's reproductive potential.

Of course, we are not suggesting a straightforward link between perceptions of health and judgements of attractiveness. A whole host of cultural and sociological factors may serve to enhance or weaken any possible relationship. For example, in contexts of low socioeconomic status, including rural South Africa, a heavier body weight may be associated with cultural perceptions of femininity, wealth, prosperity, and sexual capacity (for a review, see Swami & Furnham, 2007). In such environments, access to resources – particularly stable supplies of food – may be indexed by a heavier body weight (Furnham & Alibhai, 1983; Furnham & Baguma, 1994; Marlowe & Wetsman, 2001), which may help explain why women with higher BMIs are considered attractive in contexts of low socioeconomic status. By contrast, a high BMI is a strong indicator of poor socioeconomic status in Britain (Darmon, Ferguson, & Briend, 2002; James, Nelson, Ralph, & Leather, 1997), which helps explain the idealisation of thinness there.

However, there may also exist cultural factors that mitigate these cultural associations. In both urban and rural South Africa, for example, fear of fatness, dieting, and body image concerns have become increasingly prevalent, fuelled in part by the glorification of thin media images and celebrities (e.g., Caradas, Lambert, & Charlton, 2001; le Grange, Louw, Breen, & Katzman, 2004; le Grange, Telch, & Tibbs, 1998). This would suggest that the idealisation of thinness may be becoming more prevalent, especially among younger age groups. Indeed, Charlton, Brewitt, and Bourne (2004) have shown how South African women develop their understandings of obesity and thinness in large part by engaging with sources of mass media, which do not necessarily provide credible or accurate nutritional and dietary information. Understanding perceptions of health and attractiveness, then, will require more in-depth examinations of the way in which various sources of information about nutrition, status, health and so on are used and assimilated.

. . . but what is beautiful is healthy

We have interpreted the results in this study as support for a directional link from perceptions of health to judgements of physical attractiveness. This is based on the evolutionary psychological prediction that cues of attractiveness acts as 'windows' to a person's fitness (Buss, 1994, 1999). However, it should be pointed out that the evidence for this is somewhat equivocal. Weeden and Sabini (2005), for example, have reviewed the evidence linking health with attractiveness presented in studies conducted in relatively developed, Western setting. They report that, in general, the evidence in support of such an association is weak. This highlights the possibility of an alternative explanation for the present (and similar) results: that judgements of health are a 'halo' of perceptions of beauty.

A great wealth of evidence emphasises the fact that beauty ideals are often associated with factors quite unrelated to it. In a now-classic study, for example, Dion, Berscheid, and Walster (1972) had participants rate facial photographs that had been selected on the basis of judges' agreement that the pictured individuals differed in physical attractiveness. Participants' were found to rate individuals high in physical attractiveness more positively on a range of personality traits and probable life outcomes, such as marital happiness and career success, leading Dion and her colleagues (1972: 285) to claim that, in people's perceptions of others, 'what is beautiful is good.'

This fundamental finding has been replicated many times over the years. For instance, attractive individuals are judged as more honest (Yarmouk, 2000), less maladjusted and disturbed (Cash, Kehr, Polyson, & Freeman, 1977; Dion, 1972), and happier, more successful and having a better personality (Dion et al., 1972). Attractive people are also reported to be afforded more personal space, more likely to win arguments, more trusted with secrets, more at ease socially, considered more intelligent and generally considered *better at everything* in comparison with unattractive individuals (Horai, Naccari, & Fatoullan, 1974; Patzer, 1985).

In this light, it is quite possible that perceptions of health are an outcome of judgements concerning attractiveness. A heavier body is judged more positively in terms of health in rural South Africa because, in that environment, a heavier body is perceived as more attractive. The underlying association here may be predicated on factors quite unrelated with health differentials, such as socioeconomic status (see Swami & Tovée, 2006). This appears to be an important limitation, not only of the present study but also of similar studies that populate the literature: showing an association between health and attractiveness ratings is not necessarily the same thing as showing a directional link from health to attractiveness. Given that attractive individuals are imbued with all kinds of positive qualities, it is possible that 'what is beautiful is healthy.'

Conclusion

Pace the limitations above, our findings have two important implications for the literature. First, it is worth considering that health care strategies aimed at reducing obesity rates in South Africa are unlikely to achieve any profound success in the absence of an understanding of the way in which overweight and obese bodies are idealised (Kruger et al., 2005; Prentice, 2006; Puoane et al., 2002; van der Merwe & Pepper, 2006). Clearly, among rural communities, health care strategies that prescribe a (clinically defined) normal body weight may come up against cultural perceptions of obesity as being healthy and fertile. In such a situation, health care practitioners will need to devise more careful ways of reducing obesity rates, initially by challenging cultural assumptions of what is both healthy and attractive.

Second, our representation of what constitutes an attractive and healthy body appear to be flexible. When conditions within an environment change, or when someone moves between environments, their health preferences appear to reflect this change in the local optima for survival. Thus, when an individual moves from a rural South African environment to the relatively affluent environment of urban Britain, one would expect their health preferences to shift as a reflection of changing priorities. We believe that eventually, the preferences of the migrant population will change to become similar or identical to those of the indigenous population.

This once again highlights the importance of considering both evolutionary and sociocultural factors in understanding body weight ideals (Swami & Furnham, 2007; Tovée et al., 2006). On the one hand, cultural practices and norms have the potential to influence and define the way in which evolutionary possibilities are played out (Swami, 2006; Swami, Antonakopoulos, et al., 2006; Swami, Caprario, et al., 2006; Swami, Neto, et al., in press; Tovée et al., 2006). On the other hand, an evolutionary psychological model that accepts flexibility and malleability of preferences has the potential to unify the science of physical attraction. In short, our results suggest that health and attractiveness preferences are part of a flexible behavioural repertoire, acquired through social learning, which allow humans to adapt and respond to changing conditions within an environment or when moving between environments.

Acknowledgements

This research was supported by a Wellcome Trust award through the JIF initiative to Martin Tovée and an Overseas Research Student award from Universities UK to Viren Swami. We are greatful for the assistance of Roshila Mangalparsad with data collection in South Africa.

References

Anderson, J. L., Crawford, C. E., Nadeau, J., & Lindberg, T. (1992). Was the Duchess of Windsor right? A cross-cultural view of the socio-biology of ideals of female body shape. *Ethology and Sociobiology, 13*, 197–227.

Bernardi, L. (2002). Determinants of individual AIDS risk perception: Knowledge, behavioural control and social influence. *African Journal of AIDS Research, 1*, 111–124.

Blacker, J. (2004). The impact of AIDS on adult mortality: Evidence from national and regional statistics. *AIDS, 18*, S19–S26.

Bradshaw, D., Groenewald, P., Laubscher, R., Nannan, N., Nojilana, B., Norman, R., et al. (2003). *Initial burden of disease estimates for South Africa, 2000*. Cape Town: South African Medical Research Council.

Brown, P., & Konner, M. J. (1987). An anthropological perspective of obesity. *Annals of the New York Academy of Science, 499*, 29.

Buss, D. (1994). *The evolution of desire*. New York: Basic Books.

Buss, D. (1999). *Evolutionary psychology: The new science of the mind*. Boston: Allyn & Bacon.

Caldwell, J. C. (1997). The impact of the African AIDS epidemic. *Health Transition Review, 7*, 169–188.

Calle, E. D., Rodriguez, C., Walker-Thurmond, K., & Thun, M. J. (2003). Overweight, obesity, and mortality from cancer in a prospectively studied cohort of US adults. *New England Journal of Obesity, 348*, 1625–1638.

Caradas, A. A., Lambert, E. V., & Charlton, K. E. (2001). An ethnic comparison of eating attitudes and associated body image concerns in adolescent South African schoolgirls. *Journal of Human Nutrition and Dietetics, 14*, 111–120.

Cash, T. F., Kehr, J. A., Polyson, J., & Freeman, V. (1977). Role of physical attractiveness in peer attribution of psychological disturbance. *Journal of Consulting and Clinical Psychology, 45*, 987–993.

Charlton, K. E., Brewitt, P., & Bourne, L. T. (2004). Sources and credibility of nutrition information among black urban South African women, with a focus on messages related to obesity. *Public Health Nutrition, 7*, 801–811.

Clastres, P. (1972). The Guayaki. In M. Biccheri (Ed.), *Hunters and gatherers today* (pp. 138–174). New York: Holt, Rinehart and Winston.

Cohan, G. (1994). Malnutrition and wasting in HIV disease: A review. *Perspectives in Applied Nutrition, 2*, 10–19.

Darmon, N., Ferguson, E. L., & Briend, A. (2002). A cost constraint alone has adverse effects on food selection and nutrient density: An analysis of human diets by linear programming. *Journal of Nutrition, 132*, 3764–3771.

Dion, K. K. (1972). Physical attractiveness and evaluation of children's transgressions. *Journal of Personality and Social Psychology, 24*, 285–290.

Dion, K. K., Berscheid, E., & Walster, E. (1972). What is beautiful is good. *Journal of Personality and Social Psychology, 24*, 285–290.

Ember, C. R., Ember, M., Korotayev, A., & de Munck, V. (2005). Valuing thinness or fatness in women: Reevaluating the effect of resource scarcity. *Evolution and Human Behavior, 26*, 257–270.

European Centre for Epidemiological Monitoring of AIDS. (2003). *HIV/AIDS surveillance in Europe: Mid-year report 2003*. Saint Maurice: Institut de. Veille Sanitaire.

Fan, J., Liu, F., Wu, J., & Dai, W. (2004). Visual perception of female physical attractiveness. *Proceedings of the Royal Society of London B, 271,* 347–352.

Freese, J., & Meland, S. (2002). Seven tenths incorrect: Heterogeneity and change in the waist-to-hip ratios of *Playboy* centrefolds models and Miss America pageant winners. *Journal of Sex Research, 39,* 133–138.

Furnham, A., & Alibhai, N. (1983). Cross-cultural differences in the perception of female body-shapes. *Psychological Medicine, 13,* 829–837.

Furnham, A., & Baguma, P. (1994). Cross-cultural differences in the evaluation of male and female body shapes. *International Journal of Eating Disorders, 15,* 81–89.

Furnham, A., & Nordling, R. (1998). Cross-cultural differences in preferences for specific male and female body shapes. *Personality and Individual Differences, 25,* 635–648.

Furnham, A., Lavancy, M., & McClelland, A. (2001). Waist-to-hip ratio and facial attractiveness. *Personality and Individual Differences, 30,* 491–502.

Furnham, A., Moutafi, J., & Baguma, P. (2002). A cross-cultural study on the role of weight and waist-to-hip ratio on judgements of women's attractiveness. *Personality and Individual Differences, 32,* 729–745.

Furnham, A., Petrides, K. V., & Constantinides, A. (2005). The effects of body mass index and waist-to-hip ratio on ratings of female attractiveness, fecundity and health. *Personality and Individual Differences, 38,* 1823–1834.

Furnham, A., Swami, V., & Shah, K. (2006). Female body correlates of attractiveness and other ratings. *Personality and Individual Differences, 41,* 443–454.

Garfinkel, L. (1985). Overweight and cancer. *Annals of Internal Medicine, 103,* 1034–1036.

Henss, R. (2000). Waist-to-hip ratio and female attractiveness. Evidence from photographic stimuli and methodological considerations. *Personality and Individual Differences, 28,* 501–513.

Horai, J., Naccari, N., & Fatoullan, E. (1974). The effects of expertise and physical attractiveness upon opinion agreement and liking. *Sociometry, 37,* 601–606.

Hosegood, V., Vanneste, A. M., & Timaeus, I. M. (2004). Levels and causes of adult mortality in rural South Africa: The impact of AIDS. *AIDS, 18,* 663–671.

Hunt, S. M., McEwen, J., & McKenna, S. P. (1984). Perceived health: Age and sex comparisons in a community. *Journal of Epidemiology and Community Health, 38,* 156–160.

Hunt, S. M., McKenna, S. P., McEwen, H., Backet, E. M., Williams, J., & Papp, E. (1980). A quantitative approach to perceived health status: A validation study. *Journal of Epidemiology and Community Health, 34,* 281–286.

James, W. P. T., Nelson, M., Ralph, A., & Leather, S. (1997). Socioeconomic determinants of health: The contribution of nutrition to inequalities in health. *British Medical Journal, 314,* 1545.

Junshi, C., Campbell, T. C., Junyao, L., & Peto, R. (1990). *Diet, life-style and mortality in China.* Oxford: Oxford University Press.

Kotler, D. P., & Grunfeld, C. (1995). Pathophysiology and treatment of the AIDS wasting syndrome. *AIDS Clinical Review, 6,* 229–275.

Kruger, H. S., Puoane, T., Senekal, M., & van der Merwe, M.-T. (2005). Obesity in South Africa: Challenges for government and health professionals. *Public Health Nutrition, 8,* 491–500.

le Grange, D., Telch, C. F., & Tibbs, J. (1998). Eating attitudes and behaviors in 1,435 South African Caucasian and non-Caucasian college students. *American Journal of Psychiatry, 155,* 250–254.

le Grange, D., Louw, J., Breen, A., & Katzman, M. A. (2004). The meaning of 'self-starvation' in impoverished Black adolescents in South Africa. *Culture, Medicine and Psychiatry, 28,* 439–461.

Mann, A. E. (1981). Diet and human evolution. In R. S. O. Harding, & G. Teleki (Eds.), *Omnivorous primates* (pp. 10–36). New York: Columbia University Press.

Manson, J. E., Willet, W. C., Stampfer, M. J., Colditz, G. A., Hunter, D. J., Hankinson, S. E., et al. (1995). Body weight and mortality among women. *New England Journal of Medicine, 333,* 677–685.

Marlowe, F., & Wetsman, A. (2001). Preferred waist-to-hip ratio and ecology. *Personality and Individual Differences, 30,* 481–489.

Marlowe, F. W., Apicella, C. L., & Reed, D. (2005). Men's preferences for women's profile waist-hip-ratio in two societies. *Evolution and Human Behavior, 26,* 458–468.

Martikainen, P., Aromaa, A., Heliovaara, M., Klaukka, T., Knekt, P., Maatela, J., et al. (1999). Reliability of perceived health by sex and age. *Social Science and Medicine, 48,* 1117–1122.

Milton, K. (1984). Protein and carbohydrate resources of the Maku Indians of northwest Amazonia. *American Anthropologist, 86,* 7–27.

Nelson, L. D., & Morrison, E. L. (2005). The symptoms of resource scarcity: Judgements of food and finances influence preference for potential partners. *Psychological Science, 16,* 167–173.

O'Keefe, J. H., & Cordain, L. (2004). Cardiovascular disease resulting from a diet and lifestyle at odds with our Paleolithic genome: How to become a 21st-century hunter-gatherer. *Mayo Clinic Proceedings, 79,* 101–108.

Patzer, G. L. (1985). *Physical attractiveness phenomena.* New York: Plenum Press.

Polsky, B., Kotler, D., & Steinhart, C. (2004). Treatment guidelines for HIV-associated wasting. *HIV Clinical Trials, 5,* 50–61.

Prentice, A. M. (2006). The emerging epidemic of obesity in developing countries. *International Journal of Epidemiology, 35,* 93–99.

Puhl, R. M., & Boland, F. J. (2001). Predicting female physical attractiveness: Waist-to-hip ratio versus thinness. *Psychology, Evolution and Gender, 3,* 27–46.

Puoane, T., Steyn, K., Bradshaw, D., Laubscher, R., Fourie, J., Lambert, V., et al. (2002). Obesity in South Africa: The South African demographic and health survey. *Obesity Research, 10,* 1038–1048.

Salzano, F. M., & Callegari-Jacques, S. M. (1988). *South American Indians: A case study in evolution.* Oxford: Clarendon Press.

Shisana, O., Rehle, T., Simbayi, L. C., Parker, W., Zuma, K., Bhana, A., et al. (2005). *South African national HIV prevalence, HIV incidence, behaviour and communication survey, 2005.* Cape Town: HSRC Press.

Singh, D. (1993). Adaptive significance of female physical attractiveness: Role of waist-to-hip ratio. *Journal of Personality and Social Psychology, 65,* 292–307.

Singh, D. (2002). Female mate value at a glance: Relationship of waist-to-hip ratio to health, fecundity and attractiveness. *Human Ethology and Evolutionary Psychology, 23,* 81–91.

Singh, D. (2006). Universal allure of the hourglass figure: An evolutionary theory of female physical attractiveness. *Clinics in Plastic Surgery, 33,* 359–370.

Smith, K. L., Cornelissen, P. L., & Tovée, M. J. (2007). Color 3D bodies and judgements of human female attractiveness. *Evolution and Human Behavior, 28*, 48–54.

South African Department of Health. (1998). *The South Africa demographic and health survey.* Online publication at: http://www.doh.gov.za/facts/1998/sadhs98.

Streeter, S. A., & McBurney, D. (2003). Waist-hip ratio and attractiveness: New evidence and a critique for a 'critical test.' *Evolution and Human Behaviour, 24*, 88–98.

Sugiyama, L. S. (2004). Is beauty in the context-sensitive adaptations of the beholder? Shiwiar use of waist-to-hip ratio in assessments of female mate value. *Evolution and Human Behaviour, 25*, 51–62.

Swami, V. (2006). The influence of body weight and shape in determining female and male physical attractiveness. In M. V. Kindes (Ed.), *Body image: New research* (pp. 35–61). New York: Nova Biomedical Books.

Swami, V. (2007). *The missing arms of Vénus de Milo: Reflections on the science of physical attractiveness.* Brighton: The Book Guild.

Swami, V., & Furnham, A. (2007). *The science of physical attraction.* London: Routledge.

Swami, V., & Tovée, M. J. (2005). Male physical attractiveness in Britain and Malaysia: A cross-cultural study. *Body Image, 2*, 383–393.

Swami, V., & Tovée, M. J. (2006). Does hunger influence judgements of female physical attractiveness? *British Journal of Psychology, 97*, 353–363.

Swami, V., & Tovée, M. J. (2007). Perceptions of female body weight and shape among indigenous and urban Europeans. *Scandinavian Journal of Psychology, 48*, 43–50.

Swami, V., Antonakopoulos, N., Tovée, M. J., & Furnham, A. (2006). A critical test of the waist-to-hip ratio hypothesis of female physical attractiveness in Britain and Greece. *Sex Roles, 54*, 201–211.

Swami, V., Caprario, C., Tovée, M. J., & Furnham, A. (2006). Female physical attractiveness in Britain and Japan: A cross-cultural study. *European Journal of Personality, 20*, 69–81.

Swami, V., Gray, M., & Furnham, A. (2007). The female nude in Rubens: Disconfirmatory evidence of the waist-to-hip ratio hypothesis of female physical attractiveness. *Imagination, Cognition and Personality, 26*, 139–147.

Swami, V., Knight, D., Tovée, M. J., Davies, P., & Furnham, A. (2007). Perceptions of female body size in Britain and the South Pacific. *Body Image, 4*, 219–223.

Swami, V., Neto, F., Tovée, M. J., & Furnham, A. (in press). Preference for female body weight and shape in three European countries. *European Psychologist.*

Tassinary, L. G., & Hansen, K. A. (1998). A critical test of the waist-to-hip ratio hypothesis of female physical attractiveness. *Psychological Science, 9*, 150–155.

Tovée, M. J., & Cornelissen, P. L. (2001). Female and male perceptions of female physical attractiveness in front-view and profile. *British Journal of Psychology, 92*, 391–402.

Tovée, M. J., Maisey, D. S., Emery, J. L., & Cornelissen, P. L. (1999). Visual cues to female physical attractiveness. *Proceedings of the Royal Society of London B, 266*, 211–218.

Tovée, M. J., Reinhardt, S., Emery, J., & Cornelissen, P. (1998). Optimum body-mass index and maximum sexual attractiveness. *Lancet, 352*, 548.

Tovée, M. J., Swami, V., Furnham, A., & Mangalparsad, R. (2006). Changing perceptions of attractiveness as observers are exposed to a different culture. *Evolution and Human Behavior, 27*, 443–456.

Tovée, M. J., Hancock, P., Mahmoodi, S., Singleton, B. R. R., & Cornelissen, P. L. (2002). Human female attractiveness: Waveform analysis of body shape. *Proceedings of the Royal Society of London B, 269*, 2205–2213.

United Kingdom Department of Health. (2003). *The health survey for England – 2003.* Online publication at: http://www.dh.gov.uk/PublicationsAndStatistics/ PublishedSurvey/HealthSurveyForEngland/HealthSurveyResults/fs/en.

van der Merwe, M.-T., & Pepper, M. S. (2006). Obesity in South Africa. *Obesity Reviews, 7*, 315–322.

Varga, C. A. (1997). Sexual decision-making and negotiation in the midst of AIDS: Youth in KwaZulu-Natal, South Africa. *Health Transition Review, 7*, 45–67.

Voracek, M., & Fisher, M. L. (2002). Shapely centrefolds? Temporal change in body measures: Trend analysis. *British Medical Journal, 325*, 1447–1448.

Voracek, M., & Fisher, M. L. (2006). Success is all in the measures: Androgenousness, curvaceousness, and starring frequencies in adult media actresses. *Archives of Sexual Behavior, 35*, 297–304.

Weeden, J., & Sabini, J. (2005). Physical attractiveness and health in Western societies: A review. *Psychological Bulletin, 131*, 635–653.

Wetsman, A., & Marlowe, F. (1999). How universal are preferences for female waist-to-hip ratios? Evidence from the Hadza of Tanzania. *Evolution and Human Behaviour, 20*, 219–228.

Willet, W. C., Manson, J. E., Stampfer, M. J., Colditz, G. A., Rosner, B., Speizer, F. E., et al. (1995). Weight, weight change and coronary heart disease in women: Risk within the 'normal' weight range. *Journal of the American Medical Association, 273*, 461–465.

Wilson, J. M. B., Tripp, D. A., & Boland, F. J. (2005). The relative contributions of waist-to-hip ratio and body mass index to judgements of attractiveness. *Sexualities, Evolution and Gender, 7*, 245–267.

Woods, L. E. P. (2006). Obesity, waist-hip ratio and hunter-gatherers. *BJOG: An International Journal of Obstetrics and Gynaecology, 113*, 1110–1116.

Yarmouk, U. (2000). The effect of presentation modality on judgements of honesty and attractiveness. *Social Behavior and Personality, 28*, 269–278.

Yu, D. W., & Shepard, G. H. (1998). Is beauty in the eye of the beholder? *Nature, 396*, 321–322.

Part IV

Theory Development:
Evolutionary Perspectives

8
The Shaping of Women's Bodies: Men's Choice of Fertility or Heat Stress Avoidance?

Dorothy Einon

Beauty matters (Buss, 2004; Miller, 2001). We know from what men tell us, from the images they use when masturbating and from investigations of what men find attractive (Barber, 1995; Buss, 1994; Johnson & Franklin, 1993; Jones, 1995; Singh & Young, 1995; van den Berghe & Frost, 1986) that certain parts of women's bodies both aesthetically please, and sexually arouse, men. Men like beautiful, young women and, given a choice (Gladue & Delany, 1990), or when engaging in fantasy (Barclay, 1973), men prefer a pretty, young woman. They like to fall in love (Fisher, 1992; Jankowiak, 1995; Sprecher et al., 1994) and would order up humour, intelligence, good work habits, shared values, loyalty, and fidelity (Buss, 1989), but given an option, prefer such things (or a goodly share of them) in a pretty package. Not only are pretty women more likely to arouse men sexually, they are considered more competent, employable, generous, helpful, and intelligent (Eagly, Ashmore, Makhijani & Longo, 1991). Men gain status by the beauty of their partner (Sigall & Landy, 1973) in much the same way they do from the clothes they wear and the cars they drive.

Men the world over prefer youthful women with child-like, symmetrical faces (Johnson & Franklin, 1993). They like women with low waist-to-hip ratios (Singh, 1993), conspicuous breasts (Morris, 1967; Singh & Young, 1995), lighter skin tones (van den Berghe & Frost, 1986), and smaller feet (Barber, 1995). They prefer rounded bottoms (and in some cultures like them big; Morris, 1967) and long, slim legs (Swami, Einon, & Furnham, 2006). The ways women dress, move, and ornament themselves exaggerate these features (Miller, 2001). Men also like slim women (Tovée & Cornelisson, 1999), but just how slim is a bit of a moveable concept (Furnham & Alibhai, 1983; Swami, 2005). Grossly asymmetric bodies and faces with obvious disfigurements are disliked (Gangestad

& Thornhill, 1997), as is pockmarked, blotched, or spotty skin (Ford & Beach, 1951). While there is little doubt about men's choices (Ford & Beach, 1951), showing that men like young and pretty women does no more than state the obvious: the question is why.

Two classes of explanation

One class of explanation is that the things men find beautiful are themselves the product of evolution (Barber, 1995; Buss, 2004; Singh, 1993), or as Symons (1995) put it, 'Beauty is in the adaptations of the beholder.' In most mammals, the availability of a female for mating is a reliable guide to the availability of ova for fertilizing. This is not the case in humans. The theory of sexual selection suggests men who select women more likely to be ovulating and/or able to raise viable children had a selective advantage over those unable to make this choice (Symons, 1995), and that the aspects that men find beautiful were in the past (and remain) the best predictors of women's fertility (Singh, 1993; Symons, 1995). In choosing beauty, men also choose women who are potentially fertile, neither pregnant nor lactating, have no current health problems (nor a history of such problems) or disorders that lower fertility (Buss, 2004; Singh, 1993; Symons, 1995). If men invested more (or sooner) in women exhibiting the preferred traits, women possessing those traits would raise more children like themselves. In consequence, the desired traits would occur more frequently (and/or more extremely) in subsequent generations of women, and (if sons followed in their father's footsteps) the preference for such traits would increase in subsequent generations of men. In short, *women have breasts because men have invested more often in women with breasts, and thus women with breasts have had greater reproductive success* (RS).

A second class of explanation posits that the favoured attribute exists because of functional reasons quite unconnected with mate choice, and the aesthetic preference for gender-specific versions of an attribute reflect the observation that there are differences between men and women (Jabonski & Chaplin, 2000; van den Berghe & Frost, 1986). Men like how women look because this is the way women *are* and/or these are the characteristics men use to detect and verify the person before them is a woman, much as courtship rituals in birds act to verify the sex and species of potential partners. As in birds, stimuli that provide verification for men also induce sexual arousal. If a dimorphic characteristic directly enhances women's RS by improving metabolism (van den Berghe & Frost, 1986), or increasing the viability of pregnancy (Wolfenson, Roth,

& Meidan, 2000) or lactation (Lublin & Wolfenson, 1996), men will, in choosing 'characteristic women,' choose more fertile women; but sexual selection is not the basis for the development of the dimorphism. So, *women have breasts because breasts directly enhance women's RS* (e.g., by increasing surface area and reducing the harmful effects of heat stress to ova and embryos). Men like breasts because they help verify that this is a woman.

Visual stimuli play a major role in men's sexual arousal (Przbyla & Byrne, 1984). Areas of the brain associated with reward and the anticipation of reward are activated when men watch erotica (Karama et al., 2002). Hollis and colleagues (1997) have shown that if a visual stimulus predicts the presentation of a sexually receptive female, it becomes a conditioned stimulus (CS) for a set of responses that prepare male fish for mating. When such a CS is presented, conditioned males court sooner and in consequence father more offspring (Hollis, Pharr, Dumas, Britton, & Field, 1997). Similarly if a slide showing something neutral (such as a pile of pennies) predicts the onset of a sexually arousing film, both men and women become aroused at the sight of the pennies (Plaud & Martini, 1999), even when the neutral stimulus is presented subliminally (Hoffman, Janssen, & Turner, 2004). Both men and women show more arousal when the neutral stimuli have biological significance (Hoffman et al., 2004). By such means the arousal potential of attributes that are most characteristic of women (however selected) could prepare a man for sexual activity and, by that preparation, enhance RS.

Sexual selection

According to Miller (2000: 228), 'The manifest sexual appeal of female breasts and buttocks... seems subjectively obvious to all heterosexual male humans, and obviously is good evidence for these traits having arisen through male mate choice.' In species after species (and especially amongst birds and insects), the female is unadorned while the male is adorned in flamboyant hues that serve no apparent purpose: a comparison between the tails of peacock and peahen is but one (albeit extreme) example. Darwin (1871) distinguished between the competition between males for access to females (*intrasexual competition*) and *intersexual selection* or preferential mate choice. Two stags locked in combat are the classic example of the former; the peahen's purported preference for the peacock's fancy tail the latter. When Symons (1995) claims that 'Beauty is in the adaptations of the beholder,' it is intersexual selection that is assumed.

The evidence that males compete is well-supported (Clutton-Brock & Parker, 1995), but evidence that females systematically choose the 'best available male' is less reliable (Cronin, 1991; Small, 1993). Although women are more likely to consider 'good financial prospects' an important aspect of a potential mate (Buss, 1989), none of the societies studied considered this attribute indispensable (Buss, 1994), and in societies which allow polygamy the correlation between a man's wealth and the number of his wives is usually less than 0.4 (Strassmann, 2003).

The presence of a dimorphism is not of itself evidence that a trait has arisen as a consequence of mate choice. Dimorphisms may reflect selection pressures that have nothing to do with either male competition or female choice. For example, although it is generally assumed that size dimorphism in mammals arose as a consequence of mate choice (Alexander, Hoodland, & Howard, 1979), a viable functional alternative exists (Martin, Willner, & Dettling, 1994). Small females not only breed at an earlier age, they are less susceptible to heat stress which impairs oocyte development (Edwards & Hansen, 1997), conception (al-Katanani, Paula-Lopes, & Hansen, 2002; Edwards & Hansen, 1997; Short, 1984) and the viability of pregnancy. Heat gain is a function of volume, heat loss a function of surface area, so larger bodies retain more heat than smaller ones and larger bodies are thus more susceptible to heat stress (Aiello, 1992; Lewin, 1998). In species exposed to high ambient temperatures *smaller* females are likely to have more viable pregnancies: for males it is the larger animals with more fighting prowess that are likely to have reproductive success. There are perfectly adequate functional explanations for size dimorphism that do not rely on female choice. The correlation between body dimorphism and polygamy (Alexander et al., 1979) occurs because animals living in the open tend (for reasons that have nothing to do with mate choice) to be physically larger.

While simultaneous choice is a viable means of selecting a partner, sequential choice is unreliable. Where males display together (as grouse in a lek do), it is conceivable that females select on the basis of a male's display (although the evidence they do is not entirely convincing; Cronin, 1991). But it is very unlikely that most animals have the cognitive capacity to pick the best male by moving from territory to territory comparing the fine detail of one male with the memory of those seen previously. Logically, if the healthiest males win battles for access to, or protection of, the best territory, choosing a good territory and mating with the holder is likely to be a better way of ensuring a healthy and genetically superior mate than remembering the precise length of tail feathers or the size of a horn. Most passerine birds are territorial, notionally monogamous, and sexually dimorphic, suggesting their dimorphisms arise as a consequence of male competition for territory rather than mate choice (Partridge & Halliday, 1984). Similarly, the selection pressure that produced elaborate ornamentation in peacocks have more to do with the role of the tail in male competition (Cronin, 1991; Partridge & Halliday, 1984; Searcy, 1982) than female choice.

The ornamentations and dimorphisms of mammals tend to be characteristics such as large teeth and horns that give obvious advantages during fighting. While there is no question that male mammals compete (Clutton-Brock & Parker, 1995; Trivers, 1981), the evidence that female mammals systematically choose superior males is weak. When observed at feeding stations, female primates mate with dominant males, but away from feeding stations they mate with all the males they meet, especially males new to an area (Small, 1993). Studies of female promiscuity in monogamous birds (Birkhead, 2000), primates (Fietz, 2003; Stacey, 1982) and in those primates that form short-term consort relationships (Gagneux, Woodruff, & Boesch, 1997), reinforce suggestions that females rarely mate with a single male.

Although there is direct evidence of female choice in birds (Andersson, 1982; Burley, 1988), the choices made (widow birds choose the longest tails, zebra finches red plastic leg-rings) involve colours and characteristics females use to identify males during courtship displays (Cronin, 1991). The best examples of 'female choice' involve birds and insects that have elaborate courtship rituals, reinforcing suggestions that females are choosing the correct display for their species rather than a superior male (Cronin, 1991). As Partridge and Halliday (1984) conclude, evidence that females choose their mates is 'slight or non-existent.'

With few exceptions, females invest more in raising offspring than males and one would expect them to be more selective about their mates. Given that evidence of systematic female choice is weak, we must treat with caution claims that male preferences have shaped women's bodies (Miller, 2001). Before accepting that beauty is in the adaptations of the beholder (Symons, 1995), we must first establish that:

1. A particular claim has a basis in logic;
2. There is a viable route for its evolution, and;
3. There is no viable functional explanation for the characteristic 'of choice.'

The logic of choice for men

The need to invest

Once pregnant, a female primate is unlikely to conceive again for a number of years, while the father of her baby can father another offspring within days. Men are not exceptions to this rule. Why should men who are reported to often 'waste' sperm in nocturnal emissions and masturbation (Kinsey, Pomeroy, & Martin, 1948; Ellison Rodgers, 2002; Wellings et al., 1994) be choosier about women's youth and looks than women are about men's (Buss, 1989)? A man's rate of ejaculation (by whatever means) is related to the amount of sperm he produces; when he has more sperm, he masturbates and copulates more often (Baker & Bellis, 1995). If he does not masturbate or copulate, he is likely to expel sperm through spontaneous emissions during sleep (Baker & Bellis, 1995). This regular pattern of sperm emission ensures males inseminate females with fresh and more viable sperm (Birkhead, 2000). So the first question of logic is: why, if males need to 'clear the system' every few days, are they averse to clearing it with less than optimal females? The probability of viable fatherhood may be miniscule: but it is higher than it is for masturbation or nocturnal emission.

The usual answer is that men invest in children over a number of years and selection pressures have worked in favour of long- rather than short-term commitments. That is, in history, men who made long-term commitments raised more offspring, and if those commitments were made to young and healthy women, they had even greater RS. The underlying assumption here is that, like birds (Burley & Johnson, 2002; Møller, 2003), women cannot rear children successfully without the direct help of men (Marlowe, 2000). But is this necessarily true? Male mammals rarely provide a measurable amount of paternal care, even in socially monogamous lineages (Clutton-Brock, 1991; Komers & Brotherton, 1997). Whitten (1987) classifies human fathers as affiliation rather than intensive carers. Even the most solicitous human fathers spend less than 14 per cent of their time in contact with their children. In hunter-gatherer societies, men provide less than half of all food consumed (Hawkes, 1990, 1991; Knight, 1995).

Unlike other mammals, humans divide their labours. In hunter-gather societies, men hunt big game and women gather food. Because hunting is less reliable than gathering (men do not hunt everyday and over 90 per cent of hunts are unsuccessful), women provide about 60 per cent of the calorific needs of the family (Hawkes, 1991; Hawkes et al., 1998). Table 8.1 is based on Murdock's (1967) *Ethnographic atlas*, which

Table 8.1 The number of societies in which jobs are assigned solely to men or women, or carried out by both, based on the *Ethnographic Atlas* of Murcock (1967).

	Men's work	Women's work	Joint work[a]	% work carried out by men
Childcare[b]			0–4 %	
Daily/weekly food procurement				
Hunting large game	200	0	14	96.6
Hunting small game	128	2	18	98.6
Fishing	98	4	56	79.7
Tending animals/dairying	76	57	33	66.4
Planting, tending and harvesting	41	126	120	35.19
Gathering foodstuffs	29	162	69	28.2
Daily food preparation				
Cooking/preparing food	15	298	134	18.8
Gather water or fuel	29	208	42	17.9
Tending fire	18	62	53	18.0
Duties associated with food procurement[c]				
Clearing and preparing land	73	13	44	73.1
Burden bearing	12	57	59	32.8
Household duties (day-to-day)				
Mining and lumbering	139	9	8	91.7
House and shelter building	100	36	73	67.5
Making household objects	54	220	47	24.3
Making clothing	68	267	64	25.1
Making leather goods	60	71	25	46.8
Status and ceremony				
Body decoration	16	20	80	48.3
Making ornament	24	18	49	28.7
Weapon-making	121	0	1	99.7
Carving and ceremonial	285	24	24	92.6
Metal work	78	0	0	100
Making musical instruments	45	1	1	95.7

[a] Assumes that men carry out 50 per cent of all joint work
[b] Based on Whitten (1987)
[c] Not daily

collates the rules and norms of human societies including the work roles of men and women. As Table 8.1 shows, apart from hunting and herding, in most societies women carry out most of the daily food collection, production, and preparation. Similarly, although land clearing and house building are often men's work, tending crops, making household objects, and clothing are women's work, as is child care, water and fuel collection, and the tending of fires. While women carry out most of the tasks needed for daily survival, men engage in tasks associated with status and showing off: big-game hunting, weapon-making, making musical instruments, and carving (Hawkes, 1991). There is little evidence here that men's contribution is vital to the raising of children.

A woman exclusively breast-feeding a 1-year-old child needs about 800 extra calories per day, an active 2-year-old roughly 1100 calories a day. In brief, each year of age adds another 100 calories (Pollard, 1994). In modern Western societies, parents provision children into young adulthood, but this is (in evolutionary terms) a recent phenomenon. By 5 years of age, children in hunter-gather societies provide around 50 per cent of their own calorific needs (Howell, 1979) and girls help care for younger siblings. An active woman requires around 2700 calories, an active man around 3100 calories. Table 8.2 shows the consequences, for women and children living as hunter-gathers, of pooling resource with a man. As the table shows, far from helping women feed their children, men are often a net drain of family resources. Even when they

Table 8.2   The calories that men and women provide for their families: The disadvantages of male investment to women. The table shows the number of calories a woman must collect to provide food for herself and her children (single) or 60 per cent of the food for her family (married). For calorific needs of individuals, see text.

	Single	Married	Daily loss/gain by marriage
Woman	2700	3480	*Loss* 780 calories
Man	3100	2320	*Gain* 780 calories
Woman + breast-fed 1-year-old	3500	3960	*Loss* 460 calories
Woman + weaned 2-year-old	2800	4140	*Loss* 340 calories
Woman + weaned 3-year-old	3900	4200	*Loss* 300 calories
Woman + 4-year-old	4000	4260	*Loss* 260 calories
Woman + 5-year-old	3400	3900	*Loss* 500 calories
Woman + children 5- and 1-year(s)-old	4200	4380	*Gain* 180 calories
Woman + children 6- and 2-years-old	4550	4590	*Gain* 40 calories
Woman + children, 11-, 7- and 3-years-old[a]	4900	4740	*Loss* 160 caloris

[a] Assumes 11-year-old provides 90 per cent of their own food, and 7-year-old 60 per cent

contribute, their input is small. In practice, the game men bring home is invariably shared with all members of the society (Knight, 1995), and young unmarried men hunt more than older married men do (Hawkes, 1990, 1991).

Until recently, it was extremely difficult for women in agricultural and industrial societies to raise children without male help (Geary, 2000; Laslett, 1980; Levine & Wrighton, 1980; Rose, 1986), as it sometimes is in hunter-gatherer societies (Hill & Hurtado, 1996). But this has more to do with the laws and customs of the society, women's access to resources, the availability of work, and the level of women's wages, than the ability of women to provide for children. Women need men to help them raise children because society is constructed to ensure this. Economic surveys in Guatemala, Ghana and India show that the nutritional level of families does not rise in line with the father's income; rather, it increases in line with the mother's (Bruce, 1989). In many societies, women turn to grandmothers and other female relatives, rather than fathers, for help (Lerner & Mikula, 1994; Sear, Mace, & McGregor, 2000), as perhaps they always have (Euler & Weizel, 1996; Hawkes et al., 1998).

By marrying, a man can engage in the luxury of jobs that bring status (big-game hunting, carving and making weapons; see Table 8.1), which in turn attract women (Hawkes, 1990, 1991). If men make commitments in order to have the leisure to carry out tasks that impress other men (Sigall & Landy, 1973) and thus gain access to women (Chagnon, 1992; Hawkes, 1990, 1991; Kaplan & Hill, 1985), why choose young women? Do they perhaps gain status (Hawkes, 1991; Sigall & Landy, 1973)?

In many societies, illegitimate children and those without fathers are neglected, abandoned or killed (Blurton Jones, 1989; Hill & Kaplan, 1988; Hill & Hurtado, 1996; Laslett, 1980), as in some societies are the women who bear such children (Baker, Gregware, & Cassidy, 1999; Gilmore, 1987; Schneider, 1971; United Nations, 2002). Church records suggest that, for many years, less that 2 per cent of British illegitimate children survived (Levine & Wrighton, 1980). Apart from his legitimate children, a man's offspring by a married (and thus older) lover are the most viable. It is difficult to see, in this context, how a preference for youth and beauty evolved. If women did not gain from male investment, and few children illegitimate survived to breed, what drove the changes?

The absence of oestrus signals

The average woman takes just over six menstrual cycles to conceive (Bongaarts & Potter, 1983), is infertile during the 9 months of pregnancy and would not, traditionally, have been fertile while lactating

(Strassmann, 2003). While other primates indicate upcoming ovulation with specific signals (including olfactory signals and swellings of the vulva), sexual receptivity (accepting males) and sexual proceptivity (seeking males and sexually presenting to them), women fail to signal that they are about to ovulate, show no increase in sexual interest, nor make more frequent or persistent sexual invitations at this time. The pattern of sexual swellings in primates and the precise tissue involved vary enormously. For the majority, sexual swellings arise in the days before the onset of ovulation and rapidly subside once ovulation has occurred. In these species, signals rarely amount to more than a slight swelling and pinking of the vulva, but in many social Old World[1] primates (including chimpanzees and baboons) swellings are large, deep red, and highly conspicuous. Early in the menstrual cycle, the skin around the vulva (and sometimes the anus) begins to swell reaching a maxima in the days (or in the chimpanzee, weeks) before ovulation. Females are typically sexually receptive and proactive whenever swellings are present and many have hourly rates of copulation while their swellings are maximal (Hrdy & Whitten, 1987; Sillen-Tulberg, & Møller, 1993).

There are other primates that do not mark ovulation (Hrdy & Whitten, 1987; Sillen-Tulberg, & Møller, 1993), although most show changes in receptivity and proceptivity (Hrdy & Whitten, 1987). Other primates produce deceptive signals. Although only fertile for 7 per cent of the menstrual cycle, Bonobo chimpanzees have sexual swellings for between 25–40 per cent of the menstrual cycle, the common chimpanzee slightly less. While they have swellings, chimpanzees (of both kinds) mate almost once an hour (Takahata, Ihobe, & Idani, 1996). They also have sexual swellings during pregnancy and lactation (i.e., when infertile) and are sexually active (albeit less active) when swellings are small or absent (Hrdy & Whitten, 1987). Takahata et al. (1996) calculate that over the entire 5-year inter-birth interval, females copulate once ever 0.4 hours, which suggests that for a male chimpanzee, the odds of impregnating a female at any given copulation are rather lower than a man's. Unlike men, chimpanzees are not selective about how their mates look, nor do they make long-term investments.

Women may not signal the day of fertility, but they signal the month by menstruation (Strassmann, 1996, 1997, 2003). Menstruation indicates that a woman is in the fertile phase of her reproductive cycle (which typically lasts for about 6 months; Bongaarts & Potter, 1983). Many societies have myths and rituals that serve to draw attention to those women who are currently menstruating (Knight, 1995; Shuttle & Redgrove, 1978; Strassmann, 1996, 1997). As the Roman Historian Pliny the Elder (in Beagon, 2005) wrote:

> ... crops touched by it [menstruating women] become barren, grafts die, seeds in gardens are dried up, the fruits of trees fall off, the bright surface of mirrors in which it is merely reflected are dimmed, the edges of steel and the gleam of ivory are dulled, hives of bees die, even bronze and iron are at once seized by rust and a horrible smell fills the air.

In Italy, the belief that menstrual blood caused fruit trees to wither persisted until recent times, as did the French belief that menstruating women would sour the wine (Knight, 1995; Shuttle & Redgrove, 1978). Nor are such myths confined to those without education: in 1878, the *British Medical Journal* published letters from doctors suggesting women should not cure hams if it was their 'time of the month.' Such practices serve to draw men's attention to those women in society who are menstruating (Knight, 1995; Shuttle & Redgrove, 1978, Strassmann, 1996) and who will be fertile within a few days of the offset of menstruation. Thus, menstruation – as Strassmann (1996) suggests – provide honest signals of fertility to the entire society.

During menstruation, women lose blood together with the two superficial layers of the womb lining known as the *zona funcionalis* of the endometrium. In the first half of the menstrual cycle, the hormone ostrodial stimulates the growth of the zona funcionalis and this continues to grow until ovulation. After ovulation, progesterone prepares the endometrium for pregnancy. If conception does not occur, the endometrium sloughs 14 days after ovulation, causing the familiar menstrual bleed and the release of a third hormone, prostoglandin. It is this last hormone (or, more correctly, hormones) that dictates the degree and duration of the menstrual bleed and also inhibits the clotting of menstrual blood. A simple adjustment to prostoglandins causes periods to be slight or heavy (Heap & Flint, 1972; Short, 1984). Most primates do not menstruate externally: the waste products produced by the breakdown of their endometrium are reabsorbed.

Sexually active females risk infection from seminal fluid-born pathogens. Profet (1993) suggests that external menstruation serves to flush out the system. She suggests that if females mate relatively infrequently and with very few different males, the balance between the cost of losing blood and the cost of getting rid of pathogens is tipped towards conserving blood, and these species do not menstruate. If females mate more often (and with more males), the scales are tipped towards cleaning out the system. Of the 23 species of Old World primate in which external menstruation has been observed, 22 live in multi-male promiscuous mating groups (Hrdy & Whitten, 1987). Women are the exception to this rule: while on a primate scale they are neither promiscuous nor sexually very active (Hrdy & Whitten, 1987), their menstruation is heavier than that of any other primate.

If women were to mark ovulation with sexual swellings (swellings are incompatible with bipedal locomotion), they would need a signal which attracted males. Menstrual blood is the right colour and appears in the right place. The increase in the volume of menstrual bleeding suggests it serves as a signal to women's fertility, not at the time of fertility (for this was impossible) but a couple of weeks before ovulation. If men miss the signal, society ensures the information is broadcast (Strassmann, 2003); which begs the question of why, if menstruation provided a reliable signal of women's upcoming fertility, men use such unreliable signals for the selection of potentially fertile women, as smaller feet (Barber, 1995), certain body mass indices (Tovée & Cornelisson, 1999) or waist-hip ratios of less than 0.80 (Singh, 1993)?

A viable route for evolution

Men's attraction to breasts

Men like breasts, and from the point of view of fertility, this is a puzzle. For most mammals (including all other primates) breasts have one function: to feed babies. They develop as lactation is required and disappear after weaning. Since many primates (including all the great apes) are infertile while lactating, breasts are a perfect signal of infertility. It is difficult (if not impossible) to construct an evolutionary story of how breasts evolved from the perfect infertility signals they are in other primates to become predictors of fertility in humans. Males choosing females with flat chests would always have had greater RS than those choosing breasts. A preference for large breasts is equally puzzling. Breasts increase in size at the onset of pregnancy and again when they fill with milk. By selecting big-breasted women, a man biases his choice towards infertile women. Women's breasts store fat, but breast fat is not used to fuel pregnancy or lactation (Pond, Mattacks, Calder, & Evans, 1993). As in other primates, 'fertility fuel' is stored on the thighs, hips, and buttocks. In spite of the predictive value of fat stored on the thighs, there is no indication in the literature (or men's 'top-shelf' magazines) that men prefer fat thighs to big breasts. If selecting fertile women, clearly they should.

Men's attraction to youth

In recent decades, families and society in the West have had less control over the sexual behaviour of young people then they had in previous centuries. In consequence, the majority of women lose their virginity at (or very close to) the completion of puberty (Wellings et al., 1994). It is hard to imagine that, without the constraints imposed by their elders (Schneider, 1971), most young people would ever have voluntarily delayed the onset of sexual activity for several years. If the age gap between husbands and wives is more than 2 years, men must retain their virginity (or drastically curb their sexual activity) for longer than women; logically, there is little point in men waiting to do at 30 what they could have done at 17.

Although surveys suggest that women prefer older men and men prefer younger women (Buss, 1989), when women are free to choose their husbands (as they have been in Northern Europe for many generations (Goody, 1983), relationships are formed between couples of similar post-pubertal age. British marriage statistics for 1992 (Office of Population Census and Statistics, 1992) set the scene: the mean age difference between *all* brides and grooms in 1991 was just 2.49 years. From 1837, when British records began, until 1992, there is not a single year in which the average age gap between marriage partners is more than 3 years. In 1992, there was a difference of 1.99 years on first marriage. Only 3.8 per cent of women under 30 marry men more than 10 years older, only 0.7 per cent of men more than 15 years older. Goody (1983) suggests such age gaps have been typical of Northern Europe over many generations. If marriage is arranged by families, age gaps are often larger (Goody, 1983).

The adaptive significance of late marriage for men is unclear: labouring like fighting and hunting are young men's games and women's fertility declines very little until she reaches her early 40s (Baker & Bellis, 1995). Survival patterns for extinct and modern hunter-gatherers (Meindl, 1992) suggest that less than half of all 20-year-olds lived to 40, less than a quarter to 50. Women live longer than men. Unless older men control access to wealth and work, a father's youth is likely to have more influence on RS than a wife's age. It was only with the advent of agriculture that a man's age became indicative of wealth – and even here it is only predictive for property-owners and skilled and professional workers who require years of training. For the majority – as for hunter-gathers – when provisioning children, youth is an advantage in a man. Given the historically low life expectancy of men and women (Meindl, 1992), the low viability of illegitimate children, and the low level of provisioning of children by men, a married woman with children old enough to help provision his baby might be the better choice.

Men's attraction to youthful faces and feet

It is most unlikely that the 'baby' aspect of women's faces (Jones, 1995) or feet (Barber, 1995) gives an accurate guide to either youth or fertility. The ratio between brow-nose and nose-chin is fixed at puberty, and although it changes at the extremes of the age distribution, those changes are in the wrong direction for fertility. Those with the most 'child-like' faces are obviously children, closely followed by women old enough to have lost their back teeth, plump lips and/or the density of their jaw bones. Both Fessler and associates (Fessler et al., 2005) and Barber (1995) suggests women have smaller feet because of a history of inter-sexual selection by men for youthful feet. Although foot size both increases very slightly with age (Chantelau & Gede, 2002) and parity (Block, Hess, Timpano, & Serlo, 1985), choosing small feet is unlikely to be advantageous because women with small feet are more likely to have Caesarean sections (Frame, Moore, Peters, & Hall, 1985; van Bogaert, 1999). In as much as a Caesarean section is indicative of birth complications (Mackenzie, Cooke, and Annan, 2003), small feet are likely to have been associated with higher rates of mortality for both child and mother.

Viable alternatives to explanations based on mate choice

Skin colour

Women have lighter skin tones than men (van den Berghe & Frost, 1986), and in many cultures men prefer women with paler skin. The lighter the skin the more vitamin D is produced and the more heat is reflected; the darker the more melanin and the greater the protection from ultraviolet light. Vitamin D is needed during pregnancy and lactation; overheating causes miscarriage and birth defects (Lublin & Wolfenson, 1996; Upfold et al., 1989; Wolfenson, Roth, & Meidan, 2000). There is thus a perfectly viable explanation of why women have lighter skin than men: light-skinned women had more viable pregnancies. Just as male birds choose females exhibiting characteristics of the species (Burley, 1988), men like women with lighter skin because lighter skin enhances recognition that 'this is a woman.'

Breasts

Breast growth is one of the first signs of puberty, and an increase in the size of the breasts one of the first signs of pregnancy. Many animals living in hot dry climates (as evolving humans did) have humps, trunks, big ears, long legs, and necks to help heat dissipation: camels, elephants, and giraffes are obvious examples. The generation of heat is a function of the body volume, its dissipation a function of the surface area. Any increase in body size decreases the ratio between the surface area and body mass, and makes heat dissipation more difficult. Bergman's rule, first published in 1847, states that if a species is geographically widespread, those that live in the warmer parts of the range have smaller bodies. Allen's rule, first published in 1877, states that those in the warmest areas have the largest extremities (Lewin, 1998). Ruff (1994) suggests that if a large surface area relative to body mass facilitates heat loss, those in cold climates will tend to have a low ratio – a small surface area in relation to body mass – allowing for heat retention, while the opposite is true for those in hot climates. Thus, he predicts that peoples living in low latitudes will have narrow bodies with long limbs, and those in high latitudes wider bodies with shorter limbs. His prediction is supported by surveys of body proportions in 71 populations from different areas of the world. East African humans are tall, with relatively long limbs and short bodies; those in cold northern climates – Northern Europeans and American Plains Indians – have relatively massive bodies and short limbs (Aiello, 1992; Holliday & Fallesetti, 1995). Ruff (1994) further suggests that selection for effectiveness in carrying light loads on the back in hot climates (as women with babies frequently do) is likely to have been implicated in the evolution of human body proportions.

Maximising curves, like limb-lengthening and body-narrowing, presents a larger surface for heat loss. Consistent with this, African women have more curves than those whose ancestors lived in colder climates: East Africans have rounded buttocks, the women of the Kalahari Desert massive steatopygic buttocks (Coon, 1971) and Europeans and Orientals flatter buttocks. Breast size varies along similar lines.

Table 8.3 shows the median bra cup sizes (an indication of breast size) of 100 students attending lectures at a North London university. The first 25 students from each racial group were approached as they left lectures and asked the size and cup of their bra. For each racial group bra size ranged from 30–36, with a median of 34. Women of Southeast Asian origin (whose ancestors spent much of their history in sub-artic regions; Cavalli-Sforza & Cavalli-Sforza, 1995) had significantly smaller breasts

Table 8.3 The cup size of 100 students of different ethnic origin. If the measurement over the breasts is 2 inches more than that the measurement below the breasts, women take an A cup, if it is 4 inches more a B cup, if six inches more a C cup, eight inches more a D, cup, ten inches more an E cup, and twelve inches more a F cup. The median bra size for women in all four groups was 34, with a range between 30 and 38.

Cup size	African	South Asian	European	Southeast Asian
A	0	3	2	10
B	5	9	10	9
C	8	3	7	0
D	8	6	6	0
E	2	0	2	0
F	2	0	2	0

than the other three groups; those of African origin had significantly larger breasts than the other three groups.

It is well established that heat stress impairs oocyte development (Edwards & Hanson, 1997) and conception (al-Katanani & Hansen, 2002; al-Katanani, Paula-Lopes, & Hansen, 2002; Edwards & Hansen, 1997). It also reduces the viability of pregnancy (al-Katanani et al., 2002; Clay, Randall, Prather, & Rucker, 2006; Dutt, 1963; Roth et al., 2001; Wolfenson, Roth, & Meidan, 2000) and impairs lactation (Lublin & Wolfenson, 1996). In women, a prolonged fever of more than 104° Fahrenheit can produce foetal abnormalities including alterations in muscle tone, mental retardation, ear, eye, and facial abnormalities (Pollard, 1994). In Hong Kong (Short, 1984) and in southern areas of the United States (Huntingdon, 1938), the rate of confirmed pregnancy dips in the hottest season. Heat stress in early pregnancy causes miscarriage in sheep (Dutt, 1963) and cattle (Wolfenson et al., 2000), brain damage in guinea pigs (Upfold et al., 1989), alters the synthesis and secretion of proteins (Putney et al., 1988), has detrimental effects on cardiovascular responses in late pregnancy (Walker, Hale, Fawcett, & Pratt, 1995) and maternal hormones and blood flow to both the reproductive organs and mammary glands (Lublin & Wolfenson, 1996). It is thus likely that women exposed to heat stress would have lower reproductive success.

Humans evolved in the hot dry climate of East Africa at a time when the rain forests had receded, leaving areas of scrub and savannah in which dietary resources were less densely distributed (Isbell & Young,

1996). Because humans are rarely entirely still, they have more heat to dissipate than most mammals who spend time in the open. Grazing cattle move their jaws and occasionally take a few steps, humans gathering food in open countryside talk, laugh, dig, pull, stretch, crouch, carry, run after children, put down objects, and pick them up again. They then carry food home rather than eat it where they find it as other mammals do. It is metabolic heat generated by such movements which most influences core body temperature. The constant muscle activity of humans increases their metabolic rate and in principle makes humans more susceptible to over-heating. In addition to carrying food hunter-gathers also carry water and firewood back to their home base (Murdock, 1967). They are thus unlikely to remain in the shade throughout the day. Much of this carrying is women's work (see Table 8.1) and women also carry small children and babies. While men's testes move outside the body cavity shortly before birth (so sperm develop in the relative cool) women's ovaries and womb must remain within the body cavity. Not only is women's reproduction effort more likely to be undermined by heat stress, their role within society ensures they are more likely to be exposed to heat than men. None the less, humans are amongst the few mammals able to remain fairly active in the midday sun (Aiello, 1992; Hanna & Brown, 1979). They achieve this by efficient cooling mechanisms that stop the core of the body from overheating, and adaptations, which enhance heat loss from the body surface and reduce heat absorption. The upright stance of humans allows more efficient walking (Rodman & McHenry, 1980) between food sources and more efficient thermoregulation while exposed to the sun (Wheeler, 1994).

It is suggested here that the curves and bumps of women's bodies are mechanisms which enhance heat loss – especially in early pregnancy – directly influencing women's reproductive success. All mammals deposit fat around internal organs and in a dozen or so fat depots. These include the buttocks and upper leg, the upper back, the chest, and forearm. The bigger the animal the larger the proportion of fat stores held in external depots (Pond et al., 1993). Areas of fat (such as the camel's hump) increase the body surface more than body volume and this helps to dissipate heat. The humps of camels develop from the back fat depot, the breasts of humans from the chest fat depots. Humps or lumps on the chest are less efficient heat loss mechanisms in quadrupeds since dissipated heat would be trapped under the body (Wheeler, 1994) – which is perhaps why it is the fat deposits of the back that have expanded in other plain living species (Pond et al., 1993). The fat distribution of women who store fat on the hips, thighs, breast, and bottom (Bailey &

Katch, 1981) gives a bigger surface-to-volume ratio than the typical male pattern of storing fat on the chest and abdomen.

Bipedal locomotion increases the efficiency of heat loss mechanisms arising from the chest fat depots (Wheeler, 1994). As air flows upwards from the ground to the cooler atmosphere it passes along the surface of the human abdomen and chest and across the buttocks and back. Sweating enhances this heat loss (evaporation of sweat lowers the surface temperature of the skin), and the upward flow of air increases the efficiency of sweating (Wheeler, 1994). Adding curved buttocks to one side of the body and curved breasts to the other increases the skin surface exposed to this air flow and allows a larger surface for the evaporation of sweat. Together these enhance heat dissipation in women. Table 8.4 shows the increase in the surface area of the torso of a slim woman produced by adding breasts of four different sizes. As can be seen in the table, breasts produced an increase in the surface area of the torso of between 9 per cent and 15 per cent.

Youthful feet

The obvious reason for women's smaller feet is that women carry body mass closer to the ground than men do, which makes them more stable and less likely to topple under forward locomotion (Pawłowski & Grabar-czyk, 2003). Birds also need to avoid toppling, which is why they have relatively larger feet than mammals. Injuries to the foot are a common source of infection (Trivers, 1981): the smaller the foot the less likely the injury. Because men carry weight higher in the body and throw stones and spears when under forward locomotion, they need a longer

Table 8.4 The area beneath the breast (attachment area), the surface area of the bra cup (cup area) and the percentage increase in skin surface (% increase) that is produced by adding breasts to the body of a slim woman.[a] The final column shows the increase in surface area produced by spreading the same volume of fat tissue across the front and rear of the torso.

Cup size	Attachment	Cup area	Difference	% increase	Surface area
A	190.0	409.0	219.0	9.1	.17
B	225.6	556.8	331.2	10.0	.21
C	266.8	699.5	432.7	13.1	.33
D	311.2	858.3	547.1	16.5	.37

[a] The body size used here was the mean surface area of the torso of five different women of slim build (English size 10–12)

foot. Women carry their weight below the waist, and so their feet can be smaller. Men like small feet because they are characteristic of women.

Youth

In most societies, gender defines friendships, work, those who share gossip, and acceptable relationships. It defines the places people can go, the clothes to be worn, the rooms to be entered, and acceptable behaviour. The aspects of women's faces that men find beautiful are almost invariably the same as those that are used to classify them by gender. Apparent age is such a cue. Women store more fat beneath the skin surface than men do (Pond et al., 1993)[2] and these fat stores include the face. The fat beneath the surface of women's faces makes the skin appear smooth and the face looks younger. Dress a 39-year-old woman as a man and she looks like a boy, dress a 30-year-old man as a woman and he looks middle aged. Youthful childlike faces are characteristic of women. In choosing a 'young' face, a man is more likely to choose a woman.

This chapter has critically examined the claim that women's beauty is 'in the adaptations of the beholder' (Symons, 1995): that their bodies have been shaped by male mate choice. It has examined the logic of such claims, the viability of their evolution, and the possibility that there are functional explanations for the characteristic 'of choice'. It is concluded that claims that women's bodies have been shaped by men's choices are logically flawed, that there is not always a viable path for the evolution of a characteristic, and that functional explanations exist for many of women's dimorphic characteristics. In particular, I have examined the possibility that the development of permanent breasts at puberty is one of a number of physical changes humans have undergone that reduces the dangers of heat stress (Aiello, 1992). Ruff (1994) has argued that a large surface area relative to body mass increases heat loss, while a small surface area relative to body mass reduces heat loss. In hot, dry climates (such as East and Central Africa) women are potentially vulnerable to heat stress because their gonads remain within the body cavity. For men, the overheating of sperm is circumvented by the descent of the testes into the scrotum. The necessity for the ova (and foetus) to remain within the body provides a selection pressures for women to remain smaller (Bergman's rule) and maximise the body surface in relation to body volume (Allen's rule), especially during the maturation of ova and the early stages of foetal development. Consistent with this increased breast volume and the visibility of blood vessels close to the surface of the breasts are amongst the earliest signs of human pregnancy and could serve this purpose.

Everything about a woman's shape – from her relatively long limbs to her rounded bottom, narrow waist, and breasts (Bailey & Katch, 1981) – serves to maximise the skin surface to body mass ratio. The relatively square figures of northern women with their flatter bottoms and broader bodies reflect a historic need to conserve heat. The curves of African women reflect their origin in hotter, dryer regions. The peoples of Southeast Asia arrived in Southeast Asia via the northern artic route (Cavalli-Sforza & Cavalli-Sforza, 1995) and their body shape reflects this. They have fewer curves than African women (see Table 8.3). They coped with the hot humid climate of Southeast Asia by remaining small (Ruff, 1994).

Beautiful women have curvier bodies, more obvious breasts, narrower waists, broader hips, rounded bottoms, and relatively longer limbs. Sometimes (but rarely), their beauty is a clue to fertility; invariably, it is an indication of gender. The characteristics that men find most beautiful about women are those aspects of their bodies that place them on the female side of every sexually dimorphic characteristic. He never knows exactly which women are fertile; he always knows they are women.

Why are men aroused by female characteristics?

Male mammals are attracted to females by a combination of circulating testosterone and the sexual signals and invitations that characterise oestrus in most species. Testosterone provides the potential for sexual activity; oestrus smells and/or swellings and the sexual invitations of the female rouse him to copulate. Like all other mammals, men have the potential for sexual activity (circulating testosterone), but they do not have the oestrus smells or sexual swellings that draw the male to the female. Nor do women seek out men when about to ovulate. A man is thus like the dog with testosterone in his bloodstream and no oestrus smells on the air. In principle, he ought not to be interested in sex; in practice he thinks about sex all the time. He does not need to wait for a whiff of a certain chemical before feeling arousal, because what arouses men is women. Not just the smell of aliphatic acids or the flash of an enlarged vulva but everything that differentiates women from men: youthful faces, breasts, small waist, shapely hips, longer legs, higher pitched voices, and small feet.

Men's arousal is more subdued than that produced by the oestrus smells that draw the tomcat to the queen, so men can turn down women's advances and keep arousal under control. This does not stop most men from watching the girls. What men lack in 'signal strength' they gain in pervasiveness. The signals that arouse men are around the next corner, across every street, jogging in the park, at work and at home. Women's breasts jiggle as they pass him on the stairs, their hips sway, and a little more leg is revealed. Women are everywhere he looks and if he wants to see a little more he can buy a magazine, click on the Internet or pay to watch women wiggling their naked bottoms on little tables: and men do these things on an industrial scale. The titillation of male arousal is big business. Yet on a primate scale of things, the average man has fewer sexual partners in a lifetime than a chimpanzee does in a month (Wellings et al., 1994; Takahata et al., 1996).

The characteristics men find attractive give little insight into men's *sexual behaviour*. When we look beyond the pleasures of sexual titillation it becomes abundantly clear that sexual engagement has little to do with 'what' men like and everything to do with 'who' they love. For most men, most of the time the characteristics of a potential partner (however superior) come a very poor second to ongoing relationships – as the poetry, literature, and songs men write make abundantly clear.

On the surface, nature dealt humans a difficult hand. Women lost oestrus, men the signals that lure them into sexual activity. The downside of this is that men and women are not driven to have sex at appropriate times and must find the time and place to safely engage in their rather drawn out encounters. In principle, they could fail to initiate sex. In practice, society ensures this rarely happens. It titillates with sexy gossip, sexy images, stories, and jokes. It hands down ribald songs and sexy myths, and songs, and stories of romantic love. It allows and forbids sex, making rules we obey or disobey but never fail to notice. It says when and where and with whom we should indulge our desires. It even tells us what we can and cannot do and advises us on variations. Societies do not always make the same rules or tell the same stories, what they share is the telling of stories and the making of rules. One way or another, every society ensures their members spend more time thinking about sex than any other living creature. Such thoughts create the slow-burn sexual desire that is characteristically human and allows us to control our sexuality and that of others; we make sexual choices away from the heat of sexual passion, and create rules that allow us to invest wisely, not only for ourselves but also for our children and grandchildren.

Because desire is created by couples and arousal slow and controlled, we are able to form exclusive sexual commitments even though living in social groups. We can sit next to another man's ovulating wife without trying to lure her into sex, and trust that others will act as we do when sitting beside our partner. People can cooperate and share tasks in ways that would be impossible if women awoke some mornings with an uncontrollable and untamed desire for sex, or men awoke with the irresistible lure of 'woman' wafting on the air, if the first whiff of sex drove all thought of co-operation from our minds.

Notes

1. Primates native to Africa, the Middle East and Asia, as apposed to New World primates that are native to Central and Southern America.
2. Fat stores are necessary to maintain pregnancy and lactation. If the stores drop too low women stop ovulating.

References

Aiello, L. (1992). Allometry and the analysis of size and shape in human evolution. *Journal of Human Evolution, 22*, 127–147.

Alexander, R. D., Hoodland, J. L., & Howard, R. D. (1979). Sexual dimorphisms and breeding systems in pinnepeds, ungulates, primates and humans. In N. A. Chagnon, & W. Irons (Eds.), *Evolutionary biology and human social behaviour*. North Scitutate: Duxbury Press.

al-Katanani, Y. M., & Hansen, P. J. (2002). Induced thermotolerance in bovine two cell embryos and the role of heat shock protein 70 in embryonic development. *Molecular Reproductive Development, 62*, 174–180.

al-Katanani, Y. M., Paula-Lopes, F. F., & Hansen, P. J. (2002). Effect of season and exposure to heat stress on the oocyte competence in Holstein cows. *Journal of Dairy Science, 85*, 390–396.

al-Katanani, Y. M., Drost, M., Monson, R. L., Rutledge, J. J., Krininger, III, C. E., Block, J., et al. (2002). Pregnancy rates following timed embryo transfer with fresh or vitrified in vitro produced embryos in lactating dairy cows under heat stress conditions. *Theriogenology, 58*, 171–182.

Andersson, M. (1982). Female choice selects for extreme tail length in a widowbird. *Nature, 302*, 456.

Bailey, R. C., & Katch, V. L. (1981). The effect of body size on sexual dimorphism in fatness, volume and muscularity. *Human Biology, 53*, 337–349.

Baker, R. R., & Bellis, M. A. (1995). *Human sperm competition*. London: Chapman and Hall.

Baker, N. V., Gregware, P. R., & Cassidy, M. A. (1999). Family killing fields: Honor rationales in the murder of women. *Violence Against Women, 5*, 164–184.

Barber, N. (1995). The evolutionary psychology of physical attractiveness: Sexual selection and human morphology. *Ethology and Sociobiology, 16*, 395–424.

Barclay, A. M. (1973). Sexual fantasies in men and women. *Medical Aspects of Human Sexuality, 7*, 205–216.

Beagon, M. (2005). *The Elder Pliny on the human animal: Natural History Book 7.* Translation with introduction and historical commentary (Clarendon Ancient History Series). Oxford: Clarendon Press.

Birkhead, T. (2000). *Promiscuity.* London: Faber & Faber.

Block, R. A., Hess L. A., Timpano, E. V., & Serlo, C. (1985). Physiologic changes in the foot during pregnancy. *Journal of American Podiatry Association, 75,* 297–299.

Blurton Jones, N. G. (1989). The cost of children and the adaptive scheduling of births: Towards a sociobiological perspective on demography. In A. E. Rasa, C. Vogel, & E. Voland (Eds.), *The Sociobiology of Sexual and Reproductive Strategies.* London: Chapman & Hall.

Bongaarts, J., & Potter, R. G. (1983). *Fertility, biology and behaviour: An analysis of the proximate determinants.* New York: Academic Press.

Bruce, H. (1989). Homes divided. *World Development, 17,* 979–991.

Burley, N. (1988). Wild zebra finches have colour band preferences. *Animal Behavior, 36,* 1235–1237.

Burley, N., & Johnson, K. (2002). The evolution of avian paternal care. *Philosophical Transactions of the Royal Society of London, Series B, 357,* 241–250.

Buss, D. M. (1989). Sex difference in human mate preferences: Evolutionary hypothesis tested in 37 cultures. *Behavioural and Brain Sciences, 54,* 616–628.

Buss, D. (1994). *The evolution of desire.* New York: Basic Books.

Buss, D. M. (2004). *Evolutionary psychology: The new science of the mind.* Boston: Pearson.

Cavalli-Sforza, L. L., & Cavalli-Sforza, F. (1995). *The great human diasporas: The history and diversity of evolution.* Reading, MA: Addison Wesley Publishing.

Chagnon, N. (1992). *Yanomamo.* Fort Worth, TX: Harcourt North.

Chantelau, E., & Gede, A. (2002). Foot dimensions of elderly people with and without diabetis mellitus: A data basis for shoe design. *Gerontology, 48,* 241–244.

Clay, I., Randall, S., Prather, E. B., & Rucker, III, T. (2006). Heat stress-induced apoptosis in porcine in vitro fertilized and parthenogenetic preimplantation-stage embryos. *Molecular Reproduction and Development, 74,* 574–581.

Clutton-Brock, T. H. (1991). *The evolution of parental care.* Princeton, NJ: Princeton University Press.

Clutton-Brock, T. H., & Parker, G. A. (1995). Sexual coercion in animal societies. *Animal Behavior, 49,* 1345–1365.

Coon, C. S. (1971). *The hunting people.* Boston, MA: Little Brown.

Cronin, H. (1991). *The ant and the peacock: Altruism and sexual selection from Darwin to today.* Cambridge: Cambridge University Press.

Darwin, C. (1871). *The descent of man and selection in relation to sex.* London: Murray.

Dutt, R. H. (1963). Critical period for early embryo mortality in ewes exposed to high ambient temperatures. *Journal of Animal Science, 22,* 713–719.

Eagly, A. H., Ashmore, R. D., Makhijani, M., & Longo, L. C. (1991). What is beautiful is good, but…A meta-analytic review of research on the physical attractiveness stereotype. *Psychological Bulletin, 110,* 109–128.

Edwards, J. L., & Hansen, P. J. (1997). Differential responses of bovine oocytes and preimplantation embryos to heat shock. *Molecular Reproduction and development, 46,* 138–145.

Ellison Rodgers, J. (2002). *Sex: A natural history.* New York: Times Books.

Euler, H. A., & Weizel, B. (1996). Discriminative grandparental solicitude as reproductive strategy. *Human Nature, 7,* 39–60.

Fessler, D. M. T., Nettle, D., Afshar, Y., de Andrade Pinheiro, I., Bolyanatz, A., Borgerhoff Mulder, M., et al. (2005). A cross-cultural investigation of the role of foot size in physical attractiveness. *Archives of Sexual Behavior, 34*, 267–276.

Fietz, J. (2003). Pair living and mating strategies in the fat-tailed dwarf Lemur (*Cheirogaleus medius*). In U. H. Reichard, & C. Boesh (Eds.), *Monogamy: Mating strategies and partnerships in birds, humans and other mammals* (pp. 214–231). Cambridge: Cambridge University Press.

Fisher, H. E. (1992). *The anatomy of love: The natural history of monogamy, adultery, and divorce*. New York: W.W. Norton.

Ford, C. S., & Beach, F. A. (1951). *Patterns of sexual behaviour*. New York: Harper & Row.

Frame, S., Moore, J., Peters, A., & Hall, D. (1985). Maternal height and shoe size as predictors of pelvic disproportion: An assessment. *BJOG: An International Journal of Obstetrics and Gynaecology, 92*, 1239.

Furnham, A., & Alibhai, N. (1983). Cross cultural differences in the perception of female body shapes. *Psychological Medicine, 13*, 396–404.

Gagneux, P., Woodruff, D. S., & Boesch, C. (1997). Furtive mating in female chimpanzees. *Nature, 387*, 368–369.

Gangestad, S. W., & Thornhill, R. (1997). Human sexual selection and developmental stability. In J. A. Simpson, & D. T. Kendrick (Eds.), *Evolutionary social psychology* (pp. 169–185). Mahwah, NJ: Erlbaum.

Geary, D. (2000). Evolution and proximate expressions of human paternal investment. *Psychological Bulletin, 126*, 55–77.

Gilmore, D. D. (1987). *Honour and shame and the unity of the Mediterranean*. Washington, DC: American Anthropology Association, Special Report 2.

Gladue, B. A., & Delany, J. J. (1990). Gender differences in the perception of attractiveness of men and women in bars. *Personality and Social Psychology Bulletin, 16*, 378–391.

Goody, J. (1983). *The development of the family and marriage in Europe*. Cambridge: Cambridge University Press.

Hanna, M., & Brown, H. C. (1979). Human heat tolerance: Biological and cultural adaptations. *Yearbook of Physical Anthropology, 22*, 164–181.

Hawkes, K. (1990). Why do men hunt? Some benefits for risky strategies. In J. Cashden (Ed.), *Risk and uncertainty in tribal peasant economies* (pp. 145–166). Boulder, CO: Westview Press.

Hawkes, K. (1991). Showing off: A test of another hypothesis about men's foraging goals. *Ethology and Sociobiology, 11*, 29–54.

Hawkes, K., O'Connell, J. F., Blurton Jones, N. G., Alvarez, E. L., & Charnov, A. (1998). Grandmothering, menopause, and the evolution of human life histories. *Proceedings of the National Academy of Science, 95*, 1336–1339.

Heap, R. B., & Flint, A. P. F. (1972). *Pregnancy*. Cambridge: Cambridge University Press.

Hill, K., & Hurtado, M. (1996). *Ache life history: The ecology and demography of foraging people*. New York: Aldine & Gruyer.

Hill, K., & Kaplan, H. (1988). Tradeoffs in male and female reproductive strategies among the Ache. In L. Betzig, M. Borgerhoff Mulder, & P. Turke (Eds.), *Human Reproductive Behaviour: A Darwinian perspective*. Cambridge: Cambridge University Press.

Hoffman, M. L., Janssen, E., & Turner, S. L. (2004). Classical conditioning of sexual arousal in women and men: Effects of varying awareness and biological relevance of the conditioned stimulus. *Behavior, 33*, 43–53.

Holliday, T. W., & Fallesetti, A. B. (1995). Lower limb length of European early modern humans in relation to mobility and climate. *Journal of Human Evolution, 30*, 243–276.

Hollis, K. L., Pharr, V. L., Dumas, M. J., Britton, G. B., & Field, J. (1997). Classical conditioning provides paternity advantage for territorial male blue gouramis (*trichogaster trichopteris*). *Journal of Comparative Psychology, 111*, 219–225.

Howell, N. (1979). *Demography of the Dobe !Kung*. New York: Academic Press.

Hrdy, S. B., & Whitten, P. L. (1987). Pattering of sexual activity. In B. B. Smuts, D. L. Cheney, R. M. Seyforth, R. W. Wrangham, & T. T. Struhsaker (Eds.), *Primate societies* (pp. 370–384). Cambridge: Cambridge University Press.

Huntingdon, E. (1938). *The season of birth*. New York: John Wiley.

Isbell, L. A., & Young, T. P. (1996). The evolution of bipedalism in hominids and reduced group size in chimpanzees. *Journal of Human Evolution, 30*, 389–397.

Jabonski, N. G., & Chaplin, G. (2000). The evolution of skin coloration. *Journal of Human Evolution, 39*, 57–106.

Jankowiak, W. (1995). *Romantic passion: A universal experience?* New York: Columbia University Press.

Johnson, V. S., & Franklin, M. (1993). Is beauty in the eyes of the beholder? *Ethology & Sociobiology, 14*, 183–199.

Jones, D. M. (1995). Sexual selection, physical attractiveness and facial neotony: Cross cultural evidence and implications. *Current Anthropology, 36*, 723–748.

Kaplan, H., & Hill, K. (1985). Food sharing among the Ache foragers: Tests and explanatory hypothesis. *Current Anthropology, 26*, 233–245.

Karama, S., Lecours, A. R., Leroux, J. -M., Bourgouin, G., Joubert, S., & Beauregard, M. (2002). Areas of brain activation in males and females during viewing of erotic film exert. *Human Brain Mapping, 16*, 1–13.

Kinsey, A. C., Pomeroy, W. B., & Martin, C. E. (1948). *Sexual behavior in the human male*. Philadelphia, PA: W.B. Saunders.

Knight, C. (1995). *Blood relations: Menstruation and the origins of culture*. New Haven: Yale University Press.

Komers, P. E., & Brotherton, P. N. M. (1997). Female space use is the best predictor of monogamy in mammals. *Proceedings of the Royal Society of London B, 264*, 1261–1270.

Laslett, P. (1980). Comparing illegitimacy over timer and between cultures. In P. Laslett, K. Oosterveen, & R. M. Smith (Eds.), *Bastardy and its comparative history* (pp. 1–70). London: Edward Arnold.

Lerner, M. J., & Mikula, G. (1994). *Entitlement and the affectional bond justice in close relationships series: Critical issues in social justice*. New York: Springer.

Lewin, R. (1998). *Principles of human evolution*. Oxford: Oxford University Press.

Levine, D., & Wrighton, K. (1980). Social context of illegitimacy in early modern England. In P. Laslett, K. Oosterveen, & R. M. Smith (Eds.), *Bastardy and its comparative history* (pp. 158–175). London: Edward Arnold.

Lublin, A., & Wolfenson, D. (1996). Lactation and pregnancy effects of blood flow to mammary and reproductive system in heat stressed rabbits. *Comparative Biochemistry & Physiology, 115*, 277–285.

Mackenzie, I. Z., Cooke, I., & Annan, B. (2003). Indications for caesarean section in a consultant unit over the decades. *Journal of Obstetrics and Gynocology, 23*, 333–338.

Marlowe, F. (2000). Paternal investment and the human mating system. *Behavioural Processes, 1*, 45–61.

Martin, R. D., Willner, L. A., & Dettling, A. (1994). The evolution of sexual dimorphism in primates. In R. V. Short, & E. Balaban (Eds.), *The difference between the sexes*. Cambridge: Cambridge University Press.

Meindl, R. F. (1992). Human populations before agriculture. In S. Jones, R. Martin, & R. Pribream (Eds.), *The Cambridge encyclopaedia of human evolution* (pp. 406–410). Cambridge: Cambridge University Press.

Miller, G. F. (2000). *The mating mind: How sexual choice shaped the evolution of human nature*. New York: Doubleday.

Miller, G. (2001). *The mating mind: How sexual choice shaped the evolution of human nature*. London: Heinemann.

Møller, A. P. (2003). The evolution of monogamy: Mating relationships, paternal care and sexual selection. In U. H. Reichard, & C. Boesch (Eds.), *Monogamy: Mating strategies and partnerships in birds, humans and other mammals* (pp. 29–41). Cambridge: Cambridge University Press.

Morris, D. (1967). *The naked ape*. New York: McGraw-Hill.

Murdock, G. P. (1967). *Ethnographic atlas*. Pittsburgh, IL: University of Pittsburgh Press.

Office of Population Census and Statistics (OPCS). (1992). *1992 Marriage and divorce statistics*. London: HMSO.

Partridge, L., & Halliday, T. (1984). Mating patterns and mate choice. In J. R. Krebs, & N. B. Davis (Eds.), *Behavioral ecology an evolutionary approach*. Oxford: Blackwell Scientific.

Pawłowski, B., & Grabarczyk, M. (2003). Center of body mass and the evolution of female body shape. *American Journal of Biology, 15*, 144–150.

Plaud, J. J., & Martini, J. R. (1999). The respondent conditioning of male sexual behaviour. *Behavior Modification, 22*, 254–268.

Pollard, I. A. (1994). *Guide to reproduction: Social issues and human concerns*. Cambridge: Cambridge University Press.

Pond, C. M., Mattacks, C. H., Calder, P. C., & Evans, J. R. H. (1993). Site specific properties of human adipose depots homologous to those of other mammals. *Comparative Biochemistry, 24*, 1825–1831.

Profet, M. (1993). Menstruation as a defence against pathogens transported by sperm. *Quarterly Journal of Biology, 68*, 335–386.

Przbyla, D. P., & Byrne, D. (1984). The mediating role of cognitive processes in self reported sexual arousal. *Journal of Research in Personality, 18*, 54–63.

Putney, D., Malayer, J. R., Gross, T. S., Thatcher, W. W., Hansen P. J., & Drost, M. (1988). Heat stress-induced alterations in the synthesis and secretion of proteins and prostaglandins by cultured bovine conceptuses and uterine endrometrium. *Biology and Reproduction, 39*, 717–728.

Rodman, P. S., & McHenry, H. M. (1980). Bioenergetics of hominid bipedalism. *American Journal of Anthropology, 52*, 103–106.

Rose, L. (1986). *The massacre of the innocents: Infanticide in Britain 1800–1939*. London: Routledge & Kagan Paul.

Roth, Z., Meiden, R., Shaham-Alalancy, A., Braw-Tal, R., & Wolfenson, D. (2001). Delayed effect of heat stress on steroid production in medium-sized and preovulatory bovine follicles. *Reproduction, 121,* 745–751.

Ruff, C. B. (1994). Climatic adaption and hormonal evolution: The thermporegulation imperitive. *Evolution & Anthropology, 2,* 53–60.

Schneider, J. (1971). Of vigilance and virgins: Honor, shame and access to resources in Mediterranean societies. *Ethnology, 10,* 1–24.

Sear, R., Mace, R., & McGregor, I. A. (2000). Maternal grandmothers impose nutritional status and survival of children in rural Gambia. *Proceedings of the Royal Society of London B, 267,* 1641–1647.

Searcy, W. A. (1982). The evolutionary effects of mate selection. *Annual Review of Ecology and Systematics, 13,* 57–85.

Short, R. V. (1984). Oestrus and menstrual cycles. In C. R. Austin, & R. V. Short (Eds.), *Hormonal control of reproduction.* Cambridge: Cambridge University Press.

Shuttle, P., & Redgrove, P. (1978). *The wise wound: Menstruation and every woman.* London: Gollancz.

Sigall, H., & Landy, D. (1973). Radiating beauty: The effects of having a physically attractive partner on personal perception. *Journal of Personality and Social Psychology, 28,* 218–224.

Sillen-Tulberg, B., & Møller, A. P. (1993). The relationship between concealed ovulation and mating system in anthropoid primates: A phylogenetic analysis. *American Naturalist, 141,* 1–25.

Singh, D. (1993). Adaptive significance of female physical attractiveness: Role of waist-to-hip ratio. *Journal of Personality and Social Psychology, 65,* 292–307.

Singh, D., & Young, R. K. (1995). Body weight, waist hip ratio breasts and hips: Role of judgement of female attractiveness and desirability for relationships. *Ethology and Sociobiology, 16,* 483–507.

Small, M. F. (1993). *Female choices: Sexual behaviour in female primates.* London: Cornell University Press.

Sprecher, S., Aron, A., Hatfield, E., Cortese, A., Potopova, E., & Levitskya, A. (1994). Love: American style, Russian style and Japanese style. *Personal Relationships, 1,* 349–369.

Stacey, P. B. (1982). Female promiscuity and male reproductive success in social birds and mammals. *American Naturalist, 120,* 51–64.

Strassmann, B. (1996). Menstrual hut visits by Dogon women: A hormonal test distinguishes deceit from honest signalling. *Behavioral Ecology, 7,* 304–315.

Strassmann, B. (1997). The biology of menstruation in *Homo sapiens*: Total lifetime menses, fecundity, and nonsynchrony in a naturally fertility population. *Current Anthropology, 38,* 123–129.

Strassmann, B. I. (2003). Social monogamy in a human society: Marriage and reproductive success among the Drogon. In U. H. Reichard, & C. Boesch (Eds.), *Monogamy: Mating strategies and partnerships in birds, humans and other mammals* (pp. 29–41). Cambridge: Cambridge University Press.

Swami, V. (2005). *Evolutionary psychology and the study of human physical attractiveness: The influence of body weight and shape across cultures.* PhD Thesis, University College London.

Swami, V., Einon, D., & Furnham, A. (2006). An investigation of the leg-to-body ratio as a human aesthetic criterion. *Body Image, 3,* 317–323.

Symons, D. (1995). Beauty is in the adaptations of the beholder: The evolutionary psychology of human female sexual attractiveness. In P. R. Abrahamson, & S. D.

Pinkerton (Eds.), *Sexual nature, sexual culture* (pp. 80–118). Chicago: University of Chicago Press.

Takahata, Y., Ihobe, H., & Idani, G. (1996). Comparing copulations of chimpanzees and Bonobos: Do females exhibit proceptivity or receptivity? In W. McGrew, L. F. Marchant, & T. Nishida (Eds.), *Great ape societies*. Cambridge: Cambridge University Press.

Tovée, M. J., & Cornelisson, P. L. (1999). The mystery of human beauty. *Nature, 399*, 215–216.

Trivers, R. L. (1981). *Social evolution*. Merlo Park, CA: Benjamin Cummings.

United Nations (2002). *Working towards the elimination of crimes against women committed in the name of honour*. Geneva: United Nations.

Upfold, J. B., Smith, M. S., & Edwards, M. J. (1989). Quantitative study of the effects of maternal hypothermia on cell death and proliferation in the guinea pig brain on day 21 of pregnancy. *Teratology, 39*, 173–179.

van Bogaert, L. J. (1999). The relation between height, foot length pelvic adequacy and mode of delivery. *European Journal of Obstetrics and Gynaecology and Reproductive Behaviour, 82*, 195–199.

van den Berghe, P. L., & Frost, P. (1986). Skin colour preferences, sexual dimorphism and sexual selection. A case of gene culture co-evolution. *Ethnic and Racial Studies, 9*, 87–113.

Walker, D. W., Hale, J. R., Fawcett, A. A., & Pratt, N. M. (1995). Cardiovascular responses to heat stress in late gestation sheep. *Experimental Physiology, 80*, 755–766.

Wellings, K., Field, J., Johnson, A. M., & Wadsworth, J. (1994). *Sexual behaviour in Britain*. Harmonsworth: Penguin Books.

Wheeler, P. (1994). The thermoregulatory advantage of heat storage and shade-seeking behaviour to hominids foraging in equatorial savannah environments. *Journal of Human Evolution, 30*, 367–371.

Whitten, P. L. (1987). Infants and adult males. In B. B. Smuts, D. L. Cheney, R. M. Seyforth, R. W. Wrangham, & T. T. Struhsaker (Eds.), *Primate societies* (pp. 385–399). Cambridge: Cambridge University Press.

Wolfenson, D., Roth, Z., & Meidan, R. (2000). Impaired reproduction in heat stressed cattle: Basic and applied aspects. *Animal Reproduction Science, 60*, 535–537.

9
Interpersonal Metaperception: The Importance of Compatibility in the Aesthetic Appreciation of Bodily Cues

Kerri L. Johnson and Louis G. Tassinary

> Beauty is the proper conformity of the parts to one another and to the whole.
>
> ~ Heisenberg (1974: 183)

Psychology enjoys a rich history of theorising that is rooted in Gestalt psychology (Koffka, 1935; Köhler, 1929, 1947). Gestalt psychology has informed not only our understanding of how simple geometric objects are perceptually parsed, but also how global attitudes toward objects and individuals are formed. In both cases, one's ultimate perception is multiply determined, integrating the basic perception of a range of cues that, collectively, yield an overarching percept or attitude. In other words, each simple cue is perceived directly but contextualised by other cues that together affect a more global perception, or Gestalt.

This principle has been applied to a variety of domains including the perception of physical objects, personality traits, and interpersonal inter-actions. Three overlapping lines in one configuration can yield a percept of discontinuity, yet the same lines in a slightly different arrangement can yield the percept of a single unit – a triangle (Köhler, 1929, 1947); a colleague who is challenging, assertive, and warm may be viewed as *astute*, whereas a colleague who is challenging, assertive, but cold may be viewed as *pompous* (Asch, 1946); and a favourable attitude toward John may tarnish when one learns that John befriended a detested individual (Heider, 1946, 1958). These examples can be described as *metaperception* – the first physical, the second intrapersonal, and the last interpersonal. In each instance, the contextualised relation between two or more elemental percepts and/or attitudes ultimately yielded a Gestalt impression.

In spite of these valuable insights, the application of Gestalt theory to person construal has focused primarily on the perception of intrapersonal personality traits and on attitudes toward individual members of triads. Surprisingly, these Gestalt principles have rarely been applied to investigations of how physical cues affect basic interpersonal perception, in spite of the fact that prominent theorists have highlighted the value of such inquiry (see Neisser, 1994). Instead, the study of person perception traditionally isolated and manipulated a single physical cue to measure how it affected social perception (but cf. Sheldon, Stevens, & Tucker, 1942). Several researchers, for example, have tried to better understand the physical determinants of perceived attractiveness (e.g., bilateral symmetry, facial composites, and body shape) using this approach (e.g., Gangestad, Thornhill, & Yeo, 1994; Langlois & Roggman, 1990; Singh, 1993). Critically, this approach affords precision at the expense of breadth, and has met increasing criticism (e.g., Buller, 2005a, 2005b). Consequently, there remains no comprehensive account of how the basic perceptions of various cues ultimately coalesce to yield an evaluative social Gestalt.

Here, we adopt a broad approach to investigate how a subset of physical cues – those originating in the body – affect interpersonal metaperception. We posit that conspicuous bodily cues, such as body shape and motion, affect basic social perceptions in reliable ways that correspond to social judgements of biological sex and gender (i.e., masculinity and femininity; Unger, 1979).[1] Collectively, these basic social perceptions affect interpersonal metaperception – evaluative social judgements such as perceived attractiveness. We propose a *cue compatibility* model that accounts for these effects.

Bodily cues and evaluative social judgements

To explore how body shape affects evaluative social judgements, researchers have created line-drawn stimuli that depict men and women's bodies in various shapes and sizes (e.g., Lippa, 1983; Fallon & Rozin, 1985; Singh, 1993). Such stimuli have been used routinely to determine the particular somatotypes that people find attractive. To date, the most systematic investigations of this kind focused on a single physical cue, the waist-to-hip ratio (WHR).

Singh (1993) presented participants with a set of line-drawn women that varied both the WHR and weight. Across all weight categories, women with small WHRs were judged to be more attractive than women with larger WHRs, although body weight was a stronger inverse predictor of attractiveness (see also Tassinary & Hansen, 1998; Tovée & Cornelissen, 2001). Buttressed by biomedical research relating the WHR to health and fertility (e.g., Björntorp, 1988; Lanska, Lanska, Hartz, & Rimm, 1985; Laws, King, Haskell, & Reaven, 1993; Ostlund, Staten, Kohrt, Schultz, & Malley, 1990; Zaadstra et al., 1993), these findings were initially interpreted from a particular evolutionary perspective: the WHR, it was argued, is a biological marker of health and fecundity, and male preferences for small WHRs are adaptive (Singh, 1993). Specifically, such preferences were characterised as adaptations for mate choice (cf. Rhodes, 2006).

The WHR hypothesis became well-known by scientists and lay-people alike due in part to its widespread and continued coverage in the popular media (e.g., Chen, 2005; Cowley, 1996; Heiman, 1999; Newman, 2000; Stanish, 1996). Moreover, predictions drawn from the WHR hypothesis spawned an abundance of research to further investigate the adaptive significance of men's preferences for small WHRs (Furnham, Tan, & McManus, 1997; Furnham, Dias, & McClelland, 1998; Henss, 1995). In fact, replications and extensions of the findings abound (see Swami & Furnham, 2006 for a review).

This popular and empirical attention is not surprising. The WHR hypothesis articulated an uncomplicated supposition that was tested by manipulating a simple physical cue. This strength, however, proved ultimately to be a weakness as well. The absence of context, while affording precision, prohibited a broad understanding of how body cues *in situ* affect perceived attractiveness. Similarly, the specificity of the theory, while elegant, failed to anticipate and could not account for the contradictory data that subsequently emerged. Indeed, recent research has documented methodological shortcomings and theoretical flaws that undermine the viability of the WHR hypothesis, generally, at least in the strong form that it was originally articulated.[2]

Thus, although prior research has revealed a clear relation between body shape and perceived attractiveness, a mechanism to account for these observations has yet to be identified. Because these prior studies focused narrowly on a distal evolutionary mechanism and explored only a single physical cue, we believe a more proximal psychological mechanism may have been overlooked. From our perspective, adopting a more comprehensive approach that approaches this question from a different level of analysis – a cognitive one – is necessary to clarify how body cues affect basic social perception and interpersonal metaperception.

Bodies in balance

Characterising perceived attractiveness as interpersonal metaperception invites two critical changes to previous methodologies. First, the perspective of interpersonal metaperception highlights the fact that *multiple social judgements* are made during person perception. Second, this perspective acknowledges that *additional bodily cues* also affect social perception. These two changes may potentially uncover the evolutionary-based cognitive mechanisms that guide evaluative social judgements.

Multiple social judgements

In the vast majority of the prior research, the stimuli were readily identified as women. Thus, the judgements made by participants – whether they were ranking the stimuli by attractiveness or rating the stimuli for fecundity – were contextualised by the known biological sex of the target. Indeed, the key manipulations of the target were alterations of the body's shape and size, the *individual* was held constant across the stimuli, and the majority of the studies used a common stimulus set. In contrast, isolated judgements of attractiveness in real life rarely occur for different renderings of an individual in succession. Instead, we simultaneously make several judgements about others with great facility. Unlike the majority of laboratory studies, the category membership of each individual is judged from the available information (Allport, 1954). Among the most likely social categories to be noted, biological sex tops the list (e.g., Stangor, Lynch, Duan, & Glass, 1992; Taylor, Fiske, Etcoff, & Ruderman, 1978). In life, the perceived sex of a conspecific is a *decision* not a *given*. Subsequent social judgements are likely to be perceived in the context of this fundamental social category (Bem, 1993). Consequently, other cues that tend to covary with biological sex are likely to affect perceived gender (i.e., masculinity and femininity), and they may be deemed compatible or incompatible with the judged sex of an individual. If correct, these perceptions of sex and gender may ultimately determine the level of perceived attractiveness.

Additional bodily cues

The majority of prior research isolated a single physical cue, the WHR, while neglecting other cues that are potentially meaningful for the basic perception of sex and gender. One cue, in particular, enjoys a rich background in the arts and sciences. Artists and philosophers, for example, have written extensively about the beauty of the body's motion. Frumkin (1954) referred to body motion as a 'visual aphrodisiac'; on their 1969 album *Abby Road* and in his 1968 self-titled album, both The Beatles and James Taylor independently noted that that there is 'something in the way she moves...'; and in his *Leaves of Grass,* Whitman (1900) pointed out that, 'the expression of a well-made man appears not only in his face...it is in his walk.' Fortuitously, scientists have also noted that bodily motion in general, and gait in particular, convey important social information (see Allport & Vernon, 1933, for an early foray into this area).

A substantial scientific literature corroborates the importance of body motion for social perception. Body motion is sexually dimorphic, and these differences are evident perceptually, kinematically, and stylistically. For example, observers can accurately distinguish men from women from minimal information (e.g., point-light displays; Cutting, 1978). In addition, more shoulder twist than hip translation characterises a 'male' gait, the opposite combination characterises a 'female' gait (Cutting, 1978; Murry, Kory, & Sepic, 1970), and these motion parameters have been well-specified (Barclay, Cutting, & Kozlowski, 1978; Cutting, 1981; Cutting, Moore, & Morrison, 1988; Cutting, Proffit, & Kozlowski, 1978, Troje, 2002). Perceived differences between male and female gaits are seen in studies of kinematics, as well. Women, for example, walk at greater cadences, with greater hip flexion and pelvic motion, and with less knee extension than do men (Kerrigan, Todd, & Della Croce, 1998; Smith, Lelas, & Kerrigan, 2002). Finally, anthropologists have noted sex differences in expressive movement (e.g., dancing style, Brown et al., 2005; Eibl-Eibesfeldt, 1988; Frable, 1987). Given this abundance of evidence for the aesthetic appreciation and sex-specific nature of body motion, it is likely to contribute substantially to metaperceptual judgements.

A broad approach and cue compatibility model of interpersonal metaperception

We applied this basic principle of interpersonal metaperception to explore a range of social judgements that arise from body cues. Our stimuli varied along two dimensions – shape and motion, and our participants provided several social judgements for each target. We predicted that each physical cue would effect a basic social judgement, and that the compatibility of these cues would affect a more evaluative social judgement.

Perceived sex and gender as the foundation for interpersonal metaperception

As noted above, the body's shape and motion are, in reality, both sexually dimorphic and visually conspicuous. They are, therefore, also likely to be perceived to be gendered, and are prime candidates to affect metaperceptual judgements. In a recent series of experiments, we explored the relative importance of body shape and motion for gendered judgements that are categorical and continuous. In one set of studies (Johnson & Tassinary, 2007a), participants judged the sex and gender of humanoid animations that depicted a person walking in place. These 'walkers' varied in body shape (i.e., five WHRs from 0.5 to 0.9, see Figure 9.1) and in walk motion (i.e., five gaits from a masculine shoulder 'swagger' to a feminine hip 'sway,' see Figure 9.2).[3] As seen in Figure 9.3, sex judgements were tightly coupled to body shape, but only moderately coupled to body motion; gender judgements, in contrast, were strongly related to body motion, but were also moderately related to

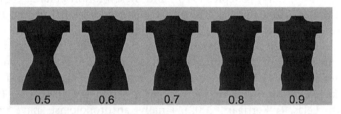

Figure 9.1   WHR from 0.5 to 0.9. Wireframe models were exported to Maya™ for accurate circumference measurements.

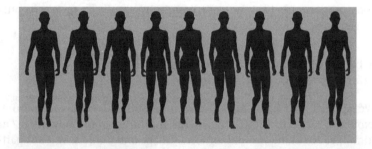

Figure 9.2   Each walker completed approximately 10 steps over 10s. Figure depicts key frames of an animation sequence. Exact motion parameters are specified in Johnson and Tassinary (2005, 2007a) and, Johnson, Gill, Reichman, and Tassinary (2007).

body shape. Thus, although related both to sex and gender judgements, the body's shape appeared to be the primary cue used to make sex category judgements.

We corroborated this finding in a set of experiments that utilised a decidedly different methodology – eye tracking (Johnson & Tassinary, 2005). In these experiments, participants viewed each of our walkers as we recorded their precise point of gaze using corneal reflection eye tracking. When we then examined the distribution of their visual scanning within four critical areas of the body – the head, the chest, the waist/hips, and the legs. We reasoned that participants would direct their visual attention toward the body regions that provided critical

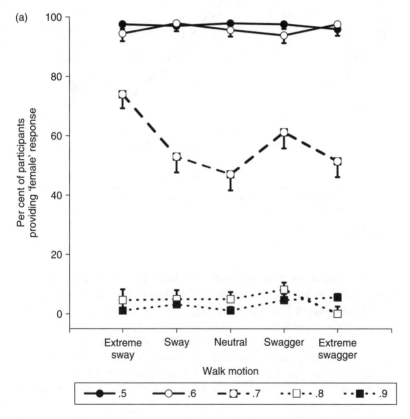

Figure 9.3 Judgements of sex (a) and gender (b) for animated walkers. One-sided error bars represent 95 per cent confidence intervals. Data from Johnson and Tassinary (2007a) were replotted using WHR and Walk Motion.

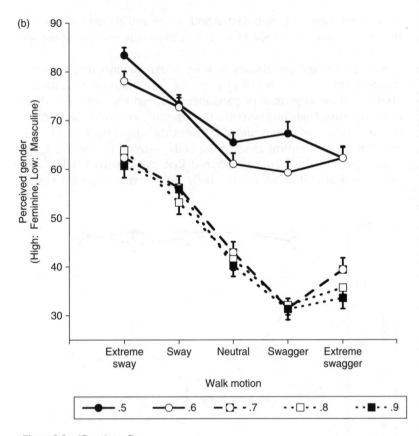

Figure 9.3 (Continued).

information for social judgements. We hypothesised that participants would concentrate their scanning within the waist and hip region, an area that was related to both sex and gender judgements in our previous studies. Indeed, participants looked longer and with a higher frequency at the waist and hip region of the walkers, data consistent with the notion that this sexually dimorphic region of the body conveyed critical information for social judgements. Yet the specificity of the information gleaned from that region remained uncertain because participants judged both sex and gender for each target.

Consequently, we next examined *why* participants concentrated their scanning within the waist and hip region of the body. We reasoned that if body shape is the primary cue to a target's sex, then preempting sex category judgements should weaken the importance of scanning the waist and hips. Said differently, when scanning the waist and hip regions no longer served a functional end (i.e., to determine a target's sex), concentrating one's scanning within the waist and hip region should no longer be necessary. As predicted, when the sex of a walker was prespecified, visual scanning of the waist and hip region dropped to chance levels, and was significantly lower than scanning of that region among a group of participants for whom the sex remained unspecified (see Figure 9.4). Thus, participants looked at the waist and hip region only when doing so was necessary to learn the targets' sex.

Based on these findings, we concluded that the body's shape is a critical visual cue to a target's sex – and for good reason. The body's shape is indeed sexually dimorphic, in both absolute and relative terms (Johnson & Tassinary, 2007b). In yet another series of experiments, we examined, among other things, whether the body shapes of men and women is,

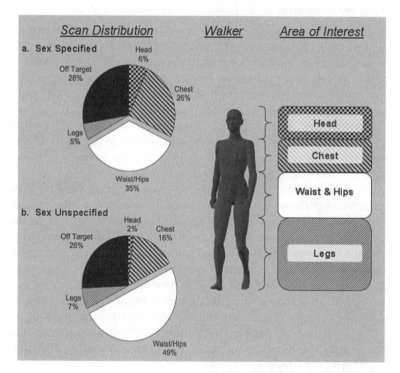

Figure 9.4 Distribution of visual scanning when the sex of a walker had been specified (a) or remained unspecified (b).

in reality, diagnostic of biological sex. First we established that the bodies of men and women varied in both absolute and relative terms. We analysed a widely used anthropometric database that contained the physical measurements of over 4,800 men and women (Clauser, Tebbetts, Bradtmiller, McConville, & Gordon, 1987–1988; Donelson & Gordon, 1988). Not surprisingly, men and women differed in their absolute body size, and classifying the sex of a target based on measures of height and weight alone would lead to accuracy nearing 86 per cent. When the relative measures of the waist and hips were included in the analyses, both independently and interactively, accuracy in classification jumped to nearly 98 per cent. Consequently, observers who use the WHR as a cue to a target's sex have a solid empirical foundation for doing so. Men's and women's bodies are dimorphic both in absolute and relative measurements.

Perceived attractiveness as interpersonal metaperception

Having found two cues that specify sex and gender, we next examined whether these cues (and indeed the very social percepts they give rise to) contextualise one another, ultimately leading to evaluative judgements such as perceived attractiveness. Because sex category judgements have been found to be obligatory, even automatic, they are also likely to be the first social percepts to emerge (Stangor et al., 1992). In our own studies, we have found a tight coupling between the body's shape and perceived sex. Therefore, sex category judgements that rely on the body's shape will likely provide a lens through which other embodied cues are perceived and evaluated (Bem, 1993).

Once a sex categorisation has occurred, other body cues are likely to be perceived as either masculine or feminine. Indeed, in our own research we have found the body's motion to relate to perceived gender. In the context of perceived sex, this gendered motion is likely to seem either typical or atypical, a contextualised perception that should affect evaluative social judgements such as perceived attractiveness. Thus, from the perspective of interpersonal metaperception, particular bodies may be deemed attractive, at least in part, because available cues specify accordant percepts (e.g., a feminine woman or a masculine man). In a series of studies we have examined this possibility with stimuli that include computer-generated animations, real human walkers, and static line drawings (Johnson & Tassinary, 2007a).

In two studies, we examined this model of interpersonal metaperception using our computer-generated animations that varied in WHR and Walk

Motion. For each walker, participants judged sex, gender, and attractiveness. As before, we found sex category judgements to be strongly related to WHR, and gender judgements to be related to both WHR and Walk Motion. Because sex categorisation is thought to be a fundamental judgement, we predicted that this would constrain the aesthetic appeal of gendered gait – ultimately determining the level of perceived attractiveness. Indeed, the predicted interaction between WHR and Walk Motion was strong and significant, and this obtained for walkers facing forward and backward (see Figure 9.5). The cues that differentially signalled sex and gender combined to determine perceived attractiveness.

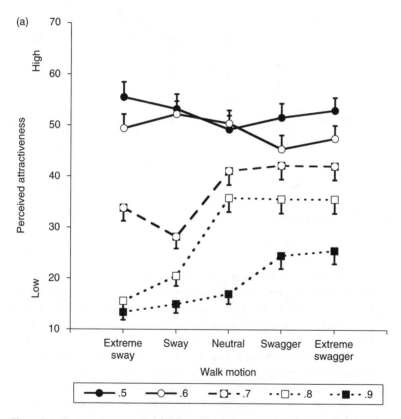

Figure 9.5 Judgements of attractiveness for walkers facing forward (a) and backward (b). One-sided error bars represent 95 per cent confidence intervals. Data from Johnson and Tassinary (2007a) were replotted using WHR and Walk Motion.

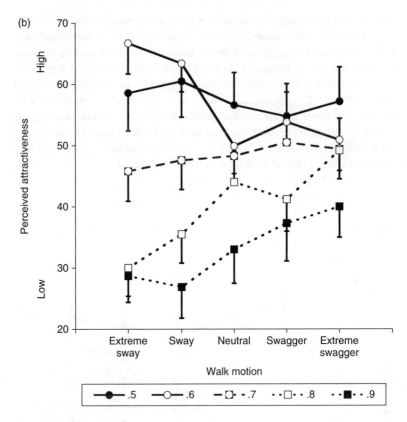

Figure 9.5 (Continued).

We interpret these effects to be consistent with our theoretical perspective of interpersonal metaperception. Though the particular cues that specify sex and gender may vary across studies, the cue that specifies perceived sex will predominate the perception of other gendered cues – and ultimately determine which bodies will be deemed attractive. This implies that it is not the physical cues, per se, but contextualised social perceptions that emerge from those cues that lead bodies to be deemed attractive. In our animated walkers, the WHR was most tightly coupled to sex category judgements, and it contextualised the perception and interpretation of the body's motion, bringing about an aesthetic Gestalt. In other stimuli that have been widely used, however, different physical parameters guide these judgements. In studies that have used the original stimuli from Singh (1993), for example, the sex of each target was not judged, but was both pre-specified and held constant. Because the sex was given, the WHR – a cue related to both sex category and gendered judgements in our own research – was perceived to be congruent or incongruent with the given category, and therefore guided judgements of attractiveness. It is in this manner that the cognitive processes described above could account for the aesthetic appeal of small WHRs for female targets.

Indeed, elsewhere we have examined these metaperceptual aspects of our approach (i.e., how the compatibility of perceived sex and gender affect perceived attractiveness). In this treatment of the data, we analysed the perceived attractiveness of our walkers as a function of perceived sex and gender (as opposed to WHR and Walk Motion as we have done here; Johnson & Tassinary, 2007a). When analysed in that way, the interaction between perceived sex and gender for judgements of attractiveness was strong and significant, just as the interaction between WHR and Walk Motion was significant.

We have replicated these findings for a range of stimuli including: (a) computer-generated animations in which we experimentally manipulated the purported sex of the target; (b) video recordings of actual men and women who were trained to move in characteristically masculine or feminine ways, and; (c) static line drawn images that depict a woman with various WHRs (i.e., the stimuli from Singh, 1993). In some cases, the sex of the target was implicit, and judged by the target (e.g., specified by WHR in some of our studies, or experimentally manipulated in others), and the gendered cue that was either compatible or incompatible was the body's motion. In other cases, the sex of the target was held constant, and the gendered cue that varied was body shape (i.e., Singh stimuli). Finally, in other cases, the sex of the target was apparent from multiple cues (e.g., videos of real people), and the gendered cue that varied across stimuli was the body's motion.

Across all of these variations, one cue (or manipulation) specified the sex of the target, and another sexually dimorphic cue varied across the range of stimuli. In spite of these variations in the stimuli, perceived attractiveness was predicted by the interaction of sex and gender in all cases. Female targets were judged to be more attractive when they were also perceived to be feminine, but the opposite was true for male targets. These findings clearly support our general proposition that body cues invoked a range of basic social percepts that coalesced to either a pleasing or unpleasant Gestalt, a global evaluation that was reflected in our participants' judgements of attractiveness.

Social categories as interpersonal metaperception

Because the cues involved in interpersonal metaperception affect multiple gendered perceptions, they may be perceived to be either typical or atypical given the perceived sex of a target. The resulting metaperceptual judgements that subsequently arise may extend beyond evaluative social judgements, also affecting other social categorisations. Specifically, gender-atypical expressive body motion and even shape has been shown to reliably predict both actual and perceived sexual orientation (Ambady, Hallahan, & Conner, 1999; Bailey & Zucker, 1995; Rieger, 2006; Rieger, Linsenmeier, Gygax, & Bailey, 2006; Sirin, McCreary, & Mahalik, 2004). Consequently, in addition to affecting perceived attractiveness (or lack thereof), perceiving sex and gender from body cues may affect presumed sexual orientation, either implicitly or explicitly. And this may or may not be related to the perceived attractiveness of the target. We addressed this possibility in a separate set of studies in which participants judged the sexual orientation of our computer-animated walkers (Johnson, Gill, Reichman, & Tassinary, 2007). Not surprisingly, perceived sexual orientation was determined by the interaction of WHR and Walk Motion. From these data we concluded that metaperceptual judgements that arise from body cues need not be restricted to evaluative judgements, but that they may also extend to other social categorisations.

Given the similarity between the findings for perceived sexual orientation and perceived attractiveness described above, we were concerned that our effects of compatibility on perceived attractiveness were somehow mediated by perceived sexual orientation. If correct, this implies that the evaluation of particular combinations of body cues were low specifically because they implied a stigmatised social category – homosexuality (Aberson, Swan, & Emerson, 1999; Herek, 1984; Sirin et al., 2004; Storm, 2001). We examined this possibility, and we reported the results in Johnson et al. (2007a). In sum, we found that the attractiveness effect remained significant after controlling for the perceived sexual orientation of each target. Thus, gender typicality's importance for judgements of attractiveness appears distinct from its importance for judgements of sexual orientation.

Practical implications

Collectively, our findings have numerous practical implications. First, our research has implications in terms of its basic approach to why/how the WHR affects judgements. Prior research has been criticised due to its repeated reliance on somewhat impoverished line drawn stimuli. Henss

(2000), for example, pointed out that because research on face recognition utilising line drawn or photographic stimuli has yielded discrepant results, one might expect the same to occur when investigating the human body. This is difficult to confirm, however, because few studies have used photographic stimuli to investigate the role of bodily cues in social judgements. The studies that have used photographs in such studies have altered the WHR by changing the relative *width* of the waist and/or the hips (Henss, 2000; Singh, 1994; Rozmus-Wrzesinska & Pawlowski, 2005; Streeter & McBurney, 2003; but for a different use of photographic stimuli, see Bateson, Cornelissen, & Tovée, Chapter 4; Tovée & Cornelissen, 2001; Tovée, Maisey, Emery, & Cornelissen, 1999). Critically, the WHR as it has been related to actual health and fecundity is a measure of circumference, not one of width (e.g., Björntorp, 1988). Because the overarching goal of previous research was to relate a social judgement (i.e., attractiveness) to a visible feature that corresponds to health and fecundity (WHR), this shortcoming is a potential lynchpin.

Our research has overcome this limitation, albeit without using photographs, by using animations of human walkers. Each of the walkers was rendered in three-dimensional space, in which the circumference of both the waist and the hips were measured (Higa, 1999). Thus, the WHR in our walkers is a more precise portrayal of the human body than can be achieved using two-dimensional width manipulations. Furthermore, the walkers were dynamic. Animation enriched the stimuli such that judgements correspond more closely to what participants experience in real life; that is, people in motion. Moreover, the androgyny of the walker pinpointed the heretofore-neglected effects of both the WHR and Walk Motion in judgements of sex. To our knowledge, only one other study has obtained sex judgements for androgynous figures (Lippa, 1983), but that study used line-drawn stimuli.

Our general approach to the study of how the WHR affects social judgements also has practical implications. Prior research investigating judgements of the human body has isolated a single physical cue and manipulated (or measured) its relation to a single dependent variable. Thus, the precise relation between the physical cue and the social judgement can be described, yet contextualising forces have been almost entirely ignored. This approach, therefore, has favoured precision over breadth. Other research investigating the accuracy of social perceptions has typically presented static or dynamic recordings of actual people to determine the accuracy of social perception. Thus, the surprising accuracy of social judgements has been demonstrated, yet the cues that inform those judgements have been intractable. In contrast to the first, this second approach has favoured breadth over precision. Our approach strikes a balance between precision and breadth that we believe will provide a foundation for future research in a variety of domains.

Finally, our approach is highly integrative. Until recently, research investigating the social perception of the body's motion and shape has occurred in isolation, uniformed by the other field's current findings and theories. Our perspective of interpersonal metaperception has, quite literally, borrowed the best of both programmes of research. By applying the gaits described in the cognitive literature to the body shapes invest-igated in the social literature, we have achieved a new level of descriptive specificity. Both shape and motion are important in basic social percep-tions, and the current research explicates how the relation of those perceptions affects interpersonal metaperception.

Theoretical implications

The conceptualisation of perceived attractiveness as interpersonal meta-perception has important theoretical implications that are both specific and general. Specifically, our model can account for the contradictory findings with respect to the WHR hypothesis. Heretofore, the psycho-logical mechanisms that triggered these discrepant results remained elusive. Our model and results fill this theoretical gap by positing a single metaperceptual mechanism, cue compatibility, which accounts for the previous effects. Moreover, our model can explain these previous find-ings in parsimonious and proximal terms without positing the presence of unique and special-purpose adaptations.

The stimulus set employed by previous researchers (e.g., Singh, 1993) permitted the emergence of the effect of WHR on judgements of attract-iveness for functional reasons unrelated to evolved signals of fecundity. As noted previously, the line-drawn Singh stimuli suffer confounds that make interpreting the results difficult. Moreover, and more important from our perspective, the sex of the targets in the Singh stimuli (and the few studies that used other stimuli) was always unambiguous. For the female targets, attractiveness was found to have an inverse rela-tionship with WHR. In the sole study of the implications of the WHR for male targets, larger WHRs that corresponded to the normal male rage were deemed more attractive (Singh, 1995). This precise pattern is predicted by the cue compatibility model. More broadly, prior studies have precontextualised attractiveness judgements by holding constant (and indeed highlighting) the targets' sex.

This basic fact has implications for the psychological processes that undergird interpersonal metaperception. When presented with a clearly female stimulus and given the task of judging her attractiveness, each participant faced a congruence problem, not a decision of reproductive potential. Those figures that were deemed to have a more gynoid shape (smaller WHRs), congruent with the unambiguous female sex, were judged to be more attractive than were those that had more android shapes (higher WHRs), and the opposite is true for clearly male targets. That is, women are judged to be attractive when they are feminine in shape and motion, and men are judged to be attractive when they are masculine in shape and motion (Johnson & Tassinary, 2007a).

This interpretation also has clear implications for cross-cultural research. Indeed, the cue compatibility model supplies a common mechanism that accounts for cross-cultural differences in preferences. When viewing line-drawn women, men from the Hadza tribe of Tanzania did not exhibit a systematic preference for any particular WHR (Wetsman & Marlowe, 1999; Marlowe & Wetsman, 2000) and the Matsigenka men from southeast Peru preferred larger WHRs (Yu & Shepard, 1998). From our perspective, it seems likely that the cultural definitions of femininity differ in these remote tribes. Based on our model, we predict that particular bodily cues have little influence over perceived gender in the Hadza and that the Matsigenka perceived large WHRs to be more feminine. The nearest examination of differences in perceived gender in remote cultures is found in anthropological descriptions of sex differences.[4] Although some research has examined cultural differences in perceived attractiveness (e.g., Swami, Antonakopoulos, Tovée, & Furnham, 2006; Swami, Caprario, Tovée, & Furnham, 2006), no systematic study has directly assessed the features perceived to be masculine and feminine in remote cultures. Instead, aesthetic preferences have been recorded for stimuli that were previously judged to be masculine or feminine by Western respondents. Matsigenka women, for example, prefer masculine (as judged by Western participants) male faces for a son-in-law, but the same women choose feminine male faces as more attractive (Yu, Proulx, & Shepard, Chapter 6). These results suggest a critical role for perceived gender in interpersonal judgements rendered by participants in remote cultures, but they are mute with respect to precisely what is perceived to be masculine or feminine by those participants.

Importantly, this highlights the primary strength of our model, but it also points to its limitation. Our model is agnostic with respect to whether preferences for specific body shapes are the result of specific mate choice adaptations, exaptations, by-products of how humans process information generally, or the product of sociocultural influence (see Rhodes, 2006). Instead, the cue compatibility model specifies a common cognitive mechanism that can result in culture-specific prefer-ences – the model is thus flexible enough to incorporate cultural vari-ability, yet specific enough to predict what will be deemed attractive.

Previous research that explained WHR preferences as due to specific mate choice adaptations used line-drawn stimuli with a lower bound of 0.70, and the sex of the target was unambiguous. Our current and prior research, in contrast, employed stimuli with WHRs as low as 0.50, and the sex of the target was ambiguous. The inclusion of more extreme stimuli has proven to be descriptively interesting and theoretic-ally meaningful for our own and our reinterpretation of others' research. Descriptively, the inclusion of these stimuli has permitted a better understanding of the boundaries and distributions of social perceptions beyond attractiveness. Theoretically, the inclusion of these stimuli has illuminated some critical asymmetries that further limit the viability of the WHR hypothesis. Specifically, previous research identified a WHR of 0.70 to be the 'ideal' female body shape, and these authors posited an adaptive model to explain their findings. Unfortunately, their limited range of WHRs obfuscated the important fact that attractiveness ratings can be even higher for *smaller* WHRs (see Tassinary & Hansen, 1998). Furthermore, we found that a substantial portion of our participants perceived walkers with a WHR of 0.70 to be men, rendering dubious the probability that this WHR is indeed the ideal female shape and the related tenability of a distal evolutionary mechanism.

Although these findings appear to contradict a prominent evolu-tionary theory, they are actually consistent with an entire class of cognitive theories on categorisation. Categorical prototypes are frequently more extreme than the exemplars experienced previously, and this has been shown to facilitate recognition of faces (e.g., Lee, Byatt, & Rhodes, 2000; Lee & Perrett, 2000; Lewis & Johnston, 1999; Mauro & Kubovy, 1992; Tversky & Baratz, 1985; cf. Rhodes & Moody, 1990, for recently presented faces), the identification of emotions (Benson, Campbell, Harris, Frank, & Tovée, 1999; Calder et al., 2000; Pollick, Hill, Calder, & Paterson, 2003), and the individuation of point-light movements (Hill & Pollick, 2000; Pollick, Fidopiastis, & Braden, 2001). Moreover, experience-based theories have described how the most appealing category members are those that are both rare and infrequent (Parducci, 1965). In other words, the 'best' exemplars for a category are extreme. Thus, both cognitive phenomenological perspectives underscore the value of including extreme stimuli in the assessment of preferences.

In addition, these findings augment recent reports that have also ques-tioned the validity of the WHR hypothesis. Specifically, Fan (Chapter 3) and Bateson et al. (Chapter 4; see also Tovée et al., 1999) have claimed that the body mass index (BMI), relative to the WHR, is a more potent cue to perceived attractiveness. We believe that our theoretical perspective shares a common foundation with the literature comparing the importance of BMI and WHR. Indeed, in both the BMI perspective and ours, judgements of both men and women arise from a common psychological mechanism, rather than a psychological adaptation that is unique to the male psychology. That said, the two perspectives do differ in their origins. In our cue compatibility model, we assume that the preference for compatibility in body cues (and social perceptions) is co-opted for evaluative judgements from other fundamental cognitive strategies, a mechanism that may have had evolutionary implications but requires no evolutionary theorising. The underpinnings of BMI preferences, in contrast, have been described almost exclusively in terms of their adaptive advantage. Thus, our perspective shares one aspect with the BMI hypothesis – an emphasis on a common mechanism, but differs in another aspect – the presumed origin of the preferences.

Like other research concerned with how the body is perceived and evaluated, the research we have described in this chapter has focused exclusively on how two body cues – its shape and motion – affect judgements of perceived attractiveness. We recognise, however, that these cues may not be the primary cues to attractiveness. In real interactions, social judgements are likely to incorporate an array of physical cues; quite possibly relying heavily on facial characteristics (see Rhodes, 2006). Thus, as researchers investigating the importance of body cues for social judgements, we must remain mindful that, at least in some circumstances, the body may come in second (or even third!).

Final thoughts

Lord Byron entitled one of his most well known poems, *She Walks in Beauty*. Like Byron, scientists have long been interested in the precise mechanisms that underlie the appreciation of beauty. A more specific understanding of this process, however, has heretofore remained elusive. By adopting a perspective of interpersonal metaperception, we have taken a first step toward a theoretical and empirical understanding for why (and how) *she* (or he) *walks in beauty*.

Author notes

This programme of research was supported in part by an NSF Presidential Faculty Fellowship to the second author. QuickTime movie files of the stimuli used in this research may be obtained from either author upon request.

Notes

1. Following the recommendations of Unger (1979), we will refer to sex judgements to indicate categorical judgements of biological sex (i.e., man or woman); we will refer to gender judgements to indicate the perceived masculinity and femininity.

2. The majority of the prior studies, for example, used an identical stimulus set (i.e., from Singh, 1993), thus raising the possibility of an artifactual interpretation. Additionally, several confounds in those stimuli limit the generalisability of previous studies. The Singh line drawings, for example, confound WHR with waist size and body weight with hip size (Tassinary & Hansen, 1998). To overcome these limitations, Tassinary and Hansen (1998) generated a new set of two-dimensional stimuli based upon anthropometric data (see Hansen, 1996). When more accurately depicted, the putative invariant relationship between the WHR and perceived attractiveness disappeared, and the authors interpreted this as 'a clear and unambiguous disconfirmation of the WHR hypothesis' (Tassinary & Hansen, 1998: 155).

   The assumption of cultural invariance, a cornerstone of the WHR hypothesis, has been discredited. Singh (1993: 305, italics added) noted the importance of cross-cultural consistency:

   > [C]ross-cultural studies should find diverse notions of what constitutes attractiveness in bodily (stature and breast size) and facial features (i.e., complexion, shape and color of teeth, shape of lips, etc.) and associated personality factors ... *WHR, as the first filter, should be culturally invariant in its significance and its relationship to female attractiveness. The fact that WHR conveys such significant information about the mate value of a woman suggests that men in all societies should favor women with a lower WHR over women with a higher WHR for mate selection or at least find such women sexually attractive.*

   Yet this assumption has been disconfirmed. Tribal Hadza men of Tanzania prefer heavier women and show no systematic WHR preference (Wetsman & Marlowe, 1999; Marlowe & Wetsman, 2000). Similarly, Matsigenka men from southeast Peru also prefer heavier women and higher WHRs (Yu & Shepard, 1998). As the populations studied become less isolated, however, judgements begin to resemble those collected from American participants (i.e., reveal a preference for a small WHR; see Swami & Furnham, 2006, for a review). Such culturally mediated findings are strikingly consistent with what is observed even for judgements of facial expressions of emotion (Sorenson, 1975; see Russell, 1994, for a review).

3. Similar silhouetted stimuli have been judged previously to be more realistic than line-drawn stimuli (Salusso-Deonier, Markee, & Pedersen, 1993). Our walkers have the added realism afforded by motion and depth cues (such as shading). Nonetheless, our walkers are not fully representative of human appearance. Notably, some of our walkers fall outside the range of human variation. But we

currently inhabit a world that validates the inclusion of such stimuli within our set of walkers. We are bombarded with images that stretch reality in a way that makes the perception of extreme images not only interesting, but also socially relevant. Little girls, for example, play with Barbie, and she is not perceived as unnatural. Instead, some have argued that she is idealised. Additionally, movies such as *Shrek* make relevant precisely what proportions are deemed by observers to be male/female. Indeed, the 'suspension of disbelief' when watching Princess Fiona (in her pre-ogre form) may have been thwarted if her WHR (approximately 0.52) had been within the normal range of human variation (see Higa, 1999, for a discussion of this issue).

That said, because our walkers depict novel combinations of WHR and walk, we assessed directly how realistic the walkers appeared relative to other stimuli that have been used in research. Participants judged one of three sets of stimuli (all walkers in our stimulus set, all Singh stimuli, or a set of five point-light displays) and made two judgements about them. The first rating assessed where the images fell on a continuum from *artificial* (1) to *lifelike* (11). The second scale assessed how well the stimuli represented humans from *not at all* (1) to *perfectly* (11). These judgements were averaged to yield an index of realism. The realism scores between the three sets of stimuli were comparable: walkers ($M = 6.65$, $SD = 1.6$, $n = 20$), Singh ($M = 6.43$, $SD = 2.0$, $n = 20$), and point-light displays ($M = 6.91$, $SD = 1.8$, $n = 13$). (We thank Randolph Blake for providing us with a set of point-light displays for this test.)

4. Eibl-Eibesfeldt (1988: 57), for example, characterised the motion of male dancers – abrupt movements oriented toward the audience – as an expression of power, and he argued that the specific poses of men served to 'enlarge the frontal appearance.' The motion of female dancers, in contrast, was described as 'coquetry,' an expression of approach and withdrawal, and he argued that the graceful motions presented the body from various angles. Others have described the 'male' and 'female' qualities of all individuals (and objects). Arve Sørum (1993) described the gendered nature of all things in the Bedamini from Papua New Guinea. Those aspects of an individual that are hard and unyielding, such as bones, are thought to be male characteristics, and are believed to be inherited from the father. In contrast, those aspects of an individual which are soft and yielding, such as flesh, are thought to be female characteristics, and are believed to be inherited from the mother. This distinction carries over into more general gender descriptions, as well. Sørum (1993: 114) notes, 'Strength and endurance are generally talked of as masculine qualities, and softness and weakness are talked of as feminine qualities. To express that a man is strong and courageous, they say that "he has got bones"...A weak man is like cooked meant, he might easily be consumed (destroyed).' These descriptions of how motion and form are perceived intimate a critical role for motion and morphology in perceived gender, although they do not explicate with precision what guides such percepts.

References

Aberson, C. L., Swan, D., & Emerson, E. P. (1999). Covert discrimination against gay men by U.S. college students. *Journal of Social Psychology, 139*, 323–334.

Allport, G. W. (1954). *The nature of prejudice*. Reading, MA: Addison Wesley.

Allport, G. W., & Vernon, P. E. (1933). *Studies in expressive movement.* New York: Macmillan.

Ambady, N., Hallahan, M., & Conner, B. (1999). Accuracy of judgements of sexual orientation from thin slices of behavior. *Journal of Personality and Social Psychology, 77,* 538–547.

Asch, S. E. (1946). Forming impressions of personality. *Journal of Abnormal and Social Psychology, 46,* 1230–1240.

Bailey, J. M., & Zucker, K. J. (1995). Childhood sex-typed behavior and sexual orientation: A conceptual analysis and quantitative review. *Developmental Psychology, 31,* 43–55.

Barclay, C. D., Cutting, J. E., & Kozlowski, L. T. (1978). Temporal and spatial factors in gait perception that influence gender recognition. *Perception and Psychophysics, 23,* 145–152.

Bem, S. L. (1993). *The lenses of gender.* New Haven: Yale University Press.

Benson, P. J., Campbell, R., Harris, T., Frank, M. G., & Tovée, M. J. (1999). Enhancing images of facial expressions. *Perception and Psychophysics, 61,* 259–274.

Björntorp, P. (1988). The associations between obesity, adipose tissue distribution and disease. *Acta Medica Scandinavica Supplement, 723,* 121–134.

Brown, W. M., Cronk, K., Grokow, K., Jacobson, A., Liu, C. K., Popovic, Z., et al. (2005). Dance reveals symmetry especially in young men. *Nature, 438,* 1148–1150.

Buller, D. J. (2005a). *Adapting minds: Evolutionary psychology and the persistent quest for human nature.* New York: Bradford Books.

Buller, D. J. (2005b). Evolutionary psychology: The emperor's new paradigm. *Trends in Cognitive Science, 9,* 277–283.

Calder, A. J., Rowland, D., Young, A. W., Nimmo-Smith, I., Keane, J., & Perrett, D. I. (2000). Caricaturing facial expressions. *Cognition, 76,* 105–146.

Chen, E. (2005, February). Rules of attraction: Size does matter. *Elle,* 157.

Clauser, C. E., Tebbetts, I. O., Bradtmiller, B., McConville, J. T., & Gordon, C. C. (1987–1988). *Measurer's handbook: US Army anthropometric survey.* Tech. Rep. NATICK/TR-88/043, AD A202 721.

Cowley, G. (1996, June 3). The biology of beauty. *Newsweek,* 61–69.

Cutting, J. E. (1978). Generation of synthetic male and female walkers though manipulation of a biomechanical invariant. *Perception, 7,* 393–405.

Cutting, J. E. (1981). Coding theory adapted to gait perception. *Journal of Experimental Psychology: Human Perception and Performance, 7,* 71–87.

Cutting, J. E., Moore, C., & Morrison, R. (1988). Masking the motions of human gait. *Perception and Psychophysics, 44,* 339–347.

Cutting, J. E., Proffit, D. R., & Kozlowski, L. T. (1978). A biomechanical invariant for gait perception. *Journal of Experimental Psychology: Human Perception and Performance, 4,* 357–372.

Donelson, S. M., & Gordon, C. C. (1988). *Anthropometric survey of US army personnel: Pilot summary statistics.* Tech. Rep. NATICK/TR-91/040, AD A241 952.

Eibl-Eibesfeldt, I. (1988). The biological foundation of aesthetics. In I. Rentschler, B. Herzberger, & D. Epstein (Eds.), *Beauty and the brain: Biological aspects of aesthetics.* Boston: Basel.

Fallon, A. E., & Rozin, P. (1985). Sex differences in perceptions of desirable body shape. *Journal of Abnormal Psychology, 94,* 102–105.

Frable, D. E. S. (1987). Sex-typed execution and perception of expressive movement. *Journal of Personality and Social Psychology, 53,* 391–396.

Frumkin, R. M. (1954). Visual aphrodisiacs. *Sexology, 20,* 481–483.

Furnham, A., Dias, M., & McClelland, A. (1998). The role of body weight, waist-to-hip ratio, and breast size in judgements of female attractiveness. *Sex Roles, 39,* 311–326.

Furnham, A., Tan, T., & McManus, C. (1997). Waist-to-hip ratio and preferences for body shape: A replication and extension. *Personality and Individual Differences, 22,* 539–549.

Gangestad, S. W., Thornhill, R., & Yeo, R. A. (1994). Facial attractiveness, developmental stability, and fluctuating asymmetry. *Ethology and Sociobiology, 15,* 73–85.

Hansen, K. (1996). *An empirical analysis of the perception of beauty, gender, and form.* Unpublished Master's thesis, Texas A&M University, College Station, Texas, USA.

Heider, F. (1946). Attitudes and cognitive organization. *Journal of Psychology, 21,* 107–112.

Heider, F. (1958). *The psychology of interpersonal relations.* New York: Wiley.

Heiman, J. D. (1999, April). The science of sexy. *US,* 55–60.

Heisenberg, W. K. (1974). *Across frontiers.* New York: Harper & Row.

Henss, R. (1995). Waist-to-hip ratio and attractiveness: Replication and extension. *Personality and Individual Differences, 19,* 479–488.

Henss, R. (2000). Waist-to-hip ratio and female attractiveness: Evidence from photographic stimuli and methodological considerations. *Personality and Individual Differences, 28,* 501–513.

Herek, G. M. (1984). Beyond 'homophobia': A social psychological perspective on attitudes toward lesbians and gay men. *Journal of Homosexuality, 10,* 1–21.

Higa, M. (1999). *Perception based character modeling and animation.* Unpublished Master's thesis, Texas A&M University, College Station, Texas, USA.

Hill, H., & Pollick, F. E. (2000). Exaggerating temporal differences enhances recognition of individuals from point light displays. *Psychological Science, 11,* 223–228.

Johnson, K. L., & Tassinary, L. G. (2005). Perceiving sex directly and indirectly: Meaning in motion and morphology. *Psychological Science, 16,* 890–897.

Johnson, K. L., & Tassinary, L. G. (2007a). Compatibility of basic social perceptions determines perceived attractiveness. *Proceedings of the National Academy of Sciences of the United States of America, 104,* 5246–5251.

Johnson, K. L., & Tassinary, L. G. (2007b). *Yin or Yang? Presumed extremity in the categorization of bodies.* Manuscript submitted for publication.

Johnson, K. L., Gill, S., Reichman, V., & Tassinary, L. G. (in press). Swagger, sway, and sexuality: Judging sexual orientation from body motion and morphology. *Journal of Personality and Social Psychology.*

Kerrigan, D. C., Todd, M. K., & Della Croce, U. (1998). Gender differences in joint biomechanics during walking: Normative study in young adults. *American Journal of Physical Medicine & Rehabilitation, 77,* 1–7.

Koffka, K. (1935). *Principles of Gestalt psychology.* Oxford, England: Harcourt Brace.

Köhler, W. (1929). *Gestalt psychology.* Oxford, England: Liveright.

Köhler, W. (1947). *Gestalt psychology: An introduction to new concepts in modern psychology.* Oxford, England: Liveright.

Langlois, J. H., & Roggman, L. A. (1990). Attractive faces are only average. *Psychological Science, 1,* 115–121.

Lanska, D. J., Lanska, M. J., Hartz, A. J., & Rimm, A. A. (1985). Factors influencing anatomic locations of fat tissue in 52,953 women. *International Journal of Obesity, 9,* 29–38.

Laws, A., King, A., Haskell, W. L., & Reaven, G. M. (1993). Metabolic and behavioral covariates of high-density lipoprotein cholesterol and triglyceride concentrations in postmenopausal women. *Journal of the American Geriatrics Society, 41,* 1289–1294.

Lee, K. J., & Perrett, D. I. (2000). Manipulation of colour and shape information and its consequence upon recognition and best-likeness judgements. *Perception, 29,* 1291–1312.

Lee, K., Byatt, G., & Rhodes, G. (2000). Caricature effects, distinctiveness, and identification: Testing the face-space framework. *Psychological Science, 11,* 379–385.

Lewis, M. B., & Johnston, R. A. (1999). A unified account of the effects of caricaturing faces. *Visual Cognition, 6,* 1–41.

Lippa, R. (1983). Sex typing and the perception of body outlines. *Journal of Personality, 51,* 667–682.

Marlowe, F., & Wetsman, A. (2000). Preferred waist-to-hip ratio and ecology. *Personality and Individual Differences, 30,* 481–489.

Mauro, R., & Kubovy, M. (1992). Caricature and face recognition. *Memory and Cognition, 20,* 433–440.

Murry, M. P., Kory, R. C., & Sepic, S. B. (1970). Walking patterns of normal women. *Archives of Physical Medicine and Rehabilitation, 51,* 637–650.

Neisser, U. (1994). Multiple systems: A new approach to cognitive theory. *European Journal of Cognitive Psychology, 6,* 225–241.

Newman, C. (2000, January). The enigma of beauty. *National Geographic,* 94–121.

Ostlund, R. E., Staten, M., Kohrt, W. M., Schultz, J., & Malley, M. (1990). The ratio of waist-to-hip circumference, plasma insulin level, and glucose intolerance as independent predictors of the HDL_2 cholesterol level in older adults. *New England Journal of Medicine, 322,* 229–234.

Parducci, A. (1965). Category judgement: A range-frequency model. *Psychological Review, 72,* 407–418.

Pollick, F. E., Fidopiastis, C., & Braden, V. (2001). Recognising the style of spatially exaggerated tennis serves. *Perception, 30,* 323–338.

Pollick, F. E., Hill, H., Calder, A., & Paterson, H. (2003). Recognising facial expression from spatially and temporally modified movements. *Perception, 32,* 813–826.

Rhodes, G. (2006). The evolutionary psychology of beauty. *Annual Review of Psychology, 57,* 199–226.

Rhodes, G., & Moody, J. (1990). Memory representations of unfamiliar faces: Coding of distinctive information. *New Zealand Journal of Psychology, 19,* 70–78.

Rieger, G. (2006). *The stickiness of sex atypicality: Movies of homosexual people from childhood and adulthood.* Unpublished doctoral thesis, Northwestern University, Evanston, IL.

Rieger, G., Linsenmeier, J. A. W., Gygax, L., & Bailey, J. M. (Manuscript Under Review). *Sexual orientation and childhood sex atypicality: Evidence from home movies.*

Rozmus-Wrzesinska, M., & Pawlowski, B. (2005). Men's ratings of female attractiveness are influenced more by changes in female waist size compared with changes in hip size. *Biological Psychology, 68,* 299–308.

Russell, J. A. (1994). Is there universal recognition of emotion from facial expression? A review of the cross-cultural studies. *Psychological Bulletin, 115,* 102–141.

Whitman, W. (1900). *Leaves of grass.* Philadelphia: McKay.

Salusso-Deonier, C. J., Markee, N. L., & Pedersen, E. L. (1993). Gender differences in the evaluation of physical attractiveness ideals for male and female body builds. *Perceptual and Motor Skills, 76,* 1155–1167.

Sheldon, W. H., Stevens, S. S., & Tucker, W. B. (1942). *The varieties of human physique.* New York: Harper.

Singh, D. (1993). Adaptive significance of female physical attractiveness: Role of waist-to-hip ratio. *Journal of Personality and Social Psychology, 65,* 293–307.

Singh, D. (1994). Is thin really beautiful and good? Relationship between waist-to-hip ratio (WHR) and female attractiveness. *Personality and Individual Differences, 16,* 123–132.

Singh, D. (1995). Female judgement of male attractiveness and desirability for relationships: Role of waist-to-hip ratio and financial status. *Journal of Personality and Social Psychology, 69,* 1089–1101.

Sirin, S. R., McCreary, D. R., & Mahalik, J. R. (2004). Differential reactions to men and women's gender role transgressions: Perceptions of social status, sexual orientation, and value dissimilarity. *Journal of Men's Studies, 12,* 119–132.

Smith, L. K., Lelas, J. L., & Kerrigan, D. C. (2002). Gender differences in pelvic motions and center of mass displacement during walking: Stereotypes quantified. *Journal of Women's Health and Gender-Based Medicine, 11,* 453–458.

Sorenson, E. R. (1975). Culture and the expression of emotion. In T. R. Willams (Ed.), *Psychological Anthropology* (pp. 361–372). Paris: Mouton Publishers.

Sørum, A. (1993). Encountering femininity: The ontogenesis of Bedaminimale selves. In V. Broche-Due, I. Rudie, & T. Bleie (Eds.), *Carved flesh cast selves: Gendered symbols and social practices* (pp. 107–127). Oxford: Berg Publishers.

Stangor, C., Lynch, L., Duan, C., & Glass, B. (1992). Categorization of individuals on the basis of multiple social features. *Journal of Personality and Social Psychology, 62,* 207–281.

Stanish, M. (1996, June 1). Hip deep in controversy: UT professor throws researchers a curve with study on waist-hip ratios. *Austin American-Statesman,* pp. C1, C12.

Storm, K. J. (2001). *Hate crimes reported in NIBRS, 1997–99* (NCJ Publication No. 186765). U.S. Department of Justice.

Streeter, S. A., & McBurney, D. H. (2003). Waist-hip ratio and attractiveness: New evidence and a critique of 'a critical test.' *Evolution and Human Behavior, 24,* 88–98.

Swami, V., & Furnham, A. (2006). The science of attraction. *The Psychologist, 19,* 362–365.

Swami, V., Antonakopoulos, N., Tovée, M. J., & Furnham, A. (2006). A critical test of the waist-to-hip ratio hypothesis of female physical attractiveness in Britain and Greece. *Sex Roles, 54,* 201–211.

Swami, V., Caprario, C., Tovée, M. J., & Furnham, A. (2006). Female physical attractiveness in Britain and Japan: A cross-cultural study. *European Journal of Personality, 20,* 69–81.

Tassinary, L. G., & Hansen, K. A. (1998). A critical test of the waist-to-hip ratio hypothesis of female physical attractiveness. *Psychological Science, 9,* 150–155.

Taylor, S., Fiske, S., Etcoff, N., & Ruderman, A. (1978). Categorical and contextual bases of person memory and stereotyping. *Journal of Personality and Social Psychology, 36,* 778–793.

Tovée, M. J., & Cornelissen, P. L. (2001). Female and male perceptions of female physical attractiveness in front-view and profile. *British Journal of Psychology, 92,* 391–402.

Tovée, M. J., Maisey, D. S., Emery, J. L., & Cornelissen, P. L. (1999). Visual cues to female physical attractiveness. *Proceedings of the Royal Society London B, 266,* 211–218.

Troje, N. F. (2002). Decomposing biological motion: A framework for analysis and synthesis of human gait patterns. *Journal of Vision, 2,* 371–387.

Tversky, B., & Baratz, D. (1985). Memory for faces: Are caricatures better than photographs? *Memory and Cognition, 13,* 45–49.

Unger, R. K. (1979). Toward a redefinition of sex and gender. *American Psychologist, 34,* 1085–1094.

Wetsman, A., & Marlowe, F. (1999). How universal are preferences for female waist-to-hip ratios? Evidence from the Hadza of Tanzania. *Evolution and Human Behavior, 20,* 219–228.

Yu, D. W., & Shepard, G. H. (1998). Is beauty in the eye of the beholder? *Nature, 396,* 321–322.

Zaadstra, B. M., Seidell, J. C., Van Noord, P. A. H., te Velde, E. R., Habbema, J. D. F., Vrieswijk, B., et al. (1993). Fat and female fecundity: Prospective study of effect of body fat distribution on conception rates. *British Medical Journal, 306,* 484–487.

10
Mate Preferences in Social Cognitive Context: When Environmental and Personal Change Leads to Predictable Cross-Cultural Variation

Leif D. Nelson, Terry F. Pettijohn II, and Jeff Galak

> Shall I compare thee to a summer's day?
> Thou art more lovely and more temperate.
> ~ Shakespeare, 1564–1616

As is common for many men, Shakespeare was idealising a woman. The search for an ideal partner was not only critical for Shakespeare – it is, by evolutionary standards, the central goal for all male and female life forms (Buss, 1985; Darwin, 1859; Vandenberg, 1972). Anthropological and psychological evidence continues to document the features women seek in a male partner (Symons, 1979), but for the purposes of this chapter we primarily focus on the features men seek in a female partner. The ideal feminine form has been characterised by painters and sculptors for as long as paintings and sculptures have existed (e.g., see Zollner & Nathan, 2003) and Shakespeare is, of course, hardly the first writer to try a verbal description.

For all of this artistic endeavor, it remains unknown whether beauty has a truly universal ideal or whether it is idiosyncratically in the eye of the beholder. Anthropologists have documented both sides of the argument, identifying those features idealised in all cultures as well as those uniquely pursued within specific cultures (e.g., Ford & Beach, 1951). Evolutionary psychologists have seized upon the former concept, and have detailed evidence supporting the universality hypothesis. Among other features, men seek youthfulness (Buss, 1989), facial averageness (Rhodes et al., 2001), a low waist-to-hip ratio (Singh, 1993; Singh & Young, 1995), and generally healthy body weights (Tovée & Cornelissen, 1999).

Many of these preferences are rooted in human evolutionary past. Darwin, after realising that various body parts on animals (e.g., the feathers on a peacock) served no survival purpose, concluded that there is a form of sexual selection (later this concept was subsumed back into natural selection) designed to elicit sexual responses in potential mates (Darwin, 1859, 1871). In other words, animals develop characteristics to attract the opposite sex. These traits often signal health and reproductive promise (Buss, 1994; Singh, 1993). For example, neotenous facial features (Cunningham, Roberts, Barbee, Druen, & Wu, 1995; Jones, 1995), a waist-to-hip ratio of about 0.70 (Singh, 1993), and a body mass index (BMI) of 20 kg/m^2 (for Caucasians) (Tovée & Cornelissen, 2001) are all positively viewed in women. The evolutionary claim essentially requires that these ideals are held by all male members of the species – a claim of universal attractiveness ideals grounded in the biological facts of natural selection. Indeed, many of the findings above have been found to be quite cross-culturally universal (for an alternative view, see Tovée, Swami, Furnham, & Mangalparsad, 2006).

The apparent exceptions then become intriguing. A variety of research has shown that variation in resource scarcity seems to reliably affect male preferences (Anderson, Crawford, Nadeau, & Lindberg, 1992; Furnham & Baguma, 1994; Symons, 1979), seemingly refuting the claims of universality. Pettijohn and Tesser (1999) have further shown that this variance persists as individual cultures change over time, such that when times are good, similar mate preferences surface as compared to a culture with plentiful resources. While the root of these two dimensions – cultural/geographic and temporal – appears to be context dependent, Nelson and Morrison (2005: 168) have shown that there is an 'implicit psychological mechanism based on the situational influence of environmental conditions' that dictates this variability. Essentially, when men feel poor or hungry, they prefer heavier women.

Why is there such variability and where does it come from? In this chapter we attempt to review the existing literature with an eye towards an integrated answer to such questions. In doing so we emphasise theory predicting variation (namely the Environmental Security Hypothesis; Pettijohn & Tesser, 1999), and consider possible psychological structure that could give rise to it (e.g., Nelson & Morrison, 2005).

Characteristics of the ideal mate

Let us return to the question of preference universality. It was long believed that standards from one culture do not generalise to others.

Even today, there are some traits that cannot be unconfounded from a given culture. For example, even the extent to which cultures value physical appearance has some meaningful between-culture variation. Male preferences emphasise physical appearance universally, but this is particularly true for cultures with high levels of pathogens (Gangestad & Buss, 1993). Even after controlling for a variety of obvious potential confounds, such as ethnicity and location, pathogen levels account for approximately 52 per cent of cross-cultural variability. Because attractiveness indicates good health, when pathogens are a serious concern, beauty indicates a healthy partner. Ford and Beach (1951: 89) showed that absence of sores and lesions are universally regarded as attractive, while poor complexion is always considered unattractive: 'Pimples, ringworm, or other disfigurements of the face or body' are universally repugnant. This suggests that cleanliness and freedom from disease are universally attractive. Aside from general notions of health, other forms of variation in physical appearance are quite predictable.

If, as aforementioned, beauty lies only partially in the eye of the beholder, it also literally lies in the eyes of the beholden. When choosing a mate, men pay particular attention to the shape and composition of women's faces. Cunningham (1986) identified a variety of measures for classifying a woman's face; most notably he identified two major categories of faces that affect mate preferences: neonate and mature. Neonate features span species and generally share features such as large eyes and forehead, smaller, rounded nose and chin, larger lips, and softer skin (Guthrie, 1976; Keating, Mazur, & Segall, 1981). Mature faces, by contrast, generally are represented by higher, wider cheekbones, and narrower eyes (Smith, 1982). For example, people believe that eyes positioned higher on a person's face, a neonate feature, indicated that the person was brighter, more sociable, and more assertive than someone with eyes positioned lower (Lorenz, 1943). Most interesting, however, is the analysis of which facial characteristic best predicted each trait attribute. With the exception of perceived fertility, which is equally predicted by a neonate and mature trait, all of the positive traits tested were more common with people who had neonate features. People with neonate features tend to be healthier and tend to be judged as more attractive (Korthase & Trenholme, 1982). What is the source of this apparently implicit preference?

Neonate features are positive indicators for infant health, and indeed parents perceive babies to be cuter if their features are more classically neonatal (Hildebrandt & Fitzgerald, 1978). Given that people prefer younger-looking adults (Enlow, 1982; Korthase & Trenholme, 1982), these findings suggest that the positive health of a baby-faced look may be guiding judgements of physical attractiveness. Alternatively, certain characteristics of a mature face, small forehead and eyes, and a large nose, prominent cheekbones and jaw, and a large chin may also be considered attractive (Symons, 1979), as they tend to represent status, power, and dominance.

Moving to a more holistic view of the body, one of the most researched traits, body weight, has been linked to a virtually universal non-appearance related attribute, perceived abundance of resources (Anderson et al., 1992; Buss & Kenrick, 1998; Furnham & Baguma, 1994; Symons, 1979). In cultures with limited resources, men prefer heavier women. As was argued about pathogen presence, body weight preferences can be grounded in an evolutionary necessity for healthy and virile mating partners. When resources are scarce, body weight may signal health and status in a potential mate (Anderson et al., 1992; Brown & Konner, 1987; Frisch, 1990). Because fat acts as a store for calories, an insulator for the body, and affects the onset and maintenance of ovulation, fatness can be a critical signal for reproductive health in a woman (Buss & Kenrick, 1998). From an evolutionary perspective, body fat is important in finding the best partner.

The relationship between body weight and resource abundance exists *within* cultures as well. In wealthy cultures, female status and obesity are negatively related, whereas in poorer cultures, female status and obesity are positively related (Sobal & Stunkard, 1989). It is interesting to note that the same stream of research showed no association between resource availability and male obesity rates, perhaps indicating that weight is less important in females' preferences for the ideal male, consistent with evolutionary theories (Buss & Kenrick, 1998).

Although body weight is a powerful predictor of female attractiveness, it is hardly the only one. For example, consider the waist-to-hip ratio (WHR), which reflects the relative circumference of a person's waist to the circumference of his or her hips. One potential reason that this metric is so important is that it helps distinguish male and female body types. At birth, males and females have identical WHRs, but at puberty increased estrogen deposits fat in the hips and the upper thighs, resulting in approximately 40 per cent of all body weight residing in this region for women (Björntorp, 1991, 1997).

This distinction suggests that female reproductive ability can be partially assessed with the WHR. Healthy women generally have a WHR between 0.67 and 0.80, whereas healthy men have a WHR closer to 1.0 (Lanska, Lanska, Hartz, & Rimm, 1985; Jones, Hunt, Brown, & Norgan,

1986). Women with a relatively high WHRs have more difficulty becoming pregnant, whereas women with a relatively low WHR have less difficulty becoming pregnant (see Singh, 1993). Furthermore, other health-related conditions such as diabetes, hypertension, and stroke have been linked to the distribution of fat in women above and beyond the absolute amount of fat (Singh, 1993). 'Good' WHRs are healthy, but are they also attractive?

A series of studies conducted by Singh (1993) revealed an inverted U-shaped relationship between body fat and attractiveness and a linear negative relationship between WHR and attractiveness. Extremes of overall body weight were judged as unattractive, but extremely low WHRs were judged as very attractive, relationships which held for judgements of images of real women, line drawings, and computer-generated illustrations (Singh, 1993). There also appears to be an optimum WHR. An analysis of *Playboy* centerfolds and beauty pageant winners within the United States found that, independent of body fat content (which was low but variable), the WHR remained constant at 0.70 (Singh, 1993).

Though there are many universals in judgements of physical attractiveness, it is equally clear that there is some meaningful cross-cultural variation. To explain this variation, be it ideals of facial features or ideals of body weight, we need a larger theoretical framework which provides a more proximal explanation for how environmental factors operate on mate preferences. One such influential theory is the Environmental Security Hypothesis (ESH; Pettijohn & Tesser, 1999), which suggests how cultural pressures might operate on evolutionarily derived preferences. Furthermore, the nature of this variability can be also attributed to an implicit contextual preference independent of culture.

Environmental security hypothesis

To explain our social preferences in environmental context, Pettijohn and Tesser (1999) developed the ESH (see Table 10.1 for a summary of study findings). Blending evolutionary and social ecological theories (Buss, 1994; Cunningham, 1986), the ESH provides a context-dependent theory of social preferences such that our perceptions of environmental security influence what we find most attractive and most desirable at different times. Since perceptions of our safety and security in our environment can vary, so too can our social preferences in order to aid in making adaptive decisions. Threatening and uncertain times elicit the desire for more fundamental, meaningful, and mature themes and items to assist with handling threat and uncertainty. In less threatening and

Table 10.1 Summaries of studies testing the Environmental Security Hypothesis.

Study	Summary
Pettijohn & Tesser (1999)	Archival investigation of popular American movie actresses from 1932–1995. When social and economic conditions were poor, actresses with small eyes and large chins were popular.
Pettijohn & Tesser (2003)	Archival investigation of popular American movie actors from 1932–1995. Actor facial features were more variable and not systematically related to social and economic conditions across time.
Pettijohn & Jungeberg (2004)	Archival investigation of *Playboy* Playmate of the Year from 1960–2000. When social and economic conditions were difficult, relatively older, heavier, taller Playmates with larger waists, smaller eyes, larger waist-to-hip ratios, and smaller body mass index values were selected.
Pettijohn & Yerkes (2004)	Archival investigation of Miss America from 1933–2002 yielding mixed results. In hard times, Miss America tended to have a lower body mass index and weigh less than in good times.
Pettijohn & Yerkes (2005)	Archival investigation of Miss Hong Kong from 1973–2003 producing mixed results. In difficult social and economic conditions, Miss Hong Kong winners were relatively older with lower BMIs, smaller chins, larger eyes, narrower faces, and larger noses.
Pettijohn & Sacco (2005)	Study of popular U.S. *Billboard* songs from 1955–2001. In hard times, popular songs were longer, and rated as slower, more meaningful, romantic, and comforting. Since 1980, popular performers were more likely to have smaller eyes in hard times.
Pettijohn & Tesser (2005)	A set of experimental studies manipulating individual threat and measuring partner eye-size preference. Participants preferred a decreased eye-size partner to a relatively greater extent in a high threat condition compared to a low threat condition.
Pettijohn, Sacco, & Yerkes (2005)	A field test of the ESH investigating ideal mate preferences. Hungry males preferred females who were relatively older, taller, heavier, and with more mature facial features and personality traits compared to males who were satiated. Female preferences were not significantly altered by hunger state.
Pettijohn, Sacco, Yerkes, & Walzer (2007)	A set of experimental studies manipulated future social and economic success in college students. Participants showed a preference for male and female models with decreased eye-size, darker male hair colour, and larger female WHR in the uncertain condition compared to the certain condition.

more certain conditions, the need for meaningful, mature themes and items to contend with threat and uncertainty is less necessary.

Therefore, less meaningful, less mature, and more carefree and fun themes and items are preferred in environmental conditions of less threat. In less threatening times, there is a different motivational state experienced where social decision-making is not as reliant on being functional as it is during threatening, uncertain times. As a result, there are less social consequences of decisions in less threatening conditions compared to conditions of threat and uncertainty. Having fun, enjoying the pleasures of life, and not worrying about serious threats are generally more reflective goals of these certain, less-threatening conditions, which produces different relative preferences.

The ESH further adapts evolutionary predictions within specific historical and cultural contexts. Evolutionary theories of mate selection suggest that males focus on female physical appearance and reproductive ability when selecting mates and females focus on male status and resources. The ESH predicts that these evolutionary main effects are moderated by individual feelings of environmental security. These moderators allow us to predict some of the cross-cultural variation we documented above. Facial features, height, weight, age, and personality preferences may vary with social and economic conditions. Males may always prefer young, thin females with large eyes, but the degree of youthfulness, thinness, and eye size may vary with environmental conditions within these evolutionary prediction ranges.

Pettijohn and Tesser (1999) first developed the ESH to explain the variability in American motion picture actress popularity. In certain years, mature-looking actresses with smaller eyes and thinner faces were popular, whereas in other years, less mature-looking actresses with larger eyes and rounder faces were popular. Could these fluctuations be predicted with the ESH? Specifically, are mature faces more popular during social and economic hard times and neotenous faces more popular during social and economic good times? As we detailed earlier, mature facial features are associated with the attributes of dominance and independence, whereas neotenous faces are associated with the attributes of submissiveness and agreeableness. Previous studies had found that men preferred women with larger eyes (see Cunningham, 1986; Cunningham et al., 1995); the ESH predicted that large-eye preferences would change as environmental conditions changed.

These hypotheses were tested using common United States social and economic statistics (unemployment rate, death rate, consumer price index, etc.) from 1932 to 1995 to create a General Hard Times Measure (variations of this measure were also used in other archival investigations). The statistics were standardised for each year and combined to create a global measure of social and economic hard times where higher values would designate more difficult social and economic times. We also utilised a consistent measure of actor popularity (the Annual Quigley Publications Poll) from 1932 to 1995 and a standardised method of facial measurement (see Cunningham, 1986; Cunningham, Roberts, Barbee, Druen, & Wu, 1995). Cunningham's method allows investigators to perform measurements to quantify eye size, facial narrowness, chin size, and a host of other facial dimensions as ratios to facial length and width so results can be compared between faces. As hypothesised, actresses with mature facial features were preferred in hard times (e.g., Marie Dressler and Janet Gaynor in the early 1930s) and actresses with neotenous facial features were preferred in good times (Ann Sheridan, Bette Davis, Judy Garland, and Rita Hayworth during the 1940s) (Pettijohn & Tesser, 1999). Although intriguing, these results raised additional questions about the influence of social and economic conditions on male facial feature preferences, the necessity for analysis of threat on an individual, experimental level, and how environmental conditions influence preferences for other types of social stimuli.

Accordingly, subsequent research showed that there was no similar relationship for male actors over the same time period (Pettijohn & Tesser, 2003) and male actors were more variable in their facial feature compositions within years. In poor social and economic times, male actors had large eyes and small eyes, large chins and small chins, thin faces and round faces. There was no consistency in preferences for male actors across the changing social and economic environments. The lack of facial feature preferences for male actors over time is largely consistent with some of the sex asymmetries in the importance placed by physical attractiveness, which we described earlier. In American society, as in other socioeconomically developed societies, much greater importance is placed on female appearance (Berscheid & Reis, 1998; Feingold, 1990), and the actor popularity likely follows suit. Therefore, female facial feature preferences are influenced by social and economic situations, but male facial features preferences are not as malleable. Other research has found that male actors were preferred to a relatively greater extent over female actors during social and economic hard times (Pettijohn, 2003). Males may naturally display greater attributes of independence, maturity, and strength compared to females by virtue of their sex, not their facial features, and these qualities are preferred during hard times.

However, this difference may only exist for male actors. Pettijohn, Sacco, Yerkes, and Walzer (2007) found support for decreased eye-size preferences in male models in uncertain conditions and increased eye-size preferences in male models in certain conditions. Further research into the complexities of this sex difference is warranted.

Looking beyond these archival findings, could the same preferences be modified at the individual level? Pettijohn and Tesser (2005) designed a set of experimental manipulations to extend the utility of the ESH. When people experienced high threat they should show a relatively greater preference for females with smaller eyes. Participants were threatened with the possibility of receiving either mild or strong electric shocks in the context of a learning exercise and chose a partner to work with from a set of female facial photographs. Male and female participants were more likely to choose a partner with small eyes under high threat than under low threat. When personality information was included with the photographs, the eye size preference effect was reduced, suggesting that individuals rely less on physical appearance when more information is available. Furthermore, when the upcoming interaction was described as being more independent, the effect was larger than when it was described as being less independent.

Pettijohn and Tesser (2005) also considered individual differences and found mixed results. Chronic perceptions of stress, anxiety, and optimism had little influence on preferences for partners in the first study, but stress and anxiety individual differences had a significant influence on partner eye-size choice in the second study. Participants who scored high on an undergraduate stress measure or high on a trait anxiety measure showed a systematic preference for the decreased eye-size partner compared to participants low in stress or low in trait anxiety. There were no differences in partner eye-size choice in relation to optimism scores. Those participants who are regularly stressed or anxious responded to our choice stimuli similarly to those in the experimental threat condition. These individual difference states may mirror experimental conditions or amplify preferences during certain and uncertain threat states. Further research is needed in this area to understand the complexity of how these and other individual differences related to threat and uncertainty fit within the ESH.

These studies found support for the ESH with respect to female facial feature preferences, but Pettijohn and Jungeberg (2004) extended the ESH to encompass female body feature and age preferences. As described above, body features and age offer additional dimensions which can provide signals of maturity and character. Tall individuals are believed to be stronger, more independent, and more dominant than shorter individuals (Adams, 1980); older individuals are believed to be more responsible and mature than younger individuals. Anderson et al. (1992) found that female body fat is considered attractive and negatively correlated with women's political power and economic resources in cultures where women have limited economic opportunities and wealth. Singh (1993) has found a preferred WHR preference of around 0.70 and other researchers report the attractiveness of curvaceousness in females to males (Barber, 1998a, 1998b). Depending on social and economic conditions, these body shape preferences and personality characteristics may become more or less important in selecting a mate or determining what makes someone desirable. When times are threatening, reproductive fitness may be less important while the ability to acquire resources and be productive may become more important (Pettijohn & Jungeberg, 2004).

In difficult times men should prefer more mature female characteristics (Pettijohn & Jungeberg, 2004). To test this hypothesis, Pettijohn and Jungeberg (2004) analysed the features of *Playboy* Playmates of the Year for the years 1960 to 2000. Similar to the previous archival investigations, United States social and economic statistics were collected, facial measurements of the models were compiled, and body measurements were taken from reported data sheets published in *Playboy* magazine. As predicted, the models were relatively older, heavier, and taller with larger waists, smaller eyes, larger WHRs, smaller bust-to-waist ratios, and lower BMIs when social and economic conditions were difficult. Mature features and body shapes were relatively more preferred in hard times.

Pettijohn and colleagues (Pettijohn, Sacco, Yerkes, & Walzer, 2007) have conducted additional experimental studies which have supported ESH predictions. In a set of studies, male and female college students read essays persuading them to feel either certain or uncertain about employment opportunities after graduation (Study 1) and participants were given positive or negative false feedback on a simulated social/economic future success test (Study 2). In both studies, participants showed a preference for male and female increased eye-size models in the certain condition and a preference for decreased male and female eye-size models in the uncertain condition. Besides eye-size preferences, participants preferred a male with black hair more in the uncertain condition, a female drawing with a 0.7 or 0.8 waist-to-hip ratio was preferred in the certain condition, and a female drawing with a 0.9 or 1.0 WHR was preferred in the uncertain condition. These studies provide additional experimental support for the ESH and extend preferences to hair colour and WHRs.

Further investigations have analysed beauty pageant contestants with intriguing (if mixed) results. Pettijohn and Yerkes (2004) considered Miss America winners between 1933 and 2002, and found that in hard times, Miss America tended to have a lower BMI and weigh less than in good times, but there was no similar relationship for other observable physical features. Over a slightly narrower range of years, however (1960 to 2002), Miss America's bust, BMI, and eye width decreased in hard times, whereas age, height, lip width, and facial narrowness increased in hard times. Pettijohn and Yerkes (2005) further investigated changes in facial and body features in a non-American sample of Miss Hong Kong from 1973 to 2003, with social and economic data from Hong Kong (i.e., unemployment rate, consumer price index, death rate, birth rate, marriage rate, divorce rate, suicide rate, and homicide rate). Overall, in difficult social and economic conditions, Miss Hong Kong winners were relatively older with lower BMIs, smaller chins, larger eyes, narrower faces, and larger noses. Furthermore, over time, Miss Hong Kong has adopted a more 'Western' ideal of beauty as her BMI and chin size have decreased and her eye size, narrowness of her face, and nose size have increased. Other researchers have noted similar changes in cultural expectations of thinness in Hong Kong (Leung, Lam, & Sze, 2001). These correlational findings provide further support for the ESH.

The ESH also makes predictions about other social preferences. For example, music preferences shift as a function of economic conditions (Pettijohn & Sacco, 2005). One investigation considered Billboard number one songs for each year from 1955 to 2003, photographs of the performers, and social and economic statistics. Raters of various ages and backgrounds listened to the songs and provided ratings (i.e., how meaningful the song was, how romantic, how comforting, etc.), another group of raters read the song lyrics and provided similar ratings, and third group of judges rated the perceived personality attributes of the performers from the photos. The relationships between social and economic conditions and the ratings of the songs, lyrical content, performer personality ratings, and the measured performer facial features were assessed. In hard times, popular songs were longer and slower, as well as more meaningful, romantic, and comforting. Furthermore, performers were rated as less agreeable during relatively poor conditions. Starting in 1980, popular performers were more likely to have smaller eyes in hard times (a relationship that corresponds to the rise of music television). The ESH may be useful in understanding a host of social preferences beyond appearance based dimensions.

Nevertheless, to better understand how the ESH contributes to social preferences will require further research. How we consciously or unconsciously process threat and uncertainty and the functional aspects of our decision-making is not completely explained in the ESH. Are attributions about stimuli (eye-size, body shape, mature themes) moderating social choices? Pettijohn and Tesser (2005) offer mixed findings on this account of how attributions are used to make social choices within the context of the ESH. They offer evidence that providing personality characteristic information overrides physical appearance preferences, but in another study, the preference for a mature partner was not stronger in a dependent interaction condition compared to an independent interaction condition. Are decisions about social stimuli preferences deliberate and cognitively intense or are these reactions automatic, quick, and implicit? Future work should address these limitations.

What types of threat lead to preferences for more mature themes, characteristics, and items? In the studies cited here, measures of social and economic well-being, individual threat of electrical shock, and individual resource scarcity priming can produce the predicted pattern of preferences. Perhaps then, any generalisable threat might lead to these effects. What types of social preferences are influenced by social threat? We demonstrated that threats changed preferences for facial and body features. Other archival investigations have shown that American societal threat increases preferences for powerful and charismatic presidential candidate preferences (Doty, Peterson, & Winter, 1991; Sales, 1972, 1973), attack dogs, strong literary character personalities, violent sporting events, and affiliation with authoritarian churches (McIntosh, Schwegler, & Terry-Murray, 2000). Additionally, when times are threatening, audiences prefer television programmes with meaningful content (McIntosh, Murray, Murray, & Manian, 2006), audiences more negatively evaluate female film characters who joke about sex, and audiences provide lower ratings of the socioeconomic status of male film characters in comedies. Finally, as described above, preferences for music artists and music content change with social and economic conditions. What moderates these effects? As described above, when additional target information is available, these effects may be reduced (Pettijohn & Tesser, 2005), whereas when the threat is made particularly salient, these effects may be enhanced (Pettijohn, Sacco, & Yerkes, 2005). Going forward it is essential to identify how these variables might operate on both global and individual levels.

Judgement-based differences in mate preferences

What are the psychological processes underlying these effects? It seems unlikely that people are drawing explicit inferences about how environmental threat should guide preferences, so perhaps an implicit mechanism can be identified. For example, because people are typically egocentric in their judgements of others (e.g., Kruger, 1999; Ross, Greene, & House, 1977), their judgements of collective resources are anchored on personal experiences and, therefore, highly variable as is the case with perceptions of the economy which are more reflective of personal political affiliation than they are of actual economic conditions (Mutz, 1998). Furthermore, it is unlikely that people could accurately report mental processes that are operating out of conscious awareness, though they often believe that they can (Nisbett & Wilson, 1997).

If people are poor judges of collective resource scarcity, then why does resource scarcity so reliably change the preferences of the collective? Nelson and Morrison (2005) hypothesised a relationship between collective and individual levels of resource scarcity. Since individual-level resource levels are generally dependent on collective-level resources, it stands to reason that people with low levels of resources believe that their status is shared by everyone else. They then implicitly use the information about themselves to infer what the norms of their society may be. This metacognitive account corresponds to the reasoning of the 'feelings as information' model, which suggests that affective state can influence thoughts and beliefs without the operation of conscious cognitive processes (Schwarz & Clore, 1983). Capitalising on this relationship, Nelson and Morrison (2005) showed that temporary affective states can produce a pattern of individual preferences that mirrors an otherwise unexplained pattern of cultural norms.

Two studies manipulated subjective judgements of personal wealth and examined changes in preferences for an idealised romantic partner. Undergraduates reported whether or not they were carrying any money and what body weight they 'personally consider ideal in a member of the opposite sex.' Experimenters manipulated the order of these two questions as a salience manipulation. As predicted, when money was salient and men did not have any money on them, they preferred heavier women. As predicted these effects were not present with the female sample (Nelson & Morrison, 2005; Study 1).

A subsequent study sought to remove the potential confound of money-possession by using a randomly assigned manipulation of financial satisfaction (Study 2). All participants reported the size of their personal savings account, but some reported this number on an 11-point scaled divided in $50 increments, from 1 ($0–$50) to 11 (over $500), whereas the remainder reported it on a similar 11-point scale divided in much larger increments, from 1 ($0–$500) to 11 (over $400,000). People infer their personal circumstances from whether they respond towards the top or bottom of a scale (Schwartz, 1999). Participants that responded towards the bottom of this scale felt poorer than subjects that responded at the top, and because of the nature of the manipulation, those participants in the small sum scale generally responded towards the top while those participants in the large sum scale generally responded towards the bottom. Consistent with this reasoning, participants were more satisfied with their personal finances after completing the $500 scale than they were after completing the $400,000 scale. Finally, participants reported the ideal weight of a potential partner. Once again, wealthy-feeling men preferred a lighter female than men who felt poor, and once again, this effect was not present for women. Furthermore, a subsequent analysis revealed that this effect was mediated by satisfaction with personal finances. However, because financial satisfaction as a construct is both culturally and temporally specific, two follow-up studies used a more general feeling of resource scarcity.

Many cultures, especially developing ones, value food as a resource far more than money, and as such, resource scarcity for them has meant a lack of food – or rather, it has meant feeling hungry (Diamond, 1997). Nelson and Morrison (2005) conducted two experiments in which participants reported their ideal partner's body weight either before or after eating dinner (Studies 3 and 4). A pattern of results emerged similar to the first two studies: hungry men preferred heavier women. Given that the construct of hunger is considered more universal than financial satisfaction as a driver of mate preferences, these two studies lend strong support to the idea that implicit cues are used when stating preferences for potential partners. These findings were further supported by a follow-up study in which men were asked to rate a series of greyscale photographs of women (Swami & Tovée, 2006). As with the Nelson and Morrison (2005) studies, men were approached either entering or leaving a campus dining hall. Consistent with those findings, hungry men preferred heavier women (higher BMI) than did satiated men.

One possibility is that these effects occur because feelings of hunger, or perhaps even the particular dining hall circumstances, were operating on a different psychological variable like self-esteem. A separate set of findings replicated the central findings of Nelson and Morrison (2005), but showed that there were no changes in self-esteem (Nelson, Sherman,

& Kim, 2006). A second concern has to do with the specificity of the effect: do hungry men prefer heavier objects in general or, as hypothesised, are the effects restricted to preferences for women? Research suggests that this is a very specific effect as hungrier men do not prefer larger sport utility vehicles (Nelson et al., 2006), milk bottles (empty or full), or anvils (Swami, Poulogianni, & Furnham, 2006). This evidence further suggests that the preference for weight is limited to potential mates and not all objects.

Lastly, if feelings of resource scarcity increase perceived environmental threat, then males should prefer mature features more generally. To test this possibility, Pettijohn, Sacco, and Yerkes (2005) measured fluctuations in preferences for ideal partner age, height, personality, and facial and body features in hungry and satiated male and female college students. If hunger was serving as a physiological threat and reminder of resource scarcity, then the ESH would predict an increased preference for more mature ideal partners. Furthermore, when participants were primed with hunger, these preferences were predicted to become stronger since the physiological threat of hunger would be more salient. In one study, experimenters positioned outside a college dining hall asked males and females to answer questions about ideal partner characteristics either immediately prior to eating dinner or immediately after eating dinner (Study 1). A subsequent study using the same procedure was used with the exception that all participants were asked about their hunger level before answering the preference questions (Study 2).

Overall, hungry males preferred females who were relatively older, taller, heavier, and with more mature facial features and personality traits compared to males who were full. Because females place greater emphasis on personality and resources in mates compared to males, personality and age attributes preferences were predicted to be influenced by hunger state. Overall, female preferences were not significantly altered by hunger state, but trends in the anticipated directions were found. In Study 2, hunger salience increased these differences, and additionally led to greater female preference for older males. WHR preferences remained stable across all conditions. These results both strengthen Nelson and Morrison's (2005) findings, and position their work within the ESH.

Conclusion

When it comes to the female form, men's preferences may not be universal but they certainly are predictable. This observation is grounded, first, in those traits for which there really is a cross-cultural consensus (e.g., Buss & Barnes, 1986), but it also extends to domains where the absent consensus is replaced by predictable variation. As we described in this chapter, there are a number of features that fall in the latter category, including facial maturity and body weight. These observations provide simultaneous empirical support for the universalist position characterised by evolutionary psychology and for a culturally idiosyncratic viewpoint essential to cultural psychology. From our perspective, the most interesting question is what makes these patterns possible? How do environmental changes operate on human preferences?

This chapter reviews some of the recent theorising about the underlying psychology of these phenomena. Pettijohn and his colleagues (e.g., Pettijohn & Tesser, 1999) start with the observation that some cross-cultural variation in preferences for females can be traced to cross-cultural variation in environmental stability (e.g., Symons, 1979). They argue that this must reflect the operation of an underlying psychological construct linking perceived environmental security to the formation of romantic preferences. In support of this ESH, they documented archival and experimental evidence suggesting that within a specific culture, temporal variation in conditions can have corresponding consequences for male preferences: in hard times men prefer a more mature looking female than they do in good times.

Can we look even closer at the underlying psychology? Nelson and his colleagues (e.g., Nelson & Morrison, 2005) have provided the broad outlines of a social cognitive mechanism to explain some of this variation. Drawing on metacognitive models of judgement, they suggest that people use feelings of deprivation (caloric or financial) to infer their environmental conditions, and that those inferences guide their preferences. In conjunction with the ESH, these findings suggest that environmental changes operate directly and unconsciously on male romantic preferences.

Nevertheless, these findings are only scratching the surface. Environmental threats operate on metacognitive processes which alter our preferences, but we have yet to uncover any of the psychology underlying the link between metacognition and preference. Peering inside that black box should offer the deepest insights into the origin of romantic preferences, in part because the black box is so influential, but also because it is so opaque. As documented above, environmental stress can reliably change preferences, but it also seems to change some underlying physiological processes, for example, making people less sensitive to pain (DeWall & Baumeister, 2006). Furthermore, we know that metacognitive processes not only operate on summary evaluations, but alter how our own judgements operate on our personal preferences (Simmons & Nelson, 2006). In short, though we are making efforts to understand the social cognition of romantic preferences, the processes at work are necessarily complex, influential, and difficult to identify.

One productive line of thinking in this domain might be to try to identify processes that readily line-up with the evolutionary theory. How can the pressures of natural selection lead to the universal preferences documented by evolutionary psychologists as well as the subtle underlying moderators captured in social psychological theory like the ESH? On the surface at least, it would seem more likely that men might have adapted a general tendency to, for example, seek youth and health in a potential mate. It seems less plausible that there is a special adaptation for the subtle preference changes we have summarised in this chapter. Though evolutionary theory of course allows for vastly more complicated and idiosyncratic processes (Tooby, Cosmides, & Barrett, 2005), it is also possible that the behaviours we are documenting are a combination of both special adaptations for reproduction and general adaptations for more general psychological life.

For example, men seem to prefer women within a certain range of body weight but there is also systematic variation regarding preferences within that range (Anderson et al., 1992; Swami, Caprario, Tovée & Furnham, 2006). It may be more fruitful to regard those as two independent processes, rather than as one single 'weight preference' adaptation. In this case then, it is worthwhile to try to further identify the independence of these processes, both at the level of behaviour, but also potentially at the level of simple biology. Granting that evolutionary pressures have led to the same general emotional and cognitive processes which guide so much of human behaviour, it would be nice if the same methodological rigour and sophistication was applied to understanding the psychological roots of the intriguing patterns of behaviour that are routinely identified by evolutionary psychologists. If natural selection is the distal universal cause, understanding these more specific processes should be a crucial aspect in identifying more proximal effects.

Once we have these tools we can start to flesh out the gaps between cultural and evolutionary psychology. In their influential review of cultural differences in social cognition, Nisbett and his colleagues argued that historically researchers have, by choosing to largely study Americans and Western Europeans, chosen to be ethnographers rather than psychologists (Nisbett, Peng, Choi, & Norenzayan, 2001). The foundational notion of this statement resides in recognising that psychologists should be studying *human* processes, but by focusing within a specific culture (typically the college student of North America) the topic of study ends up being the culture itself. In many respects this is close to the same argument evolutionary psychologists would make: because evolutionary history dwarfs modern cultural history, basic psychological processes should not be influenced by the idiosyncrasies of culture (cf. Buss & Kenrick, 1998). So from two different (and typically oppositional) perspectives, these two groups are after the same thing – an identification of a human psychology.

Going forward, then, it may be useful to conceive of cross-cultural variation in terms of what it might mean for evolutionary psychology. In the very narrow domains we review in this chapter, we report findings that very neatly suggest that some cultural differences may emerge as the result of individual level responses to environmental change. This possibility is consistent with some reasoning about the interplay of self and culture (Kim & Markus, 1999) and suggests a potentially fruitful method for conceiving human behaviour. Perhaps for some characteristics it is not the culture which shapes the individual, but instead, as the environment alters the individual, it is the individual who shapes the culture.

Author note

This article represents an equal contribution from the three authors. We would like to thank Ginny Naples, Lauren McDermott, and Amy Walzer for their assistance with reviewing the manuscript.

References

Adams, G. R. (1980). Social psychology of beauty: Effects of age, height, and weight on self-reported personality traits and social behavior. *Journal of Social Psychology, 112*, 287–293.

Anderson, J. L., Crawford, C. B., Nadeau, J., & Lindberg, T. (1992). Was the Duchess of Windsor right? A cross-cultural review of the socioecology of ideals of female body shape. *Ethology & Sociobiology, 13*, 197–227.

Barber, N. (1998a). Secular changes in standards of bodily attractiveness in American women: Different masculine and feminine ideals. *Journal of Psychology: Interdisciplinary and Applied, 132*, 87–94.

Barber, N. (1998b). The slender ideal and eating disorders: An interdisciplinary telescope model. *International Journal of Eating Disorders, 23*, 295–307.

Berscheid, E., & Reis, H. T. (1998). Attraction and close relationships. In D. T. Gilbert, S. T. Fiske, & G. Lindzey (Eds.), *The handbook of social psychology, Vol. 2* (4th ed., pp. 193–281). New York, NY: McGraw Hill.

Björntorp, P. (1991). Adipose tissue distribution and function. *International Journal of Obesity, 15,* 67–81.

Björntorp, P. (1997). Body fat distribution, insulin resistance and metabolic disease. *Nutrition, 13,* 795–803.

Brown, P. J., & Konner, M. (1987). An anthropological perspective of obesity. *Annals of the New York Academy of Science, 499,* 29–46.

Buss, D. M. (1985). Human mate selection. *American Scientist, 73,* 47–51.

Buss, D. M. (1989). Sex differences in human mate preferences: Evolutionary hypotheses tested in 37 cultures. *Behavioral and Brain Sciences, 12,* 1–49.

Buss, D. M. (1994). *The evolution of desire: Strategies of human mating.* New York, NY: Basic Books.

Buss, D. M., & Barnes, M. (1986). Preferences in human mate selection. *Journal of Personality and Social Psychology, 50,* 559–570.

Buss, D. M., & Kenrick, D. T. (1998). Evolutionary social psychology. In D. T. Gilbert, S. T. Fiske, & G. Lindzey (Eds.), *The handbook of social psychology, Vol. 2* (4th ed., pp. 982–1026). New York, NY: McGraw-Hill.

Cunningham, M. R. (1986). Measuring the physical in physical attractiveness: Quasi-experiments on the sociobiology of female facial beauty. *Journal of Personality and Social Psychology, 50,* 925–935.

Cunningham, M. R., Roberts, A. R., Barbee, A. P., Druen, P. B., & Wu, C. H. (1995). 'Their ideas of beauty are on the whole the same as ours.' Consistency and variability in the cross-cultural perception of female physical attractiveness. *Journal of Personality and Social Psychology, 68,* 261–279.

Darwin, C. (1859). *On the origin of the species by means of natural selection, or, preservation of favoured races in the struggle for life.* London: Murray.

Darwin, C. (1871). *The descent of man and selection in relation to sex.* London: Murray.

DeWall, N. C., & Baumeister, R. F. (2006). Alone but feeling no pain: Effects of social exclusion on physical pain tolerance and pain threshold, affective forecasting, and interpersonal empathy. *Journal of Personality and Social Psychology, 91,* 1–15.

Diamond, J. (1997). *Guns, germs, and stell: The fates of human societies.* New York, NY: W. W. Norton.

Doty, R. M., Peterson, B. E., & Winter, D. G. (1991). Threat and authoritarianism in the united states, 1978–1987. *Journal of Personality and Social Psychology, 61,* 629–640.

Enlow, D. M. (1982). *Handbook of facial growth* (2nd ed.). Philadelphia, PN: Saunders.

Feingold, A. (1990). Gender differences in effects of physical attractiveness on romantic attraction: A comparison across five research paradigms. *Journal of Personality and Social Psychology, 59,* 981–993.

Ford, C. S., & Beach, F. A. (1951). *Patterns of sexual behavior.* New York: Harper.

Frisch, R. E. (1990). Body fat, menarche, fitness, and fertility. In R. E. Frisch (Ed.), *Adipose tissue and reproduction* (pp. 1–26). Basel: Karger.

Furnham, A., & Baguma, P. (1994). Cross-cultural differences in the evaluation of male and female body shapes. *International Journal of Eating Disorders, 15,* 81–89.

Gangestad, S. W., & Buss, D. M. (1993). Pathogen prevalence and human mate preferences. *Ethology and Sociobiology, 14,* 89–96.

Guthrie, R. D. (1976). *Body hotspots.* New York, NY: Van Nostrand Reinhold.

Hildebrandt, K. A., & Fitzgerald, H. E. (1978). Adult's responses to infants varying in perceived cuteness. *Behavioral Processes, 212,* 46–54.

Jones, D. (1995). Sexual selection, physical attractiveness, and facial neoteny: Cross-cultural evidence and implications. *Current Anthropology, 36,* 723–748.

Jones, P. R. M., Hunt, M. J., Brown, T. P., & Norgan, N. G. (1986). Waist-hip circumference ratio and its relation to age and overweight in British men. *Human Nutrition: Clinical Nutrition, 40,* 239–247.

Keating, C. F., Mazur, A., & Segall, M. H. (1981). A cross cultural exploration of physiognomic traits of dominance and happiness. *Ethnology and Sociobiology, 2,* 41–48.

Kim, H., & Markus, H. R. (1999). Deviance or uniqueness, harmony or conformity? A cultural analysis. *Journal of Personality and Social Psychology, 77,* 785–800.

Korthase, K. M., & Trenholme, I. (1982). Perceived age and perceived physical attractiveness. *Perceptual and Motor Skills, 54,* 1251–1258.

Kruger, J. (1999). Lake wobegon be gone! The 'below-average effect' and the egocentric nature of comparative ability judgments. *Journal of Personality and Social Psychology, 77,* 221–232.

Lanska, D. J., Lanska, M. J., Hartz, A. J., & Rimm, A. A. (1985). Factors influencing anatomical location of fat tissue in 52,953 women. *International Journal of Obesity, 9,* 29–38.

Leung, F., Lam, S., & Sze, S. (2001). Cultural expectations of thinness in Chinese women. *Eating Disorders: The Journal of Treatment and Prevention, 9,* 339–350.

Lorenz, K. (1943). Die angeborenen formen moglicher arfahrung. *Zietschrift Für Tierpsychologie, 5,* 233–409.

McIntosh, W. D., Schwegler, A. F., & Terry-Murray, R. M. (2000). Threat and television viewing in the United States, 1960–1990. *Media Psychology, 2,* 35–46.

McIntosh, W. D., Murray, J. D., Murray, R. M., & Manian, S. (2006). Sexual humor in Hollywood films: Influences of social and economic threat on the desirability of male and female characters. *Mass Communication & Society, 9,* 239–254.

Mutz, D. (1998). *Impersonal influences: How perceptions of mass collectives affect political attitudes.* New York, NY, US: Cambridge University Press.

Nelson, L. D., & Morrison, E. L. (2005). The symptoms of resource scarcity: Judgments of food and finances influence preferences for potential partners. *Psychological Science, 16,* 167–173.

Nelson, L. D., Sherman, D. K., & Kim, H. S. (2006). *Effect of sex and hunger on mate preference, self-esteem, and SUVs.* Unpublished Raw Data.

Nisbett, R. E., & Wilson, T. D. (1997). Telling more than we can know: Verbal reports on mental processes. *Psychological Review, 13,* 279–301.

Nisbett, R. E., Peng, K., Choi, I., & Norenzayan, A. (2001). Culture and systems of thought: Holistic versus analytic cognition. *Psychological Review, 108,* 291–310.

Pettijohn, T. F., II. (2003). Relationships between U.S. social and economic hard times and popular motion picture actor gender, actor age, and movie genre preferences. *North American Journal of Psychology, 5*(1), 61–66.

Pettijohn, T. F., II, & Jungeberg, B. J. (2004). *Playboy* playmate curves: Changes in facial and body feature preferences across social and economic conditions. *Personality and Social Psychology Bulletin, 30,* 1186–1197.

Pettijohn, T. F., II, & Sacco, D. F., Jr. (2005, May). *Popular U.S. music preferences across time and social and economic conditions.* Poster presented at the 17th Annual American Psychological Society Convention, Los Angeles, CA.

Pettijohn, T. F., II, & Tesser, A. (1999). Popularity in environmental context: Facial feature assessment of American movie actresses. *Media Psychology, 1,* 229–247.

Pettijohn, T. F., II, & Tesser, A. (2003). History and facial features: The eyes have it for actresses but not for actors. *North American Journal of Psychology, 5,* 335–343.

Pettijohn, T. F., II, & Tesser, A. (2005). Threat and social choice: When eye size matters. *Journal of Social Psychology, 145*(5), 547–570.

Pettijohn, T. F., II, & Yerkes, M. J. (2004, May). *Miss America facial and body feature changes across social and economic conditions.* Poster presented at the 16th Annual American Psychological Society Convention, Chicago, IL.

Pettijohn, T. F., II, & Yerkes, M. J. (2005, May). *Miss Hong Kong facial and body feature changes across social and economic conditions and time.* Poster presented at the 17th Annual American Psychological Society Convention, Los Angeles, CA.

Pettijohn, T. F., II, Sacco, D. F., Jr., & Yerkes, M. J. (2005, May). *Hungry men prefer more mature women: A field test of the environmental security hypothesis.* Poster presented at the 17th Annual American Psychological Society Convention, Los Angeles, CA.

Pettijohn, T. F., II, Sacco, D. F., Jr., Yerkes, M. J., & Walzer, A. S. (2007). *The effect of anticipated uncertainty on physical and personality characteristic preferences.* Unpublished manuscript.

Rhodes, G., Zebrowitz, L. A., Clark, A., Kalick, S. M., Hightower, A., & McKay, R. (2001). Do facial averageness and symmetry signal health? *Evolution and Human Behavior, 22,* 31–46.

Ross, L., Greene, D., & House, P. (1977). The false consensus effect: An egocentric bias in social perception and attribution processes. *Journal of Experimental Social Psychology, 13,* 279–301.

Sales, S. M. (1972). Economic threat as a determinant of conversion rates in authoritarian and nonauthoritarian churches. *Journal of Personality and Social Psychology, 23,* 420–428.

Sales, S. M. (1973). Threat as a factor in authoritarianism: An analysis of archival data. *Journal of Personality and Social Psychology, 28,* 44–57.

Schwartz, N. (1999). Self reports: How the questions shape the answers. *American Psychologist, 54,* 93–105.

Schwarz, N., & Clore, G. L. (1983). Mood, misattribution, and judgments of well-being: Information and directive functions of affective states. *Journal of Personality and Social Psychology, 45*(3), 513–523.

Simmons, J. P., & Nelson, L. D. (2006). Intuitive confidence: Choosing between intuitive and nonintuitive alternatives. *Journal of Experimental Psychology: General, 135,* 409–428.

Singh, D. (1993). Adaptive significance of female physical attractiveness: Role of waist-to-hip ratio. *Journal of Personality and Social Psychology, 65,* 293–307.

Singh, D., & Young, R. K. (1995). Body weight, waist-to-hip ratio, breasts, and hips: Role in judgments of female attractiveness and desirability for relationships. *Ethology and Sociobiology, 16,* 483–507.

Smith, D. M. (1982). *Recognizable patterns of human malformation.* Philadelphia, PN: Saunders.

Sobal, J., & Stunkard, A. J. (1989). Socioeconomic status and obesity: A review of the literature. *Psychological Bulletin, 105,* 260–275.

Swami, V., & Tovée, M. J. (2006). Does hunger influence judgements of female physical attractiveness? *British Journal of Psychology, 97,* 353–363.

Swami, V., Poulogianni, K., & Furnham, A. (2006). The influence of resource availability on preferences for human body weight and non-human objects. *Journal of Articles in Support of the Null Hypothesis, 4,* 17–28.

Swami, V., Caprario, C., Tovée, M. J., & Furnham, A. (2006). Female physical attractiveness in Britain and Japan: A cross-cultural study. *European Journal of Personality, 20,* 69–81.

Symons, D. (1979). *The evolution of human sexuality.* Oxford: Oxford University Press.

Tooby, J., Cosmides, L., & Barrett, H. C. (2005). Resolving the debate on innate ideas: Learnability constraints and the evolved interpenetration of motivational and conceptual functions. In P. Carruthers, S. Laurence, & S. Stich (Eds.), *The innate mind: Structure and contents.* (pp. 305–337). New York, NY: Oxford University Press.

Tovée, M. J., & Cornelissen, P. L. (1999). The mystery of human beauty. *Nature, 399,* 215–216.

Tovée, M. J., & Cornelissen, P. L. (2001). Female and male perceptions of female physical attractiveness in front-view and profile. *British Journal of Psychology, 92,* 391–402.

Tovée, M. J., Swami, V., Furnham, A., & Mangalparsad, R. (2006). Changing perceptions of attractiveness as observers are exposed to a different culture. *Evolution and Human Behavior, 27,* 443–456.

Vandenberg, S. G. (1972). Assortative mating, or who marries whom? *Behavior Genetics, 2,* 127–157.

Zollner, F., & Nathan, J. (2003). *Leonardo Da Vinci: The complete paintings and drawings.* Los Angeles, CA: Taschen.

Part V

Theory Development: Sociocultural Perspectives

11
The Roles of Stereotypes and Group Norms on Perceptions of Bodily Attractiveness

Tom Hildebrandt and Janet D. Latner

Research on social stereotypes has enjoyed a long history in psychology and related fields. Although many definitions of a stereotype exist, researchers generally believe that 'stereotypes are qualities perceived to be associated with particular groups or categories of people' (Schneider, 2004: 24). Many have used stereotypes to understand the impact of attractiveness on social situations or personality (Eagly, Ashmore, Makhijani, & Longo, 1991; Feingold, 1992). The overwhelming majority of research on the attractiveness stereotype has focused on how individuals perceive attractive people or how well attractiveness correlates with a range of traits or behaviours. However, the social processes that contribute to attractiveness stereotyping are of equal theoretical importance.

Social processes as they relate to body image and body satisfaction have received a fair amount of attention in the body image literature and are commonly aimed at determining the ways in which individuals adopt unrealistic bodily attractiveness ideals (Thompson, Heinberg, Altabe, & Tantleff-Dunn, 1999). Group norm development (i.e., attractiveness ideal development) is a rather complex phenomenon with multiple individual and group-level variables of interest. In particular, the role of peer groups in the development and maintenance of body image disturbance has provided some insight into how peer group participation influences adoption of exaggerated attractiveness ideals (e.g., Jones & Crawford, 2006). Other researchers have focused on the consequences of unrealistic group norms, in particular the social stigma associated with excess body weight (Latner, Stunkard, & Wilson, 2005). Thus, the interplay between individual and group is often cited as a source of norm development and is an important level of analysis for understanding individual perceptions of attractiveness, as well as group endorsement of attractiveness ideals and its consequences.

The study of groups in social psychology is often complicated by fragmenting social processes into individual meaning (e.g., individual perception of attractiveness) while still attempting to understand the process as a group level phenomenon (i.e., development of attractiveness norms). Bond and Kenny (2002) suggest that individual phenomena are interdependent upon membership in an identified group. When applied to our understanding of physical attractiveness, this theory suggests that individual self-reports of attractiveness tell us little about how attractiveness is perceived in different social contexts or the effects of attractiveness at a group level. Rather, individual perceptions of attractiveness may be understood as functional contributions to group creation of idealised attractiveness norms.

Attractiveness stereotypes and attractiveness norms

A considerable amount of research has shown that men and women tend to ascribe a range of unrelated positive attributes to individuals who are perceived as attractive. In their classic meta-analysis, Eagly et al. (1991) found that social competence attributions were the greatest contributor to the attractiveness stereotype (i.e., the difference between attractive and unattractive individuals). Other moderate contributors to the attractiveness stereotype included potency, adjustment and intellectual competence. Such evidence suggests that men and women largely perceive physically attractive individuals to be more extraverted, able to manage social situations, and more likely to experience positive outcomes related to this trait (e.g., popularity). In general, the most robust aspect of the attractiveness stereotype is the perception that attractive individuals have the ability to successfully navigate common social experiences and consequently enjoy these experiences and benefit from them more often.

Relatively few studies report on the predictive validity of attractiveness in social situations, leading some to argue that the data supporting this link are mixed (Ashmore & Longo, 1995). For example, Anderson, John, Keltner, and Kring (2001) examined the effects of personality, physical attractiveness, and gender on social status among college fraternity, sorority, and mixed-sex dormitory floor members in a series of studies. They found strong relationships between the Big Five personality factor of Extraversion, physical attractiveness, and social status in male fraternity members. However, only Extraversion was related to social status in female sorority members. When these relationships were examined longitudinally in mixed-sex groups, physical attractiveness was only predictive of social status in men and Extraversion was predictive of status for both genders. These findings suggest that the relationship between attractiveness and social outcomes is likely complex and potentially indirect. For instance, attractiveness may only affect attractiveness through increased extraversion or social efficiency, and it is likely that attractiveness alone is not adequate for the achievement of high social status. Swami, Greven, and Furnham (2007) have made a similar argument, finding significant interactions between personality and body weight, and personality and waist-to-hip ratio, in the prediction of participant-rated female attractiveness.

In addition to social competence, attractive individuals are also believed to be generally more intelligent and higher achievers than unattractive individuals (Chai, Allred, Grossnickle, & Lee, 1998; Clifford, 1975). The impact of these attributes are found in research indicating that teachers rate attractive students as more intelligent and are more likely to attribute achievement to an attractive individual's actual ability as opposed to luck (Kanazawa & Kovar, 2004; Rich, 1975). Potency and adjustment are similarly important aspects of the attractiveness stereotype. For example, Feingold (1992) indicated in his meta-analyses that attractive individuals were perceived to have better mental health (e.g., less depressed, anxious, or neurotic), although his findings suggest that objective attractiveness is weakly correlated with most of these attributes, with the exception of certain aspects of social competency (e.g., popularity). Interestingly, Feingold (1992) found that self-perceived attractiveness, which is poorly correlated with objective attractiveness, was significantly related to a wide range of positive attributions.

Attractiveness attributions extend beyond trait-based beliefs about behaviour or social skills. An important aspect of the attractiveness stereotype is the set of attributions about physical status, health, and reproductive potential. Correlational research largely suggests that attractive individuals are perceived to be healthier, have sex more often, and have greater reproductive potential (Eagly et al., 1991; Feingold, 1992; Singh, 1994, 2004). The validity of these associations was examined by Weeden and Sabini (2005), and they concluded that there was little support for the predictive validity of many proposed aspects of physical attractiveness. Generally, they found that weight and waist-to-hip ratio (WHR) were predictive of health, reproductive outcomes, and attractiveness in women, suggesting a health-attractiveness link, but found little evidence for this relationship in men. Such research suggests that the link between attractiveness and health in men may be less important. Clearly, more prospective research designs are needed to understand how well objective indicators of attractiveness predict health and reproductive outcomes.

Although research on the attractiveness stereotype generally supports halo effects, or the linking of generally unrelated positive traits through a stereotype, it would appear that there is mixed support for the validity of this attractiveness stereotype. This, however, does not suggest that there is no link between attractiveness and traits associated with the attractiveness stereotype. Rather, the current state of research on these factors generally suggests that there is little evidence for a direct causal link between attractiveness (and certain aspects of attractiveness such as body symmetry) and traits associated with attractiveness. More research is needed to determine whether attractiveness is a good predictor of social, psychological, health-, or reproductive-related outcomes. Furthermore, the social contexts where attractiveness is important need to be elucidated with careful attention to understand how attractiveness and the attractiveness stereotype affect these outcomes.

If there is little support for the validity of the attractiveness stereotype, questions remain as to where, or in what context, the attractiveness stereotype is validated. Cultural and group norms are one potential source of information regarding physical attractiveness. It is generally accepted that Western cultures idealise exaggerated thinness in females, and muscularity and leanness in males (Pope, Phillips, & Olivardia, 2000; Thompson et al., 1999). There are a series of studies that have examined the anthropometric measurements of culturally idealised figures. For example, Barbie has often been criticised as possessing an unrealistically thin body (Brownell & Napolitano, 1995; Norton, Olds, Olive, & Dank, 1995). Similar research exists supporting the exaggerated muscularity and leanness of male idealised figures, such as G. I. Joe (Pope, Olivardia, Gruber, & Borowiecki, 1999). Although there is still some debate as to whether these cultural icons are accurate representations of physical attractiveness, what is clear is that these idealised figures are associated with a wide range of positive attributions in media content (Smith, McIntosh, & Bazzini, 1999), and their bodily dimensions fall outside the realm of optimal health and reproductive value.

Social mechanisms of stereotype/group norm development

There have been a great number of investigations into the processes of group and cultural norm development. As discussed above, it is not enough to assume that the attractiveness stereotype or idealised attractiveness norms have evolved out of strong predictive validity. Surprisingly, very little research has examined the social mechanisms specific to attractiveness stereotyping or attractiveness norm development. However, body image researchers mainly concerned with the development of body dissatisfaction and its consequences, such as extreme weight and shape control behaviours (e.g., excessive dieting, anabolic steroid use, etc.), have begun to investigate some of these mechanisms through the study of adolescent peer groups.

While it cannot be assumed that body image and body dissatisfaction are the same as physical attractiveness, many relevant clues to attractiveness stereotyping and norm development may be gleaned from our understanding of these features of body image. For example, body dissatisfaction is often determined by some measure of the distance between perceived self and perceived body ideal. Thus, measuring body dissatisfaction takes into account an individual's perception of what is ideally attractive. At least for women, the majority of studies indicates that ideal bodies and attractive bodies represent the same physical standard (Fingeret, Gleaves, & Pearson, 2004; Hildebrandt, & Walker, 2006). This may not be true for male bodies, with ideal bodies representing more muscular and lean body types than are believed to be optimally attractive by men or women (Hildebrandt, & Walker, 2006).

Peer groups represent an important social context for the development and validation of beliefs regarding attractiveness and appearance. In part, peer groups represent an important context because of their role in norm development for a variety of behaviours, such as smoking and alcohol use (Jackson, 1997). Similar mechanisms are likely at work in developing norms about physical attractiveness. These attractiveness norms are thought to develop within peer groups in what is understood as a peer-specific appearance culture (Jones & Crawford, 2006). For instance, Paxton, Shultz, Wertheim, and Muhr (1999) found that participation in specific peer groups led to the development of extreme forms of dieting and weight loss behaviour and contributed to the internalisation of unrealistically thin ideals among adolescent girls. Other research has supported this finding, suggesting that peers' influence is also important to adolescent boys (Jones, 2004; McCabe, & Ricciardelli, 2003). As a social context, adolescents tend to develop their own peer group culture, governed by implicit and explicit rules, social events and processes, and environmental conditions and structure.

There are several proposed mechanisms by which the adolescent appearance culture among peer groups leads to body image norms, including the identification of attractiveness. Perhaps the most researched mechanism for development of individual body image norms is social comparison. This mechanism, originally described by Festinger (1954), has four main tenets: (a) individuals have a drive to evaluate their opinions, beliefs, and attitudes for purposes of self-evaluation; (b) in the absence of defined structure or standards of comparison, individuals intentionally compare themselves to others; (c) individuals prefer to compare themselves to others who are perceived as similar, and; (d) individuals prefer to make upward comparisons in order to find ways to improve themselves.

Although social comparison theory has been expanded and improved since Festinger's (1954) description, it remains an important theoretical mechanism for understanding how individuals' perceptions are shaped by groups. Some important refinements have been made to this theory, most importantly that social comparisons can be automatic as opposed to intentional (Morse & Gergen, 1970) and occur with similar as well as dissimilar people (Gilbert, Giesler, & Morris, 1995). Thus, comparisons between individuals and peers on aspects of attractiveness are likely to be automatic as well as intentional, and may occur with peers who occupy different social groups.

Recent research has also sought to understand the consequences of social comparison processes. Lyubomirsky and Ross (1997) found that happy individuals' moods were not responsive to feedback about peers who performed better than they did on performance tasks, but rather their moods were attenuated only by feedback about inferior peer performance. For unhappy individuals, feedback about both inferior and superior peer performance attenuated their moods, suggesting that unhappy individuals are more sensitive to social comparison processes. Perceived threat also appears to be an important part of the social comparison process. As Taylor and Lobel (1989) suggested, individuals under threat tend to make downward comparisons (i.e., comparing oneself to unattractive individuals) to improve self-esteem, but make upward (i.e., comparing oneself to more attractive individuals) for a source of motivation. Although untested in attractiveness-based social comparisons, these data suggest that social comparison not only plays a role in group conformity and motivation for improved performance, but is also moderated by individual differences in temperament, mood, and perceived threat of a given social context.

Social comparison processes and body image: Cross-sectional and experimental studies

Research on body image generally supports the integral role of peers in determining the relevant outcomes to the social comparison process. For example, Heinberg and Thompson (1992b) found that college women rate comparisons with peers as more important than family, general population members, and fashion models. This finding has been replicated and extended by McCabe and Ricciardelli (2003), who found that feedback from a participants' best friend had a significant impact on body image as well as body changing behaviours in both adolescent boys and girls. Furthermore, Schultz, Paxton, and Wertheim (2002) found that the frequency of social comparisons increased with age of adolescent girls, stressing their importance in the development of peer group norms. Finally, Paxton et al. (1999) found that body image concerns and extreme weight control behaviours were clustered in specific peer friendship cliques. Thus, the social context of peer groups appears to be where social comparisons have the greatest impact on the development of attractiveness stereotypes and norms.

Experimental studies of social comparison suggest that body dissatisfaction increases after exposure to excessively thin female figures (e.g., Heinberg & Thompson, 1995) and that *in vivo* comparisons to thin peers leads to increased body dissatisfaction (Krones, Stice, Batres, & Orjada, 2005). In a classic experiment by Heinberg and Thompson (1992a), participants were given feedback about their weight relative to other peers. Participants were randomised to receive positive or negative feedback and were compared to same-college peers or an average person in the United States. Results suggested that regardless of the feedback, participants reported greater body image disturbance when compared to peers. This finding indicates that the most salient factor for body comparison is the comparison target; in this case, peer comparisons had the greatest impact upon individuals' self-perceived attractiveness.

Lin and Kulik (2002) extended these findings in efforts to determine whether upward or downward comparisons affected college women's perception of their own level of attractiveness. Their results suggested that women who made upward comparisons (i.e., compared to an extremely thin peer) experienced a decrease in self-perceived attractiveness, increased anxiety, and consequently rated a potential male partner as less attractive. In addition, boyfriend status moderated the effect on

anxiety suggesting that women who are not in a relationship experience more anxiety in response to upward comparisons. Interestingly,
downward comparisons did not produce an increase in self perceived
attractiveness. One potentially important conclusion to be drawn from
the work of Lin and Kulik (2002) is that social comparisons (specifically,
upward comparisons) can influence self-reported attractiveness of the
opposite-sex.

In addition to appearance-based social comparisons, Stice, Maxfield,
and Wells (2003) presented evidence that hearing a thin confederate
describe concerns with being overweight and disclose intentions to lose
weight led college women to be more dissatisfied with their bodies. These
data indicate that comparisons between self and ideal attractiveness may
be modeled by peers and ultimately affect an individual's perception
of attractiveness. This type of peer pressure may be an indirect form of
social comparison that similarly helps to increase conformity to group
attractiveness norms.

What remains to be investigated in experimental studies of social
comparison is the effect of social comparison processes on attractiveness norm development. While it is clear that social comparison
with peers that have attributes of idealised attractiveness (e.g., very
thin females) leads to body dissatisfaction (i.e., self-perceived attractiveness), it is unclear how this process affects individuals' perception of same-sex attractiveness ideals (i.e., group attractiveness norms).
Although not explored explicitly in the literature, it is likely that peer-
based social comparison, particularly among those with more negative
affect, leads to perceptions of ideal attractiveness that fall outside the
realm of health. This would not only increase body dissatisfaction, but
also motivate an individual to try extreme forms of weight control
behaviour.

Social comparison processes and body image: Longitudinal studies

There are few longitudinal investigations of social comparison and body
image; however, those that exist support its role in body image disturbance. As with experimental studies, these investigations do not directly
assess perceptions of physical attractiveness, but the presence of body
image disturbance is likely influenced by the adoption of unrealistically thin or lean and muscular attractiveness ideals (Thompson et al.,
1999). All of the longitudinal data on body image and social comparison
processes has been conducted on adolescent and collegiate populations,

thus little is known about whether these processes continue to influence attractiveness norms into adulthood.

In a prospective study of body image among adolescent boys and girls, Jones (2004) found that both appearance conversations and appearance based social comparisons predicted changes in body dissatisfaction for adolescent girls but only greater 'internalization of a muscular ideal' predicted body dissatisfaction one year later for adolescent boys. These data are consistent with previous longitudinal investigations of body dissatisfaction which suggest that social comparison processes are unique contributors to change in body dissatisfaction in female adolescents over time (Stice, 2001; Stice & Whitenton, 2002). In fact, evidence from Presnell, Bearman, and Stice (2004) found in a longitudinal study of body dissatisfaction and eating pathology in adolescent girls and boys that pressure from peers to be thin predicted changes in body dissatisfaction whereas thin-ideal internalisation did not. Thus, pressure to conform to a group norm appeared to be more important to the development of body dissatisfaction.

In a study by McCabe and Ricciardelli (2003), only messages about weight control strategies from same-sex individuals (same-sex parent and same-sex best friend) predicted extreme weight control behaviours in adolescents. Consistent with social comparison theory, those perceived as most relevant for comparisons provided information viable to motivate extreme weight control behaviour. As Bearman, Martinez, and Stice (2006) note in their recent longitudinal study of adolescent body image, parent and peer support deficits were better predictors of body dissatisfaction than thin-ideal internalisation. This finding generally suggests that the social context where comparisons occur must be supportive in order for comparisons to be used as healthy motivation. On the other hand, social comparison processes in environments with poor support are likely to reinforce poor self-image.

There are limitations to the longitudinal study of social comparison processes. For example, a majority of studies have used self-report measures of the frequency of comparisons or the importance of specific types of comparisons. While these aspects of social comparison are likely to be related to changes in the perception of self-reported attractiveness ideals, they may not be measuring the most important aspects of the social comparison process. It could be hypothesised that upward comparisons to similar peers are likely to motivate individuals to behave in certain ways (e.g., extreme weight control). Furthermore, it could be hypothesised that downward comparisons generally protect individuals from developing an unrealistically thin or lean and muscular ideal. To our knowledge, these aspects of the social comparison process have not been examined in longitudinal designs.

A second important limitation to this research is the unit of analysis. In all of the prospective designs, individuals' responses were analysed as if they were independent. This may not be the case, as evidence from Paxton et al. (1999) suggested that attitudes about attractiveness ideals and weight control clustered in certain peer groups. It would be reasonable to assume that the endorsement of certain attractiveness ideals and the behaviours associated with pursuing these ideals are dependent upon group membership. Future research would benefit from considering individual as well as group-level attractiveness ideal outcomes. For example, do attractiveness norms change within friendship peer cliques over time?

Finally, social comparison is unlikely to be the only aspect of peer group participation that affects the development of attractiveness norms. Individual variables such as participants' objective attractiveness and personality are likely to have an impact on how group level attractiveness norms are developed. For example, a group of athletically inclined adolescent boys may develop an attractiveness ideal that is consistent with the body that functions ideally for their relative sport. In essence, swimmers may develop attractiveness ideals based on the body that proves best suited for swimming (i.e., low weight and lean), whereas football players may develop an attractiveness ideal that is best suited for football (i.e., muscular and lean). Thus, the makeup of the social group may have a significant impact upon the perception of attractiveness ideals.

Other social processes: Room for expanded understanding of attractiveness ideals

While social comparison does provide an important social mechanism related to the development of body dissatisfaction, it has not been explicitly examined in the development of attractiveness stereotypes or norms. There are other peer processes that deserve further investigation. Specifically, appearance-related teasing, social contagion, peer modeling, and social reinforcement have been examined in relationship to body image development (Crandall, 1988; Lieberman, Gauvin, Bukowski, & White, 2001; Stice & Bearman, 2001; Stromer & Thompson, 1996). The common denominator to these mechanisms is that they are all potential catalysts to norm development within same-sex peer groups.

Jones and Crawford (2006) put these social mechanisms into a larger context and described three major social contributors: (a) appearance culture; (b) appearance evaluation, and; (c) peer acceptance concerns. They considered appearance culture to include the discussion of appearance among friends and body change talk (either dieting or increasing muscularity). Appearance evaluation consisted of peer appearance pressures, direct appearance teasing, and vicarious appearance teasing. Finally, peer acceptance concerns were defined as appearance-based acceptance and peer appearance comparisons. Overall, Jones and Crawford (2006) found evidence for significant relationships between each of these aspects of peer group participation and body dissatisfaction.

Social stigma and obesity

One of the more damaging consequences of group attractiveness norms is the stigma, bias, and discrimination aimed at overweight individuals. Theoretical accounts suggest that social consensus may be at the root of weight bias, just as it may be a causal influence for other prejudices (Sechrist & Stangor, 2005). Other psychological mechanisms are also likely to contribute to obesity stigma, such as attribution theory (Crandall, 1994) and the justification-suppression model (Crandall & Eshleman, 2003), which suggest that viewing overweight individuals as responsible for their condition leads to disliking them or to justifying the expression of prejudice even though it may be socially undesirable.

However, social consensus may be particularly promising as a theory to explain weight bias because of its ability to change it. Both weight bias and racial prejudices can be ameliorated by changing participants' perceptions of the social norms of these biases (Puhl, Schwartz, & Brownell, 2005; Stangor, Sechrist, & Jost, 2001). Perhaps as a result of the widespread consensus on physical attractiveness norms, weight bias is similarly widespread. It also has important consequences for psychosocial functioning and health. The expression and consequences of weight bias are examined in this section.

Obesity stigma: Sources and settings

Weight bias against adults

Discrimination against overweight and obese adults is evident in multiple settings. The interpersonal treatment of overweight individuals in employment and health care settings may be particularly affected by weight-related prejudices (Puhl & Brownell, 2001; Fikkan & Rothblum,

2005; Fabricatore, Wadden, & Foster, 2005; Roehling, 1999). Participants asked to make hypothetical hiring decisions rate overweight job applicants (identified by photos or with written descriptions of weight) as having more negative characteristics than non-overweight applicants; this prejudice can also result in decisions not to hire overweight individuals (Klesges et al., 1990; Larkin & Pines, 1979; Polinko & Popovich, 2001). For example, despite equal qualifications, overweight applicants viewed on videotape were labeled as having poorer work habits, lower self-control, and lower discipline than non-overweight applicants (Klesges et al., 1990).

Although the above studies of prejudice have relied primarily on university student samples, disparities in income among overweight people in the actual workforce, particularly women, may be associated with weight bias (Gortmaker, Must, Perrin, Sobol, & Dietz, 1993). Lower income has been found among overweight women in the United States (Register & Williams, 1990), Finland (Sarlio-Lähteenkorva, Silventoinen, & Lahelma, 2004), and Britain (Sargent & Blanchflower, 1994). Surprisingly, lower income was present even if women had been overweight only during adolescence and were no longer heavy in adulthood.

Weight bias in medical settings has been documented using several research approaches: assessing negative attributions about obesity among health care workers, assessing implicit stereotypes among these professionals, and assessing experiences of stigma among obese patients. Surveys have found that doctors (Klein, Najman, Kohrman, & Munro, 1982), nurses (Bagley, Conklin, Isherwood, Pechiulis, & Watson, 1989), nutrition professionals (Maiman, Wang, Becker, Finlay, & Simonson, 1979), and medical students (Blumberg & Mellis, 1980) endorse negative attitudes about obesity and obese patients. Among primary care physicians, over 50 per cent felt that obese individuals are awkward, ugly, and non-compliant (Foster et al., 2003). These negative attitudes could potentially decrease obese patients' quality of care and, in turn, increase their risk of comorbid illnesses. It is unfortunate that a population already prone to increased medical conditions should be subject to this additional potential health risk.

High rates of weight bias have been shown among health care professionals, despite a possible reluctance among some to admit prejudices due to social desirability effects. However, methods of assessing implicit attitudes are specifically designed to get around this problem. Using procedures of implicit attitude measurement, even health care professionals who specialise in working with obese patients were more likely to associate being fat with attributes such as 'bad,' 'lazy' and 'worthless' (Schwartz, O'Neal, Brownell, Blair, & Billington, 2003; Teachman & Brownell, 2001). Some research has also shown that obese individuals feel they have been treated disrespectfully by health care workers, although the number of patients reporting this has differed across studies (Anderson & Wadden, 2004; Rand & MacGregor, 1990). Qualitative research has also suggested that some parents of overweight children feel blamed and are held responsible by health care providers for their child's weight status (Edmunds, 2005).

Overweight adults are also stigmatised in interpersonal situations. Overweight adults are least preferred as sexual partners, even less preferred than mentally ill partners or those with sexually transmitted diseases (Chen & Brown, 2005). Women were more harshly targeted by this stigma. Similarly, obese women are judged as less desirable, skilled, and warm in intimate relationships (Reagan, 1996). On a reliable and valid measure of anti-fat attitudes, a physical/romantic unattractiveness subscale yielded somewhat higher scores among both men and women than the measure's two other subscales, social/character disparagement and weight control/blame (Lewis, Cash, Jacobi, & Bubb-Lewis, 1997).

Weight bias against children

Obesity stigma's effect on children was first investigated in the 1960s, when overweight children were repeatedly found to be liked the least among children with various disabilities, by children from different ethnic backgrounds, socioeconomic status, and children who were disabled (Richardson, Goodman, Hastorf, & Dornbusch, 1961). Adults showed the same bias, including those who worked with physically disabled children (Goodman, Dornbusch, Richardson, & Hastorf, 1963), who were obese, and from diverse ethnic backgrounds (Maddox, Back, Liederman, 1968). Subsequent studies using various research designs have found similar prejudices (Latner & Schwartz, 2005). Despite the rising prevalence rates of childhood obesity (Wang & Lobstein, 2006), the stigma against overweight children appears to have increased in the past 40 years (Latner & Stunkard, 2003). Common sources of this stigma may include peers, family members, and individuals involved in children's education.

As early as age three, children are more likely to attribute negative characteristics to overweight children, such as stupid, ugly, and mean, loud and lazy, and to prefer thin to overweight peers as playmates (Cramer & Steinwert, 1998; Brylinsky & Moore, 1994). This trend continues, and even worsens, over the course of development, when weight bias strengthens. For example, studies have shown increases in negative stereotyping of overweight peers across grades 2, 4 and 6 (Lawson, 1980), and across the ages of 5 to 6, 14 to 15, and 19 to 20 years (Lerner & Korn, 1972). However, weight bias towards peers may level off or decrease over development into late adolescence and adulthood. Adolescents and adults view a wider range of body sizes as acceptable compared to elementary school children (Rand & Wright, 2000), and college students show greater liking for overweight peers than 5th and 6th-grade children (Latner, Stunkard, & Wilson, 2005). However, studies revealing implicit bias among adults (e.g., Schwartz, Vartanian, Nosek, & Brownell, 2006) suggest that bias is still strong in adulthood, despite a possible increased awareness of social desirability over the course of development.

A surprisingly common source of weight bias is from parents and family members. Among 4,746 adolescents, 47 per cent of very overweight girls and 34 per cent of very overweight boys reported weight-based teasing by family members at least a few times a year (Neumark-Sztainer et al., 2002). Among 2,449 adult overweight women and 222 men, weight bias was reported to have been perpetrated by 44 per cent of participants' mothers and 34 per cent of fathers (Puhl & Brownell, 2001). Overweight girls have been found to receive less financial support for college from their parents than average-weight girls, regardless of parental income, family size or education (Crandall, 1991).

Educators may be another common source of weight bias in the lives of children. Among 115 school teachers, nurses, and social workers, over half believed that obesity is caused primarily by one's own behaviours, and 20 to 25 per cent believed that obese persons are more emotional, less tidy, less likely to succeed at work, and have different personalities and more family problems (Neumark-Sztainer, Story, & Harris, 1999). Physical education (PE) teachers have reported that overweight children have poorer social, reasoning, physical, and cooperation skills than non-overweight children (Greenleaf & Weiller-Abels, 2005), and students training to become PE instructors showed significantly more negative implicit attitudes compared to a matched sample of non-PE students (O'Brien, Hunter, & Banks, 2007). This might be damaging to school performance as well as health, given the importance of physical activity for overweight children. Weight criticism during physical activities was related to reduced enjoyment of sports and lower self-reported amounts of activity performed among 5th to 8th grade children (Faith, Leone, Ayers, Moonseong, & Pietrobelli, 2002). Overweight middle school students have also reported that teachers' negative comments about their physical abilities led children to avoid physical education classes (Bauer, Yang, & Austin, 2004).

Transmission of weight bias

Less is known about how cultural norms about obesity are transmitted to young children, but limited evidence suggests that parents may transmit the notion that overweight is unacceptable. When asked to tell a story to their preschool child about an overweight, average-weight, or handicapped child, more negative descriptions and less successful outcomes were applied to the overweight child, and peer reactions to the overweight child were presented as deeply disapproving (Adams, Hicken, & Salehi, 1988). Parents' encouragement to lose weight, along with peer interactions focused on body shape and weight, predicted negative stereotypes about overweight people among 9-year-old girls (Davison & Birch, 2004).

Weight stereotypes may also be transmitted through the media. On popular television shows, heavier characters have fewer romantic interactions, positive social interactions, and are more likely to be objects of humor (Greenberg, Eastin, Hofschire, Lachlan, & Brownell, 2003). Heavier female characters on situation comedies receive more negative comments regarding her weight or body from male characters and stronger audience laughter (both live and 'laugh-tracked'; Fouts & Burggraf, 2000). Among 1st to 3rd grade boys, more television viewing is associated with greater stereotyping of overweight girls (e.g., lower ratings of nice, smart, clean, tell the truth and have a lot of friends; Harrison, 2000).

Consequences of weight bias

Interpersonal consequences

During adolescence, the consequences of weight stigma may be particularly damaging. A sophisticated study of friendship networks among 90,118 adolescents found that overweight adolescents were more socially isolated, less often selected as friends or best friends, and more likely to receive zero friendship nominations from peers (Strauss & Pollack, 2003). Obese adolescent girls experience more relational victimisation (exclusionary and hurtful treatment by 'friends'), and obese boys experience more overt victimisation than their non-obese peers (Pearce, Boergers, & Prinstein, 2002). Other research has shown that both overweight boys and girls of nearly all preadolescent and adolescent ages were more likely than non-overweight children to experience overt and relational victimisation (Janssen, Craig, Boyce, & Pickett, 2004).

Psychological consequences

Research has begun to investigate the psychological effects of experiences of stigmatisation. According to retrospective studies with overweight adults, more frequent exposure to obesity stigmatisation by others is associated with poor body image, low self-esteem, and greater psychological distress (Annis, Cash, & Hrabosky, 2004; Friedman, Reichmann, Costanzo, & Musante, 2002; Myers & Rosen, 1999). Body image may be particularly affected by weight-related stigma, especially teasing, among youth. Prospective studies of adolescents, as well as retrospective studies of adults, have found that weight-based teasing predicted body dissatisfaction (Grilo, Wilfley, Brownell, & Rodin, 1994; Cattarin & Thompson, 1994). Teasing about weight is also related to the development of eating disturbances (Thompson, Coovert, Richards, Johnson, & Cattarin, 1995).

Other prospective research has also shown that self-esteem can be adversely affected by weight bias. Among girls, experiences of weight-related peer teasing and parental criticism about weight mediated the association between higher BMI and lower self-concept (Davison & Birch, 2002). Obese children who believe that they are responsible for their weight problem may be the most likely to have low self-esteem (Pierce & Wardle, 1997), suggesting that self-blame or internalisation of weight stigma may be an important consequence of societal prejudices.

An unfortunate consequence of the negative psychological repercussions of weight stigma may be increased risk of depression. In a large sample of adolescents, weight-based teasing was related to increased likelihood of depression (Eisenberg et al., 2003). Once teasing history was controlled, weight itself was no longer significantly associated with depression and most other measures of emotional well-being. These researchers also found that girls and boys who were teased about their weight were over twice as likely to experience suicidal ideation as those who were not teased. Among the girls who experienced weight-based teasing from peers or family members, 51 per cent had thought about suicide, compared with 25 per cent among those who had not been teased.

Quality of life and health

Given these findings, it may not be surprising that the quality of life of obese individuals is impaired, in both psychological and physical domains (Kushner & Foster, 2000). Quality of life scores in obese children were lower than non-overweight children in the areas of physical health, psychosocial health, emotional functioning, behaviour, social functioning, general health, and school functioning, and their scores were similar to the scores of children with cancer (Friedlander, Larkin, Rosen, Palermo, & Redline, 2003; Schwimmer, Burwinkle, & Varni, 2003). Results are mixed, however, with other research showing overweight in adolescents to be associated only with physical, and not with psychological, quality of life impairment (Swallen, Reither, Haas, & Meier, 2005). It is possible that the link between obesity and quality of life may be associated with or mediated by stigma, either as perpetrated by others or as internalised by the overweight individual. Research is needed to identify the association between experiences of weight bias and quality of life in children and adults.

Integration of sociocultural theory and evolutionary theories of physical attractiveness

In their classic meta-analytic study, Langlois et al. (2000) found that a majority of studies supported evolutionary hypotheses as opposed to sociocultural hypotheses of physical attractiveness, indicating that men and women largely agree on physical attractiveness across cultures, ages, and different contexts. In particular, Langlois et al. (2000) suggested that reliability in attractiveness ratings across cultures was evidence that attractiveness is not a culture-bound phenomenon. While this finding is somewhat controversial, we believe that the two theories are not inconsistent on this issue. For instance, both sociocultural and evolutionary theories predict the *flexibility* of attractiveness preferences across contexts. Specifically, there are individual and culture-bound variables that influence mate preferences or, in the case of sociocultural theorists, attractiveness ideals.

Mate selection theory

Mate selection theory is a primary component of evolutionary theory and distinguishes between two types of competition that effect mate preferences, namely intrasexual (between-sex) and intersexual (within-sex) competition (Buss, 1992). Mate preference has been linked to physical attractiveness based on observed relationships between reproductive value and physical attractiveness and the assumption that preference (perceived attractiveness) influences behaviour (mate choice; Miller,

1998). Both forms of competition are theorised to maximise an individual's preferences for reproductive value and much of the support for these mechanisms derives from evidence of cross-cultural similarities in mating strategies and trait preferences (e.g., Buss, 1989).

However, the social mechanisms that reflect intrasexual and intersexual competition have received less attention in the evolutionary literature, with exceptions contained to individual phenomenon such as long-term versus short-term mating strategies (e.g., Buss & Schmidtt, 1993) or macro-level phenomenon such as the impact of sex-ratio on between-sex selection strategies (e.g., Pedersen, 1991). In particular, the process of within-sex competition and its direct consequences on perceptions of attractiveness has not received much attention. Rather, the existing data and theory has focused on mate choice (i.e., between-sex competition) because it is more directly related to reproductive outcomes.

Sociocultural theory

Primary to sociocultural theories are the relative influence of mechanisms such as social stereotyping, group norms, and social comparisons to the development of preferences for attractive individuals. In particular, body image researchers have focused on how participation in different groups leads to exaggerated preferences for ideal body types, which in many cases fall outside the range of reproductive advantage. A range of social mechanisms have been indicated in this process that suggests subgroups of teenage girls create an 'appearance culture' where social status and communication centers around appearance control and value (Jones & Crawford, 2006). Not only does this culture lead to increased competition between same-sex adolescents, but may have the consequence of exaggerated attractiveness norms. Similarly, this culture facilitates discrimination against unattractive individuals (Pearce et al., 2002; Strauss & Pollack, 2003). Despite such evidence, sociocultural theorists have not provided strong theoretical evidence for why individuals cluster into same-sex cliques or why there is a seemingly innate tendency for social comparison and group norm development.

Theory integration

Because both sociocultural and evolutionary theory allow flexibility in mate preference (ideal attractiveness) either through social mechanisms (Thompson et al., 1999) or through adaptation to different environmental and mate selection pressures (Sugiyama, 2005), there is ample justification to integrate both theories of physical attractiveness.

Specifically, we believe that social comparison, group norm development, and social stereotyping are social mechanisms that constitute special forms of within-sex competition. Appropriately, all three social mechanisms have been shown to influence attractiveness norms within groups and contribute to the negative treatment and perception of unattractive individuals.

In fact, recent evidence suggests that social stereotyping may be more important for linking unattractiveness to negative attributions than attractiveness to positive attributions (Griffin & Langlois, 2006). Such processes are also likely then to be flexible enough to adapt to environmental pressures. For instance, one could argue that the increasing focus on thinness as an attractiveness norm for women is in part a reaction to escalating rates of obesity, in essence, an adaptive function of the environmental pressures associated with an abundance of food. Such adaptations, and its relative influence on behaviour, allows for much quicker adjustments in mate preferences than relying entirely on the genetic transmission as a function of mate choice. Relying completely on mate choice, then, would be a poor strategy for survival where information about important environmental pressures (i.e., poor health associated with excess body weight) is discovered relatively quickly.

Between-sex competition (i.e., mate choice) is also affected by these sociocultural processes; mate choices must produce adequate variability for adaptation. Thus, the presence of universal agreement on attractiveness may ultimately be less important than variability in attractiveness perceptions. Such flexibility, or the ability to choose mates that do not have ideal attractiveness features, allows rapid adjustment to potential environmental or contextual variables that may increase potential for reproductive success. For instance, the lack of body hair might lead to very high risk of skin cancer due to increases in ultraviolet radiation. Knowledge of this phenomenon may lead to changes in perceptions of hairy individuals and give them a distinct social advantage over those with less body hair. Social mechanisms such as social comparisons between same-sex individuals, group norm development, and stereotyping/stigmatisation may facilitate these selection processes by motivating individuals to highlight their body hair, allowing body hair to influence social status, and attributing positive traits to those with body hair and attributing negative traits to those without body hair. This between-sex flexibility in mate choice, thus, allows for existing within-sex social mechanisms to facilitate mate choices that have the greatest reproductive value.

Summary

Social groups clearly play an important role in the development of attractiveness ideals, whether they simply support pre-existing preferences for mate value or develop in response to a range of social demands. Existing literature has focused on individual responses to social mechanisms and could benefit from understanding individual responses as a function of membership in specific groups. Nonetheless, it appears as though several social mechanisms are important to physical attractiveness including social comparison, group norm development, and social stereotyping/stigmatisation. These mechanisms not only have significant impact on the development of self-perceived attractiveness, but may facilitate prejudice against unattractive individuals, in particular those who are overweight or obese. Similarly, these mechanisms may be appropriately considered specific evolutionary mechanisms that facilitate within-sex and between-sex competition.

To our knowledge, no one has formally attempted to integrate both theories of physical attractiveness, but both theories are likely to benefit from such integration. Namely, sociocultural theories would benefit from a greater understanding of *why* such social processes exist and *why* attractiveness plays such an important role in these processes. Similarly, evolutionary theories would benefit from an expanded understanding of *how* mate preferences result in mate choices and *how* social groups can facilitate both convergence upon attractiveness ideals and the adaptability of such convergence.

References

Adams, G. R., Hicken, M., & Salehi, M. (1988). Socialization of the physical attractiveness stereotype: Parental expectations and verbal behaviors. *International Journal of Psychology, 23*, 137–149.

Anderson, D. A., & Wadden, T. A. (2004). Bariatric surgery patients' views of their physicians' weight-related attitudes and practices. *Obesity Research, 12*, 1587–1595.

Anderson, C., John, O. P., Keltner, J. D., & Kring, A. M. (2001). Who attains social status? Effects of personality and physical attractiveness in social groups. *Journal of Personality and Social Psychology, 81*, 116–132.

Annis, N. M., Cash, T. F., & Hrabosky, J. I. (2004). Body image and psychosocial differences among stable average weight, currently overweight and formerly overweight women: The role of stigmatizing experiences. *Body Image, 1*, 155–167.

Ashmore, R. D., & Longo, L. C. (1995). Accuracy stereotypes: What research on physical attractiveness can teach us. In Y. Lee, L. J. Jussim, & C. R. McCauley

(Eds.), *Stereotype accuracy: Toward appreciating group differences* (pp. 63–86). Washington, DC: American Psychological Association.

Bagley, C. R., Conklin, D. N., Isherwood, R. T., Pechiulis, D. R., & Watson, L. A. (1989). Attitudes of nurses toward obesity and obese patients. *Perceptual and Motor Skills, 68*, 954.

Bauer, K. W., Yang, Y. W., & Austin, S. B. (2004). 'How can we stay healthy when you're throwing all of this in front of us?' Findings from focus groups and interviews in middle schools on environmental influences on nutrition and physical activity. *Health Education and Behavior, 31*, 34–46.

Bearman, S. K., Martinez, E., & Stice, E. (2006). The skinny on body dissatisfaction: A longitudinal study of adolescent girls and boys. *Journal of Youth and Adolescence, 35*, 217–229.

Blumberg, P., & Mellis, L. P. (1980). Medical students' attitudes toward the obese and morbidly obese. *International Journal of Eating Disorders, 4*, 169–175.

Bond, C. F., Jr., & Kenny, D. A. (2002). The triangle of interpersonal models. *Journal of Personality and Social Psychology, 83*, 355–366.

Brownell, K. D., & Napolitano, M. A. (1995). Distorting reality for children: Body size proportion of Barbie and Ken dolls. *International Journal of Eating Disorders, 18*, 295–298.

Brylinsky, J. A., & Moore, J. C. (1994). The identification of body build stereotypes in young children. *Journal of Research in Personality, 28*, 170–181.

Buss, D. M. (1989). Sex differences in human mate preferences: Evolutionary hypotheses tested in 37 cultures. *Behavioral and Brain Sciences, 12*, 1–49.

Buss, D. M. (1992). Mate preference mechanisms: Consequences for partner choice and intrasexual competition. In J. Barkow, L. Cosmides, & J. Tooby (Eds.), *The adapted mind: Evolutionary psychology and the generation of culture* (pp. 556–579). New York: Oxford University Press.

Buss, D. M., & Schmidtt, D. P. (1993). Sexual strategies theory: An evolutionary perspective on human mating. *Psychology Review, 100*, 204–232.

Cattarin, J. A., & Thompson, J. K. (1994). A three-year longitudinal study of body image, eating disturbance, and general psychological functioning in adolescent females. *Eating Disorders: Journal of Treatment & Prevention, 2*, 114–125.

Chai, R. C., Allred, L. J., Grossnickle, W. F., & Lee, G. W. (1998). Effects of attractiveness and gender on achievement-related variables. *The Journal of Social Psychology, 138*, 471–477.

Chen, E. Y., & Brown, M. (2005). Obesity stigma in sexual relationships. *Obesity Research, 13*, 1393–1397.

Clifford, M. M. (1975). Physical attractiveness and actual performance. *Child Study Journal, 5*, 201–209.

Cramer, P., & Steinwert, T. (1998). Thin is good, fat is bad: How early does it begin? *Journal of Applied Developmental Psychology, 19*, 429–451.

Crandall, C. S. (1988). Social contagion of binge eating. *Journal of Personality and Social Psychology, 55*, 588–598.

Crandall, C. S. (1991). Do parents discriminate against their heavyweight daughters? *Personality and Social Psychology Bulletin, 21*, 724–735.

Crandall, C. S. (1994). Prejudice against fat people: Ideology and self-interest. *Journal of Personality and Social Psychology, 66*, 882–894.

Crandall, C. S., & Eshleman, A. (2003). A justification-suppression model of the expression and experience of prejudice. *Psychological Bulletin, 129*, 414–446.

Davison, K. K., & Birch, L. L. (2002). Processes linking weight status and self-concept among girls from ages 5 to 7 years. *Developmental Psychology, 38,* 735–748.

Davison, K. K., & Birch, L. L. (2004). Predictors of fat stereotypes among 9-year-old girls and their parents. *Obesity Research, 12,* 86–94.

Eagly, A. H., Ashmore, R. D., Makhijani, M. G., & Longo, L. C. (1991). What is beautiful is good, but...: A meta-analysis of research on the physical attractiveness stereotype. *Psychological Bulletin, 110,* 109–128.

Edmunds, L. D. (2005). Parents' perceptions of health professionals' responses when seeking help for their overweight children. *Journal of Family Practice, 22,* 287–292.

Eisenberg, M. E., Newmark-Sztainer, D., & Story, M. (2003). Associations of weight-based teasing and emotional well-being among adolescents. *Archives of Pediatric and Adolescent Medicine, 157,* 733–738.

Fabricatore, A. N., Wadden, T. A., & Foster, G. D. (2005). Bias in health care settings. In K. D. Brownell, R. M. Puhl, & M. B. Schwartz (Eds.), *Weight bias: Nature, consequences and remedies* (pp. 29–41). New York: Guilford Publications.

Faith, M. S., Leone, M. A., Ayers, T. S., Moonseong, H., & Pietrobelli, A. (2002). Weight criticism during physical activity, coping skills, and reported physical activity in children. *Pediatrics, 110,* E23.

Feingold, A. (1992). Good-looking people are not what we think. *Psychological Bulletin, 111,* 304–341.

Festinger, L. (1954). A theory of social comparison processes. *Human Relations, 7,* 117–140.

Fikkan, J., & Rothblum, E. D. (2005). Weight bias in employment. In K. D. Brownell, R. M. Puhl, & M. B. Schwartz (Eds.), *Weight bias: Nature, consequences and remedies* (pp. 15–28). New York: Guilford Publications.

Fingeret, M., Gleaves, D. H., & Pearson, C. A. (2004). On the methodology of body image assessment: The use of figural rating scales to evaluate body dissatisfaction and the ideal body standards of women. *Body Image, 2,* 207–212.

Foster, G. D., Wadden, T. A., Makris, A. P., Davidson, D., Sanderson, R. S., Allison, D. B., et al. (2003). Primary care physicians' attitudes about obesity and its treatment. *Obesity Research, 11,* 1168–1177.

Fouts, G., & Burggraf, K. (2000). Television situation comedies: Female weight, male negative comments, and audience reactions. *Sex Roles, 42,* 925–932.

Friedlander, S. L., Larkin, E. K., Rosen, C. L., Palermo, T. M., & Redline, S. (2003). Decreased quality of life associated with obesity in school-aged children. *Archives of Pediatric and Adolescent Medicine, 157,* 1206–1211.

Friedman, K. E., Reichmann, S. K., Costanzo, P. R., & Musante, G. J. (2002). Body image partially mediates the relationship between obesity and psychological distress. *Obesity Research, 10,* 33–41.

Gilbert, D. T., Giesler, R. B., & Morris, K. A. (1995). When comparisons arise. *Journal of Personality and Social Psychology, 69,* 227–236.

Goodman, N., Dornbusch, S. M., Richardson, S. A., & Hastorf, A. H. (1963). Variant reactions of physical disabilities. *American Sociological Review, 28,* 429–435.

Gortmaker, S. L., Must, A., Perrin, J. M., Sobol, A. M., & Dietz, W. H. (1993). Social and economic consequences of overweight in adolescence and young adulthood. *The New England Journal of Medicine, 329,* 1008–1012.

Greenberg, B. S., Eastin, M., Hofschire, L., Lachlan, K., & Brownell, K. D. (2003). Portrayals of overweight and obese individuals on commercial television. *American Journal of Public Health*, *93*, 1342–1348.

Greenleaf, C., & Weiller-Abels, K. (2005). *Perceptions of youth obesity among physical educators*. Conference presentation AAHPERD national convention, April 2005.

Griffin, A. M., & Langlois, J. H. (2006). Stereotype directionality and attractiveness stereotyping: Is beauty good or ugly bad? *Social Cognition*, *24*, 187–206.

Grilo, C. M., Wilfley, D. E., Brownell, K. D., & Rodin, J. (1994). Teasing, body image, and self-esteem in a clinical sample of obese women. *Addictive Behaviors*, *19*, 443–450.

Harrison, K. (2000). Television viewing, fat stereotyping, body shape standards, and eating disorder symptomatology in grade school children. *Communication Research*, *27*, 617–640.

Heinberg, L. J., & Thompson, J. K. (1992a). The effects of figure size feedback (positive vs. negative) and target comparison group (particularistic vs. universalistic) on body image disturbance. *International Journal of Eating Disorders*, *12*, 441–448.

Heinberg, L. J., & Thompson, J. K. (1992b). Social comparison: Gender, target importance ratings, and relation to body image disturbance. *Journal of Social Behavior and Personality*, *7*, 335–344.

Heinberg, L. J., & Thompson, J. K. (1995). Body image and televised images of thinness and attractiveness: A controlled laboratory investigation. *Journal of Social and Clinical Psychology*, *7*, 335–344.

Hildebrandt, T., & Walker, D. C. (2006). Evidence that ideal and attractive figures represent different constructs: A replication and extension of Fingeret, Gleaves, and Pearson (2004). *Body Image*, *3*, 173–182.

Jackson, C. (1997). Initial experimental stages of tobacco and alcohol use during late childhood: Relation to peer, parent, and personal risk factors. *Addictive Behaviors*, *22*, 685–698.

Janssen, I., Craig, W. M., Boyce, W. F., & Pickett, W. (2004). Associations between overweight and obesity with bullying behaviors in school-aged children. *Pediatrics*, *113*, 1187–1194.

Jones, D. C. (2004). Body image among adolescent girls and boys: A longitudinal study. *Developmental Psychology*, *40*, 823–835.

Jones, D. C., & Crawford, J. K. (2006). The peer appearance culture during adolescence: Gender and body mass variations. *Journal of Youth and Adolescence*, *35*, 243–255.

Kanazawa, S., & Kovar, J. L. (2004). Why beautiful people are more intelligent. *Intelligence*, *32*, 227–243.

Klein, D., Najman, J., Kohrman, A. F., & Munro, C. (1982). Patient characteristics that elicit negative responses from family physicians. *Journal of Family Practice*, *14*, 881–888.

Klesges, R. C., Klem, M. L., Hanson, C. L., Eck, L. H., Ernst, J., O'Laughlin, D., et al. (1990). The effects of applicant's health status and qualifications on simulated hiring decisions. *International Journal of Obesity*, *14*, 527–535.

Krones, P. G., Stice, E., Batres, C., & Orjada, K. (2005). In vivo thin-ideal peer promotes body dissatisfaction: A randomized experiment. *International Journal of Eating Disorders*, *38*, 134–142.

Kushner, R. F., & Foster, G. D. (2000). Obesity and quality of life. *Nutrition*, *16*, 947–952.

Langlois, J. H., Halakanis, L., Rubenstein, A. J., Larson, A., Hallam, M., & Smoot, M. (2000). Maxims or myths of beauty: A meta-analytic and theoretical review. *Psychological Bulletin, 126,* 390–423.

Larkin, J., & Pines, H. (1979). No fat persons need apply: Experimental studies of the overweight stereotype and hiring preference. *Sociology of Work and Occupations, 6,* 312–327.

Latner, J. D., & Schwartz, M. B. (2005). Weight bias in a child's world. In K. D. Brownell, R. M. Puhl, M. B. Schwartz, & L. Rudd (Eds.), *Weight bias: Nature, consequences and remedies* (pp. 54–67). New York, NY: Guilford Press.

Latner, J. D., & Stunkard, A. J. (2003). Getting worse: The stigmatization of obese children. *Obesity Research, 11,* 452–456.

Latner, J. D., Stunkard, A. J., & Wilson, T. G. (2005). Stigmatized students: Age, sex, and ethnicity effects in the stigmatization of obesity. *Obesity Research, 13,* 1226–1231.

Lawson, M. C. (1980). Development of body build stereotypes, peer ratings, and self-esteem in Australian children. *The Journal of Psychology, 104,* 111–118.

Lerner, R. M., & Korn, S. J. (1972). The development of body-built stereotypes in males. *Child Development, 43,* 908–920.

Lewis, R. J., Cash, T. F., Jacobi, L., & Bubb-Lewis, C. (1997). Prejudice toward fat people: The development and validation of the antifat attitudes test. *Obesity Research, 5,* 297–307.

Lieberman, M., Gauvin, L., Bukowski, W. M., & White, D. R. (2001). Interpersonal influence and disordered eating behaviors in adolescent girls: The role of peer modeling, social reinforcement, and body-related teasing. *Eating Behaviors, 2,* 215–236.

Lin, L. F., & Kulik, J. A. (2002). Social comparison and women's body satisfaction. *Basic and Applied Social Psychology, 24,* 115–123.

Lyubomirsky, S., & Ross, L. (1997). Hedonic consequences of social comparison: A contrast of happy and unhappy people. *Journal of Personality and Social Psychology, 23,* 1141–1157.

Maddox, G. L., Back, K. W., & Liederman, V. R. (1968). Overweight as social deviance and disability. *Journal of Health and Social Behavior, 9,* 287–298.

Maiman, L. A., Wang, V. L., Becker, M. H., Finlay, J., & Simonson, M. (1979). Attitudes toward obesity and the obese among professionals. *Journal of the American Dietetic Association, 74,* 331–336.

McCabe, M. P., & Ricciardelli, L. A. (2003). Sociocultural influences on body image and body changes among adolescent boys and girls. *The Journal of Social Psychology, 143,* 5–26.

Miller, G. F. (1998). How mate choice shaped human nature: A review of sexual selection and human evolution. In C. Crawford & D. L. Kribs (Eds.), *Handbook of evolutionary psychology* (pp. 87–129). Mahwah, NJ: Erlbaum.

Morse, S., & Gergen, K. J. (1970). Social comparison, self-consistency, and the concept of the self. *Journal of Personality and Social Psychology, 16,* 148–156.

Myers, A., & Rosen, J. D. (1999). Obesity stigmatization and coping: Relation to mental health symptoms, body image, and self-esteem. *International Journal of Obesity, 23,* 221–230.

Neumark-Sztainer, D., Story, M., & Harris, T. (1999). Beliefs and attitudes about obesity among teachers and school health care providers working with adolescents. *Journal of Nutrition Education, 31,* 3–9.

Neumark-Sztainer, D., Falkner, N., Story, M., Perry, C., Hannan, P. J., & Mulert, S. (2002). Weight-teasing among adolescents: Correlations with weight status and disordered eating behaviors. *International Journal of Obesity, 26*, 123–131.

Norton, K. I., Olds, T. S., Olive, S., & Dank, S. (1995). Ken and Barbie at life size. *Sex Roles, 34*, 287–294.

O'Brien, K. S., Hunter, J. A., & Banks, M. (2007). Implicit anti-fat bias in physical educators: Physical attributes, ideology, and socialization. *International Journal of Obesity, 31*, 308–314.

Paxton, S. J., Shultz, H., Wertheim, E. H., & Muhr, S. L. (1999). Friendship clique and peer influences on body image concerns, dietary restraint, extreme weight-loss behaviors and binge eating in adolescent girls. *Journal of Abnormal Psychology, 108*, 255–266.

Pearce, M. J., Boergers, J., & Prinstein, M. J. (2002). Adolescent obesity, overt and relational peer victimization, and romantic relationships. *Obesity Research, 10*, 386–393.

Pedersen, F. A. (1991). Secular trends in human sex ratios: Their influence on individual and family behavior. *Human Nature, 2*, 271–291.

Pierce, J. W., & Wardle, J. (1997). Cause and effect beliefs and self-esteem of overweight children. *Journal of Child Psychology & Psychiatry, 38*, 645–650.

Polinko, N. K., & Popovich, P. M. (2001). Evil thoughts by angelic actions: Responses to overweight job applicants. *Journal of Applied Social Psychology, 31*, 905–924.

Pope, H. G., Jr., Phillips, K. A., & Olivardia, O. (2000). *The Adonis complex: The secret crisis of male body obsession.* New York: The Free Press.

Pope, H. G., Jr., Olivardia, R., Gruber, A., & Borowiecki, J. (1999). Evolving ideals of male body image as seen through action toys. *International Journal of Eating Disorders, 26*, 65–72.

Presnell, K., Bearman, S. K., & Stice, E. (2004). Risk factors for body dissatisfaction in adolescent boys and girls: A prospective study. *International Journal of Eating Disorders, 36*, 389–401.

Puhl, R., & Brownell, K. D. (2001). Bias, discrimination, and obesity. *Obesity Research, 9*, 788–805.

Puhl, R., Schwartz, M. B., & Brownell, K. D. (2005). Impact of perceived consensus on stereotypes about obese people: New avenues for bias reduction. *Health Psychology, 24*, 517–525.

Rand, C. S. W., & Wright, B. A. (2000). Continuity and change in the evaluation of ideal and acceptable body sizes across a wide age span. *International Journal of Eating Disorders, 28*, 90–100.

Rand, C. S., & MacGregor, A. M. (1990). Morbidly obese patients' perceptions of social discrimination before and after surgery for obesity. *Southern Medical Journal, 83*, 1390–1395.

Reagan, P. C. (1996). Sexual outcasts: The perceived impact of body weight and gender on sexuality. *Journal of Applied and Social Psychology, 26*, 1803–1815.

Register, C. A., & Williams, D. R. (1990). Wage effects of obesity among young workers. *Social Science Quarterly, 71*, 130–141.

Rich, J. (1975). Effects of children's physical attractiveness on teachers' evaluations. *Journal of Educational Psychology, 67*, 599–609.

Richardson, S. A., Goodman, N., Hastorf, A. H., & Dornbusch, S. M. (1961). Cultural uniformity in reaction to physical disabilities. *American Sociological Review, 26*, 241–247.

Roehling, M. V. (1999). Weight-based discrimination in employment: Psychological and legal aspects. *Personnel Psychology, 52,* 969–1017.

Sargent, J. D., & Blanchflower, D. G. (1994). Obesity and stature in adolescence and earnings in young adulthood. *Archives of Pediatric and Adolescent Medicine, 148,* 681–687.

Sarlio-Lähteenkorva, S., Silventoinen, K., & Lahelma, E. (2004). Relative weight and income at different levels of socioeconomic status. *American Journal of Public Health, 94,* 468–472.

Schneider, D. J. (2004). *The psychology of stereotyping.* New York: Guilford Press.

Schultz, H. K., Paxton, S. J., & Wertheim, E. H. (2002). Investigation of body comparison among adolescent girls. *Journal of Applied Social Psychology, 32,* 1906–1937.

Schwartz, M. B., Vartanian, L. R., Nosek, B. A., & Brownell, K. D. (2006). The influence of one's own body weight on implicit and explicit anti-fat cias. *Obesity, 14,* 440–448.

Schwartz, M. B., O'Neal, H., Brownell, K. D., Blair, S., & Billington, C. (2003). Weight bias among health professionals specializing in obesity. *Obesity Research, 11,* 1033–1039.

Schwimmer, J. B., Burwinkle, T. M., & Varni, J. W. (2003). Health-related quality of life of severely obese children and adolescents. *Journal of the American Medical Association, 289,* 1813–1819.

Sechrist, G. B., & Stangor, C. (2005). Social consensus and the origins of stigma. In K. D. Brownell, R. M. Puhl, M. B. Schwartz, & L. Rudd (Eds.), *Weight bias: Nature, consequences and remedies* (pp. 97–108). New York: Guilford Publications.

Singh, D. (1994). Is thin really beautiful and good? Relationship between waist-to-hip ratio (WHR) and female attractiveness. *Personality and Individual Differences, 16,* 123–132.

Singh, D. (2004). Mating strategies of young women: Role of physical attractiveness. *Journal of Sex Research, 41,* 43–54.

Smith, S. M., McIntosh, W. D., & Bazzini, D. G. (1999). Are the beautiful good in Hollywood? An investigation of the beauty-as-goodness stenotype in film. *Basic and Applied Social Psychology, 21,* 69–80.

Stangor, C., Sechrist, G. B., & Jost, J. T. (2001). Changing beliefs by providing consensus information. *Personality and Social Psychology Bulletin, 27,* 486–496.

Stice, E. (2001). A prospective test of the dual-pathway model of bulimic pathology: Mediating effects of dieting and negative affect. *Journal of Abnormal Psychology, 110,* 124–135.

Stice, E., & Bearman, S. K. (2001). Body-image and eating disturbances prospectively predict increases in depressive symptoms in adolescent girls: A growth curve analysis. *Developmental Psychology, 37,* 597–607.

Stice, E., & Whitenton, K. (2002). Risk factors for body dissatisfaction in adolescent girls: A longitudinal investigation. *Developmental Psychology, 38,* 669–678.

Stice, E., Maxfield, J., & Wells, T. (2003). Adverse effects of social pressure to be thin on young women: An experimental investigation of the effects of 'fat talk.' *International Journal of Eating Disorders, 34,* 108–117.

Strauss, R. S., & Pollack, H. A. (2003). Social marginalization of overweight children. *Archives of Pediatric and Adolescent Medicine, 157,* 746–752.

Stromer, S. M., & Thompson, J. K. (1996). Evaluations of body image disturbance: A test of maturational status, negative verbal commentary, social comparison, and sociocultural hypotheses. *International Journal of Eating Disorders, 19,* 193–202.

Sugiyama, L. S. (2005). Physical attractiveness in adaptations perspective. In D. M. Buss (Ed.). *Handbook of evolutionary psychology* (pp. 292–343). Hoboken, NJ: John Wiley & Sons.

Swallen, K. C., Reither, E. N., Haas, S. A., & Meier, A. M. (2005). Overweight, obesity, and health-related quality of life among adolescents: The national longitudinal study of adolescent health. *Pediatrics, 115,* 340–347.

Swami, V., Greven, C., & Furnham, A. (2007). More than just skin-deep? A pilot study integrating physical and non-physical factors in the perception of physical attractiveness. *Personality and Individual Differences, 42,* 563–572.

Taylor, S. E., & Lobel, M. (1989). Social comparison activity under threat: Downward evaluation and upward contacts. *Psychological Review, 96,* 569–575.

Teachman, B. A., & Brownell, K. D. (2001). Implicit anti-fat bias among health professionals: Is anyone immune? *International Journal of Obesity, 25,* 1525–1531.

Thompson, J. K., Heinberg, L. J., Altabe, M., & Tantleff-Dunn, S. (1999). *Exacting beauty: Theory, assessment, and treatment of body image disturbance.* Washington, DC: American Psychological Association.

Thompson, J. K., Coovert, M. D., Richards, K. J., Johnson, S., & Cattarin, J. (1995). Development of body image, eating disturbance, and general psychological functioning in female adolescents: Covariance structure modeling and longitudinal investigations. *International Journal of Eating Disorders, 18,* 221–236.

Wang, Y., & Lobstein, T. (2006). Worldwide trends in childhood overweight and obesity. *International Journal of Pediatric Obesity, 1,* 11–25.

Weeden, J., & Sabini, J. (2005). Physical attractiveness and health in Western societies: A review. *Psychological Bulletin, 131,* 635–653.

12

Feminism and Body Image

Linda Smolak and Sarah K. Murnen

Body image is defined as one's perception of, affective reaction to, and cognitive appraisal of one's body. It has become evident that the process of developing a body image as well as the nature of these perceptions and appraisals are marked by considerable gender differences. In addition, the consequences of negative body image seem to differ for men and women. More specifically, in the United States and in a variety of other countries (e.g., Grogan, 1999; Luo, Parish, & Laumann, 2005), women are more likely to be interested in obtaining a thin body while men are more interested in obtaining a muscular body.

Women and girls may be more likely to take action to change their bodies when they are dissatisfied (Grogan, 1999). They are certainly more likely to engage in dangerous calorie-restrictive dieting and to develop life-threatening eating disorders (American Psychiatric Association, 2000; Ricciardelli & McCabe, 2004). This is true in childhood as well as in adulthood (Bryant-Waugh, 2006; Smolak & Levine, 2001). Men are more likely to engage in exercise than dieting to control their weight (though not necessarily at higher levels than women do) and to build muscle (Ricciardelli & McCabe, 2004). Boys and men are more likely than girls and women to use steroids and food supplements to build muscles (e.g., Field et al., 2005). Women are more likely to submit to body reshaping cosmetic surgeries, such as liposuction and breast enhancement. For example, 287,932 women compared to 35,673 men underwent liposuction in 2005 (American Society of Plastic Surgeons, 2006). Thus, although a small group of men engage in dangerous body shaping activities (e.g., steroids and food supplements), a larger group of women use extreme and even life-threatening means (e.g., self-starvation, liposuction) to try to achieve a particular body type.

236

For males especially, some of this investment in body shape is attributable to functional interests, such as the strength to participate in sports or to perform certain 'masculine' activities (e.g., Grogan & Richards, 2002; Smolak & Stein, 2006). Furthermore, both men and women report some health-related motives for weight loss (e.g., Grogan & Richards, 2002). However, it is also clear that both men and women, and indeed girls and boys, are motivated to participate in body shaping activities such as dieting, exercise, weight-lifting, and steroid use in order to be attractive.

The question addressed by this chapter is whether the roots of gender differences in the definitions of and the pressure to adopt standards of attractiveness are better explained by biological theories or sociocultural theories. We begin with a feminist analysis of behavioural evolutionary and genetic theories of attractiveness. We then present sociocultural theories, and more explicitly feminist theories and research, to help interpret these gender differences.

A feminist critique of evolutionary psychology and genetic theories of female attractiveness

Evolutionary psychology

Evolutionary psychology posit that mate selection to maximise reproductive success is the driving force behind gender-differentiated behaviours (Singh, 1993). A woman's reproductive fitness is equated with her fertility and her ability to mother while a man's is signaled by his potential to provide material resources. Hence, a woman should look for indications that a man has a high status while a man should seek evidence that a woman will be fecund. The best indicators of the latter are body cues, aspects of women's body's shape that has come to be equated with physical attractiveness (Singh, 1993).

Thus, in evolutionary psychological theory, women's physical attractiveness is valued because it indicates that she will be able to bear and rear children (Buss, 1994). Some of this attractiveness simply reflects good health, an ability to resist pathogens. But what is presumably more crucial is the presence of the 'gynoid' body shape. This body shape is marked by fat deposition that is associated with normal adult female levels (as opposed to male levels) of circulating estrogen (Singh, 1993). In their original formulations, evolutionary theorists pointed out that this gynoid body shape resulted in a waist-to-hip ratio (WHR) that normally fell in the range of 0.67 to 0.80, whereas for 'android' shaped men a normal WHR was 0.85 to 0.95 (e.g., Singh, 1993, 1994).

There have been data supporting this perspective (e.g., Singh, 1993). However, WHR and body mass index (BMI) were often confounded in the methodology used in the research (Swami & Tovée, 2005a). Furthermore, even very thin women, including those in the anorexic range who are amenorrheic, can maintain a gynoid WHR. Therefore, some evolutionary theorists shifted focus to arguing that a healthy BMI is the key indicator of attractiveness, again because of its association with reproductive fitness (Swami & Tovée, 2005a). Other chapters in this volume examine some of the specific methodological and empirical issues related to the evolutionary psychological perspective in detail. Our purpose is to briefly present three feminist criticisms of the theory and then to focus on alternative feminist explanations of how attractiveness is defined and learned.

Feminist critiques

Status

While feminists offer a variety of critiques of evolutionary psychology, three are particularly relevant for our purposes. First, evolutionary psychological theory confuses what exists in society with what is natural or inherent. Socially pervasive roles, inculcated from infancy, can appear to be natural because we perform them without thinking. An alternative theory that has generated much empirical support is Social Roles Theory (SRT; Eagly, 1987; Eagly, Wood, & Diekman, 2000; Eagly, Wood, & Johannesen-Schmidt, 2004). According to SRT, the social roles that people occupy in society produce traits and behaviours that, in turn, support the role. In gender-segregated cultures, women and men take on different societal roles that lead to gender-differentiated behaviour. In many societies, women are associated with the domestic role while men are associated with the employee or work role (Eagly et al., 2004).

Eagly argues that the origins of gender-differentiated roles likely resulted from physical differences between women and men (e.g., men's larger body size, women's ability to bear children) that interacted with social and ecological conditions. Once established, roles are reinforced through various societal and psychological forces, even though the physical differences may be of marginal significance. For example, if women are more likely to be placed in care-taking roles in society due to the fact that they bear children and can breast-feed them, they are more likely to develop skills such as nurturance to help them fulfill that role. Individuals see women perform this role and develop stereotypes that women are more nurturing than men.

Women often behave in ways consistent with the gender stereotype because failure to do so creates a risk of negative social consequences. In addition, observers tend to remember behaviour that is consistent with stereotypes and act in ways to elicit stereotype-consistent behaviours from others, thus further perpetuating the stereotypes (Eagly et al., 2000). Thus, we enact gender roles in the smallest details and the largest themes of our daily lives in an almost automatic manner. This makes them appear innate. But the question is whether the basis for such behaviours is biological (evolutionary, genetic, hormonal) or whether it is rooted in status differences in society.

Buss et al. (1990) suggested that because the pattern of women selecting men of high status as partners existed across 37 different cultures, it must be innate in the human species. But Eagly and Wood (1999) demonstrated that the strength of this pattern varied with the status of women in the society. Similarly, researchers have found that women's investment in a particular body shape is related to their perception that the body shape will gain them status (Becker & Fay, 2006). For example, Becker (2004) reported that girls in Fiji who thought that weight loss would gain them economic opportunities and upward social mobility were the ones who tried to emulate body shapes of the newly introduced television medium. Similarly, Anderson-Fye (2004) found eating disordered behaviour only among Belize teenagers working in the tourist industry whose families thought that the girls' 'Westernised' bodies would gain them more customers. Cases of anorexia nervosa in Curacao were found only among mixed ethnicity women who thought that thinness would bring them greater acceptance in the White community (Katzman et al., 2004).

Thus, women – and men – may select marital partners based on status. A beautiful woman may be a status symbol for men whereas a wealthy husband may be important to women when they cannot earn their own resources. Furthermore, status and investment in definitions of attractiveness appear to be intertwined. Women will invest in a particular definition of physical attractiveness if it gains them resources. This may be because in many societies women's attractiveness continues to be their main currency.

Parenting

Second, evolutionary psychology continues to suggest that women are designed to be active parents while men are not. We might begin by noting that the animal data indicate that females are sometimes good mothers and sometimes reject the maternal role; circumstances are crucial in determining the likelihood that females will parent their offspring (Hrdy, 1999). Among humans, it is evident that men are not only interested in parenting, beginning with 'engrossment' with their newborns (Greenberg & Morris, 1974), but that they can play an important role in the cognitive and social development of children that is not simply redundant to the role mothers play (e.g., Hart, Newell, & Olsen, 2003). Both men and women are capable of providing physical, emotional, and social support to children. Men simply do it less frequently than women do. Again, this leads to a confusion of what is 'natural' with what is 'common.' Eagly's SRT, for example, can again explain this phenomenon.

Male attractiveness

Finally, and perhaps most importantly for this chapter, the evolutionary psychological perspective suggests that men's attractiveness is of limited importance. Until the 1990s, much body image and eating problems research focused exclusively on girls and women. This was partially because of the long-held finding that the major eating disorders, anorexia nervosa (AN) and bulimia nervosa (BN), are 8 to 9 times more common in women than in men (American Psychiatric Association, 2000), though recent research suggests a slightly lower ratio (Hudson, Hiripi, Pope, & Kessler, 2007). Research examining body dissatisfaction focused on the symptoms associated with AN and BN, namely drive for thinness and dieting, and found that women, and even young girls, were much more likely to be body dissatisfied and to engage in weight management techniques than were men and boys (e.g., Smolak & Levine, 2001; Smolak & Murnen, 2004). Women are also more likely than men to report that their body shape is important to their self-definition (e.g., Reichborn-Kjennerud et al., 2004).

However, more recent research has clearly demonstrated that, if both interest in losing weight and in gaining muscle are considered, then men show about as much body dissatisfaction as women do (e.g., Ricciardelli & McCabe, 2004). Furthermore, boys and men will engage in potentially dangerous practices, including the use of food supplements and steroids, in order to gain muscle (e.g., Cafri et al., 2005; Smolak, Murnen, & Thompson, 2005). Although this is less common than dieting and eating disorders among women, it does underscore men's commitment to obtain a particular body type.

Men's desire to be muscular could be viewed as consistent with evolutionary psychological theory since, arguably, muscularity might be associated with strength and health and hence reproductive fitness. As with definitions of women's attractiveness, however, men's definitions of and investment in attractiveness appear to be substantially socioculturally influenced. Although the research concerning men is limited, like women, men's commitment to a muscular ideal of attractiveness seems to vary by culture. For example, gay men seem more invested in body shape than straight men do (Rothblum, 2002); while Swami and Tovée (2005b) reported that chest size is the more important determinant of attractiveness among urban men, but BMI is more important among rural men. Researchers have also found that investment in muscularity is correlated with perceived media and peer pressures (e.g., Ricciardelli & McCabe, 2004; Smolak et al., 2005). Interestingly, investment in male gender role may be related to drive for muscularity in boys and men (e.g., McCreary, Saucier, & Courtenay, 2005; Smolak & Stein, 2006), a finding that is consistent with Eagly's SRT.

Genetic theories

During the past decade, genetic research and theorising concerning eating disorders has grown immensely (e.g., Bulik & Tozzi, 2004; Mazzeo, Landt, van Furth & Bulik, 2006). As part of this effort, researchers have examined individual components and symptoms of eating disorders, including body dissatisfaction, to assess their possible heritability. Several studies have reported a significant additive genetic component of body dissatisfaction in older adolescent girls and women. For example, Klump, McGue, and Iacono (2000) found a heritability estimate (h^2) of 0.23 in 17-year-old girls after BMI had been considered. Similarly, Wade, Martin, and Tiggemann (1998) reported that genetics were more important than the environment in determining shape concerns among adult (30 to 45 years old) women.

These studies only included female participants. In a recent study by Keski-Rahkonen et al. (2005), both male and female Finnish young adults (aged 22 to 27) completed the Eating Disorders Inventory (EDI) Body Dissatisfaction scale. This large sample ($n = 4,667$) study included both monozygotic and dizygotic twins. The results suggested that additive genetics accounted for a little more than 59 per cent of the variance in body dissatisfaction among the women but that body dissatisfaction among the men was completely determined by environmental forces.

This finding is consistent with the frequent historical claim that women's bodies (and minds) are more controlled by nature (e.g., reproductive hormones), while men's are more controlled by rationality (e.g., Bordo, 1993). Indeed, scientific data have often been marshaled to demonstrate women's biological 'problems' (e.g., Shields, 1975). Feminist analysis shows how scientific research traditions can be biased to yield such results (e.g., McHugh, Koeske, & Frieze, 1986).

The genetic research examining body dissatisfaction, and much of the work on eating disorders, is quantitative behavioural genetics. Molecular genetic sites for body dissatisfaction, or concepts similar to body dissatisfaction, have not been identified. Thus, critiques that generally apply to quantitative behavioural genetics research (e.g., Gottlieb, 1995) are applicable here. So, for example, this research does not explicitly permit a role for gene-environment interactions in their equations. Rather, they typically assume that genes determine environments rather than vice versa and hence include the variance associated with the interactions under the genetic component (Gottlieb, 1995). Given that environments can indeed influence genetic expression, this assumption may result in an inflated heritability estimate.

Returning to the Keski-Rahkonen et al. (2005) study of gender differences in the heritability of body dissatisfaction, the EDI body dissatisfaction scale served as the dependent variable. This scale does not tap body dissatisfaction in males as effectively as it does in females because it does not assess concerns about muscularity. Thus, the researchers did not fully consider the gendered nature of body image in designing their study.

Furthermore, genetic researchers, like evolutionary psychologists, may be conflating what is common with what is innate. Some geneticists (e.g., Turkheimer, 2000) claim that every behaviour is genetically based. Clearly this is an overstatement. It is important to distinguish behaviours that are rooted in genetic predispositions, including, perhaps, some gender differences, from those that are socioculturally determined. There may, indeed, be some small percentage of variance in attractiveness associated with either evolution or genetics; for example, there may be a preference for faces or body shapes that fall within the 'average' range that is indicative of good health (e.g., Langlois et al., 2000). But the current Caucasian American ideal body shape for women does not represent good health and is not easily obtained by healthy methods. Rather, attractiveness ideals, and the body dissatisfaction that accrues by perceived failures to meet those standards, are more likely to be explained by sociocultural than genetic influences.

Sociocultural explanations of attractiveness

If one rejects biological explanations of gender differences in definitions and implications of attractiveness, then typically cultural factors are cited as causative. Indeed, sociocultural theories are probably the most popular explanations of attractiveness, body dissatisfaction, and eating disorders. There are many sociocultural theories (e.g., Cash & Pruzinsky, 2002; Thompson, Heinberg, Altabe, & Tantleff-Dunn, 1999). They commonly point to media, parents, and/or peers as influencing the development of an 'ideal' body type which, when compared to the individual's appraisal of her own body often results in body dissatisfaction. In the case of women, body dissatisfaction can become weight concerns, a focus, perhaps even an obsession, with avoiding gaining even 2 to 5 pounds for fear that it will negatively impact one's well-being (Wertheim, Paxton, & Blaney, in press). For men, this body dissatisfaction may take the form of concern about overweight or it may be expressed as a drive for muscularity (e.g., McCreary & Sasse, 2000).

Sociocultural theories generally seek to explain how people learn and internalise the cultural ideals of attractiveness. For most American ethnic groups, the cultural ideal for females is the 'thin ideal' (Grabe & Hyde, 2006). Many researchers have pointed out that an unrealistically thin ideal for women is promoted in various media (Groesz, Levine, & Murnen, 2002; Levine & Smolak, 2006). *Playboy* centrefold models, Miss America contestants, female television characters, and models in magazines have all become thinner across time (Mazur, 1986; Silverstein, Perdue, Peterson, & Kelly, 1986), whereas American women have become heavier. The thin ideal for girls is linked with beauty and attractiveness, both aspects of current norms for femininity (Mahalik et al., 2005), as well as with social, educational, and economic success.

The current American ideal male body is muscular and V-shaped. Parallel to changes in the body ideal for women, in the last 20 years *Playgirl* centrefold models and action figures have become more muscular (Leit, Pope, & Gray, 2001; Pope, Olivardia, Gruber, Borowiecki, 1999). The muscular image is associated with power and masculinity (Grogan & Richards, 2002; McCreary et al., 2005; Smolak & Stein, 2006). While extreme muscularity of the sort associated with body builders or portrayed in 'action figures' (e.g., Pope et al., 1999) is unattainable by most men without resorting to artificial and dangerous means, the general form of the muscular ideal is much more consistent with the 'normal' adult male physique than the thin ideal is with the 'normal' adult female physique. Thus, puberty moves boys towards the male ideal but takes girls away from the female ideal. This difference in the similarity between the ideal and the norm also reflects the patriarchal system's power differential.

Thompson et al.'s (1999) Tripartite Model of Body Dissatisfaction is an example of a sociocultural theory. In this theory, three sociocultural influences – media, peers, and parents – are seen as the primary causal determinants of the body ideal. However, this will not translate to body dissatisfaction unless the girl has internalised the thin ideal or is high on social comparison of physical attributes. If she possesses these mediating characteristics, then she is likely to develop body dissatisfaction. There has been some support for this model with adolescent girls and boys (Keery, van den Berg, & Thompson, 2004; Smolak & Stein, 2006).

Feminist critique

Why not just continue to develop the sizeable body of literature on sociocultural factors? What can feminist perspectives add to the discussion? First and foremost, most sociocultural theories do not explicitly consider gender, despite the gendered nature of attractiveness ideals, body image, and eating problems. Gender differences need to be faced and explained directly. This is particularly important given the growing trend to explain eating problems and even body dissatisfaction in terms of genetics and neuropsychology (e.g., Bulik & Tozzi, 2004; Kaye, Frank, Bailer, & Henry, 2005) and to treat body image and eating problems pharmacologically. Feminist theories highlight gender and the meaning of gender.

Furthermore, feminists emphasise that the experience of growing up and living as a male is very different from the 'lived experience' of being female. The power and status of men differs from the power and status of women. Analysing these differences may lead to a focus on different potential causal factors. For example, non-feminist sociocultural theorists often do not discuss sexual violence or sexual harassment as causative in body image or eating disorders (e.g., Stice's, 2002, meta-analysis of risk factors for eating disorders), variables that feminist theories argue need substantial attention. Indeed, traditional empiricists might claim that these variables cannot be considered as causal factors because they cannot be experimentally manipulated and are rarely studied prospectively. Feminists suggest that this argument exemplifies how the power structure of science has developed to minimise, and even negate, women's experiences. Thus, feminist explanations adopt a different position when analysing and interpreting theory, method, and data.

The influence of feminist theory on psychological theory and research

Feminist theorists argue that the patriarchal structure of society is reproduced through societal institutions and the everyday behaviours of individuals. Women's bodies and the treatment of women's bodies are believed to be an important site for oppression. In a patriarchal culture, women do not have control over their own bodies. The main value of women's bodies is to appear attractive to men. Attractiveness and 'sexiness' are important aspects of current definitions of femininity. Mahalik and colleagues (2005) recently developed a measure of feminine norms in dominant American culture. Five of the eight norms deal with appearance and relationships. Women are supposed to be 'nice in relationships,' maintain romantic relationships, exhibit sexual fidelity, invest in appearance, and be thin.

These norms are encouraged in a variety of ways. For example, Ward (1995) found that the most common theme among television shows popular to adolescents is that women attract men through their physical appearance. The sexual subordination that is part of women's role helps maintain women's lower status in at least two ways. First, while women who comply with the cultural demand for sexual subordination are seen as non-threatening, they also are not likely to increase their status (Matschiner & Murnen, 1999). Furthermore, many theorists have noted that the beauty work required to maintain the thin ideal is believed to represent a form of 'backlash' against the rights that women have gained (Bordo, 1993). To the extent that women need to exert energy to try to meet beauty ideals, they will have less energy to fight oppression. Indeed, researchers have documented that focusing on one's body interferes with cognitive functioning (e.g., Fredrickson, Roberts, Noll, Quinn, & Twenge, 1998; Hebl, King, & Lin, 2004). Also, to the extent that women do not meet these ideals, they will experience body dissatisfaction and self-doubt.

In addition to the work required to aspire to societal notions of sexual attractiveness and 'beauty,' daily social interactions provide continual reminders to women that they do not control their own bodies. Theorists have discussed the role of objectification, degradation, harassment, abuse, and assault. For example, one ubiquitous reminder is the objectification of women. Objectification involves treating women as bodies to be looked, primarily for men's sexual pleasure. Men's bodies, on the other hand, are defined as agentic and functional, as acting to accomplish things rather than simply to be enjoyed by others

(Fredrickson & Roberts, 1997). Thus, being attractive becomes the *raison d'etre* for the female body.

Objectification of the female body is demonstrated in a variety of ways including the way the media display and sometimes dismember female bodies, using them to sell products. In a recent review, Ward (2003) concluded that women were objectified in the mass media more than men. Objectification is present in many realms including fashion and fitness magazines (Rudman & Verdi, 1993); music television videos (Sommers-Flanagan, Sommers-Flanagan, & Davis, 1993); and prime-time television shows and commercials (Lin, 1998). In a recent meta-analysis, Levine, Murnen, Smith, and Groesz (2006) found that the correlations between the frequency of use of various media and amount of body image dissatisfaction were stronger among women than men. Similarly, exposure to the thin body ideal in experimental research is consistently linked to increased body dissatisfaction in women (Groesz et al., 2002).

Objectification Theory

The feminist psychological theory about the body that has received the most empirical attention is Objectification Theory. Both Fredrickson and Roberts (1997) and McKinley and Hyde (1996) have developed psychological theories that tie the societal objectification of women to self-objectification. In self-objectification, women have internalised the gaze of the outside observer/evaluator. This means women will judge and monitor their own bodies to make sure that they are sufficiently attractive, that they meet societal standards. Even elementary school girls are aware of and have internalised these standards. A substantial minority of elementary school girls – studies commonly report 40 per cent by 4th and 5th grade – are concerned about being or becoming too fat (see Smolak & Levine, 2001, for a review). Self-objectification is believed to have psychological consequences, including body shame, anxiety, lack of 'peak' emotional states, and lack of internal body awareness. These phenomena, in turn, are predicted to put women at risk for eating disorders.

Fredrickson and Roberts' (1997) model has been tested through correlational and experimental research. Many correlational studies have found that self-objectification scores are related to eating disorder scale responses, a relationship mediated by amount of body shame (Calogero, Davis, & Thompson, 2005; Fredrickson et al., 1998; Greenleaf, 2005; Miner-Rubino, Twenge, & Fredrickson, 2002; Muehlenkamp & Saris-Baglama, 2002; Noll & Frederickson, 1998; Slater & Tiggemann, 2002;

Tiggemann & Kuring, 2004; Tiggemann & Lynch, 2001; Tiggemann & Slater, 2001; Tylka & Hill, 2004).

McKinley and Hyde (1996) developed the Objectified Body Consciousness (OBC) Scale as a way to measure a similar set of ideas. They argued that objectification increases as girls develop sexually during puberty and that over time some women internalise the objectification, resulting in self-surveillance. Because the beauty standards are so unrealistic, self-surveillance can lead to body shame. Women are told they are responsible for how they look, so they think they should control their bodies which leads to the third dimension of control beliefs. Thus, the three components measured by their scale are body surveillance, body shame, and appearance-control beliefs. OBC scores have been linked to low body esteem (McKinley, 1998, 1999; McKinley & Hyde, 1996; Noll & Frederickson, 1998) and eating problems (Fredrickson et al., 1998; McKinley, 1999; Muehlenkamp & Saris-Baglama, 2002; Noll & Frederickson, 1998; Slater & Tiggemann, 2002, Tiggemann & Lynch, 2001; Tiggemann & Slater, 2001), supporting their model.

Experimental manipulations have been designed to determine the effects of self-objectification. These studies are crucial because they allow us to assess the potential role of self-objectification as a causal risk factor (Kraemer et al., 1997) for body image problems. Fredrickson et al. (1998) asked college women to try on a swimsuit or sweater supposedly to measure consumer choice, but in reality to induce self-objectification. Compared to women who tried on a sweater, those in the swimsuit condition reported higher levels of body shame which predicted restrained eating on another task. Gapinski, Brownell, and LaFrance (2003), as well as Hebl et al. (2004), have replicated this finding. Roberts and Gettmann (2004) manipulated self-objectification through a sentence scramble task involving objectification-related words and found increases in self-surveillance. Finally, Calogero (2004) led women participants to believe that they would be interacting with a man for five minutes of 'small talk.' Just the thought of this interaction led women to experience higher body shame and social physique anxiety than the expectation that they would be interacting with a woman. These studies show that self-surveillance can be induced by cultural forces, and its prompting leads women to experience negative feelings about their bodies.

Prospective studies are another way of establishing the nature of risk factors (Kraemer et al., 1997). Aubrey (2006) found that exposure to sexually objectifying television correlated with trait self-objectification one year later in both college men and women. This finding, along with some experimental data (e.g., Hebl et al., 2004), demonstrates that it is possible to induce self-objectification in both men and women. This strengthens the argument that self-objectification and its accompanying characteristics (e.g., body shame, self-survelliance) are neither genetic nor evolutionary in nature. Rather, a particular lived cultural experience leads to self-objectification. When men are treated the way that women are routinely treated, they will behave like women commonly do. It is simply the case that in today's Western societies, women are more likely to encounter objectifying experiences.

For example, in one study college, women and men kept diaries of sexist experiences (Swim, Hyers, Cohen, & Ferguson, 2001). Women experienced more incidents such as demeaning comments and sexual objectification than men did. Women experienced sexist events having a personal impact once or twice per week. Sexual harassment has been linked to body image disturbance in adolescent girls and college women (e.g., Harned, 2000; Weiner & Thompson, 1997). Sexual harassment is related to body esteem in elementary school girls but not boys (Murnen & Smolak, 2000). Sexual harassment serves as a reminder of the potential for rape. Both child sexual abuse (CSA) and rape victimise women more frequently than men. CSA and rape have been related to the development of eating problems in girls and women (Faravelli, Giugni, Salvatori, & Ricca, 2004; Smolak & Levine, in press; Smolak & Murnen, 2002). Thus, girls and women may learn to monitor and be ashamed of their bodies through direct, body shape-related messages (e.g., comments from peers) or through other 'lived experiences' of being female (e.g., CSA or rape).

Furthermore, there are individual differences in self-objectification/ self-surveillance that support the idea that the culture helps influence these phenomena. Tiggemann and Slater (2001) found that former dancers were higher on self-objectification than non-dancers. McKinley and Hyde (1996) indicated that women in highly feminine activities showed elevated OBC scores. Daubenmeier (2005) reported that yoga participants showed less self-objectification, greater satisfaction with physical appearance, and fewer disordered eating attitudes than non-participants.

As women age they are believed to experience less objectification, so it is not surprising that there are age differences in many of the constructs described in Objectification Theory. Tiggemann (2003) reviewed the research on age differences in body constructs and found that there is stability in women's body dissatisfaction across age. Across all age groups, women want to be thinner, show concerns about weight and diet, and experience low body satisfaction. However, the importance of appearance decreases as women age. So even though women grow further from the ideal, it does not result in greater body dissatisfaction. McKinley (1999) found that mothers of undergraduate women showed lower body surveillance than their daughters. Self-objectification, body monitoring, and appearance anxiety decreased with age in another cross-sectional study (Tiggemann & Lynch, 2001). In a 10-year follow-up study of college women and their mothers, McKinley (2006) found that body esteem increased across time among the younger women, perhaps the result of less objectification, indicated by lower body surveillance, and an increased focus on other roles. Overall, then, objectification indices appear to be highest among young women who are arguably the target of the sexualised ideal and the attention it brings. Nonetheless, middle age women are not immune to the effects of objectification.

Summary

The empirical support for Objectification Theory shows that it is possible to link societal phenomena identified by feminist theories to psychological processes. Furthermore, the presence of experimental and longitudinal data supporting major tenets of the theory strengthens the arguments that (a) gender differences in the definition and meaning of attractiveness are socioculturally rooted; (b) the status differences between the genders in patriarchal societies are crucial to understanding the roots of body image and eating problems, including the gendered nature of these problems; and (c) feminist strategies in research, treatment, and prevention will be necessary to understand and address these problems. Specifically, future research should continue to examine the effect of various disempowering experiences on women's bodies and their lives.

Feminist perspectives help us understand more about how various 'lived experiences' of women, including sexual violence and discrimination, affect their bodies and their status in society. Such factors have frequently been ignored in previous sociocultural research but objectification theory data have begun to call attention to their importance. Such findings may be useful in attempts to design programmes aimed at preventing body image and eating problems.

Prevention

The cost of body image problems is substantial, particularly given the causal relationship of these problems to eating disorders, cosmetic surgery, steroid and food supplement abuse, excessive exercise, extreme calorie restrictive dieting, and other potentially dangerous forms of body shaping techniques (e.g., Ricciardelli & McCabe, 2004; Stice, 2002; Wertheim et al., in press). Arguably, the most effective way to eliminate or at least substantially reduce body image and eating problems is through prevention programmes (Levine & Smolak, 2006). Although there are numerous approaches to prevention and there are ongoing debates about which are most effective, it is evident that prevention programmes for body image and eating problems can indeed work (Levine & Smolak, 2006).

The adoption of feminist perspectives holds promise for prevention. In one of the earliest feminist programmes, Niva Piran (1999) instituted a longitudinal prevention programme in a residential ballet school. Piran's approach emphasised establishing respectful relationships with the students that allowed them to voice their concerns about the elements of their school environment that were damaging to body image. Piran then worked with the students and the staff to actually change the school environment. This is a crucial piece of the feminist approach. If we assume that the root causes of body image and eating problems lie in women's status and the societal treatment of women, then it is status and social treatment that must change. Although there was no control comparison group in Piran's study, over the course of the 9 years of the study, the prevalence of anorexia nervosa dropped tenfold and there were no new cases of bulimia nervosa, as well as declines in rates of other extreme body shaping techniques.

Other feminist prevention programmes have also been tested. Full of Ourselves (Steiner-Adair et al., 2002), a programme for middle school girls to help them gain assertiveness as well as to critically evaluate cultural messages, has resulted in improved body satisfaction. Another feminist-based programme for 12 to 14 year old girls, GirlTalk, also led to increased body esteem (McVey, Lieberman, Voorberg, Wardrope, & Blackmore, 2003) though a replication attempt was not successful (McVey, Lieberman, Voorberg, Wardrope, Blackmore, & Tweed, 2003). In a study using college women, very brief exposure (15 minutes) to feminist principles resulted in increased self-identification as a feminist and in improved appearance satisfaction. Furthermore, changes in feminist identity were positively related to changes in body image (Peterson, Tantleff-Dunn, & Bedwell, 2006).

These successes, limited though they are, underscore the potential value of a feminist approach to prevention. Larkin and Rice (2005) argue that we should 'mainstream body equity' into our prevention programmes and promote an acceptance of diverse body types. Similarly, Piran (1999) has argued that we should focus on the many disempowering experiences that women have, including sexual harassment and prejudice. Piran (e.g., Piran & Cormier, 2005) has further drawn attention to the various ways that women express their disengagement from their bodies ('disembodiment') through behaviours such as smoking for weight control, plastic surgery, self-harm behaviour (e.g., 'cutting'), risky sexual behaviours, and unhealthy weight management practices. In order to fully address such behaviours, we need to add a critique of the culture to our current prevention efforts.

Individuals who develop a critical perspective of the culture through feminism may be better able to cope with some potentially disempowering experiences. For example, Sabik and Tylka (2006) found that synthesis and active commitment aspects of feminist identification buffered the effects of perceived sexist events on eating disorders. Rubin, Nemeroff, and Russo (2004) spoke with self-identified feminist college women to try to understand their experiences with their bodies. The women reported that feminist attitudes helped them develop strategies to resist cultural messages about the body. Feminism did not entirely change their thoughts about their bodies, though. The authors stated that, 'Rejecting beauty ideals is a radical act, particularly for college-age women for whom appearance norms may be most salient...' (Rubin et al., 2004: 28). Similarly, Swami and Tovée (2006) found that self-reported feminism was not related to preferred body shape (for others) in a sample of predominantly college age lesbian and straight women. Finally, Tiggemann & Stevens (1999) examined the influence of self-esteem and feminist attitudes on body image across the lifespan. In women aged 30 to 49, though not in those under 30, feminist attitudes were negatively related to weight concerns.

Thus, we are left with a complex picture concerning the role of feminism as a protective factor for body image. Some prevention and correlational research suggest that feminism is protective. Indeed, there may be more data supporting feminism as a protective factor than for any other variable. Yet, there are several studies that fail to find this relationship, particularly when the sample consists of college-age women. More research is needed to document the circumstances under which feminist identification and cognitive schema serve to ameliorate the impact of sociocultural influences on body image.

Conclusion

Biologically-based explanations of attractiveness and body image conflate what is common with what is 'natural.' Closer examination suggests that these common trends are actually rooted in cultural prescriptions that are associated with specific gender roles. These gender roles result in gender differences in body image as well as in the adoption and use of techniques to achieve a particular body shape, including the development of eating disorders. While there have long been sociocultural theories to explain body image development and functioning, few of these have fully addressed the gender issues. In particular, they have often skirted the root cause of the gender difference: the status of men and women in society. This is the focus, and contribution, of feminist theory.

Feminist approaches, particularly objectification theory, have received some empirical attention. Correlational data support the relationship between a wide range of objectification experiences and body image problems as well as the protective nature of feminist ideology. Perhaps more importantly, there are now limited experimental and prospective data supporting objectification theory. Furthermore, some prevention programmes based on feminist theory have positively affected body satisfaction; these too may be viewed as experimental evidence of the efficacy of feminist explanations.

Taken together, these data are beginning to build a strong, consistent argument for feminist explanations of body image development and functioning. Feminism provides a more parsimonious explanation of gender differences in body image than does either evolutionary psychology or genetics. It also provides a theoretical basis for successful prevention programmes. While much work remains to be done, feminist theory clearly holds promise as both an etiological and clinical framework in understanding body image.

References

American Psychiatric Association (2000). *Diagnostic and statistical manual of mental disorders* (4th ed., Text Revision). Washington DC: American Psychiatric Association.

American Society of Plastic Surgeons (2006). *2005 gender quick facts: Cosmetic plastic surgery*. Online publication at www.plasticsurgery.org. Retrieved September 1, 2006.

Anderson-Fye, E. P. (2004). A 'Coca-Cola' shape: Cultural change, body image, and eating disorders in San Andres, Belize. *Culture, Medicine, and Psychiatry, 28*, 561–594.

Aubrey, J. S. (2006). Effects of sexually objectifying media on self-objectification and body surveillance in undergraduates: Results of a 2-year panel study. *Journal of Communication, 56*, 366–386.

Becker, A. E. (2004). Television, disordered eating, and young women in Fiji: Negotiating body image and identity during rapid social change. *Culture, Medicine and Psychiatry, 28,* 533–559.

Becker, A. E., & Fay, K. (2006). Sociocultural issues and eating disorders. In S. Wonderlich, J. Mitchell, M. de Zwaan, & H. Steiger (Eds.), *Annual review of eating disorders, Part 2 – 2006* (pp. 35–63). Oxford: Radcliffe Publishing.

Bordo, S. (1993). *Unbearable weight: Feminism, Western culture, and the body.* Berkeley, CA: University of California Press.

Bryant-Waugh, R. (2006). Eating disorders in children and adolescents. In S. Wonderlich, J. Mitchell, M. de Zwaan, & H. Steiger (Eds.), *Annual Review of Eating Disorders, Part 2 – 2006* (pp. 131–144). Oxford: Radcliffe Publishing.

Bulik, C., & Tozzi, F. (2004). Genetics in eating disorders: State of the science. *CNS Spectrums, 9,* 511–515.

Buss, D. (1994). *The evolution of desire.* New York: Basic Books.

Buss, D. M., Abbott, M., Angleitner, A., Asherian, A., Biaggio, A., Blanco-Villa Senor, A., et al. (1990). International preferences in selecting mates: A study of 37cultures. *Journal of Cross-Cultural Psychology, 21,* 5–47.

Cafri, G., Thompson, J. K., Ricciardelli, L., McCabe, M., Smolak, L., & Yesalis, C. (2005). Pursuit of the muscular ideal: Physical and psychological consequences and putative risk factors. *Clinical Psychology Review, 25,* 215–239.

Calogero, R. M. (2004). A test of Objectification Theory: The effect of the male gaze on appearance concerns in college women. *Psychology of Women Quarterly, 28,* 16–21.

Calogero, R. M., Davis, W. N., & Thompson, J. K. (2005). The role of self-objectification in the experience of women with eating disorders. *Sex Roles, 52,* 43–50.

Cash, T., & Pruzinsky, T. (2002). *Body image: A handbook of theory, research and clinical practice.* New York: Guilford.

Daubenmeier, J. J. (2005). The relationship of yoga, body awareness, and body responsiveness to self-objectification and disordered eating. *Psychology of Women Quarterly, 29,* 207–219.

Eagly, A. H. (1987). *Sex differences in social behavior: A social-role interpretation.* Hillsdale, NJ: Lawrence Erlbaum Associates.

Eagly, A. H., & Wood, W. (1999). The origins of sex differences in human behavior: Evolved dispositions versus social roles. *American Psychologist, 54,* 408–423.

Eagly, A. H., Wood, W., & Diekman, A. B. (2000). Social role theory of sex differences and similarities: A current appraisal. In T. Eckes, & H. M. Taunger (Eds.), *The developmental social psychology of gender* (pp. 123–174). Mahwah, NJ: Erlbaum.

Eagly, A. H., Wood, W., Johannesen-Schmidt, M. C. (2004). Social Role Theory of sex differences and similarities: Implications for the partner preferences of women and men. In A. H. Eagly, A. E. Beall, & R. J. Sternberg (Eds.), *The psychology of gender* (2nd ed., pp. 269–295). New York, NY: Guilford Press.

Faravelli, C., Giugni, A., Salvatori, S., & Ricca, V. (2004). Psychopathology after rape. *American Journal of Psychiatry, 161,* 1483–1485.

Field, A., Austin, S. B., Camargo, C., Taylor C. B., Striegel-Moore, R., Loud, K., et al. (2005). Exposure to the mass media, body shape concerns, and use of supplements to improve weight and shape among male and female adolescents. *Pediatrics, 116,* 214–220.

Fredrickson, B. L., & Roberts, T. A. (1997). Objectification Theory: Toward understanding women's lived experiences and mental health risks. *Psychology of Women Quarterly, 21,* 173–206.

Fredrickson, B. L., Roberts, T. A., Noll, S. M., Quinn, D. M., & Twenge, J. M. (1998). That swimsuit becomes you: Sex differences in self-objectification, restrained eating, and math performance. *Journal of Personality and Social Psychology, 75,* 269–284.

Gapinski, K. D., Brownell, K. D., & LaFrance, M. (2003). Body objectification and 'fat talk': Effects on emotion, motivation, and cognitive performance. *Sex Roles, 48,* 377–387.

Gottlieb, G. (1995). Some conceptual deficiencies in 'developmental' behavioral genetics. *Human Development, 38,* 131–141.

Grabe, S., & Hyde, J. S. (2006). Ethnicity and body dissatisfaction among women in the United States: A meta-analysis. *Psychological Bulletin, 132,* 622–640.

Greenberg, M., & Morris, N. (1974). Engrossment: The newborn's impact upon the father. *American Journal of Orthopsychiatry, 44,* 520–531.

Greenleaf, C. (2005). Self-objectification among physically active women. *Sex Roles, 52,* 51–62.

Groesz, L. M., Levine, M. P., & Murnen, S. K. (2002). The effect of experimental presentation of thin media images on body satisfaction: A meta-analytic review. *International Journal of Eating Disorders, 31,* 1–16.

Grogan, S. (1999). *Body image: Understanding body dissatisfaction, in men, women and children.* London: Routledge.

Grogan, S., & Richards, H. (2002). Body image: Focus groups with boys and men. *Men and Masculinities, 4,* 219–232.

Harned, M. (2000). Harassed bodies: An examination of the relationships among women's experiences of sexual harassment, body image, and eating disturbances. *Psychology of Women Quarterly, 24,* 336–348.

Hart, C., Newell, L., & Olsen, S. (2003). Parenting skills and social-communicative competence in childhood. In J. Greene, & B. Burleson (Eds.), *Handbook of communication and social interaction skills* (pp. 753–797). Mahwah, NJ: Lawrence Erlbaum Associates.

Hebl, M., King, E., & Lin, J. (2004). The swimsuit becomes us all: Ethnicity, gender, and vulnerability to self-objectification. *Personality and Social Psychology Bulletin, 30,* 1322–1331.

Hrdy, S. B. (1999). *Mother Nature: Maternal instincts and how they shape the human species.* New York: Ballantine.

Hudson, J., Hiripi, E., Pope, H., & Kessler, R. (2007). The prevalence and corelates of eating disorders in the National Comorbidity Survey replication. *Biological Psychology, 61,* 348–358.

Katzman, M., Hermans, K., Van Hoeken, D., & Hoek, H. (2004). Not your typical island woman: Anorexia nervosa is reported only in subcultures in Curacao. *Culture, Medicine and Psychiatry, 28,* 463–492.

Kaye, W., Frank, G., Bailer, U., & Henry, S. (2005). Neurobiology of anorexia nervosa: Clinical implications of alterations of the function of serotonin and other neuronal systems. *International Journal of Eating Disorders, 37,* S15–S19.

Keery, H., van den Berg, P., & Thompson, J. K. (2004). An evaluation of the Tripartite Influence Model of body dissatisfaction and eating disturbance with adolescent girls. *Body Image, 1,* 237–251.

Keski-Rahkonen, A., Bulik, C., Neale, B., Rose, R., Rissanen, A., & Kaprio, J. (2005). Body dissatisfaction and drive for thinness in young adult twins. *International Journal of Eating Disorders, 37*, 188–199.

Klump, K., McGue, M., & Iacono, W. (2000). Age differences in genetic and environmental influences on eating attitudes and behaviors in preadolescent and adolescent female twins. *Journal of Abnormal Psychology, 109*, 239–251.

Kraemer, H., Kazdin, A., Offord, D., Kessler, R., Jensen, P., & Kupler, D. (1997). Coming to terms with the terms of risk. *Archives of General Psychiatry, 54*, 337–343.

Langlois, J., Kalakanis, L., Rubenstein, A., Larsen, A., Hallam, M., & Smoot, M. (2000). Maxims or myths of beauty? A meta-analysis and theoretical review. *Psychological Bulletin, 126*, 390–423.

Larkin, J., & Rice, C. (2005). Beyond 'health eating' and 'healthy weights': Harassment and the health curriculum in middle schools. *Body Image, 2*, 219–232.

Leit, R. A., Pope, H. G., Gray, J. J. (2001). Cultural expectations of muscularity in men: The evolution of Playgirl centerfolds. *International Journal of Eating Disorders, 29*, 90–93.

Levine, M. P., & Smolak, L. (2006). *The prevention of eating problems and eating disorders: Theory, research and practice.* Mahwah NJ: Lawrence Erlbaum Associates.

Levine, M. P., Murnen, S. K., Smith, J., & Groesz, L. M. (2006). *Meta-analytic examination of studies of the correlation between negative body image, disordered eating, and extent of exposure to mass media.* Barcelona, Spain: Paper presented at the annual meeting of the International Academy of Eating Disorders.

Lin, C. A. (1998). Use of sex appeals in prime-time television commercials. *Sex Roles, 38*, 461–475.

Luo, Y., Parish, W., & Laumann, E. (2005). A population-based study of body image concerns among urban Chinese adults. *Body Image, 2*, 333–345.

Mahalik, J. R., Mooray, E. B., Coonerty-Femiano, A., Ludlow, L. H., Slattery, S. M., & Smiler, A. (2005). Development of the conformity to feminine norms inventory. *Sex Roles, 52*, 417–435.

Matschiner, M., & Murnen, S. K. (1999). Hyperfemininity and influence. *Psychology of Women Quarterly, 23*, 631–642.

Mazur, A. (1986). U.S. trends in feminine beauty and overadaptation. *Journal of Sex Research, 22*, 281–303.

Mazzeo, S., Landt, M., van Furth, E., & Bulik, C. (2006). Genetics of eating disorders. In S. Wonderlich, J. Mitchell, M. de Zwaan, & H. Steiger (Eds.), *Annual review of eating disorders, Part 2 – 2006* (pp. 17–33). Oxford: Radcliffe Publishing.

McCreary, D. R., & Sasse, D. K. (2000). An exploration of the drive for muscularity in adolescent boys and girls. *Journal of American College Health, 48*, 297–304.

McCreary, D. R., Saucier, D., & Courtenay, W. (2005). The Drive for muscularity and masculinity: Testing the associations among gender-role traits, behaviors, attitudes, and conflicts. *Psychology of Men and Masculinity, 6*, 83–94.

McHugh, M., Koeske, R., & Frieze, I. (1986). Issues to consider in conducting nonsexist psychological research: A guide for researchers. *American Psychologist, 41*.

McKinley, N. M. (1998). Gender differences in undergraduates' body esteem: The mediating effect of objectified body consciousness and actual/ideal weight discrepancy. *Sex Roles, 39*, 113–123.

McKinley, N. M. (1999). Women and objectified body consciousness: Mothers' and daughters' body experience in cultural, developmental, and familial context. *Developmental Psychology, 35,* 760–769.

McKinley, N. M. (2006). The developmental and cultural contexts of objectified body consciousness: A longitudinal analysis of two cohorts of women. *Developmental Psychology, 42,* 679–687.

McKinley, N. M., & Hyde, J. S. (1996). The objectified body consciousness scale: Self-objectification, body shame, and disordered eating. *Psychology of Women Quarterly, 22,* 623–636.

McVey, G., Lieberman, M., Voorberg, N., Wardrope, D., & Blackmore, E. (2003). School-based peer support groups: A new approach to the prevention of eating disorders. *Eating Disorders: The Journal of Treatment and Prevention, 11,* 169–185.

McVey, G., Lieberman, M., Voorberg, N., Wardrope, D., Blackmore, E., & Tweed, S. (2003). Replication of a peer support prevention program designed to reduce disorder eating: Is a life skills approach sufficient for all middle school students? *Eating Disorders: The Journal of Treatment and Prevention, 11,* 187–195.

Miner-Rubino, K., Twenge, J. M., & Fredrickson, B. L. (2002). Trait self-objectification in women: Affective and personality correlates. *Journal of Research in Personality, 36,* 147–172.

Muehlenkamp, J. J., & Saris-Baglama, R. N. (2002). Self-objectification and its psychological outcomes for college women. *Psychology of Women Quarterly, 26,* 371–379.

Murnen, S. K., & Smolak, L. (2000). The experience of sexual harassment among grade-school students: Early socialization of female subordination? *Sex Roles, 43,* 1–17.

Noll, S. M., & Frederickson, B. L. (1998). A mediational model linking self-objectification, body shame, and disordered eating. *Psychology of Women Quarterly, 22,* 623–636.

Peterson, R., Tantleff-Dunn, S., & Bedwell, J. (2006). The effects of exposure to feminist ideology on women's body image. *Body Image, 3.*

Piran, N. (1999). Eating disorders: A trial of prevention in a high risk school setting. *Journal of Primary Prevention, 20,* 75–90.

Piran, N., & Cormier, H. C. (2005). The social construction of women and disordered eating patterns. *Journal of Counseling Psychology, 52,* 549–558.

Pope, H., Olivardia, R., Gruber, A., & Borowiecki, J. (1999). Evolving ideas of male body image as seen through action toys. *International Journal of Eating Disorders, 26,* 65–72.

Reichborn-Kjennerud, T., Bulik, C., Kendler, K., Roysamb, E., Tambs, K., Torgersen, S., et al. (2004). Undue influence of weight on self-evaluation: A population-based twin study of gender differences. *International Journal of Eating Disorders, 35,* 123–132.

Ricciardelli, L. A., & McCabe, M. P. (2004). A biopsychosocial model of disordered eating and the pursuit of muscularity in adolescent boys. *Psychological Bulletin, 130,* 179–205.

Roberts, T. A., & Gettmann, J. Y. (2004). Mere exposure: Gender differences in the negative effects of priming a state of self-objectification. *Sex Roles, 51,* 17–27.

Rothblum, E. (2002). Gay and lesbian body images. In T. Cash, & T. Pruzinsky (Eds.), *Body image: A handbook of theory, research, and clinical practice* (pp. 257–268). New York: Guilford.

Rubin, L. R., Nemeroff, C. J., Russo, N. F. (2004). Exploring feminist women's body consciousness. *Psychology of Women Quarterly, 28*, 27–37.

Rudman, W. J., & Verdi, P. (1993). Exploitation: Comparing sexual and violent imagery of females and males in advertising. *Women and Health, 20*, 1–14.

Sabik, N. J., & Tylka, T. L. (2006). Do feminist identity styles moderate the relation between perceived sexist events and disordered eating? *Psychology of Women Quarterly, 30*, 77–84.

Shields, S. (1975). Functionalism, Darwinism, and the psychology of women: A study in social myth. *American Psychologist, 30*.

Silverstein, B., Perdue, L., Peterson, B., & Kelly, E. (1986). The role of the mass media in promoting a thin standard of bodily attractiveness for women. *Sex Roles, 14*, 519–532.

Singh, D. (1993). Adaptive significance of female physical attractiveness: Role of waist-to-hip ratio. *Journal of Personality and Social Psychology, 65*, 293–307.

Singh, D. (1994). Ideal female body shape: Role of body weight and wait-to-hip ratio. *International Journal of Eating Disorders, 16*, 283–288.

Slater, A., & Tiggemann, M. (2002). A test of Objectification Theory in adolescent girls. *Sex Roles, 46*, 343–349.

Smolak, L., & Levine, M. P. (in press). Trauma and eating problems and disorders. In S. Wonderlich, J. Mitchell, M. de Zwaan, & H. Steiger (Eds.), *Annual review of eating disorders, Part 3 – 2007*. Oxford, UK: Radcliffe Publishing.

Smolak, L., & Levine, M. P. (2001). Body image in children. In J. K. Thompson, & L. Smolak (Eds.), *Body image, eating disorders, and obesity in youth: Theory, assessment, and practice* (pp. 41–66). Washington DC: American Psychological Association.

Smolak, L., & Murnen, S. K. (2002). A meta-analytic examination of the relationship between child sexual abuse and eating disorders. *International Journal of Eating Disorders, 31*, 136–150.

Smolak, L., & Murnen, S. K. (2004). A feminist approach to eating disorders. In J. K. Thompson (Ed.), *Handbook of eating disorders and obesity* (pp. 590–605). New York: Wiley.

Smolak, L., & Stein, J. A. (2006). The relationship of drive for muscularity to sociocultural factors, self-esteem, physical attributes gender role, and social comparison in middle school boys. *Body Image, 3*, 121–129.

Smolak, L., Murnen, S. K., & Thompson, J. K. (2005). Sociocultural influences and muscle building in adolescent boys. *Psychology of Men and Masculinity, 6*, 227–239.

Sommers-Flanagan, R., Sommers-Flanagan, J., & Davis, B. (1993). What's happening on music television? A gender role content analysis. *Sex Roles, 28*, 745–753.

Steiner-Adair, C., Sjostrom, L., Franko, D., Pai., S., Tucker, R., Becker, A., et al. (2002). Primary prevention of eating disorders in adolescent girls: Learning from pratice. *International Journal of Eating Disorders, 32*, 401–411.

Stice, E. (2002). Risk and maintenance factors for eating pathology: A meta-analytic review. *Psychological Bulletin, 128*, 825–848.

Swami, V., & Tovée, M. (2005a). Female physical attractiveness in Britain and Malaysia: A cross-cultural study. *Body Image, 2*, 115–128.

Swami, V., & Tovée, M. (2005b). Male physical attactiveness in Britain and Malaysia: A cross-cultural study. *Body Image, 2*, 383–393.

Swami, V., & Tovée, M. (2006). The influence of body weight on the physical attractiveness preferences of feminist and non-feminist heterosexual women and lesbians. *Psychology of Women Quarterly, 30,* 252–257.

Swim, J. K., Hyers, L. L., Cohen, L. L., & Ferguson, M. J. (2001). Everyday sexism: Evidence for its incidence, nature, and psychological impact from three daily diary studies. *Journal of Social Issues, 57,* 31–53.

Thompson, J. K., Heinberg, L., Altabe, M., & Tantleff-Dunn, S. (1999). *Exacting beauty: Theory, assessment, and treatment of body image disturbance.* Washington, DC: American Psychological Association.

Tiggemann, M. (2003). Media exposure, body dissatisfaction and disordered eating: Television and magazines are not the same! *European Eating Disorders Review, 11,* 418–430.

Tiggemann, M., & Kuring, J. K. (2004). The role of body objectification in disordered eating and depressed mood. *British Journal of Clinical Psychology, 43,* 299–311.

Tiggemann, M., & Lynch, J. E. (2001). Body image across the life span in adult women: The role of self-objectification. *Developmental psychology, 37,* 243–253.

Tiggemann, M., & Slater, A. (2001). A test of Objectification Theory in former dancers and non-dancers. *Psychology of Women Quarterly, 25,* 57–64.

Tiggemann, M., & Stevens, A. (1999). Weight concern across the life-span: Relationship to self-esteem and feminist identity. *International Journal of Eating Disorders, 26,* 103–106.

Turkheimer, E. (2000). Three laws of behavior genetics and what they mean. *Current Directions in Psychological Science, 9,* 160–164.

Tylka, T. L., & Hill, M. S. (2004). Objectification Theory as it relates to disordered eating among college women. *Sex Roles, 51,* 719–730.

Wade, T., Martin, N., & Tiggemann, M. (1998). Genetic and environmental risk for the weight and shape concerns characteristic of bulimia nervosa. *Psychological Medicine, 28,* 761–771.

Ward, L. M. (1995). Talking about sex: Common themes about sexuality in the prime-time television programs children and adolescents view most. *Journal of Youth and Adolescence, 24,* 595–615.

Ward, L. M. (2003). Understanding the role of entertainment media in the sexual socialization of American youth: A review of empirical research. *Developmental Review, 23,* 347–388.

Weiner, K. E., & Thompson, J. K. (1997). Overt and covert sexual abuse: Relationship to body image and eating disturbance. *International Journal of Eating Disorders, 22,* 273–284.

Wertheim, E., Paxton, S., & Blaney, S. (in press). Body image in girls. In L. Smolak & J. K. Thompson (Eds.), *Body image, eating disorders, and obesity in youth* (2nd ed.). Washington DC: American Psychological Association.

13
The Impact of Western Beauty Ideals on the Lives of Women: A Sociocultural Perspective

Rachel M. Calogero, Michael Boroughs, and J. Kevin Thompson

I'm tired of all this nonsense about beauty being only skin-deep. That's deep enough. What do you want – an adorable pancreas?
~ Jean Kerr

It is amazing how complete is the delusion that beauty is goodness.
~ Leo Tolstoy

I wanted to get rid of my stomach, but [I have] no money... [I] asked my doctor, 'Don't you have a pill to give me bulimia?'
~ Dillaway (2005: 13)

According to a recent survey of 3,300 girls and women across 10 countries, 90 per cent of all women aged 15 to 64 worldwide want to change at least one aspect of their physical appearance, with body weight ranking the highest (Etcoff, Orbach, Scott, & D'Agostino, 2004). This finding suggests that women's anxiety about their appearance is a global phenomenon, observed in every country studied from Saudi Arabia to the United States. Beyond body dissatisfaction, a stunning 67 per cent of all women aged 15 to 64 worldwide reported that they actually withdraw from life-engaging, life-sustaining activities due to feeling badly about their looks. These activities include giving an opinion, meeting friends, exercising, going to work, going to school, dating, and going to the doctor.

Body dissatisfaction is considered 'normative' in the experience of girls and women in Western cultures (Rodin, Silberstein, & Striegel-Moore, 1984; Smolak, 2006). Children as young as 6 to 9 years old express body dissatisfaction and concerns about their weight (Flannery-Schroeder & Chrisler, 1996; Schur, Sanders, & Steiner, 2000; Smolak & Levine, 1994).

Drawing on a sociocultural theoretical model, considerable research has demonstrated the powerful influence of societal factors on these disturbances in girls' and women's lives (Hesse-Biber, Leavy, Quinn, & Zoino, 2006; Levine & Smolak, 1996; Thompson, 1992; Thompson, Heinberg, Altabe, & Tantleff-Dunn, 1999). In particular, ample empirical research is available documenting associations between idealised images of female beauty and negative effects on women's physical, psychological, and social well-being (Thompson et al., 1999).

A variety of perspectives have been offered to explain the nature of female beauty ideals. For example, female beauty ideals may provide information about fertility (Buss, 1989), reflect the distribution of economic and political power in society (Hesse-Biber, 1996), and/or negotiate gender role identity (Nagel & Jones, 1992). Consistent with a sociocultural approach, the common element among these various perspectives is the idea that beauty ideals contain information about more than mere external appearance. However, where individual perspectives may be limited in their capacity to explain the unrealistic nature of beauty ideals and their negative consequences for individuals, groups, and societies, applying a sociocultural framework offers a more comprehensive account for the systematic and significant reductions in the physical, mental, and social well-being of girls and women (Heinberg, 1996; Thompson et al., 1999).

In the following sections, we review the variation in beauty ideals over time and the consequences of these ideals on the lives of women and men within a sociocultural framework. Although the focus will be primarily on ideals for body weight and shape in Western culture, examples of beauty ideals that go beyond weight and shape and represent other cultures will be included where appropriate. Particular attention is given to the effects of the promotion and pursuit of these cultural beauty ideals on the lives of women, and increasingly men, across the world. We begin with an in-depth analysis of women because the great majority of research over the years has involved an examination of women.

A history of beauty ideals

> The ideal beauty is a fugitive which is never found.
> ~ Joan Rivers

External appearance is extremely important in Western cultures (Bartky, 2003; Bordo, 1993). The external body has been described as a 'text of culture: it is a symbolic form upon which the norms and practices of a society are inscribed' (Lee, 2003: 82). Broadly defined, beauty ideals represent culturally prescribed and endorsed 'looks' that incorporate various features of the human face and body, and thus define the standards for physical attractiveness within a culture. According to Zones (2000: 87), at any given time and place, there are fairly 'uniform and widely understood models of how particular groups of individuals "should" look.'

A review of the history of beauty ideals provides the clearest demonstration of the importance of beauty and appearance in the lives of women. Surviving texts, artifacts, and images from ancient Egypt showcase the immense amount of time and effort women invested toward the perfection of their bodies (Watterson, 1991). The following review provides considerable evidence that this crusade for thinness, beauty, and youth among ancient Egyptian women continues 5000 years later among modern Western women.

Between 1400 and 1700, the ideal for female beauty was fat and full. This is best exemplified in the popular art of this era. For example, in Botticelli's *The Birth of Venus*, the goddess of beauty was endomorphic in shape, with a round face and pear-shaped body (see Swami, 2007). In the 19th century, we see a shift toward restricting women's fullness. In fact, this period seems to represent the early stages of the mass 'standardising' of female beauty in Western culture, and the promotion of unrealistic, unnatural body ideals. Corsets, the restrictive garment of choice, actually originated much earlier and were compulsory for aristocratic women around the 16th century; however, by the 19th century they had become a hallmark of fashion for women of nearly all classes. Corseted waistlines gave the illusion of voluptuousness by propping up, pushing out, and holding in the fuller features of women's bodies, whittling some women down to a 15 inch waist (Kunzle, 2004). This idealised hourglass figure was not possible without special garments, and thus required women to 'work' at making their bodies conform to unnatural measurements.

The sheer extremity of corseting must be underscored. *The Lancet*, a preeminent British medical journal, published more than an article a year on the medical dangers of corseting from the late 1860s to the early 1890s. Late 19th century women's corseting practices included sleeping and bathing in corsets (using steel bolts to flatten the waist at the sides) to permanently reduce and maintain smaller waists (between 14 and 20 inches if possible) (Kunzle, 2004). Corseting is not an arcane beauty practice relegated to particular historical contexts, however. Even within the last decade, there are notable examples of women adhering to these beauty practices. Born in 1937, Cathie Jung has worn a corset for virtually every hour of the day and night since 1983. The only time that she is not wearing a corset is for the hour it takes her to shower and dry herself thoroughly. Her waist was 26 inches when she began serious 'waist training,' 23 hours a day, every day of the week. Today, at a height of 5 feet, 6 inches, and a weight of 135 pounds, Cathie's uncorseted waist is 21 inches around, and she wears a 15-inch corset (*Guinness World Records*, 2006).

During the mid-19th century there was an additional conflict in the portrayal of ideal female beauty. Banner (1983) identified two, distinct (but both corseted) beauty ideals. On the one hand, there was the image of the 'steel engraving lady,' so named for the illustrative process used to create her by Currier and Ives. This image embodied frailty by accentuating a slight shape, sloped shoulders, small waist, tapered fingers, and tiny, delicate feet. In short, she was anything but 'steel,' and instead depicted a vision of ill-health and weakness. This delicate image was associated not only with beauty, but with high social status and moral values. On the other hand, there was the image of the 'voluptuous woman,' which gained popularity toward the end of the century. This image embodied a full-figured, fleshy female that was consonant with European nude art during this period (Renoir bathers) and the body shapes of popular American theatre performers, such as Lillian Russell. In contrast to the unhealthy appearance described above, this image of beauty depicted a vision of good health, with broadened bottoms and large-boned figures.

At the end of the 19th century and into the early 20th century, these conflicting images seemed to morph into a new ideal, which is best known as the 'Gibson Girl.' Appearing about 1890, this new beauty ideal contained features from the 'steel engraving lady' and the 'voluptuous woman,' and added a few of her own. The Gibson Girl was slender in the waist and legs, but still curvy with wide hips and large breasts. Corseting and padding were still used to obtain this image, and in particular to form the breast into a 'monobosom' (Mazur, 1986). This ideal embodied athletic features as well, as depicted by the rounded calves, erect posture, and sports attire.

At the end of World War I, waistlines were loosened and skirts were shortened. The 1920s saw the exchange of padding and corsets for different undergarments that bound the breasts to create a flat-chested, boy-like appearance (Caldwell, 1981). Referred to as the 'flapper' era, the beauty ideal of this period had shifted to an almost exclusive focus on a cosmetically decorated face and slender legs. Miss America pageants emerged in 1921. Mary Campbell, who was Miss America in 1922–1923, was 5 feet, 7 inches, and weighed 140 pounds, which was thin for this era. Without the adulation of curves, and with the unveiling of the legs, women of this era embarked on a quest to reduce any signs of secondary sex characteristics. According to Silverstein, Peterson, and Perdue (1986), this required the use of rolling machines, iodine, starvation diets, and strenuous exercise to lose weight. Interestingly, in 1926, the New York Academy of Science convened to study the 'outbreak' of eating disorders (Fallon, 1990).

The proliferation of mass media in the 1920s, and throughout the 20th century, ensured the perpetuation of standardised beauty ideals, and the homogenisation of Western culture. Motion pictures, magazines, and singular Hollywood stars informed women and men about what was beautiful. The period of the Great Depression saw a return to longer hemlines and narrow waist, and a resurging emphasis on secondary sex characteristics. While a slender figure was still ideal, a flat stomach was emphasised as well as long legs. Moving into the 1940s, legs were the focal point of ideal beauty, as depicted in the popular World War II pinup of Betty Grable and her 'million dollar legs' and rear end. Legs were enhanced and emphasised with hemmed stockings, garters, and high-heeled shoes. In addition, bust size was growing in the 1940s, and eventually breasts would assert themselves as the dominant feature of the female beauty ideal.

This trend toward larger busts and an hourglass figure can be observed throughout the 1940s, '50s, and '60s in the Hollywood and fashion industry. During this period, waist size declined so that the body exhibited conspicuous curves, with measurements of 36-23-36. *Playboy* magazine glorified full-breasted women (Garner, Garfinkel, Schwartz, & Thompson, 1980), with Hollywood stars such as Marilyn Monroe and Jane Mansfield exemplifying the proper bust-to-waist-to-hip-ratios. Since 1950, almost all Miss America winners have had bust-hip symmetry. The beauty ideal of the 1950s and '60s seemed to exemplify the same slender but voluptuous figure of the 19th century. During this period, researchers reported that women desired smaller ideal body sizes and larger ideal breast sizes compared to their actual self-rated body and breast sizes (Jourard & Secord, 1955). Notably, DuPont introduced Lycra in 1960, which made the use of whalebone or metal frames used in corsets obsolete, but not the corset itself. In effect, the corset became the girdle.

Then came Twiggy. Debuting in the United States in 1966, the 17-year old model was spread across the pages of *Seventeen* and *Vogue*, with skeletal measurements of 31-22-32. She was described by Newsweek as 'four straight limbs in search of a woman's body' (Fallon, 1990). Twiggy's flat-chested, hipless, anorexic image peaked in popularity in 1976, but never completely dominated the female beauty ideal. However, the trend toward increasingly slender bodies had taken hold. Although the movement toward a thinner ideal body shape was obvious merely by scanning fashion magazines, researchers quantified and confirmed this change in shape. Garner et al. (1980) revealed similar trends in the body measurements of *Playboy* centrefold models and Miss America pageant contestants. Specifically, between 1959 and 1978, average weights (based on age and height), bust measurements, and hip size decreased, whereas height and waist size increased. Other research has confirmed this slenderisation trend. The body shapes of English fashion models showed similar decreases in bust and hip measurements with corresponding increases in waist size and height between 1967 and 1987 (Morris, Cooper, & Cooper, 1989). This particular combination of measurements was described as creating a 'tubular' body shape. By comparison, the body measurements of average women during this time period were significantly higher than the body measurements of models and pageant winners.

In the 1970s, the focus shifted more explicitly from breasts to buttocks, and small buttocks were preferred over large breasts by both men and women (Fallon, 1990). In the 1980s, a more muscular image of female beauty had emerged, as depicted by celebrities such as Jane Fonda and Victoria Principal. Jane Fonda, feminine and attractive, became the prototype of the fit American woman with her fitness videos that first came out in 1982. Broad shoulders were in vogue, and shoulder pads were everywhere. However, the focus remained on a thin, slender body shape. Silverstein, Perdue, Peterson, and Kelly (1986) demonstrated significant decreases in the bust-to-waist ratios of models portrayed in *Ladies Home Journal* and *Vogue* magazines between the 1970s and 1990s. An update of Garner et al. (1980) showed that the trend in women's body size did not reverse itself between 1979 and 1988, but either stabilised at a below average weight as observed for *Playboy* centrefold models or continued to decrease as observed for Miss America contestants (Wiseman, Gray, Mosimann, & Ahrens, 1992). Wiseman et al. (1992) demonstrated that 69 per cent of *Playboy* centrefold models and 60 per cent of Miss American contestants were 15 per cent or more below their expected weight for their height, indicating that these 'ideals' of female beauty met one of the central criteria for anorexia nervosa based on the *Diagnostic and Statistical Manual for Mental Disorders – Fourth*

Edition (American Psychiatric Association, 1994). The high percentage of these ideal images displaying below normal weights corresponded with an increase in magazine articles focused on weight loss (diet-for-weight-loss, exercise, diet-exercise) in popular women's magazines during this period, with exercise articles surpassing the prevalence of diet articles after 1983 (Wiseman et al., 1992).

By the 1990s, the female beauty ideal was synonymous with the 'thin ideal' (Owen & Laurel-Seller, 2000). Spitzer, Henderson, and Zivian (1999) updated and extended the research by Garner et al. (1980) and Wiseman et al. (1992), demonstrating that the body sizes (based on measures of BMI) of Miss America pageant contestants continued to decrease throughout the 1990s, whereas *Playboy* centrefold models remained below average weight. Recently, Seifert (2005) confirmed this trend toward increased thinness in *Playboy* centrefold models over the last 50 years (1953–2003); however, based on analyses of anthropometric measurements, WHR did not vary over time, suggesting that the models did not become less curvaceous over this period. According to Sypeck et al. (2006), there were fewer *Playboy* centrefold models below normal weight between 1989 and 1999 (10–15 per cent) compared to between 1979 and 1988 (13–19 per cent). These researchers suggest that the downward trend in the weights of the models may have stabilised as indicated by Wiseman et al. (1992), and possibly begun to reverse itself. In addition, they did not confirm Seifert's findings regarding WHR, and rather supported the increased prevalence of a 'tubular' shape.

The *Psychology Today* surveys have documented an increasing shift toward a more muscular female body ideal over the last three decades (Garner, 1997). Women's dissatisfaction with their muscle tone has increased over time, rising from 30 per cent in 1972, to 45 per cent in 1985, and to 57 per cent in 1997. In the 1997 survey, 43 per cent of the entire sample, and 67 per cent of the women in the sample with pre-existing body dissatisfaction, reported that 'very thin or muscular models' made them feel insecure. Recent research indicates a discrepancy between women's actual and ideal level of muscularity, with women wishing to be more muscular than they actually are (Cafri & Thompson, 2004). When making social comparisons with specific celebrities, college women selected Brittany Spears most frequently, followed by Christina Aguilera and Angelina Jolie (Strahan, Wilson, Cressman, & Buote, 2006). Thus, while the current Western ideal for female beauty continues to glorify thinness, this ultra lean figure also includes a flat stomach, thin waist, boyish hips, long legs, well-developed breasts, well-defined muscles, and flawless skin (Groesz, Levine, & Murnen, 2002; Harrison, 2003).

Negative consequences of promoting and pursuing cultural beauty ideals

> No object is so beautiful that, under certain conditions, it will not look ugly.
>
> ~ Oscar Wilde

Exposure to beauty ideals

Virtually every form of media exposes individuals to information about thinness and ideal female beauty (Levine & Harrison, 2004), including magazines (Englis, Solomon, & Ashmore, 1994), television shows (Harrison & Cantor, 1997), television advertisements (Richins, 1991), music television (Tiggemann & Slater, 2003), popular films (Silverstein, Perdue, et al., 1986), children's fairy tales (Baker-Sperry & Grauerholz, 2003), and children's videos (Herbozo, Tantleff-Dunn, Gokee-Larose, & Thompson, 2004). A meta-analytic review of the immediate impact of experimental exposure to the thin beauty ideal revealed a significant association between exposure to media images of the thin ideal and negative body image in girls and women (Groesz et al., 2002). Other evidence indicates that exposure to non-media-based messages about the thin beauty ideal also produces adverse effects on women. For example, college women reported higher body dissatisfaction after exposure to 'fat talk' among peers (Stice, Maxfield, & Wells, 2003) and after *in vivo* exposure to an attractive peer who typified the thin beauty ideal (Krones, Stice, Batres, & Orjada, 2005). These associations between exposure to idealised images of women and increased body image disturbances have been well-established across research designs, including correlational (e.g., Harrison & Cantor, 1997), quasi-experimental (e.g., Turner, Hamilton, Jacobs, Angood, & Dwyer, 1997), experimental (e.g., Irving, 1990), longitudinal (Hargreaves & Tiggemann, 2003a), prospective (e.g., Stice & Whitenton, 2002), and meta-analytic studies (Stice, 2002).

In addition to body image variables, exposure to media images has also been linked to the disproportionate prevalence among women of disordered eating attitudes (e.g., McCarthy, 1990), dieting and bulimic pathology (e.g., Stice, 2002), and actual eating behaviours (e.g., Strauss, Doyle, & Kreipe, 1994; Harrison, Taylor, & Marske, 2006; but see Jansen & de Vries, 2002, for non-significant effects with subliminal primes).

For example, Harrison et al. (2006) exposed women and men to overt media images that were presented with congruent text or incongruent text. Results revealed significant reductions in the actual eating behaviour of women and men when images were presented alone or with congruent text, but not when presented with incongruent text, and only in the presence of high body-related self-discrepancies between how they see themselves and what they believe their peers expect of them. Thus, the accumulated evidence indicates that exposure to idealised images of female beauty is a causal risk factor for body image and eating disturbances among women in Western cultures (Cusumano & Thompson, 1997; Polivy & Herman, 2004; Thompson et al., 1999).

Even for individuals who do not purposely expose themselves to media sources of these beauty ideals, the negative impact of these sources still seems virtually unavoidable. For example, exposure to ideal-body television images was associated with preferences for thinness and approval of plastic surgery even for individuals who expressed no interest in viewing television shows with topics such as dieting, nutrition, fitness, and exercise (Harrison, 2003). In other research, high school boys who reported a mid-range level of appearance schematicity (extent of investment in appearance as basis for self-evaluation) rated attractiveness as significantly more important in a potential girlfriend after viewing appearance-based versus non-appearance-based commercials (Hargreaves & Tiggemann, 2003b).

Thus, direct and indirect exposure to cultural beauty ideals does have serious negative consequences for women, although as discussed next, not all women are equally affected.

Internalisation of thin ideal

Researchers have established that people associate beauty with goodness: 'What is beautiful is good' (Dion, Berscheid, & Walster, 1972; Seid, 1989). Attractive people are assumed to be better liked, more sociable, independent, exciting, less deviant, and less stigmatised (e.g., Eagly, Ashmore, Makhijani, & Longo, 1991). Dellinger and Williams (1997) found that American women who adhere to cultural standards of female attractiveness (e.g., wearing make-up to work) are more likely to be viewed as heterosexual, healthy, and competent. This research is consistent with Wolf's (1991: 14) writings, which assert that beauty ideals are 'always actually prescribing behaviour rather than appearance.' These associations between beauty and goodness and beauty and behaviour is well-illustrated in a recent advertisement for *Shape* magazine, which offers a free guide with each new magazine subscription focused on how to perfect the abdominal area entitled, *Absolution* (Shape, 2006).

People's chronic exposure to these idealised images reinforces the associations among thinness, beauty, and social rewards (Cash, 1990; Eagly et al., 1991; Evans, 2003). For example, women reported that they expected their lives would change in important and positive ways if they looked like the ideal portrayals of women in the media (Engeln-Maddox, 2006), such as being happier, better adjusted, more socially competent, romantically successful, and improving job opportunities.

Such an emphasis on idealised images and their associated rewards can lead to a personal acceptance or internalisation of cultural beauty ideals (Heinberg, Thompson, & Stormer, 1995; but see Engeln-Maddox, 2006, for slightly different interpretation). *Thin-ideal internalisation* refers to the extent to which individuals cognitively accept the thin societal standard of attractiveness as their own personal standard and engage in behaviours designed to help them meet that standard (Thompson et al., 1999). Women who have internalised cultural beauty ideals are more vulnerable to experiencing the negative outcomes associated with exposure to beauty ideals than women who have not internalised these ideals. For example, while all women exposed to appearance-based images (versus non-appearance based) reported higher levels of anger, anxiety, depression, and overall appearance dissatisfaction (Cattarin, Thompson, Thomas, & Williams, 2000), these effects were stronger for women who reported pre-existing thin-ideal internalisation, high body dissatisfaction, and interest in appearance-based television programmes. Dittmar and Howard (2004a) found that adult, professional women who reported higher levels of thin-ideal internalisation experienced more body anxiety following exposure to thin-ideal media than women with lower levels of internalisation. In addition, women working in secondary schools reported less body-focused anxiety when exposed to average-size models compared to no models, whereas women working in fashion advertising reported no such benefits (Dittmar & Howard, 2004b).

Recent studies have differentiated the use of media as an informational source for how to be attractive from the internalisation of media ideals, with the former demonstrating weaker, albeit significant, associations with measures of body dissatisfaction in non-clinical and eating disorders samples (Calogero, Davis, & Thompson, 2004; Thompson, van den Berg, Roehrig, Guarda, & Heinberg, 2004). Empirical evidence has linked thin-ideal internalisation to experiences of self-objectification, negative affect, negative body image, and disordered eating in young girls, college women, and women with eating disorders (e.g., Calogero,

Davis, & Thompson, 2005; Heinberg et al., 1995; Sands & Wardle, 2003; Stice, Schupak-Neuberg, Shaw, & Stein, 1994), and it is considered a causal risk factor for body image and eating disturbances (Stice, 2002; Thompson & Stice, 2001).

Recent longitudinal research suggests that thin-ideal internalisation may not stem directly or exclusively from media influences (e.g., television and magazine exposure). In a 1-year study of prepubescent girls, television viewing at Time 1 was associated with the desire for a thin body as an adult and disordered eating at Time 2, but did not predict a current desire for a thin body at Time 2 (Harrison & Hefner, 2006). These researchers note that the girls' current preferences for thin body shape were already quite thin, which suggests that a thin ideal had already been internalised. These findings are consistent with other research on body and eating-related disturbances in preadolescent samples. For example, parental feedback has been identified as an important source for conveying sociocultural ideals and attitudes about appearance to preadolescent girls (Levine & Smolak, 1996; McCabe & Ricciardelli, 2003). Smolak, Levine, and Schermer (1999) demonstrated that the body esteem scores of elementary school girls were related to both maternal dieting and parental complaints about their own weight. McKinley (1999) provided further evidence that mothers' experiences with their own bodies may influence daughters' experiences with their own bodies in a sample of 151 undergraduate women and their middle-aged mothers. Specifically, McKinley demonstrated significant, positive relationships between mothers' and daughters' body esteem and body surveillance. In addition, higher body shame in mothers was associated with lower body esteem in daughters, and daughters' perceptions that her family approved of her appearance significantly predicted her body esteem. Phares, Steinberg, and Thompson (2004) found that, compared to boys, girls exhibited greater body image concern, received more information regarding weight and dieting from their parents, and tried more actively to stay thin. Thus, it is clear that the thin ideal is not promoted exclusively by the media as the role of parents and peers appear to be powerful contributing factors to thin-ideal internalisation in preadolescent girls. However, family and peer groups live in the same cultural context, and therefore are not immune to the exposure, pressures, and internalisation of female beauty ideals. An important area of future research is to investigate thin-ideal internalisation within family and peer-based groups to improve knowledge about how beauty ideals are indirectly transmitted to young girls.

Broader societal patterns: Discrepancy and objectification

Two broader societal patterns can be gleaned from this historical evidence regarding the evolution, prevalence, and internalisation of beauty ideals: cultural beauty ideals perpetuate chronic discrepancies in women and the chronic objectification of women. These patterns are interrelated, and each of these patterns promotes and produces negative effects for women's lives, which will be delineated in the sections below.

Chronic discrepancy

Considerable evidence highlights the *discrepancy* that is concomitant with striving toward ideal beauty standards. The majority of women's bodies have always been, and will continue to be, discrepant from the contemporary ideals of female beauty. Between the 19th and 21st century, women have tried to have no waist but large hips, to be full-figured but thin, to have no breasts but lower body curves, and today, to have sizable breasts and muscle, but no body fat. Female beauty ideals have almost always promoted the attainment of physically incompatible body attributes. Indeed, the current beauty ideal may represent the ultimate in unrealistic and unnatural attributes for female beauty: ultra thinness and large breasts (Thompson & Tantleff, 1992). This 'curvaceously thin' ideal for women is virtually impossible to achieve without some form of surgical modification, which makes the current standards of female beauty particularly dangerous (Harrison, 2003).

The obvious biological reality is that breasts are composed of fat tissue (Sherwood, 1993), and therefore breast fat is positively correlated with total body fat (Katch et al., 1980). It is impossible to lose body fat (in attempt to meet the thin standard) and maintain breast size (in attempt to meet the bust size standard) because as fat disappears, so does breast tissue. In addition, some bodies are just not compatible with current ideals because of their particular somatotype, or body shape (Brownell, 1991). In short, the beauty ideals themselves contain obvious biological discrepancies for most female bodies, and thus culture and physiology are in perpetual conflict. As Harrison (2003) describes, to meet the current 'curvaceously thin' ideal, women are at risk for doing 'double damage' to their bodies as they try to reduce and reshape the lower half through disordered eating and exercise practices while trying to enlarge and reshape the upper half through surgical practices and drug use (e.g., herbal supplements). In fact, Harrison's research demonstrates that body image and eating disturbances are not the only potential adverse outcomes of exposure to contemporary standards for female beauty: both women and men were more likely to express approval for body-altering surgical procedures after exposure to ideal body television images. Considering these patterns of behaviour, it could be argued that the corset and the girdle have been replaced with diet, exercise, and plastic surgery. Considering this perpetual conflict between culture and physiology, Thompson et al. (1999) observed that, 'culture appears to be winning.'

As early as 6-years-old, children report discrepancies between how they actually look and how they wished they looked, and this discrepancy increases over time with children preferring smaller ideal body sizes as they get older, especially girls (Gardner, Sorter, & Friedman, 1997). When asked to rate different figures representing varying sizes of women's bodies, 72 per cent of 1,056 adolescent girls defined their ideal body as smaller than their actual body (Wertheim, Paxton, & Tilgner, 2004). The average American woman is 5 feet, 4 inches tall, and weighs 140 pounds whereas the average American model is 5 feet, 11 inches tall, and weighs 117 pounds (National Eating Disorders Association [NEDA], 2002). NEDA also reports that fashion models are thinner than 98 per cent of American women. If the infamous Barbie doll's measurements were extrapolated to that of an average woman, she would lack the necessary 17 to 22 per cent body fat for menstruation, and her measurements would be 39-21-33, which is dangerously unattainable (Turkel, 1998). The probability of a woman attaining Barbie's measurements is less than 1 in 100,000 (Norton, Olds, Olive, & Dank, 1996). Researchers have consistently acknowledged that only 5 to 10 per cent of women can actually acquire and easily maintain the desired fat-free body, which means 90 to 95 per cent of women cannot naturally acquire it.

Despite this reality, girls are socialised to believe that they can manipulate and change their bodies if they try hard enough (Becker & Hamburg, 1996). Repeated exposure to the sheer prevalence of these idealised images of women, and media's blurred boundaries between fictitious and real women, fosters the belief that these images are actually attainable and realistic (Freedman, 1984; Holstrom, 2004). Evidence exists documenting that health, beauty, and fashion products are strategically marketed to create an awareness of a 'gap' between the consumer and the ideal, and then to provide the solution in a product (see Becker, 2004). Evidence also exists documenting that media images of women are often computer-merged images of different models, and require a tremendous investment of time and finances from multiple professionals/trainers (e.g., agent, clothing, make-up, hair, and exercise/diet) to control and manipulate appearance, which is unrealistic for the average woman;

however, many women still consider these images to be appropriate comparisons for what they should look like (Heinberg, 1996; Wolf, 1991).

According to social comparison theory (Festinger, 1954), people tend to make downward social comparisons with relevant comparison targets to enhance their self-image. That is, people prefer to compare themselves to social others who may be worse off or rated more negatively on some variable in order to feel better about themselves. However, many women report that they make upward social comparisons with media-presented models as comparative targets when evaluating their physical appearance (e.g., Irving, 1990; Wertheim, Paxton, Schutz, & Muir, 1997). These patterns run counter to the literature on self-enhancement and social comparison theory.

A recent experimental investigation offers some explanation for this phenomenon (Strahan et al., 2006). First, compared to men, women demonstrated more spontaneous irrelevant, upward social comparisons and evaluated themselves more negatively, but only for appearance and not other domains, such as social skills. Second, when beauty ideals were made salient, both women and men evaluated their appearance more negatively and made upward social comparisons with irrelevant (professional models) versus relevant (peers) targets. The salience of the beauty ideals alone, and not necessarily their personal endorsement of them, was enough to influence participants' self-appraisal processes. These researchers suggest that women chronically engage in upward social comparisons with irrelevant targets such as fashion models and celebrities because the cultural norms for appearance imply that these standards are attainable, relevant, and appropriate by all women.

It is important to note that all participants in this study were exposed to only three advertisements reflecting gender-specific cultural beauty ideals. Being exposed to the same number of images related to cultural beauty standards seemed to equalise the effects of exposure to these ideals on men and women. However, we know that women are bombarded with messages about their appearance whereas the same messages are not as ubiquitous for men, and thus we can imagine the effects on women in the real world (Andersen & DiDomenico, 1992). On the basis of this cumulative evidence, then, it is not surprising that appearance-related comparisons occur regularly in the lives of women, and they are associated with sizable self-discrepancies that contribute to depression, anxiety, body dissatisfaction, body shame, and eating disordered behaviours (Markham, Thompson, & Bowling, 2005; Durkin & Paxton, 2002; Stormer & Thompson, 1996).

Chronic objectification

The prevalence of idealised images of women's bodies throughout history and across media provides the clearest evidence of the pervasive objectification of women. As defined by Bartky (1990: 26), 'a person is sexually objectified when her sexual parts or sexual functions are separated out from the rest of her personality and reduced to the status of mere instruments or else regarded as if they were capable of representing her.' Reducing women's bodies to the status of objects renders them available for visual inspection, measurement, evaluation, and manipulation. Examples of this pervasive sexual objectification include catcalls, 'checking out' or gazing at women's bodies, sexual comments about appearance, sexualised visual depictions across media, pornography, sexual harassment, and sexual violence (e.g., Fredrickson & Roberts, 1997; Lin, 1998; Rudman & Verdi, 1993; Swim, Hyers, Cohen, & Ferguson, 2001; Thompson et al., 1999). Murnen and Smolak (2000) demonstrated that a remarkable 75 per cent of elementary school girls (3rd through 5th grade) reported experiences of sexual harassment. In recent qualitative research, Eck (2003) illustrated the differential responses of women and men to viewing nude media images of women and men, confirming that familiar cultural scripts exist for viewing, evaluating, and commenting on women's bodies, but not for men's bodies. Among grade-school girls and boys between the ages of 6 and 12, girls are already demonstrating more consistent responses to objectified images of women that relate to how they feel about their bodies, whereas boys are not displaying these response patterns (Murnen, Smolak, Mills, & Good, 2003). In a recent study of 52,677 heterosexual adults aged 18 to 65 based on survey data collected by *Elle* magazine, women reported greater dissatisfaction with their appearance and were more likely to avoid situations where their bodies were on display, such as wearing a swimsuit in public, compared to men (Frederick, Peplau, & Lever, 2006). This study also found that while men felt better about their bodies than women across most of the weight span, among underweight individuals the women felt better than men, reflecting the difference in cultural standards for female and male beauty.

The societal emphasis on women's appearance and its association with women's achievement has contributed to women valuing how they look more than how they feel or what they can do. As early as the 1950s, adolescent girls were listing 'good looks' as a top aspiration when asked to write essays on the sort of person they would like to be when they grow up (Crane, 1956). Indeed, 'women are encouraged to...feel pleasure through their own bodily objectification, especially being looked at and identified as objects of male desire' (Lee, 2003: 88). Researchers have consistently observed stronger links among weight satisfaction, appearance, and general self-worth in girls compared to boys (e.g., Bowker, Gadbois, & Cornock, 2003; Tiggemann & Rothblum, 1997). More recently, Tiggemann (2005) demonstrated that adolescent women who were not overweight, but perceived themselves as overweight or felt dissatisfied with their current weight, reported lower self-esteem over a 2-year period.

Theories of objectification and objectified body consciousness have articulated the pervasive nature of women's objectification and delineated many of the negative psychological consequences it brings to women (Berger, 1972; Fredrickson & Roberts, 1997; McKinley & Hyde, 1996; Moradi, Dirks, & Matteson, 2005; Roberts & Gettman, 2004). Chronic exposure to objectified images of women and personal experiences of objectification encourage women to internalise the objectifying gaze of others, and to turn this gaze on themselves, referred to as self-objectification (Fredrickson & Roberts, 1997). Watching the self as an object requires a psychic distancing between the self and the body, which may explain how so many women are able to break and bruise skin, cut to shape themselves, rearrange or amputate body parts, and/or starve their bodies continuously in an effort to meet the current standards of beauty. Little empirical research is available that examines the influence of sexual and self-objectification on the type and degree of women's behavioural adherence to beauty ideals. The severity of these practices described above underscores the importance of investigating these relationships in future research.

Considerable evidence indicates that women who chronically self-objectify, or women who experience self-objectifying situations (i.e., where there bodies are on display), are vulnerable to a variety of negative consequences: These consequences include increased levels of body shame, physique anxiety, depression, disordered eating, and decreased levels of intrinsic motivation, self-efficacy, and cognitive performance in women across age, ethnic, and clinical groups (e.g., Calogero, 2004; Calogero et al., 2005; Fredrickson et al., 1998; Gapinski, Brownell, & LaFrance, 2003; Hebl, King, & Lin, 2004; McKinley & Hyde, 1996; Miner-Rubino, Twenge, & Fredrickson, 2002; Noll & Fredrickson, 1998; Slater & Tiggemann, 2002; Tiggemann & Kuring, 2004; Tiggemann & Lynch, 2001).

Particularly insidious are the effects of self-objectification on cognitive performance, indicating that the emphasis on how one looks affects more than body dissatisfaction, or even disordered eating; it affects how well women will perform and meet their potential across a multitude of personal, academic, and social contexts. For example, Fredrickson et al. (1998) demonstrated that women wearing a swimsuit reported more negative affect, performed worse on a math test, and ate less food compared to women wearing a sweater and men wearing either type of clothing, with these effects even more pronounced in women reporting high trait levels of self-objectification. A similar induced state of self-objectification disrupted the attentional focus of undergraduate women when performing a standard Stroop-colouring name task (Quinn, Kallen, Twenge, & Fredrickson, 2006). Researchers have also demonstrated that body-related thoughts persist after women are removed from self-objectifying situations, and the amount of shame experienced mediates the relationship between self-objectification and subsequent body-related thoughts (Quinn, Kallen, & Cathey, 2006). These findings suggest that rumination about the body continues to tap cognitive resources for some period of time even when women are removed from the self-objectifying situation. The real-world implications of this research are underscored by Puwar's (2004) interviews conducted with women members of the British parliament, which revealed that the legitimacy of these women in the legislature required suffering constant sexual remarks, being sexually objectified, and chronically monitoring their appearance to convey the right amount of femininity; thereby making it difficult to be effective in government. As Hesse-Biber (1996: 14) points out, 'Even a woman with a successful and lucrative career may fear that her success comes at the expense of her femininity.' If we imagine the multitude of seemingly innocuous environments in which girls and women may be exposed to objectifying experiences, the effects on women's achievement and potential are far-reaching.

Beyond weight and shape: The most beautiful bodies are unchanged

There are aspects to the female beauty ideal that have not been explicitly articulated, but are clearly associated with Westernised female beauty: contemporary standards of female beauty incorporate the attributes of youth, whiteness, and flawlessness (Zones, 2000). Historically, research on the effects of exposure to and internalisation of Western beauty ideals has predominantly focused on young, non-disabled, White, European American women. Research that examines other populations will be reviewed here.

Non-white populations

Increasing attention has been given to the responses and experiences of ethnic minority women to cultural beauty ideals (Altabe, 1998; Parker et al., 1995). Research has demonstrated that African American women have more flexible conceptions of beauty and reject White ideals, which is linked to higher levels of body image and self-esteem and less guilt about body size, despite their objectively higher body weights (Bond & Cash, 1992; Lovejoy, 2001; Makkar & Strube, 1995; Molloy & Herzberger, 1998; Stevens, Kumanyika, & Keil, 1994). More recently, experimental research extended the effects of state self-objectification to other ethnic groups (Hebl, King, & Lin, 2004), demonstrating that wearing a swimsuit versus a sweater negatively affects women across ethnic groups (African American, Hispanic, Asian American) and men (although not to the same degree), not only European American women. State self-objectification increased body shame and reduced self-esteem and math performance across all ethnic groups, with Hispanic women reporting the highest level of body shame and the lowest level of self-esteem when wearing a swimsuit. Although still negatively affected by state self-objectification, this research demonstrated that African American women are least likely to internalise culturally objectifying gazes, and thus may be least vulnerable to the negative effects of trait and state self-objectification.

Differences between Euro-American and Latina women in the effects of beauty ideals may be less pronounced. This may be due to the fact that Latinos are the largest ethnic minority in the United States, and therefore they are exposed to the same socialisation practices related to body weight and shape. In fact, research has indicated that Latina women born in the United States endorse an even thinner ideal body size than European American women whereas Latina women who immigrated to the United States endorsed a larger body ideal (Lopez, Blix, & Blix, 1995). This is consistent with research demonstrating that children of immigrants in the United States may utilise the media as a 'cultural guide' to negotiate social strategies (Suarez-Orozco & Suarez-Orozco, 2001). Both Latina and White women have reported that bodily self-control is their primary means to exert control in the social world (Goodman, 2002).

Recent research has identified 'the whiter the better' ideal of beauty as increasingly problematic for Latin American women in Latin American countries (Casanova, 2004), where female beauty is equated with whiteness, delicate features, straight, light hair, and light eyes. Qualitative interviews and quantitative assessments of young, Ecuadorian women in rural and urban settings revealed that the dominant ideal for female beauty is white, although they do apply more flexible criteria to real Ecuadorian people who reflect a continuum of blackness. Despite the acknowledged acceptance of this white ideal, 65 per cent of participants from two different samples did not report that they compare themselves to idealised versions of white or Latina beauty. However, the majority of participants reported that it was compulsory to look good because it affected job and romantic opportunities, and this was associated with lower body and self-esteem scores in the rural sample. In addition, there was considerable preoccupation with appearance, with young women reporting, 'You always have to think about what others will think of you' (Casanova, 2004: 300). Casanova states that women chronically anticipate reactions to their appearance by the *los demás,* which refers to all the people, known and unknown, with whom a person comes into contact on a daily basis, as well as people who may know of her or hear something about her. With the increasing emphasis on idealised images of Latina women such as Jennifer Lopez, Latina models in swimsuit issues of *Sports Illustrated,* and the winners of Miss Universe contests from Puerto Rico (reigning) and the Dominican Republic (former), this pervasive self-objectification among Latin American women can be expected to increase, and should continue to be investigated in future research.

The cross-cultural work of Ann Becker and colleagues demonstrates the impact of Westernised media imagery on adolescent girls in Fiji. Since the introduction of television in 1995, young Fijian girls have expressed an increased desire to be thin. Between 1995 and 1998, a cross-sectional, two-wave cohort study revealed increased eating disordered attitudes and behaviours among ethnic Fijian adolescents (Becker, Burwell, Gilman, Herzog, & Hamburg, 2002). This is remarkable considering that the traditionally revered body in Fiji is large and robust; yet, there is no corresponding preoccupation with attaining this robust ideal and an almost explicit disinterest in reshaping the body (Becker, 1995). The narrative responses of adolescent Fijian girls reveal that young girls admire and accept Western ideals of beauty portrayed in the media, and they associate thinness with success and social mobility (Becker, 2004). In addition, these young girls report increased identification with television characters as role models, preoccupation with weight loss, greater motivation to reshape their bodies through dieting and exercise, and disordered eating behaviours. According to Becker (2004: 553), 'Fijian self-presentation has absorbed new dimensions related to buying into Western styles of appearance and the ethos of work on the body.'

Western beauty ideals have not pervaded every part of the globe, however. Recent cross-cultural research provides evidence for the adverse effects of internalising beauty ideals that do not embody thinness, but rather fatness. Utilising a figural rating scale, a sample of 249 Moroccan Sahraoui women rated their ideal body size as significantly *larger* than their rating of a healthy body size (Rguibi & Belahsen, 2006). The desire to lose weight was very low, even among the majority of obese women, and educational level did not affect desire to lose weight. Women who reported dissatisfaction with their body size were more likely to report trying to gain weight. Consistent with the literature on thin-ideal internalisation, the internalisation of a fat-ideal was associated with maternal feedback, men's approval, and culturally prescribed clothing, and it is implicated in the prevalence of obesity among women. Similar results have been reported in samples of Samoans (Brewis, McGarvey, Jones, & Swinburn, 1998), Malaysians (Swami & Tovée, 2005), and many African societies (Tovée, Swami, Furnham, & Mangalparsad, 2006; Treloar et al., 1999).

The cross-cultural differences in perceptions of female beauty described above are consistent with prior research that has documented differential associations between socioeconomic status (SES) and perceptions of physical attractiveness in developing vs. developed countries. In a review of 144 studies across several continents, Sobal and Stunkard (1989) observed a positive association between obesity and SES for women in developing countries, with similar associations observed for men and children as well. These results support the idea that obesity is often viewed positively as the feminine beauty ideal in developing countries (Anderson, Crawford, Nadeau, & Lindberg, 1992; Brown & Konner, 1987). In contrast, a negative association was observed between obesity and SES for women in developed countries (Sobal & Stunkard, 1989). Specifically, obesity was six times more prevalent in women of lower SES compared to women of higher SES. This reverse pattern in developed countries was not demonstrated for men or children, confirming the unique association between thinness and beauty for women in developed countries, and the corresponding association between obesity and stigma, especially for women with the resources to manipulate weight. Researchers have suggested that thinner, less curvaceous body types are highly valued in societies where women are in competition with men for the same resources, mainly jobs (Barber, 1998). This view suggests that in societies where economic opportunities are not available to women, a more curvaceous ideal is dominant in order to secure economic resources by attracting men.

The cross-cultural differences in perceptions of female beauty described above are also challenge the idea that WHR is a universal indicator of female beauty. Some researchers have suggested that women's mean WHR (calculated by dividing the circumference of the waist by the circumference of the hips) is the universal indicator of ideal female beauty because particular distributions of body fat reflect a women's ability to produce healthy, abundant offspring (Buss, 1989; Singh, 1993). However, other researchers suggest that WHR may not vary with fertility to the same degree that body mass index (BMI) varies with fertility (Swami & Tovée, 2005). For example, comparisons of amenorrheic women with anorexia and healthy women have shown little distinction in terms of WHR, which demonstrates that women with effectively zero fertility can have the same WHR as women with effectively normal fertility (Tovée, Maisey, Emery, & Cornelissen, 1999). In addition, as WHR increases there is a corresponding increase in BMI, which suggests that this emphasis on WHR in women may be confounded by variations in body mass index (BMI). Swami and Tovée recently demonstrated that BMI, and not WHR, is the primary predictor of female attractiveness across samples of British and Malayasian subgroups, accounting for 75 per cent of the variance in attractiveness ratings. Thus, while body shape cues do seem to be associated with perceived male attractiveness (Maisey, Vale, Cornelissen, & Tovée, 1999), female attractiveness is apparently judged based on fatness across cultures (Furnham, Tan, & McManus, 1997; Puhl & Boland, 2001; Tovée & Cornelissen, 2001).

Age

As a symbolic marker of bodily change and loss of reproduction, it has been argued that aging women find themselves in contradiction with contemporary beauty ideals (Dillaway, 2005; Markson, 2003). Little systematic research has examined how older women respond to contemporary beauty ideals (Pliner, Chaiken, & Flett, 1990). Among a sample of women aged 61 to 92, Hurd Clarke (2002a) reported that weight and appearance are still central to women's identity and their perceived social value. The majority of women reported some degree of body dissatisfaction, a desire to lose weight for appearance reasons, and varying degrees of dieting behaviour. However, in samples of older women, appearance concerns seem to stem more from socialisation practices and pervasive social norms for female beauty than media messages per se; and they appear to reject extreme thin ideals, preferring more rounded female bodies and emphasise inner beauty (Hurd Clarke,

2002b). Managing appearance concerns is difficult for older women because they have internalised the importance of looking good, but a focus on appearance is considered vain later in life, and thus appearance concerns become embedded in weight and health discourse. According to Pliner et al. (1990), 'The need outwardly to deny the importance of appearance, and instead to emphasise the health benefits of staying slim, undoubtedly reinforce existing cultural norms about the relationship between women's appearances and their social value' (770).

Disfigurement and disability

Little research is available that examines the impact of cultural beauty ideals on individuals with varying types of disfigurement or disability. As with aging bodies, disfigured or disabled bodies contradict contemporary standards of beauty. Scholars have discussed the perpetuation of negative perceptions of disfigurement or disability across various media (Bowman & Jaeger, 2004). Evil characters in children's stories are portrayed as ugly or disfigured (e.g., evil queens and stepmothers; Scar in *The Lion King*) whereas good characters are portrayed as beautiful (e.g., Snow White), and these messages continue in adult stories and films (e.g., Freddy Kruger in *Nightmare on Elm Street*; Partridge, 1990; Smith, McIntosh & Bazzini, 1999). Quite often when characters in films become ugly, they are often turning bad or evil (e.g., *The Fly*, *The Exorcist*). Individuals who contradict the norms of beauty are often viewed as societal deviants and experience dehumanising treatment by others (e.g., Solomon, 1998). For example, adults with visible burns are perceived as significantly less attractive, less sociable, and lacking a sense of humour compared to adults without visible burns (Franks & Goodrick-Meech, 1997). The recent development of measures to assess the perceptions of stigma among adult burn victims highlights the importance of addressing societal effects on populations who are unable to meet cultural beauty ideals (Lawrence, Fauerbach, Heinberg, Doctor, & Thombs, 2006).

Pregnancy

Pregnant women in Western cultures are not immune to the pressures of attaining contemporary standards of beauty. Indeed, medical and cultural pressures encourage women to gain minimal weight during pregnancy in order to regain their pre-pregnancy shape/weight as quickly as possible (Dworkin & Wachs, 2004). Leifer (1977) found that body image changes during pregnancy evoked negative feelings in women regardless of how satisfied women were with their body prior to pregnancy. Similarly, Fairburn and Welch (1990) found that 40 per cent of the pregnant women in their sample expressed fear of weight gain in pregnancy and 72 per cent expressed a fear that they would not be able to return to their pre-pregnancy body weight. In a sample of healthy pregnant women, Skouteris, Carr, Wertheim, Paxton, and Duncombe (2005) reported that most women do adapt to the changes in their bodies; however, sociocultural pressures to be thin and appearance comparisons with other people were significant predictors of body image disturbance over the course of the pregnancy.

Robin Wallace (2003), journalist for Fox News, offered her experience while sitting in her doctor's office when she was 8 and 1/2 months pregnant. She was flipping through a fashion magazine and saw a full-page nude picture of a 5-month pregnant model:

> As if women were not already held to an impossible standard of media-defined beauty, now there is a pregnant ideal that we're expected to achieve, and it is an image of Cindy or Demi with their barely-there bumps. It may be the cruellest standard of all. As impossible as it will ever be for my body to resemble Cindy's under normal circumstances, it's a thousand times less likely-truly beyond impossible-in our respective pregnant forms... I can relate to pregnant Cindy about as much as I can when she's on the cover of *Vogue*.

Beauty ideals as oppressive practices

> The beauty practices that women engage in, and which men find so exciting, are those of political subordinates... The fact that some women say that they take pleasure in the practices is not inconsistent with their role in the subordination of women.
>
> ~ Jeffreys (2005: 26–27)

We would be remiss if we did not acknowledge what these detrimental beauty practices are ultimately conveying about the conditions of the social world within which women live (Hesse-Biber et al., 2006; Katzman & Lee, 1997; Thompson et al., 1999). It has been argued that the most powerful, and most devastating, impact of these narrow, unrealistic, and ever changing beauty ideals on women is oppression. In applying a sociocultural approach to examine dangerous beauty-related practices, it seems critical to consider the effects of the promotion and adherence to these beauty ideals on the legitimation of gender inequality (Baker-Sperry & Grauerholz, 2003; Lorber, 1994).

According to Dworkin (1974: 112, emphasis in original):

> Standards of beauty describe in precise terms the relationship that an individual will have to her own body. They prescribe her mobility, spontaneity, posture, gait, the uses to which she can put her body. *They define precisely the dimensions of her physical freedom.*

Indeed, the promotion and pursuit of beauty ideals is considered oppressive because of 'the guise of free will and choice' that is created by the media with regard to women's appearance (Callaghan, 1994). A survey by *Glamour* magazine in 1995 uncovered this guise (Haiken, 1997). *Glamour* asked men, 'If it were painless, safe, and free, would you encourage your wife or girlfriend to get breast implants?' More than half of the men sampled (55 per cent) answered 'yes.' The pressure to meet current beauty ideals, by surgically altering one's body, is clearly present and supported within the culture, and raises the question of women's *choice*.

Internalised beauty ideals and objectified gazes create a context in which women are vulnerable to the ubiquitous cultural messages regarding female beauty. The beauty industry renders women even more vulnerable by portraying real women's bodies as deficient and in constant need of alteration. According to Wolf (1991), over 20 billion dollars are spent in America each year on beauty products. Wolf demonstrated that an alternative use of this incredible sum over one year could fund 400,000 4-year university scholarships, 20 million airline tickets around the world, one million well-paid home health aides for homebound elderly, 75,000 women's music, art, or film festivals, and 33,000 battered women's shelters. This chronic emphasis and valuing of appearance in women not only usurps and wastes precious cognitive and physical resources (e.g., time, physical energy, cognitive capacity) that could be utilised for achievement-based activities, but it requires a considerable financial investment that can drain the average woman's economic resources, and thus become disempowering over time. As noted by Tiggemann and Rothblum (1997: 592):

> Given that billions of dollars are spent annually on diets, diet foods, and weight-loss surgery, there would be a considerable economic impact (and backlash against women) should women cease to be focused on thinness. The economy has much to gain to keep women blaming themselves (and other women) for their weight.

Cross-cultural evidence exists supporting this association between the subordination of women and adherence to beauty ideals. The Karen women of upland Burma are known in Europe as 'giraffe-necked' women. This is because the females of this group are required by local beauty norms to start wearing brass neck rings from an early age. Initially, five brass rings are fixed around the neck, and this number is increased gradually each year to a total of 24 rings. Brass rings are also put on the arms and legs, so that a woman might carry between 50 to 60 pounds of brass while walking long distances and working in the fields. In an attempt to artificially lengthen the neck, this custom stretches the cervical muscles in the neck and pulls apart the neck vertebrae to such a degree that women's necks cannot support their own heads if the rings are removed (Fallon, 1990; Morris, 1985).

The practice of foot binding in China dates back to at least 900 AD, and continued until the 20th century (Fallon, 1990; Jeffreys, 2005). From as early as age 2, girls were forced to bind their toes to the soles of their feet. A wide bandage was wrapped around the four small toes, bending them back on themselves, and then woven tightly around the heel to pull the toes and heel together. Large stones were placed on the top of the foot to crush the arch. Girls were required to walk on their bound feet in order to force the feet into their new, buckled shape. Smaller pairs of shoes were worn every few days. By the time these girls were adults they were permanently crippled, unable to walk normally – they had to be carried or crawl to move. A Chinese woman whose feet had not been bound would not be married. Bound feet were considered the most beautiful and erotic feature of a woman. Writer Jung Chang (1993) describes the experience of her grandmother in China whose feet were bound at the age of two by her mother. Chang explains that when the feet were bound and the bones were crushed:

> My grandmother screamed in agony and begged her [mother] to stop. Her mother had to stick a cloth into her mouth to gag her…For years my grandmother lived in relentless, excruciating pain. When she pleaded with her mother to untie the bindings, her mother would weep and tell her that unbound feet would ruin her entire life, and that she was doing it for her own future happiness. (p. 24)

Both of these examples clearly reflect the absolute rejection of women's natural body parts and sizes, and the eroticisation of artificially modified (mutilated) body parts which become necessary to obtain in order to attain social and economic rewards. The perpetuation of extreme beauty practices is evident across Western cultures as well. Indeed, scholars have articulated the similarities between contemporary beauty practices for women in the West (e.g., labiaplasty) and the mutilation and subordination of women's bodies in non-Western cultures (e.g., female genital mutilation; see Jeffreys, 2005). For example, in earlier centuries, small feet had been a dominant feature of Western female beauty, and some women did have their small toes amputated to fit their feet into smaller, more pointed shoes (Brownmiller, 1984). Wearing high-heeled, pointed shoes creates opportunities for short and long-term deformity, increases the risks of twisted ankles, strained backs, shortened tendons, and torn ligaments, and requires increased vigilance and energy to avoid uneven paths, pavement cracks, elevator grids, and sidewalk gratings. The bound foot and the high-heeled foot impose problems of grace and self-consciousness 'on what would otherwise be a simple art of locomotion, and in this artful handicap lies its subjugation and supposed charm' (Brownmiller, 1984: 186).

Body modification in the form of plastic surgery is an estimated $8 billion-dollar per year industry in the United States. Based on reports from the American Society for Aesthetic Plastic Surgery (2004), a remarkable 1.8 million elective surgical procedures and a little over 7 million minimally invasive procedures (e.g., Botox injections, chemical peels) were performed in 2003, with 80 per cent performed on women. Breast augmentation increased 114 per cent between 1997 and 2001, and 80 per cent of these surgeries were done on healthy women to change their breast size – not as part of a postmastectomy. Over one billion dollars was spent on silicone breast enlargement in 2004 (Hesse-Biber et al., 2006). Between 2001 and 2003, buttock lifts increased by 78 per cent, tummy tucks by 61 per cent, and Botox injections by 267 per cent.

These remarkable increases in plastic surgery resonate with Morgan's (1991) assertion that the severity of pressure experienced by women to be 'perfect' will eventually render women who refuse to have plastic surgery as deviant. Indeed, the normalisation of plastic surgery is most clearly evident in mainstream television shows, such as *Extreme Makeover* and *The Swan,* which have large prime-time audiences. People on these shows compete to undergo large numbers of surgical procedures to modify their appearance to make it more acceptable and closer to cultural beauty ideals. This normalised practice of surgically modifying the body to meet beauty standards has caused deadly infections, gangrene, nerve damage, loss of sensation, loss of body parts, mutilated body parts, and death: these deleterious effects of plastic surgery on women's physical health and psychological well-being have been reported for decades (Haiken, 1997).

Future trends and shifting focus

Recent research has identified a shifting trend in the responses of over 3,000 college women and men between 1983 and 2001 across multiple dimensions of body image (Cash, Morrow, Hrabosky, & Perry, 2004). Specifically, whereas body image dissatisfaction increased among non-Black women between 1983 and the early to mid-1990s, body-image dissatisfaction, overweight preoccupation, and investment in appearance decreased among non-Black and Black women from the mid-1990s onward. Men's body image remained relatively stable over this time period. Perhaps paradoxically, these apparent improvements in body image have coincided with actual increases in body weight during this period (Flegal, Carroll, Ogden, & Johnson, 2002). As of yet, it is unclear whether these trends will continue and how they can be understood within the current cultural climate of increasingly extreme pressures and methods to meet unrealistic beauty ideals.

It is possible that societal awareness and public consciousness of body image and eating disturbances is growing, and programmatic efforts to enhance media literacy may empower women to reject unrealistic beauty ideals and the dangerous behaviours required to meet them (Irving & Berel, 2001; Levine & Piran, 2004; Levine & Smolak, 2001, 2002). Meta-analytic and literature reviews have indicated that some types of interventions that target internalisation of cultural beauty ideals, such as dissonance-based models, produce marked improvements in body dissatisfaction (Stice & Shaw, 2004; Thompson & Stice, 2001). However, not all intervention studies have demonstrated positive effects. Irving, DuPen, and Berel (1998) found that a media literacy-based intervention decreased thin-ideal internalisation and perceived realism of media images, but there was no corresponding reduction for body dissatisfaction or the desire to look like the media images. In fact, some researchers have demonstrated that critically viewing idealised media images may increase the extent to which they are processed, thereby increasing body dissatisfaction (Botta, 2003; Milkie, 1999; Nathanson & Botta, 2003).

It seems clear that women are quite capable of critiquing the current standards for beauty and the images portraying these standards, but they continue to feel bound by them and motivated to attain them. This may not be surprising when we consider that there is no evidence of a reduction in the cultural messages conveying contemporary standards of female beauty at the societal level (Tiggemann, 2002). Many women continue to engage in beauty practices and perceive being 'beautiful' as empowering; this is despite the widely held view that female beauty ideals are oppressive and contribute to the objectification, devaluation, and subordination of women. According to the United Nations (1995), harmful cultural practices against women are identified as: (1) being harmful to the health of women and girls; (2) arising from the material power differences between the sexes; (3) being for the benefit of men; (4) creating stereotyped masculinity and femininity which damage the opportunities of women and girls, and; (5) being justified by tradition. Thus, it can be argued that beauty practices in Western culture represent harmful, cultural practices against girls and women.

Furthermore, the World Health Organization [WHO] (2006) defines human health as 'a state of complete physical, mental, and social well-being, and not merely the absence of disease or infirmity.' Based on the evidence reviewed in this chapter, a considerable number of women in Western culture, and increasingly other cultures, are not meeting the WHO's definition of human health; that is, many women do not embody a state of complete physical, mental, and social well-being because of these harmful, cultural beauty practices. The evidence reviewed in this chapter stands as a stark call to action for researchers, practitioners, and community members to systematically identify the negative effects of cultural beauty ideals and eliminate detrimental beauty practices from the lives of girls and women.

Men's body image: The emergence of the muscular ideal, and beyond

Men's body image has emerged in recent years as a focus of empirical inquiry on a par with women's body image (Thompson & Cafri, 2007). Over the past three decades, increasing body dissatisfaction among men has been documented (see Thompson & Cafri, 2007; Thompson et al., 1999), with the focus on a drive for muscularity (Cafri, Blevins, & Thompson, 2006). Researchers have demonstrated marked increases in the presentation of muscular male physiques in Playgirl centre-folds (Ginsberg & Gray, 2007) over the past 25 to 30 years. Indeed, a casual scan of magazine shelves at bookstores, grocery and convenience stores reveals a wealth of magazines with numerous images of hyper-muscular male bodies. Similar to research on female beauty ideals, Thompson and Cafri (2007) demonstrated that men exposed to ads illustrating the male body ideal (a mesomorphic physique) reported greater body dissatisfaction than men exposed to neutral ads. Other beauty practices among men are becoming popularised including body depilation (Boroughs, Cafri, & Thompson, 2005; Boroughs & Thompson, 2002), which is the removal of hair in rather non-traditional places for men such as arms, legs, or genital area. Cosmetic procedures for men have increased 44 per cent between 2000 and 2005 (American Society of Plastic Surgeons, 2004). As is the case for women, this exacting male beauty ideal has required men to spend a great deal more money in recent years on a variety of appearance enhancing and modification strategies. Now that men's attractiveness issues receive almost as much research attention as women's, it will be fascinating to track the trends of the two sexes in the coming years.

References

Altabe, M. (1998). Ethnicity and body image: Quantitative and qualitative analysis. *International Journal of Eating Disorders, 23*, 154–159.

American Psychiatric Association (1994). *Diagnostic and statistical manual of mental disorders* (4th ed.). Washington, DC: Author.

American Society for Aesthetic Plastic Surgery (2004). *Plastic Surgery Statistics*. One publication at http://www.plasticsurgery.org.

American Society of Plastic Surgeons (2004). 2000/2001/2002/2003 *National plastic surgery statistics: Cosmetic and reconstructive procedure trends*. Online publication at: http://www.plasticsurgery.org/public_education/2003statistics. cfm. Retrieved September 15, 2006.

Andersen, A. E., & DiDomenico, L. (1992). Diet vs. shape content in popular male and female magazines: A dose-response relationship to the incidence of eating disorders? *International Journal of Eating Disorders, 11*, 283–287.

Anderson, J. L., Crawford, C. E., Nadeau, J., & Lindberg, T. (1992). Was the Duchess of Windsor right? A cross-cultural view of the socio-biology of ideals of female body shape. *Ethology and Sociobiology, 13*, 197–227.

Baker-Sperry, L., & Grauerholz, L. (2003). The pervasiveness and persistence of the feminine beauty ideal in children's fairy tales. *Gender and Society, 15*, 711–726.

Banner, L. (1983). *American beauty*. New York: Knopf.

Barber, N. (1998). Secular changes in standards of bodily attractiveness in women: Tests of a reproductive model. *International Journal of Eating Disorders, 23*, 449–453.

Bartky, S. (1990). *Femininity and domination*. New York: Routledge.

Bartky, S. L. (2003). Foucault, femininity, and the modernization of patriarchal power. In Rose Weitz (Ed.), *The politics of women's bodies: Sexuality, appearance and behaviour*. (2nd ed.). New York: Oxford University Press.

Becker, A. E. (1995). *Body, self, society: The view from Fiji*. Philadelphia, PN: University of Pennsylvania Press.

Becker, A. E. (2004). Television, disordered eating, and young women in Fiji: Negotiating body image and identity during rapid social change. *Culture, Medicine, and Psychiatry, 28*, 533–559.

Becker, A. E., & Hamburg, P. (1996). Culture, the media, and eating disorders. *Harvard Review of Psychiatry, 4,* 163–167.

Becker, A. E., Burwell, R. A., Gilman, S. E., Herzog, D. B., & Hamburg, P. (2002). Eating behaviors and attitudes following prolonged television exposure among ethnic Fijian adolescent girls. *British Journal of Psychiatry, 180,* 509–514.

Berger, J. (1972). *Ways of seeing.* London: BBC/Harmondsworth: Penguin.

Bond, S., & Cash, T. (1992). Black beauty: Skin color and body images among African American college women. *Journal of Applied Social Psychology, 22,* 874–888.

Bordo, S. (1993). *Unbearable weight.* Berkley: University of California Press.

Boroughs, M., & Thompson, J. K. (2002). Body depilation in males: A new body image concern? *International Journal of Men's Health, 1,* 247–257.

Boroughs, M., Cafri, G., & Thompson, J. K. (2005). Male body depilation: Prevalence and associated features of body hair removal. *Sex Roles, 52,* 637–644.

Botta, R. (2003). For your health? The relationship between magazine reading and adolescents' body image and eating disturbances. *Sex Roles, 48,* 389–399.

Bowker, A., Gadbois, S., & Cornock, B. (2003). Sport participation and self-esteem: Variations as a function of gender and gender role orientation. *Sex Roles, 49,* 47–58.

Bowman, C. A., & Jaeger, P. T. (2004). *A guide to high school success for students with disabilities.* Westport, CT: Greenwood Press.

Brewis, A. A., McGarvey, S. T., Jones, J., & Swinburn, B. A. (1998). Perceptions of body size in Pacific Islanders. *International Journal of Obesity and Related Metabolic Disorders, 22,* 185–189.

Brown, P. J., & Konner, M. (1987). An anthropological perspective of obesity. *Annals of the New York Academy of Sciences, 499,* 29–46.

Brownell, K. (1991). Dieting and the search for the perfect body: Where physiology and culture collide. *Behavior Therapy, 22,* 1–12.

Brownmiller, S. (1984). *Femininity.* New York: Ballentine Books.

Buss, D. M. (1989). Sex differences in human mate preferences: Evolutionary hypotheses tested in 37 cultures. *Behavior and Brain Sciences, 12,* 1–49.

Cafri, G., & Thompson, J. K. (2004). Evaluating the convergence of muscle appearance attitude measures. *Assessment, 11,* 224–229.

Cafri, G., Blevins, N., & Thompson, J. K. (2006) The drive for muscle leanness: A complex case with features of muscle dysmorphia and eating disorder not otherwise specified. *Eating and Weight Disorders, 11,* 117–118.

Caldwell, D. (1981). *And all was revealed: Ladies underwear 1907–1980.* New York: St. Martin's Press.

Callaghan, C. A. (1994). *Ideals of feminine beauty: Philosophical, social, and cultural dimensions.* Westport, CT: Greenwood Press.

Calogero, R. M. (2004). A test of objectification theory: Effect of the male gaze on appearance concerns in college women. *Psychology of Women Quarterly, 28,* 16–21.

Calogero, R. M., Davis, W. N., & Thompson, J. K. (2004). The sociocultural attitudes toward appearance questionnaire: Reliability and normative comparisons of eating disordered patients. *Body Image, 1,* 193–198.

Calogero, R. M., Davis, W. N., & Thompson, J. K. (2005). The role of self-objectification in the experience of women with eating disorders. *Sex Roles, 52,* 43–50.

Casanova, E. M. (2004). 'No ugly women': Concepts of race and beauty among adolescent women in Ecuador. *Gender & Society, 18,* 287–308.

Cash, T. F. (1990). The psychology of physical appearance: Aesthetics, attributes, and images. In T. F. Cash, & T. Pruzinsky (Eds.), *Body images: Development, deviance, and change* (pp. 51–79). New York: Guilford.

Cash, T. F., Morrow, J. A., Hrabosky, J. I., & Perry, A. A. (2004). How has body image changed? A cross-sectional investigation of college women and men from 1983 to 2001. *Journal of Consulting and Clinical Psychology, 72,* 1081–1089.

Cattarin, J. A., Thompson, J. K., Thomas, C., & Williams, R. (2000). Body image, mood, and televised images of attractiveness: The role of social comparison. *Journal of Social and Clinical Psychology, 19,* 220–239.

Chang, J. (1993). *Wild swans: Three daughters of China.* London: Flamingo.

Crane, A. R. (1956). Stereotypes of the adult held by early adolescents. *Journal of Education Research, 50,* 227–230.

Cusumano, D. L., & Thompson, J. K. (1997). Body image and body shape ideals in magazines: Exposure, awareness and internalization. *Sex Roles, 37,* 701–721.

Dellinger, K., & Williams, C. L. (1997). Makeup at work: Negotiating appearance rules in the workplace. *Gender & Society, 11,* 151–177.

Dillaway, H. (2005). (Un)changing menopausal bodies: How women think and act in the face of a reproductive transition and gendered beauty ideals. *Sex Roles, 53,* 1–17.

Dion, K. K., Berscheid, E., & Walster, E. (1972). What is beautiful is good. *Journal of Personality and Social Psychology, 34,* 285–290.

Dittmar, H., & Howard, S. (2004a). Thin-ideal internalization and coial comparison tendency as moderstors of emdia models' impact on women's body-focused anxiety. *Journal of Social and Clinical Psychology, 23,* 768–791.

Dittmar, H., & Howard, S. (2004b). Professional hazards? The impact of models' body size on advertising effectiveness and 477 women's body-focused anxiety in professions that do and do not emphasize the cultural ideal of thinness. *British Journal of Social Psychology, 43,* 477–497.

Durkin, S. J., & Paxton, S. J. (2002). Predictors of vulnerability to reduced body image satisfaction and psychological well-being in response to exposure to idealized female media images in adolescent girls. *Journal of Psychosomatic Research, 53,* 995–1005.

Dworkin, A. (1974). *Women hating.* New York: E. P. Dutton.

Dworkin, S., & Wachs, F. L. (2004). 'Getting your body back': Postindustrial fit motherhood in Shape Fit Pregnancy Magazine. *Gender & Society, 18,* 610–625.

Eagly, A. H., Ashmore, R. D., Makhijani, M. G., & Longo, L. C. (1991). What is beautiful is good, but … A meta-analytic review of research on the physical attractiveness stereotype. *Psychological Bulletin, 110,* 109–128.

Eck, B. A. (2003). Men are much harder: Gendered viewing of nude images. *Gender & Society, 17,* 691–710.

Engeln-Maddox, R. (2006). Buying a beauty standard or dreaming of a new life? Expectations associated with media ideals. *Psychology of Women Quarterly, 30,* 258–266.

Englis, B. G., Solomon, M. R., & Ashmore, R. D. (1994). Beauty before the eyes of the beholder: The cultural encoding of beauty types in magazine advertising and music television. *Journal of Advertising, 23,* 49–64.

Etcoff, N., Orbach, S., Scott, J., & D'Agostino, H. (2004). *Beyond stereotypes: Rebuilding the foundation of beauty beliefs: Findings of the 2005 Dove Global Study.* Online publication at: http://www.campaignforrealbeauty.com/Dove BeyondStereotypesWhitePaper.pdf. Retrived September 10, 2006.

Evans, P. C. (2003). 'If only I were thin like her, maybe I could be happy like her': The self-implications of associating a thin female ideal with life success. *Psychology of Women Quarterly, 27*, 209–214.

Fairburn, C. G., & Welch, S. L. (1990). The impact of pregnancy on eating habits and attitudes to weight and shape. *International Journal of Eating Disorders, 9*, 153–160.

Fallon, A. (1990). Culture in the mirror: Sociocultural determinants of body image. In T. F. Cash, & T. Pruzinsky (Eds.), *Body images: Development, deviance, and change* (pp. 80–109). New Tork: Guilford Press.

Festinger, L. (1954). A theory of social comparison processes. *Human Relations, 1*, 117–140.

Flannery-Schroeder, E., & Chrisler, J. C. (1996). Body esteem, eating attitudes, and gender-role orientation in three age groups of children. *Current Psychology: Developmental, Learning, Personality, Social, 15*, 235–248.

Flegal, K. M., Carroll, M. D., Ogden, C. L., & Johnson, C. L. (2002). Prevalence and trends in obesity among US adults, 1999–2000. *Journal of the American Medical Association, 288*, 1723–1727.

Franks, T., & Goodrick-Meech, A. (1997). Society's perceptions of visibly burned adults and the implications for occupational therapy. *British Journal of Occupational Therapy, 60*, 320–324.

Frederick, D. A., Peplau, L. A., & Lever, J. (2006). The swimsuit issue: Correlates of body image in a sample of 52,677 heterosexual adults. *Body Image, 3*, 413–419.

Fredrickson, B. L., & Roberts, T. (1997). Objectification theory: Toward understanding women's lived experiences and mental health risks. *Psychology of Women Quarterly, 21*, 173–206.

Fredrickson, B. L., Roberts, T. A., Noll, S. M., Quinn, D. M., & Twenge, J. M. (1998). That swimsuit becomes you: Sex differences in self-objectification, restrained eating, and math performance. *Journal of Personality and Social Psychology, 75*, 269–284.

Freedman, R. (1984). Reflections on beauty as it relates to health in adolescent females. *Women and Health, 9*, 29–45.

Furnham, A., Tan, T., & McManus, C. (1997). Waist-to-hip ratio and preferences for body shape: A replication and extension. *Personal and Individual Differences, 22*, 539–549.

Gapinski, K. D., Brownell, K. D., & LaFrance, M. (2003). Body objectification and 'fat talk': Effects on emotion, motivation, and cognitive performance. *Sex Roles, 48*, 377–388.

Gardner, R. M., Sorter, R. G., & Friedman, B. N. (1997). Developmental changes in children's body images. *Journal of Social Behavior and Personality, 12*, 1019–1036.

Garner, D. M. (1997, February). Survey says: Body image poll results. *Psychology Today*. Retrieved September 21, 2006, from http://www.psychologytoday.com/articles/pto-19970201-000023.html.

Garner, D. M., Garfinkel, P. E., Schwartz, D., & Thompson, M. (1980). Cultural expectations of thinness in women. *Psychological Reports, 47*, 483–491.

Ginsberg, R., & Gray, J. (2007). The muscular ideal: Social, cultural, and psychological perspectives. In J. K. Thompson, & G. Cafri (Eds.), *The muscular ideal: Psychological, social, and medical perspectives*, Washington, DC: American Psychological Association.

Goodman, R. (2002). Flabless is fabulous: How Latina and Anglo women read and incorporate the excessively thin body ideal into every experience. *Journalism and Mass Communication Quarterly, 79*, 712–727.

Groesz, L. M., Levine, M. P., & Murnen, S. K. (2002). The effect of experimental presentation of thin media images on body satisfaction: A meta-analytic review. *International Journal of Eating Disorders, 31*, 1–16.

Guinness World Records (2006). Online publication at: http://www.guinnessworld records.com/content_pages/ Retrived September 25, 2006.

Haiken, E. (1997). *Venus envy: A history of cosmetic surgery.* Baltimore, MD: The Johns Hopkins University Press.

Hargreaves, D. A., & Tiggemann, M. (2003a). Longer-term implications of responsiveness to 'thin-ideal' television: Support for a cumulative hypothesis of body image disturbance? *European Eating Disorders Review, 11*, 465–477.

Hargreaves, D. A., & Tiggemann, M. (2003b). Female 'thin ideal' media images and boys' attitudes toward girls. *Sex Roles, 49*, 539–544.

Harrison, K. (2003). Television viewers' ideal body proportions: The case of the curvaceously thin woman. *Sex Roles, 48*, 255–264.

Harrison, K., & Cantor, J. (1997). The relationship between media consumption and eating disorders. *Journal of Communication, 47*, 40–67.

Harrison, K., & Hefner, V. (2006). Media exposure, current and future body ideals, and disordered eating among preadolescent girls: A longitudinal panel study. *Journal of Youth and Adolescence, 35*, 153–163.

Harrison, K., Taylor, L. D., & Marske, A. L. (2006). Women's and men's eating behaviour following exposure to ideal-body images and text. *Communication Research, 33*, 1–23.

Hebl, M. R., King, E. B., & Lin, J. (2004). The swimsuit becomes us all: Ethnicity, gender, and vulnerability to self-objectification. *Personality and Social Psychology Bulletin, 30*, 1322–1331.

Heinberg, L. J. (1996). Theories of body image: Perceptual, developmental, and sociocultural factors. In J. K. Thompson (Ed.), *Body image, eating disorders, and obesity: An integrative guide for assessment and treatment* (pp. 27–48). Washington, DC: American Psychological Association.

Heinberg, L. J., Thompson, J. K., & Stormer, S. (1995). Development and valid-ation of the sociocultural attitudes towards appearance questionnaire. *International Journal of Eating Disorders, 17*, 81–89.

Herbozo, S., Tantleff-Dunn, S., Gokee-Larose, J., & Thompson, J. K. (2004). Beauty and thinness messages in children's media: A content analysis. *Eating Disorders: The Journal of Treatment and Prevention, 12*, 21–34.

Hesse-Biber, S. J. (1996). *Am I thin enough yet? The cult of thinness and commercial-ization of identity.* New York: Oxford University.

Hesse-Biber, S., Leavy, P., Quinn, C. E., & Zoino, J. (2006). The mass marketing of disordered eating and eating disorders: The social psychology of women, thinness, and culture. *Women's Studies International Forum, 29*, 208–224.

Holstrom, A. J. (2004). The effects of the media on body image: A meta-analysis. *Journal of Broadcasting and Electronic Media, 48*, 196–218.

Hurd Clarke, L. (2002a). Older women's perceptions of ideal body weights: The tensions between health and appearance motivations for weight loss. *Ageing & Society, 22*, 751–773.

Hurd Clarke, L. (2002b). Beauty in later life: Older women's perceptions of phys-ical attractiveness. *Canadian Journal on Ageing, 21*, 429–442.

Irving, L. (1990). Mirror images: Effects of the standard of beauty on the self- and body-esteem of women exhibiting varying levels of bulimic symptoms. *Journal of Social and Clinical Psychology, 9*, 230–242.

Irving, L. M., & Berel, S. R. (2001). Comparison of media–literacy programs to strengthen college women's resistance to media images. *Psychology of Women Quarterly, 25*(3), 103–111.

Irving, L. M., DuPen, J., & Berel, S. (1998). A media literacy program for high school females. *Eating Disorders: The Journal of Treatment and Prevention, 6*(2), 119–131.

Jansen, A., & de Vries, M. (2002). Pre-attentive exposure to the thin female beauty ideal does not affect women's mood, self-esteem, and eating behaviour. *European Eating Disorders Review, 10*, 208–217.

Jeffreys, S. (2005). *Beauty and misogyny: Harmful cultural practices in the West.* New York: Routledge.

Jourard, S. M., & Secord, P. F. (1955). Body-cathexis and personality. *British Journal of Psychology, 46*, 130–138.

Katch, V. L., Campaigne, B., Freedson, P., Sayd, S., Katch, F. L., & Behnke, A. R. (1980). Contribution of breast volume and weight to body fat distribution in females. *American Journal of Physical Anthropology, 53*, 93–100.

Katzman, M. A., & Lee, S. (1997). Beyond body image: The integration of feminist transcultural theories in the understanding of self-starvation. *International Journal of Eating Disorders, 22*, 385–394.

Krones, P. G., Stice, E., Batres, C., & Orjadam, K. (2005). In vivo social comparison to a thin-ideal peer promotes body dissatisfaction: A randomized experiment. *International Journal of Eating Disorders, 38*, 134–142.

Kunzle, D. (2004). *Fashion and fetishism: A social history of the corset, tight-lacing and other forms of body-sculpture in the West.* Phoenix Mill: Sutton Publishing.

Lawrence, J. W., Fauerbach, J. A., Heinberg, L. J., Doctor, M., & Thombs, B. D. (2006). The reliability and validity of the perceived stigmatization questionnaire (PSQ) and the social comfort questionnaire (SCQ) among an adult burn survivor sample. *Psychological Assessment, 18*, 106–111.

Lee, J. (2003). Menarche and the (hetero)sexualization of the female body. In R. Weitz (Ed.), *The politics of female bodies: Sexuality, appearance, and behavior* (pp. 82–99). New York: Oxford University Press.

Leifer, M. (1977). Psychological changes accompanying pregnancy and motherhood. *Genetic Psychological Monographs, 95*, 55–96.

Levine, M. P., & Harrison, K. (2004). Media's role in the perpetuation and prevention of negative body image and disordered eating. In J. K. Thompson (Ed.), *Handbook of eating disorders and obesity* (pp. 695–717). New York: John Wiley.

Levine, M. P., & Piran, N. (2004). The role of body image in the prevention of eating disorders. *Body Image: An International Journal of Research, 1*, 57–70.

Levine, M. P., & Smolak, L. (1996). Media as a context for the development of disordered eating. In L. Smolak, M. P. Levine, & R. Striegel-Moore (Eds.), *The developmental psychopathology of eating disorders* (pp. 183–204). Mahwah, NJ: Erlbaum.

Levine, M. P., & Smolak, L. (2001). Primary prevention of body image disturbances and disordered eating in childhood and early adolescence. In J. K. Thompson, & L. Smolak (Eds.), *Body image, eating disorders, and obesity in youth: Assessment, prevention, and treatment* (pp. 237–260). Washington, DC: American Psychological Association.

Levine, M. P., & Smolak, L. (2002). Ecological and activism approaches to the prevention of body image problems. In T. F. Cash, & T. Pruzinsky (Eds.), *Body image: A handbook of theory, research, and clinical practice* (pp. 497–505). New York: Guilford Press.

Lin, C. A. (1998). Use of sex appeals in prime-time television commercials. *Sex Roles, 38*, 461–475.

Lopez, E., Blix, G. G., & Blix, A. G. (1995). Body image of Latinas compared to body image of non-Latina White women. *Health Values: The Journal of Health, Behavior, Education, and Promotion, 19*, 3–10.

Lorber, J. (1994). *Paradoxes of gender.* New Haven, CT: Yale University Press.

Lovejoy, M. (2001). Disturbances in the social body: Differences in body image and eating problems among African American and white women. *Gender & Society, 15*, 239–261.

Maisey, D. M., Vale, E. L. E., Cornelissen, P. L., & Tovée, M. J. (1999). Characteristics of male attractiveness for women. *Lancet, 353*, 1500.

Makkar, J. K., & Strube, M. J. (1995). Black women's self-perceptions of attractiveness following exposure to white versus Black beauty standards: The moderating role of racial identity and self-esteem. *Journal of Applied Social Psychology, 25*, 1547–1566.

Markham, A., Thompson, T., & Bowling, A. (2005). Determinants of body-image shame. *Personality and Individual Differences, 38*, 1529–1541.

Markson, E. W. (2003). The female aging body through film. In C. Faircloth (Ed.), *Aging bodies: Images and everyday experiences* (pp. 77–102). Walnut Creek, CA: AltaMira Press.

Mazur, A. (1986). US trends in feminine beauty and overadaptation. *Journal of Sex Research, 22*, 281–303.

McCabe, M., & Ricciardelli, L. (2003). Sociocultural influences on body image and body changes among adolescent boys and girls. *The Journal of Social Psychology, 143*, 5–26.

McCarthy, M. (1990). The thin ideal, depression, and eating disorders in women. *Behaviour Research and Therapy, 28*, 205–214.

McKinley, N. M. (1999). Women and objectified body consciousness: Mothers' and daughters; body experience in cultural, developmental, and familial context. *Developmental Psychology, 35*, 760–769.

McKinley, N. M., & Hyde, J. S. (1996). The Objectified Body Consciousness Scale: Development and validation. *Psychology of Women Quarterly, 20*, 181–215.

Milkie, M. (1999). Social comparisons, reflected appraisals, and mass media: The impact of pervasive beauty images on black and white girls' self concepts. *Social Psychology Quarterly, 62*(2), 190–210.

Miner-Rubino, K., Twenge, J. M., & Fredrickson, B. L. (2002). Trait self-objectification in women: Affective and personality correlates. *Journal of Research in Personality, 36*, 147–172.

Molloy, B. L., & Herzberger, S. D. (1998). Body image and self-esteem: A comparison of African-American and Caucasian women. *Sex Roles, 38*, 631–644.

Moradi, B., Dirks, D., & Matteson, A. (2005). Roles of sexual objectification experiences and internalization of standards of beauty in eating disorder symptomatology: A test and extension of objectification theory. *Journal of Counseling Psychology, 52*, 420–428.

Morgan, K. P. (1991). Women and the knife: Cosmetic surgery and the colonization of women's bodies. *Hypatia, 6*, 25–53.

Morris, D. (1985). *Bodywatching: A field guide to the human species.* New York: Crown.

Morris, A., Cooper, T., & Cooper, P. J. (1989). The changing shape of female fashion models. *International Journal of Eating Disorders, 8,* 593–596.

Murnen, S. K., & Smolak, L. (2000). The experience of sexual harassment among grade-school students: Early socialization of female subordination? *Sex Roles, 43,* 1–17.

Murnen, S. K., Smolak, L., Mills, J. A., & Good, L. (2003). Thin, sexy women and strong, muscular men: Grade-school responses to objectified images of women and men. *Sex Roles, 49,* 427–437.

Nagel, K. L., & Jones, K. H. (1992). Sociological factors in the development of eating disorders. *Adolescence, 27,* 107–113.

Nathanson, A. I., & Botta, R. A. (2003). Shaping the effects of television on adolescents' body image disturbance. *Communication Research, 30,* 304–331.

National Eating Disorders Association [NEDA] (2002). Online publication at http://www.nationaleatingdisorders.org. Retrieved September 15, 2006.

Noll, S. M., & Fredrickson, B. L. (1998). A mediational model linking self-objectification, body shame, and disordered eating. *Psychology of Women Quarterly, 22,* 623–636.

Norton, K. I., Olds, T. S., Olive, S., & Dank, S. (1996). Ken and Barbie at life size. *Sex Roles, 34,* 287–294.

Owen, P. R., & Laurel-Seller, E. (2000). Weight and shape ideals: Thin is dangerously in. *Journal of Applied Social Psychology, 30,* 979–990.

Parker, S., Nichter, M., Nichter, M., Vuckovic, N., Sims, C., & Ritenbaugh, C. (1995). Body images and weight concerns among African American and white adolescent females: Differences that make a difference. *Human Organization, 54,* 103–114.

Partridge, J. (1990). *Changing faces: The challenge of facial disfigurement.* London: Penguin.

Phares, V., Steinberg, A., & Thompson, J. (2004). Gender differences in peer and parental influences: Body image disturbance, self-worth, and psychological functioning in preadolescent children. *Journal of Youth and Adolescence, 33,* 421–429.

Pliner, P., Chaiken, S., & Flett, G. L. (1990). Gender differences in concern with body weight and physical appearance over the life span. *Personality and Social Psychology Bulletin, 16,* 263–273.

Polivy, J., & Herman, C. P. (2004). Sociocultural idealization of thin female body shapes: An introduction to the special issue on body image and eating disorders. *Journal of Social and Clinical Psychology, 23,* 1–6.

Puhl, R. M., & Boland, F. J. (2001). Predicting female physical attractiveness: Waist-to-hip ratio versus thinness. *Psychology, Evolution and Gender, 3,* 27–46.

Puwar, N. (2004). *Space invaders: Race, gender, and bodies out of place.* Oxford: Berg Publishers.

Quinn, D. M., Kallen, R. W., & Cathie, C. (2006). Body on my mind: The lingering effect of state self-objectification. *Sex Roles, 55,* 869–874.

Quinn, D. M., Kallen, R. W., Twenge, J. M., & Fredrickson, B. L. (2006). The disruptive effect of self-objectification on performance. *Psychology of Women Quarterly, 30,* 59–64.

Rguibi, M., & Belahsen, R. (2006). Body size preferences and sociocultural influences on attitudes towards obesity among Moroccan Sahraoui women. *Body Image, 3,* 395–400.

Richins, M. L. (1991). Social comparison and the idealized images of advertising. *Journal of Consumer Research, 18,* 71–83.

Roberts, T., & Gettman, J. Y. (2004). Mere exposure: Gender differences in the negative effects of priming a state of self-objectification. *Sex Roles, 51,* 17–27.

Rodin, J., Silberstein, L., & Striegel-Moore, R. (1984). Women and weight: A normative discontent. *Nebraska Symposium on Motivation, 32,* 267–308.

Rudman, W. J., & Verdi, P. (1993). Exploitation: Comparing sexual and violent imagery of females and males in advertising. *Women and Health, 20,* 1–14.

Sands, E., & Wardle, J. (2003). Internalization of ideal body shapes in 9–12-year-old girls. *International Journal of Eating Disorders, 33,* 193–204.

Schur, E. A., Sanders, M., & Steiner, H. (2000). Body dissatisfaction and dieting in young children. *International Journal of Eating Disorders, 27,* 74–82.

Seid, R. P. (1989). *Never too thin: Why women are at war with their bodies.* Toronto: Prentice-Hall.

Seifert, T. (2005). Anthropometric characteristic of centerfold models: Trends towards slender figures over time. *International Journal of Eating Disorders, 37,* 271–274.

Shape. (2006). *Absolution.* Online publication at http://www.shape.com. Retrieved September 27, 2006.

Sherwood, L. (1993). *Human physiology: From cells to systems.* St. Paul, MN: West Publishing.

Silverstein, B., Peterson, B., & Perdue, L. (1986). Some correlates of the thin standard of bodily attractiveness for women. *International Journal of Eating Disorders, 5,* 895–905.

Silverstein, L. R., Perdue, L., Peterson, B., & Kelly, E. (1986). The role of mass media in promoting a thin standard of bodily attractiveness for women. *Sex Roles, 14,* 519–532.

Singh, D. (1993). Adaptive significance of female physical attractiveness: Role of waist-to-hip ratio. *Journal of Personality and Social Psychology, 65,* 293–307.

Skouteris, H., Carr, R., Wertheim, E. H., Paxton, S. J., & Duncombe, D. (2005). A prospective study of factors that lead to body dissatisfaction during pregnancy. *Body Image, 2,* 347–361.

Slater, A., & Tiggemann, M. (2002). A test of objectification theory in adolescent girls. *Sex Roles, 46,* 343–349.

Smith, S. M., McIntosh, W. D., & Bazzini, D. G. (1999). Are the beautiful good in Hollywood? An investigation of the beauty and goodness stereotype on film. *Basic and Applied Social Psychology, 21,* 69–80.

Smolak, L. (2006). Body image. In J. Worell, & C. D. Goodheart (Eds.), *Handbook of girls' and women's psychological health: Gender and well-being across the lifespan.* Oxford series in clinical psychology (pp. 69–76). New York, NY: Oxford University Press.

Smolak, L., & Levine, M. P. (1994). Critical issues in the developmental psychopathology of eating disorders. In L. Alexander-Mott, & D. B. Lumsden (Eds.), *Understanding eating disorders: Anorexia nervosa, bulimia nervosa, and obesity* (pp. 37–60). Philadelphia, PN: Taylor & Francis.

Smolak, L., Levine, M., & Schermer, F. (1999). Parental input and weight concerns among elementary school children. *International Journal of Eating Disorders, 25,* 263–271.

Sobal, J., & Stunkard, A. J. (1989). Socioeconomic status and obesity: A review of the literature. *Psychological Bulletin, 105,* 260–275.

Solomon, S. E. (1998). On an island by myself: Women of color with facial distinctions. *Journal of Burn Care & Rehabilitation, 19,* 268–278.

Spitzer, B. L., Henderson, K. A., & Zivian, M. T. (1999). Gender differences in population versus media body sizes: A comparison over four decades. *Sex Roles, 40,* 545–565.

Stevens, J., Kumanyika, S. K., & Keil, J. E. (1994). Attitudes towards body size and dieting: Differences between elderly Black and White women. *American Journal of Public Health, 84,* 1322–1325.

Stice, E. (2002). Risk and maintenance factors for eating pathology: A meta-analytic review. *Psychological Bulletin, 128,* 825–848.

Stice, E., & Shaw, H. (2004). Eating disorder prevention programs: A meta-analytic review. *Psychological Bulletin, 130,* 206–227.

Stice, E., & Whitenton, K. (2002). Risk factors for body dissatisfaction in adolescent girls: A longitudinal investigation. *Developmental Psychology, 38,* 669–678.

Stice, E., Maxfield, J., & Wells, T. (2003). Adverse effects of social pressure to be thin on young women: An experimental investigation of the effects of 'fat talk.' *International Journal of Eating Disorders, 34,* 108–117.

Stice, E., Schupak-Neuberg, E., Shaw, H. E., & Stein, R. I. (1994). Relation of media exposure to eating disorder symptomatology: An examination of mediating mechanisms. *Journal of Abnormal Psychology, 103,* 836–840.

Stormer, S. M., & Thompson, J. K. (1996). Explanations of body image disturbance: A test of maturational status, negative verbal commentary, social comparison, and sociocultural hypotheses. *International Journal of Eating Disorders, 19,* 193–202.

Strahan, E. J., Wilson, A. E., Cressman, K. E., & Buote, V. M. (2006). Comparing to perfection: How cultural norms for appearance affect social comparisons and self-image. *Body Image, 3,* 211–227.

Strauss, J., Doyle, A. E., & Kreipe, R. E. (1994). The paradoxical effect of diet commercials on reinhibition of dietary restraint. *Journal of Abnormal Psychology, 103,* 441–444.

Suarez-Orozco, C., & Suarez-Orozco, M. M. (2001). *Children of immigration.* Cambridge, MA: Harvard University Press.

Swami, V. (2007). *The Missing Arms of Vénus de Milo: Reflections on the Science of Physical Attractiveness.* Brighton: The Book Guild Publishing.

Swami, V., & Tovée, M. J. (2005). Female physical attractiveness in Britain and Malaysia: A cross-cultural study. *Body Image, 2,* 115–128.

Swim, J. K., Hyers, L. L., Cohen, L. L., & Ferguson, M. J. (2001). Everyday sexism: Evidence for its incidence, nature, and psychological impact from three daily diary studies. *Journal of Social Issues, 57,* 31–53.

Sypeck, M. F., Gray, J. J., Etu, S. F., Ahrens, A. H., Mosimann, J. E., & Wiseman, C. V. (2006). Cultural representations of thinness in women, redux: Playboy magazine's depiction of beauty from 1979 to 1999. *Body Image, 3,* 229–235.

Thompson, J. K. (1992). Body image: Extent of disturbance, associated features, theoretical models, assessment methodologies, intervention strategies, and a proposal for a new DSM-IV diagnostic category-Body image disorder. In M. Hersen, R. M. Eisler, & P. M. Miller (Eds.), *Progress in behavior modification.* 28 (pp. 3–54). Sycamore, IL: Sycamore.

Thompson, J. K., & Cafri, G. (2007). *The muscular ideal: Psychological, social, and medical perspectives.* Washington, DC: American Psychological Association.

Thompson, J. K., & Stice, E. (2001). Thin-ideal internalization: Mounting evidence for a new risk factor for body-image disturbance and eating pathology. *Current Directions in Psychological Science, 10,* 181–183.

Thompson, J. K., & Tantleff, S. (1992). Female and male ratings of upper torso: Actual, ideal, and stereotypical conceptions. *Journal of Social Behavior and Personality, 7,* 345–354.

Thompson, J. K., Heinberg, L. J., Altabe, M., & Tantleff-Dunn, S. (1999). *Exacting beauty: Theory, assessment, and treatment of body image disturbance.* Washington, DC: American Psychological Association.

Thompson, J. K., van den Berg, P., Roehrig, M., Guarda, A. S., & Heinberg, L. J. (2004). The Sociocultural Attitudes Toward Appearance Scale–3 (SATAQ-3): Development and validation. *International Journal of Eating Disorders, 35,* 293–304.

Tiggemann, M. (2002). Media influences on body image development. In T. F. Cash & T. Pruzinsky (Eds.), *Body image: A handbook of theory, research, and clinical practice* (pp. 91–98). New York: Guilford Press.

Tiggemann, M. (2005). Body dissatisfaction and adolescent self-esteem: Prospective findings. *Body Image, 2,* 129–135.

Tiggemann, M., & Kuring, J. K. (2004). The role of body objectification in disordered eating and depressed mood. *British Journal of Clinical Psychology, 43,* 299–311.

Tiggemann, M., & Lynch, J. E. (2001). Body image across the life span in adult women: The role of self-objectification. *Developmental Psychology, 37,* 243–253.

Tiggemann, M., & Rothblum, E. D. (1997). Gender differences in internal beliefs about weight and negative attitudes towards self and others. *Psychology of Women Quarterly, 21,* 581–593.

Tiggemann, M., & Slater, A. (2003). Thin ideals in music television: A source of social comparison and body dissatisfaction. *International Journal of Eating Disorders, 35,* 48–58.

Tovée, M. J., & Cornelissen, P. L. (2001). Female and male perceptions of female physical attractiveness in front-view and profile. *British Journal of Psychology, 92,* 391–402.

Tovée, M. J., Maisey, D. S., Emery, J. L., & Cornelissen, P. L. (1999). Visual cues to female physical attractiveness. *Proceedings of the Royal Society of London B, 266,* 211–218.

Tovée, M. J., Swami, V., Furnham, A., & Mangalparsad, R. (2006). Changing perceptions of attractiveness as observers are exposed to a different culture. *Evolution and Human Behavior, 27,* 443–456.

Treloar, C., Porteous, J., Hassan, F., Kasniyah, N., Lakshmandu, M., Sama, M., et al. (1999). The cross cultural context of obesity: An INCLEN multicentre collaborative study. *Health and Place, 5,* 279–286.

Turkel, A. R. (1998). All about Barbie: Distortions of a transitional object. *Journal of the American Academy of Psychoanalysis and Dynamic Psychiatry, 26,* 165–177.

Turner, S. L., Hamilton, H., Jacobs, M., Angood, L. M., Dwyer, D. H. (1997). The influence of fashion magazines on the body image satisfaction of college women: An exploratory analysis. *Adolescence, 32,* 603–614.

United Nations. (1995). *Fact sheet No. 23 on harmful traditional practices affecting the health of women and children.* Geneva: United Nations.

Wallace, R. (2003, March 18). *Taking a pregnant pause in media beauty ideals.* Retrieved September 21, 2006, from http://www.foxnews.com/story/0, 2933, 81456, 00.html.

Watterson, B. (1991). *Women in ancient Egypt.* New York: St. Martin's Press.

Wertheim, E. H., Paxton, S. J., & Tilgner, L. (2004). Test–retest reliability and construct validity of Contour Drawing Rating Scale scores in a sample of early adolescent girls. *Body Image: An International Journal of Research, 1,* 199–205.

Wertheim, E. H., Paxton, S. J., Schutz, H. K., & Muir, S. L. (1997). Why do adolescent girls watch their weight? An interview study examining sociocultural pressures to be thin. *Journal of Psychosomatic Research, 42,* 345–355.

Wiseman, C. V., Gray, J. J., Mosimann, J. E., & Ahrens, A. H. (1992). Cultural expectations of women: An update. *International Journal of Eating Disorders, 11,* 85–89.

Wolf, N. (1991). *The beauty myth.* New York: William Morrow.

World Health Organization [WHO]. (2006). Online publication at http://www.who. int/about/en/ Retrieved September 25, 2006.

Zones, J. S. (2000). Beauty myths and realities and their impacts on women's health. In M. B. Zinn, P. Hondagneu-Sotelo, & M. Messner (Eds.), *Gender through the prism of difference* (2nd ed., pp. 87–103). Boston, MA: Allyn and Bacon.

Index